THE PROMISE
OF DIVERSITY

THE PROMISE OF DIVERSITY

Over 40 Voices Discuss
Strategies for Eliminating
Discrimination
in Organizations

Coeditors

Elsie Y. Cross

Judith H. Katz

Frederick A. Miller

Edith Whitfield Seashore

Professional Publishing
Burr Ridge, Illinois
New York, New York

Senior sponsoring editor: Cynthia A. Zigmund
Project editor: Jean Lou Hess
Production manager: Bob Lange
Interior designer: Larry J. Cope
Cover designer: Tim Kaage
Jacket photo: M. Angelo/West Light
Compositor: Carlisle Communications, Ltd.
Typeface: 10.5/12 Palatino
Printer: Book Press, Inc.

Library of Congress Cataloging-in-Publication Data

The promise of diversity : over 40 voices discuss strategies for
  eliminating discrimination in organizations / co-editors, Elsie Y.
  Cross . . . [et al.].
      p.   cm.
  Includes bibliographical references and index.
  ISBN 0-7863-0307-7
    1. Minorities—Employment—United States—Case Studies.
  2. Organizational change—United States—Case Studies.
  3. Multiculturalism—United States—Case studies.   I. Cross, Elsie
  Y.
  HF5549.5.M5P76   1994
  331.6'0973—dc20   94–4772

Printed in the United States of America
  3 4 5 6 7 8 9 0 BP 1 0 9 8 7 6 5 4

This book is dedicated to those who are no longer with us on the journey toward ameliorating oppression in organizations. In particular we dedicate this book to: Ken Benne, Nancy Campbell, Bob Chin, Kaleel Jamison, Hal Kellner, and Alice Sargent. Without them, we would not have progressed to where we are today.

Acknowledgments

In September 1991, the board of directors and staff of NTL Institute for Applied Behavioral Sciences (NTL) voted to sponsor the creation and publication of a book on diversity. They were interested in this topic because of its importance to organizations and because little had been written to make this topic accessible for managers and the general public. It was also in keeping with NTL's longtime interest in and commitment to providing important resource information to organizations, communities, human-resource professionals, organizational consultants, managers, and leaders.

Lennox Joseph, who is NTL's chief executive officer, and Nanci Appleman-Vassil, its director of programs, asked Frederick A. Miller, a member of NTL and a widely recognized leader in the field of diversity, to lead the project. He accepted and invited three other leaders to join him: Elsie Y. Cross, Judith H. Katz and Edith Whitfield Seashore. The coeditors are all pioneers with a long history of hands-on experience in working with organizations. All have worked together previously for NTL. Each agreed to participate in the project *pro bono*, with the proceeds from the book earmarked for NTL scholarships.

We, the coeditors, would like to thank the NTL Institute's 1991 board of directors for their wisdom and foresight in commissioning this volume: Darya Funches (chair), Barbara Brewer, Michael Broom, Leon Butler, Argentine Saunders Craig, Amanda Fouther, Sherman Kingsbury, Bernard Lubin, Robert J. Marshak, Srinivasan Umapathy, Julie A. C. Virgo, and Jane Magruder Watkins (vice chair).

We would especially like to acknowledge the authors who contributed their time, energy and dedication to the articles that appear in this book.

The chapter "A Perspective on the Struggle to Ameliorate Oppression and to Support Diversity in United States Organizations" would not have been possible without the cooperation, input, and insight from the people interviewed by Clare C. Swanger: Mark A. Chesler, Price Cobbs, Elsie Y. Cross, Janice Eddy, Robert Hayles, Evangelina Holvino, Bailey Jackson, Judith H. Katz, Mel King, Marilyn Loden, Frederick A. Miller, Henry Morgan, Judith Palmer, Henry Roberts, Edith Whitfield Seashore, Barry Stein, Robert Terry, Barbara Walker, David C. Wigglesworth, and Orion Worden.

We would also like to express our appreciation to those who supported and assisted us in the preparation of the book: from NTL, Lennox Joseph, Nanci Appleman-Vassil, and Kathy Crabbs, and Robin

Mayers for her hard work in obtaining a publisher; Martha N. Johnson and Clare C. Swanger for their efforts in coordinating the project in its beginning and middle stages; Mary Helen Moses for historical research; Bob Kopcha and Jennifer French for their suggestions for enhancing the final manuscript; Sandy Fastert for administrative assistance; Gail Simmons for word processing; Catherine Warren-Muller for her work on the index; Alan Moorse for reviewing and improving the final manuscript; Laura Johnson and Brent Foulke for logistical, managerial, and clerical support; Roger Gans for rewrites; Pauline Kamen Miller for proofreading assistance and support of the manuscript team; Joanne Stiles for working with the authors in the last stages of the project and editing the final manuscript; and Joan Buccigrossi for managing the manuscript team and tracking the countless details of this monumental project.

To one and all, we are truly grateful.

Contents

About the Editors

ELSIE Y. CROSS, COEDITOR

Elsie Y. Cross is founder and president of Elsie Y. Cross Associates, Inc., an organization development consulting firm in Philadelphia, Pennsylvania, and publisher of *The Diversity Factor,* a quarterly journal. Since 1970, she has consulted to organizations in Europe, Africa, and the Caribbean, as well as to U.S. corporations and national, state, and local governmental agencies. The firm consults on organization development, managing diversity, team building, strategic planning, and conflict resolution.

Elsie is a member of the NTL Institute and a former chair of the NTL board of directors. She holds a bachelor of science degree in business administration and master's degrees in business and in psychoeducational processes from Temple University.

Elsie and her associates have pioneered an approach to the amelioration of racism and sexism that is unique in the field. The approach is premised on the view that values and norms that perpetuate racism and sexism are embedded in organizations and are inherited by successive generations of managers. The client organizations that work with her firm embark on a process of culture change that aims to promote the full inclusion of men and women of color and white women by removing barriers to their full participation and extending the enablers that are experienced by white men. This culture-change process also involves the integration of work and family issues for all employees.

JUDITH H. KATZ, COEDITOR

Judith H. Katz has focused her 20-year career in organization development on systemic change processes to address oppression and build high-performing, culturally inclusive organizations. Her work as a consultant, educator, and author has consistently pioneered new arenas in the field. Her book *White Awareness: Handbook for Antiracism Training* (1978) earned an international reputation as one of the first works to address racism from a white perspective. Her second book, *No Fairy Godmothers, No Magic Wands: The Healing Process after Rape* (1984), broke new ground in the field of gender-based oppression. Judith received her doctorate in education at the University of

Massachusetts and has served on the faculties of the University of Oklahoma and San Diego State University. A vice president of the Kaleel Jamison Consulting Group, Inc., since 1985, Judith serves on the boards of directors of the Kaleel Jamison Foundation and the Group for Cultural Documentation. She previously served on the board of NTL Institute. Currently, Judith is concentrating on helping organizations address downsizing while developing and retaining diversity. She also works with organizations to integrate and link diversity efforts with such strategic initiatives as quality, leadership, empowerment, and teamwork.

FREDERICK A. MILLER, MANAGING EDITOR

Since 1985, Frederick A. Miller has been president of the Kaleel Jamison Consulting Group, Inc., specialists in developing High Performing Inclusive^{SM} organizations through strategic cultural change. He began his career in organization development and training in 1972 at Connecticut General Life Insurance Company (now CIGNA), where he was responsible for their pioneering diversity effort. Since joining The Kaleel Jamison Consulting Group in 1979, he has been involved in numerous large systems-change efforts in Fortune 100 companies and has worked with clients in the United States, Europe, and Asia. He has also been actively involved with managers, consultants, and students of change in the former Soviet Union. Fred has pioneered methodologies for the inclusion of the diverse talents and perspectives of all people in an organization and has authored many articles on leadership, cultural diversity, racism, individual and team development, high performance, and the inclusive workplace. He is a member of the NTL Institute and a past member of its board of directors. Currently, he is a member of the board of directors of Ben & Jerry's Homemade, Inc., the Living School, the National Organization Development Network, and the Institute of Development Research.

EDITH WHITFIELD SEASHORE, COEDITOR

Edith Whitfield Seashore is a leading organization development consultant and pioneer in the field of cultural diversity. She entered this field in 1972, assisting AT&T with racial and gender training following a landmark consent decree. Since then, she has worked for scores of organizations in the private, public, and not-for-profit sectors. Edie is a member of the NTL Institute and served as its president from 1974 to 1979. She is also a member of the Society for the Psychological Study of Social Issues of the American Psychological Association.

In addition to her consulting, Edie teaches organization development, conflict resolution, and consulting skills at Johns Hopkins, American, Georgetown, and George Washington universities. In 1979, she received the Citation of Merit for Outstanding Contribution to the Applied Behavioral Sciences from the University of Southern California, School of Public Administration. Edie received a BA from Antioch College and an MA from Columbia University. She is the author, with Charles N. Seashore and Gerald M. Weinberg, of *What Did You Say? The Art of Giving and Receiving Feedback* (1991).

Editors' Introduction

This book is about the struggle against oppression in organizations and the promise of diversity. We who engage in this struggle for democracy have visions of what our institutions could be like in a world where no person or group of people would ever be oppressed.

Significant numbers of organizations have focused on diversity and the elimination of discrimination, but the strong grip of racism, sexism and other forms of oppression persists in many of our institutions. And for large numbers of people, the workplace is a hostile environment. Our institutions have failed to eliminate harassment and ongoing discrimination against women of color, men of color, white women, gays, lesbians, people with disabilities, older workers, younger workers, and others who are systematically excluded.

Those who struggle against oppression in organizations and move toward achieving the promise of diversity have experienced many phases of pessimism and optimism. We have seen some organizations work to transform themselves and, in fact, enjoy moments of success. We have seen some individuals move from being oppressors to champions, from victims to the empowered, from adversaries to allies. However, we are also witness to the power of resistance and the persistence of the status quo. We continue to feel the effects of a legacy of oppression: slavery, genocide, indentured servitude, denial of basic human rights, disenfranchisement, and deep-seated hatred, fear, and violence against those who are different. Now is the time for the courage and risk-taking required to make systemic, personal, behavioral, and conceptual changes that will begin to ameliorate oppression and allow us to truly live the democratic ideals of our heterogeneous nation.

Many more people need to join in the struggle against the powerful forces that impede our progress toward that ideal. We believe that individuals, groups, communities, and institutions must act now because the oppressed cry out for immediate action. The volume of these voices indicates the magnitude of change required to answer their call. We must dramatically shift the power dynamics in our relationships and change many of our policies and practices. We must develop new ways of thinking, new behaviors, and new skills.

In order to change the current one-up/one-down framework in which we find ourselves, we need to create a new frame, one that (1) holds that inclusion of people who are different does not mean that they must fit in with, or assimilate into, the dominant group, (2) does not try merely to create acceptance or tolerance, but that values each person's unique identity and group identities, and (3) substantially changes current modes of dealing with conflict and power to achieve greater creativity, organizational productivity, and an inclusive, respectful environment.*

The promise of diversity cannot be achieved through simplistic means. Achieving the promise of diversity requires much more than:

- Eating ethnic food.
- Role-playing being blind or being confined to a wheelchair.
- Walking briefly in each others' shoes.
- Understanding different cultures.
- Giving a speech or attending a symposium.
- Teaching people to conform.
- Developing more-effective listening skills.
- Creating the business case.
- Declaring a level playing field.
- Establishing networks and support groups.
- Placing some of the "new" people in visible positions.
- Changing the words *melting pot* to *salad, mosaic,* or *stew.*
- Writing a sexual-harassment policy.
- Implementing hiring bonuses.
- Conducting a cultural audit.
- Reading articles.
- Attending awareness workshops.
- Providing day care, flextime, and elder care.
- Adding the word *diversity* to the mission statement.
- Arranging brown-bag lunches.
- Calling in consultants.
- Reading this book.

We must address issues of oppression through actions that will eliminate racism, sexism, heterosexism, classism, ableism, and other forms of discrimination at the individual, identity group, and systems levels. The promise of diversity and the struggle against oppression in organizations call for redefining, reexamining, rethinking, and restructuring many aspects of our institutions and our lives.

---

*"One-up/one-down" refers to the zero-sum notion that for one person to be superior, another one must be inferior; for one to succeed, another must fail. A one-up/one-down framework is a hierarchy in which power and privilege are the "natural right" of those who are "up."

We hope this book moves the dialogue and actions forward. It contains the following:

A perspective. A review of efforts to address racism, sexism, and other forms of discrimination over the last 30 years.

Articles. By leaders, researchers and practitioners who are actively working to address issues of oppression and diversity in organizations.

Visions. The hopes, fears, and dreams of leading change agents regarding the promise and perils of diversity.

Further readings. A review of the current literature in the field and an annotated list of suggested further readings.

Index. The people, places, concepts, terms, and organizations in this book.

As we delved into this project, it became evident that this book—with its various authors, styles, points of view, colors, textures, and voices—is itself a living example of diversity. It has become multifaceted and multidimensional, without a neat beginning, middle, and end. It ranges from the obvious to the formidable, and not everyone is going to agree with the range of viewpoints expressed. We hope the readers will be stimulated by some voices and influenced by several. It contains the best and latest thinking on diversity and the amelioration of oppression by the people who are defining the field, and therein will lie its value and contribution.

As we struggle against oppression, it is important that we see and build upon our collective efforts for change. We hope this book will inform and stimulate the reader to take action for change. We hope it provides a positive springboard for us all to see *what is possible* as we struggle to address *what is.*

Elsie Y. Cross
Judith H. Katz
Frederick A. Miller
Edith Whitfield Seashore

WHY WE CHOSE TO ADDRESS OPPRESSION

Frederick A. Miller
Managing Editor

Among my responsibilities as managing editor of this book was to oversee revising the final manuscript to address various concerns of the publishers. To best judge what might need to be addressed, the publishers engaged several teams of reviewers to critique an earlier draft of the manuscript. The following is an excerpt from one of the reviews:

> This is a monumental book. One filled with so much source material that it will be valuable to future students of equal employment opportunity and the human condition in organizations for a very long time. Obviously, much effort went into compiling these "voices," and much can be learned from hearing them. In every chapter, there is some insight into how we have all hurt, underestimated and done some wrong to each other. These personal reflections, as well as perspectives, often "hit" with power and poignancy. These reviewers respect the editors' desire to understand how oppression and discrimination have affected the workplace. And therein lies our major comment on this work.
>
> Oppression and discrimination pervade the tone of this book. The word *racism* appears often, and anecdotes of discrimination abound. We share with the editors and authors of this work the disappointments and injustices reflected in their voices. These are important, often emotional, statements. But *they are not reflective of consensus thinking about diversity. This is not a book about the "Promise of Diversity" but a book about "The Shame of Discrimination."* [emphasis mine—Ed.]
>
> This NTL viewpoint is very much present throughout this work; after all, this is an NTL book. But this viewpoint is not a majority view of the issue of diversity. Those responsible for diversity programs have stressed that diversity does not mean "pointing a finger." It does not mean equal employment opportunity. It does not mean the study of discrimination and oppression. It is a celebration of individual differences and the strengths these differences bring to the workplace.
>
> Diversity should not have the negative tone so prevalent in this book, but be a positive approach to understanding and exemplifying how human differences add to satisfaction in the workplace as well as to business performance. Overall, this book takes the exact opposite approach. This is not a book about diversity as we understand it. Will other readers feel the same way? We think so. Executives reading this book would probably say, "Those diversity people are really EEO people after all." We would not be happy with

this reaction after all the work done to convince them that diversity is a performance issue, not one where blame is needed . . .[1]

Upon reading this critique, it struck me that the need for addressing that point of view was exactly why we wanted to put this book together in the first place!

At the heart of the matter lie some very different assumptions about "diversity" and the path to change. There is a belief that diversity should be about individual differences. We might call this the Individual Differences perspective. But there is also a belief that diversity should be about correcting the injustices visited upon people and groups. We might call this the Social Justice perspective.[2]

The Individual Differences perspective assumes the fundamental issue of diversity is to create understanding between different individuals. But it too often includes an underlying assumption that addressing discrimination and oppression will result in "pointing fingers of blame" rather than providing a basis for common ground. The reviewers, and many Individual Differences advocates, would have us forget the past and relegate issues of discrimination and oppression to a box labeled "affirmative action/equal employment opportunity."

The reviewers point out that diversity is a performance issue that can provide a positive richness to an organization, a view that the editors of this book fervently share. Where the editors diverge from the reviewers' perspective is in our belief that social justice issues must be addressed in order to achieve the *potential* of diversity. We feel you cannot skip over injustice to get there. Celebrating everyone's differences won't lead to higher performance from your work force if the suffering experienced because of those differences must remain under wraps before, during, and after the celebration.

The editors of this book all believe that celebrating individual differences is important. But we also believe that many individuals and identity groups are blocked from being fully included in today's organizations by systems and practices that favor some people at the expense of others. Individuals of certain races, genders, ethnicities, sexual orientations, and physical abilities are burdened with the weight of being seen as different and therefore not as good.

To people who benefit, the biases in our organizations' and our society's systems and practices can be as unnoticeable and as intangible as air. But to people who are thwarted every day in their attempts to contribute (and to have *their* differences celebrated), the biases are as tangible as a brick wall.

Granted, this may not be the "majority view of the issue of diversity." It is a view that has been obscured by the preponderance of programs celebrating diversity and individualism. But those who hold the majority view are not the only ones who may object to the views represented in this book. There are many people so deeply hurt, angered, and blocked by oppressions of various sorts that they feel rooting out oppression can be the *only* worthy task.

The Social Justice perspective calls for addressing discrimination and oppression head-on: identifying what they are, where they are, how they work, what mechanisms perpetuate them, and how to eliminate them. For many people who have experienced pain and suffering, the feeling is that if that leads to pointing fingers, so be it. And until we've dealt with discrimination, they often feel, it's pointless to address performance. To them, this book will barely scratch the surface.

Clearly, there are many sincere people who raise their voices in the celebration of individualistic diversity. Just as clearly, there are many sincere people who raise their voices in a call for social justice. But when individuals from these different groups meet, too often their dialogue achieves little beyond the raising of their voices.

An Imaginary Conversation We Have Heard and Felt Many Times . . .

The Voice of an Individual Differences Person

Why do you keep holding onto the past? Are you trying to make me feel guilty? Don't you see all the opportunities open to you and your kind? There are more white women and women and men of color in Congress than ever before. More in executive positions than ever before. More making six-digit salaries than ever before. The Americans with Disabilities Act is working. Gays and lesbians in the military have a new policy that's better than the old ban. Can't you see all the progress that's being made?

The Voice of a Social Justice Person

Wait a minute, don't talk to me about progress. Talk to me about right here and right now. What's going on *here?* There aren't *enough* white women, men and women of color, "out" gays and lesbians, and people with disabilities in positions of authority right here in *this* organization.

Individual Differences Voice

Come on! Look at all the recruiting we've done. Look where you are in the pipeline. In a few more years, you'll be even further along. Don't be upset at us. We have good intentions. We've done lots of good things, and with some ups and downs, we will succeed. Just give us some more time.

Social Justice Voice

What matters to me is the effect on me and people like me. When I see there are no women and people of color in strategic positions in the organization, that's what I'm focused on. Your pipeline sounds like a pipedream. If you trample my foot, your intent doesn't matter to me. My toe's broken. What are you going to do about it?

Diversity clearly is a hot topic today. But the more people talk about it, the more clear it is how many people disagree about it, even those who are actively working to ameliorate oppression and include the widest possible bandwidth of individual and identity group differences in organizations. Unfortunately, many of today's disagreements about diversity are preventing potential allies from joining forces to bring about the societal and organizational changes to which both sides are so deeply committed.

Ironically (and tragically), voices for Social Justice and voices for Individual Differences often regard each other as obstacles to achieving the better society that both sides want.

Just Listen . . .

Individual Differences Voice

If you didn't carry this burden of your whole group around with you all the time, you could focus better on what you need to do to be successful. Look at me. I try to do everything as an individual, and I've been very successful at that. You're unique, you're special, you're very talented. Why do you act as though you can't do things as an individual?

Social Justice Voice

There's no way in the world in which I live that I'm just an individual and not also a white woman, woman of color, man of color, someone born outside the United States, a gay, a lesbian, someone with a disability, someone who speaks with an accent, too old, too young, or from the wrong ethnic group. If I'm a woman, the fact that I can't jog safely at night says that I'm not just an individual. If my car breaks down in the road, I'm at risk no matter whose neighborhood I'm in. I'm part of an identity group that bad things happen to. And too often I'm seen not as an individual but as one of "those" people who are dangerous or weak or inferior or lazy or emotional or slow.

To acknowledge progress on the individual level is fine. But to deny that there are still "isms" operating in our world is foolish. Classism, ageism, sexism, and, yes, racism are still very much alive.

Individual Differences Voice

Come on, you're just adding fuel to the fire with this class conflict stuff. Your anger and hostility are counterproductive. We leveled the playing field in the 1960s and '70s. This is the 1990s.

Social Justice Voice

Conceptually, and with some laws, we may have moved in that direction. But our systems, practices, and attitudes are far from where they need to be. In school, having teachers call on white, male students significantly more often than everyone else tells me that the field still isn't level.

A significantly larger percentage of African Americans are denied disability claims than whites. The same is true with mortgages. As a rational person, you can point to it and say it's not a systemic problem, they're all individual cases. But these rates hold even when the people have the same degree of injury or the same levels of income and employment history. Can't you see the evidence right in front of you?

But you won't even consider the possibility that your success might be due, *even in part,* to the deck being stacked in your favor and against people from other identity groups. You don't want to think there's not a level playing field because it affects all the other assumptions you have about the world, especially your assumption that your individual success is based solely on your own merit.

Neither of these voices is completely wrong. Each has validity in its context, but each refuses to accept that there are simultaneous realities, and that the realities can coexist. The present system does, in fact, work for some people—and does not work for many, many others.

To achieve the promise of diversity, we need to hear, understand, and appreciate the voice of Individual Differences *and* the voice of Social Justice. We need to recognize that both voices are not only valid but necessary. *Both* must be heard and acted upon to bring about an inclusive organizational culture. Mutual listening, respect, and understanding are required to make a true dialogue possible. And once a dialogue has begun, it becomes *possible* to partner with each other to create an effective plan for change that *includes, values, and taps* the differences and similarities of every member and every identity group.

Developing the dialogue and building the partnership may not be easy or quick. But by hearing the voices, valuing their experiences, and respecting their points of view, the dialogue finally becomes possible. And that's where all progress begins.

NOTES

1. This prepublication review was prepared for Irwin Professional Publishing by an independent team consisting of a director of human resource development, a manager of diversity training, and a corporate general manager.

2. The discussions of the perspectives of social justice and individual differences as presented in this article were inspired by the work of Bailey Jackson and Rita Hardiman. I also want to thank Judith H. Katz for her contributions to the concept and to this article and Karen A. Moran for her work on this article, especially for creating the voices approach to presenting the concept.

THE PROMISE
OF DIVERSITY

HISTORY OF OPPRESSION AND DIVERSITY IN ORGANIZATIONS

1

Chapter One

Clare C. Swanger

Perspectives on the History of Ameliorating Oppression and Supporting Diversity in United States Organizations

Clare C. Swanger

■

Clare C. Swanger is senior researcher and strategic writer for The Kaleel Jamison Consulting Group, having joined the firm in 1991. She designs case studies about client interventions and develops materials and technologies for the firm. Since 1977, she has focused her consulting work on strategic management, executive development, marketing, and environmental management. She is also executive director of the Taos Land Trust, New Mexico. Ms. Swanger has an MBA from Stanford University Graduate School of Business.

T his perspective is intended to set a historical context regarding diversity work in organizations. In order to understand where we are today and where we want to go in the future, we need to know where we've been.

The data were gathered from publicly available literature and through interviews with 20 people who pioneered work in diversity and the amelioration of oppression in the 1960s and 1970s. It is not meant to be a fully detailed history but to capture major events and trends and the perspectives of selected leaders in the field.

The focus is on the pioneers—individuals and organizations— because so little has been written about the forces that catalyzed organizations to begin addressing discrimination or about the organizations' efforts themselves. Although these issues can be traced back a century or more in organizations, this perspective focuses on the time frame from the 1960s to 1993, with a brief overview of major catalyzing events prior to that time.

It is important to remember the long and difficult history of the United States in respect to discrimination and oppression; the atrocities that have been perpetrated on different groups of people; and the efforts to end segregation and discrimination, to ameliorate oppression, and to create a "level playing field" for all people regardless of race, religion, gender, nationality, age, sexual orientation, ability, or other differences.

In organizations, formal efforts to eliminate discrimination generally started in the late 1960s as a response to legislative mandate or civil unrest or as a commitment to social and moral justice. The belief was that if white women and blacks, Latinos, Asians, and other people of color gained access to the workplace, they would advance equally with white men. This proved to be untrue, however, due to discrimination and prejudice embedded within individuals and organizational systems.

In recent years, issues of diversity have catapulted to the forefront of organizational consciousness and activity. The casual observer might believe that these issues arose only recently—for example, with the publication of *Workforce 2000* by the Hudson Institute in 1987.[1] *Workforce 2000* portrayed demographic shifts in the United States that would have wide-ranging effects on our society and institutions. In reality, however, organizations and individuals have been grappling with discrimination and diversity for many decades.

Today, in the eyes of an increasing number of leaders and managers, diversity within organizations has become an imperative for organizational success. Astute leaders and managers realize that for their organizations to be the best they can be, to thrive in the current environment of "permanent white water," as Peter Vaill terms it,[2] everyone's talents and input must be actively sought and fully utilized in ways that are conducive to all people contributing their fullest to reaching the goals of the organizations.

As this perspective is explained, the reader would do well to keep in mind several major points. First, many of the people whose perspectives are included in this essay emphasized the importance of the civil rights and women's movements in forcing organizations to address issues of discrimination. Mel King, community activist, put it this way: "Organizations were forced to deal with discrimination by the civil rights movement and then civil rights legislation that mandated equal employment opportunity and led to affirmative action. The impetus came out of the streets . . . not the suites, not the schools."

Second is the psychological perspective. Robert Terry, consultant and author, says: "Diversity was never the issue . . . Diversity is a fact. The question is about inclusion or exclusion of whom, on what terms, and for what purpose? The issue is about fear: our fear of the other, our fear of the stranger, our shadow side, our fear of change, our fear of failure."

Third, according to Elsie Y. Cross, consultant: "People of color and women have difficulty getting ahead not because they are not qualified or smart, but because racism and sexism exist in individual managers and are built in to the way businesses are operated, such as recruiting and promotional processes . . ."

Fourth, according to Orian Worden, consultant and researcher, diversity is a fact of life in organizations today. "The workplace is the one place where people of diverse backgrounds come together on a daily basis. People continue, for the most part, to live separately according to race, ethnicity, etc. The workplace is a lab for people to learn how to live with differences."

SETTING THE STAGE: WATERSHED EVENTS OF THE 1930s, '40s, '50s, AND '60s

The movement against segregation and discrimination on the basis of race in the United States began to gather strength in the 1930s, when blacks gained a modicum of economic leverage through the formation of all-black unions. In 1941, A. Philip Randolph, president of the Brotherhood of Sleeping Car Porters, conferred with other black leaders and organized a march on Washington, D.C. Labor solidarity had a political effect: President Roosevelt, in response to the threatened march, issued Executive Order 8802, ordering an end to discrimination in defense industries and government employment.[3] That order was reissued by all subsequent presidents.

Legal barriers to full participation in American life also began to topple during this time. In 1944, the Supreme Court mandated that all labor unions represent employees without regard to race, even though as private organizations they could still deny membership on that basis.[4] That same year, the Supreme Court held that the Fifteenth Amendment prohibited racial discrimination in primary elections. President Truman issued an executive order that provided for equality of treatment in the armed services.[5] He also created a civil rights committee to recommend civil rights programs and proposed legislation based on the committee's recommendations. Much of this legislation was finally enacted in the 1960s.

Societally, the 1950s marked the height of the melting-pot paradigm. Many people believed that newcomers and people of different cultures and races would, and should, assimilate into the mainstream of the Western European–based white culture of the United States. It was pointed out that succeeding waves of immigrants—many from Western European countries—had come to the United States, worked hard, bettered themselves, raised their standard of living, and melted into society. To succeed, however, some of these people had had to change their names, identities, religions, and other attributes. In addition, successful assimilation was largely based on skin color—that is, white. For African Americans, Latinos, Asians, Native Americans, and others, the path toward acceptance and equality was not straightforward or, in most cases, successful.

In the mid-1950s, the efforts against discrimination and segregation finally led to monumental legislative and social changes. In 1954, in *Brown* v. *Board of Education*,[6] the Supreme Court overturned the separate-but-equal doctrine that had stood since 1896, when it had ruled to allow separate train cars for the races.[7] The court stated that separation necessarily meant inequality and that segregation in government-supplied services—in this case, public education—was forbidden by the Fourteenth Amendment's equal-protection clause. In another decision in the same case a year later, the Supreme Court ordered that the states must make a prompt start toward desegregating public schools.[8] The landmark case, argued by Thurgood Marshall, then head of the NAACP's Legal Defense and Educational Fund, culminated nearly three decades of patient legal effort on the part of the NAACP and other organizations. According to Judge A. Leon Higginbotham, Jr., "[T]he significance of the victory in the *Brown* case cannot be overstated. *Brown* changed the moral tone of America; by eliminating the legitimization of state-imposed racism it implicitly questioned racism wherever it was used."[9]

The *Brown* decision gave impetus to the civil rights movement. There is broad agreement that the movement began with the arrest of Rosa Parks in Montgomery, Alabama, in 1955, when Mrs. Parks, a black woman, broke the law by refusing to give up her seat on the bus to a white man. The black community, led by the young minister Dr. Martin Luther King, Jr., rallied around her. Dr. King, who espoused peaceful, nonviolent resistance, instituted a boycott of the bus system that lasted a full year, ending only after the Montgomery bus system was ordered to be desegregated.

For the next 10 years, peaceful efforts similar to the Montgomery boycott resulted in court-ordered remedies time and time again. Congress also responded by passing a series of laws that legislated the end of racial discrimination in the United States. Foremost among these were the:

- Civil Rights Act of 1960, which enabled court-appointed officials to protect voting rights and made it a federal offense to obstruct a court order.
- Civil Rights Act of 1964, the strongest civil rights legislation since the Civil War, which prohibited discrimination based on race, gender, national origin, and religion in employment, education, public accommodations, and federally assisted programs.

- Voting Rights Act of 1965, which eliminated the poll tax and mandated the Civil Rights Division of the Justice Department to intervene when voter registration rolls fell beneath a certain level.
- Fair Housing Act of 1968, which prohibited race discrimination in housing and real estate.

At the same time, to provide broader-based remedies for discrimination, the Supreme Court revived the civil rights acts that had been passed after the Civil War and limited by earlier Supreme Courts.

Critical as these changes were because they eliminated de jure (legally sanctioned) segregation, many people felt that the nonviolent process was too slow in eliminating de facto (societally sanctioned) segregation and other forms of racism. By 1965, the mood of the country became more restless and violent. The nonviolent approach to civil rights came under pressure from those who saw little or no tangible, systemic change. Stokely Carmichael, Malcolm X, and many others espoused "black power" as a viable strategy for the black community to focus on empowerment and leverage its economic base. The assassinations of President Kennedy, Dr. Martin Luther King, Jr., Malcolm X, and the murders of other social justice leaders, civil rights workers, and innocent children increased the tension. There was increasing recognition of the need to enhance economic and political power among blacks and other "disadvantaged" groups in order to achieve equality for all. As Dr. King stated, "I worked to get these people the right to eat hamburgers, and now I've got to do something to help them get the money to buy them."[10]

Driven by frustration, anger, poverty, overcrowding, high unemployment, rampant crime, and promises and dreams deferred, the people of the Watts area of Los Angeles lashed out in the summer of 1965. Thirty-four people were killed, many by the police, and more than 1,000 were injured. Over the next three summers, in response to specific events—such as the beatings of civil rights workers and the assassination of Dr. Martin Luther King, Jr.—more urban insurrections occurred: in Chicago, San Francisco, and Atlanta in 1966; in 23 cities, large and small, in 1967, including Newark (26 people killed, 1,200 injured) and Detroit (43 dead, 7,200 arrested); and in Boston, Detroit, Chicago, Philadelphia, San Francisco, Toledo, Pittsburgh, and Washington, D.C., in 1968.[11]

The Kerner Commission, convened to prepare a report on the causes of and solutions to the violence, stated, "What white Americans have never fully understood—but what the Negro can never forget—is that white society is deeply implicated in the ghetto. White institutions created it, white institutions maintain it, and white society condones it."[12] The Kerner Commission report signaled a fundamental shift from a focus on individual acts to recognition that white institutions and the inaction of white society were part of the causes of the problem. "What the Kerner Commission was weaker on," according to Milton Viorst in *Fire in the Streets,* "was what white society had to do about it."[13]

While the civil rights movement tried to ameliorate oppression based on race, women were also challenging their oppression. The publication of *The Feminine Mystique* by Betty Friedan in 1963 catalyzed an entire generation of women. Friedan pointed out that women had played an important role during World War II, both in the factories in the United States and in the U.S. military; but, when the war ended, a fundamental assumption resurfaced: that women could only be housewives or caretakers or hold low-level jobs. *The Feminine Mystique* pointed out the reality of discrimination that was keeping women out of the country's organizations and leadership positions and energized a generation of women into challenging that assumption. Not since the suffragist movement that had led to the passage of the Nineteenth Amendment in 1920, giving women the right to vote, had women had such a motivating cause.

In 1964, as Congress worked to pass the landmark Civil Rights Act, feminists insisted that women be included in Title VII, the employment provision of the statute. Congress resisted including women within the protections of the law because the Equal Pay Act of 1963, which mandated equal pay for men and women when performing equal work, was deemed sufficient protection for women in the workplace. An amendment adding the word *sex* to the classifications protected by the statute was proposed at the last minute on the floor of the House, in an effort, many believed, to derail the entire bill.[14]

Nonetheless, the statute—which forbids discrimination in employment based on race, color, religion, national origin, *and* sex—passed. This was not the only time that women's rights were piggybacked onto social-change initiatives based on race. Responsibility for handling initial complaints of discrimination went to the newly created Equal Employment Opportunity Commission (EEOC). During the first two years of the agency's operation, women filed about 4,000 complaints, or roughly 25 percent of the total.[15] Flooded with complaints, the EEOC developed a backlog of cases almost from its inception. Impatient with the progress of the law to ameliorate sex discrimination, a handful of leading activists founded in 1966 the National Organization for Women (NOW), with Betty Friedan as president. Its goal was "to take the actions needed to bring women into the mainstream of American society."[16]

It was Title VII of the Civil Rights Act of 1964—the first federal equal employment opportunity law that required compliance from nonpublic entities—that placed the most pressure on organizations. Strongly supported by the NAACP, Title VII instructed organizations to stop discriminating. Organizations with 25 or more employees were covered when the statute became effective on July 1, 1965; two years later, organizations with 15 or more employees came under its umbrella. The statute's proscription against discrimination was enforceable through private litigation as well as suits brought by the EEOC's Enforcement Division. For the first time, there was legal clout behind the antidiscrimination movement. Although the EEOC focused initially on African Americans, it also began to address issues related to Asians, Latinos, Native Americans, other people of color, white women, and others. The Enforcement Division's emphasis in many cases was on goals, targets, and timetables, particularly as to hiring. Affirmative action plans were an important result of this activity, and organizations were forced to examine their work forces and consider diversity as an imperative.

PIONEERING ORGANIZATIONAL EFFORTS

With legal imperatives driving them, organizations began trying to hire more African Americans and white women for entry-level professional, supervisory, and managerial jobs. Prior to the mid-1960s, African Americans had held only menial jobs in major corporations, though African Americans were doctors, lawyers, and other professionals in their own communities. White women, who had worked in the factories in World War II, were for the most part cleaning or clerical workers, nurses, teachers, or retail clerks.

During the 1940s and 1950s, a research base was developed on the dynamics of gangs, groups, and organizations. In the late 1950s, organizational development technology began to encompass large-systems change in addition to the small-group work already well under way. Some of the key people involved included Chris Argyris, Richard Beckard, Ken Benne, Lee Bradford, and Ron Lippitt. The Tavistock Institute in London, of which Harold Bridger is a founding member, also played a key part in this drama. Its work during World War II and afterward has been in the action research mode and has led, in particular, to a greater understanding of organizations as open sociotechnical systems. These efforts resulted in techniques that were particularly relevant and useful for organizations in the late 1960s as they tried to figure out how to eliminate discrimination.

In response to the need for legislative compliance, the executives of major organizations developed a variety of remedies for change. Organizations took one or more of several approaches, including trying to hire more African Americans and white women, changing recruiting practices and policies, and conducting educational sessions for employees. The direction educational sessions took often depended on whether people needed exposure, dialogue, or techniques to reduce tension in the organization. Many organizations brought training and development programs in-house. The programs were largely geared to individuals, to create shifts in awareness and ethics. Training groups (T-groups) were viewed as a way to reduce people's prejudices. The late 1960s also saw a proliferation of black-white encounter groups and racism-reduction processes. Price Cobbs, a well-known African American psychiatrist and consultant and the author of *Black Rage* (1968), noted that his African American clients expressed feelings of dismay, tension, pain, and restriction as a result of both overt and covert discrimination. He said, "In the early days in organizations, people didn't know what they wanted, beyond reducing tensions . . ."

It is important to note that in the late 1960s and the 1970s government agencies were focused on the *number* of "affected-class" members represented in the workplace, not on systems and organizational change; therefore, it was numbers that organizations worked to improve. Although the civil rights and equal employment opportunity laws of the United States forbade discrimination in jobs, voting, and housing, many organizations resisted the laws and continued to discriminate. Affirmative action became the strategy used to force organizations to comply with the law. Every company with more than 25 employees needed a plan stipulating what affirmative action it would take and its goals regarding recruiting, hiring, and promotion of people of color and of white women. The government could no longer enter into contracts with organizations that didn't have affirmative action plans in place. Led by Eleanor Holmes Norton, President Johnson's EEOC head, the government also began to bring organizations under court order when they were not in compliance.

The focus at this time was to get people of color and white women into organizations. The predominant belief was that once people became aware of the issues, everything else would change. There were a number of approaches used by organizations to address the difficulties of getting people in the door, giving them opportunities, and getting them into significant positions. Several models and examples are profiled below.

Two of the earliest corporate efforts occurred at KLH R & D and at the Polaroid Corporation. KLH—under the direction of Henry Morgan, a white man who later became president, and was then minority recruiter—instituted a minority hiring program in 1962 that included efforts to lower the barriers to employment by decreasing the entry requirements and then training the workers.

Polaroid's founder, Dr. Edwin Land, and two of the company's senior vice presidents shared a strong commitment to social justice. They hired Henry Morgan in 1968 and generated goals for the company. In the spring of 1969, Morgan initiated workshops of mixed-level, -race, and -gender participants to try to create among Polaroid employees an understanding of other people's values.

In the summer of 1970, emotions escalated around the United States about apartheid in South Africa, with pressure being placed on corporations to eliminate their business in and with South Africa. Polaroid had a distributor there, and the company's black employees were agitated. In response, Polaroid established a study committee, 80 percent of whom had been in the workshops together. Two whites and two blacks visited South Africa and set up guidelines for the distributor: Polaroid products could not be used for identity cards, and a percentage of profits had to go to the education of blacks in South Africa. Shortly thereafter, Polaroid discovered a violation of the guidelines and withdrew its business from South Africa.

Many U.S. companies responded to the urban unrest of 1968. Property insurance companies, in particular, had a vested interest. With property being destroyed and claims having to be paid, it was in these companies' best interests to address racism.

Henry Roberts, the president of Connecticut General Life Insurance Company (CG), believed that variety provided an opportunity to become a better company, that "diversity was an asset to be captured, not a problem to be controlled." Providing leadership from the top, Roberts recalled, "Rather than stressing altruism and do-goodness, it was better to think in terms of the objective: to be effective. As president, I was on surer ground in directing the company regarding these issues and efforts . . ."

CG was seen as a progressive company and an excellent place to work at this time. Their advertising slogan "We do things a little differently" summed it up. Roberts attended an NTL T-group in 1968 that was facilitated by Carl Rogers. He came away with the view that there should be no teaching at CG, but rather a learning experience where people got into groups to learn about and become comfortable with one another. He also believed it was easier to change people's behaviors than their attitudes. He hired Billie Alban and Herb Shephard to assist in cultural-change efforts.

Richard Kremer, a white manager at CG, was assigned to deal with the feeling among the black employees that their performance ratings underrepresented their value to the company. In February 1972, under Kremer's direction, CG held its first black-white workshop, titled "Intergroup Cooperation and Understanding." The experiential learning session helped to improve understanding and communication. After the sessions, the participants formed problem-solving groups to address issues, such as performance appraisals, mentoring, and recruiting policies, and to plan reunions and newsletters. One of the attendees at the second workshop was Frederick A. Miller, an African American. Kremer soon asked Miller to join the staff for workshops and co-direct the effort.

In December 1972, Connecticut General started workshops for men and women, similar to its black-white workshops. Kremer and Miller hired Edith Whitfield Seashore and Kaleel Jamison to help design and conduct the workshops.

Many other interventions revolved around urban issues. One of the consultants in this field was Robert Terry, a white man who was involved with groups responding to the Detroit riots of 1967. He worked with Doug Fitch, an African American, who pushed Terry to focus on what it meant to be white. Terry recalled, "I realized that I didn't have to think about what it means to be white, which is a paradox, because once I realized this, I *could* think about it." Terry wrote the book *For Whites Only*, a pioneering examination of whites' attitudes toward racism and the privilege and power whites enjoy because they are white.

Also in the late 1960s, Mark Chesler, a white academician at the University of Michigan, received funding from the Ford Foundation to conduct organizational interventions involving interracial and intergenerational conflict in urban secondary schools. Working with a diverse team, he went into eight schools across the country that were largely comprised of black and Hispanic students. As Chesler recalls:

> We worked with the kids, the parents, and the community. Dialogue and education occurred, but [there was] really no long-term change because the work did not address systemic issues. At this time, the country was just beginning to pay attention to race as a serious matter. The danger became that *everything* would be defined as racial and that situations of poor management would be missed. Other conflicts, in addition to the interracial and intergenerational ones that we were addressing, couldn't be ignored . . .

Around this time, Bailey Jackson was at the Center for Humanistic Education at the State University of New York at Albany. Noticing that there weren't many black people there, he said, "This was strange for me since I was from New York City." After attending workshops that Jackson recalled were "white and male, and not relevant to me and the other blacks," he eventually received a grant for experiential Black on Black Workshops, designed to address the specific interests and concerns of blacks.

At universities, there were pockets of activity supported by liberal social scientists. As more blacks enrolled in universities, racial tensions heightened, professors got confronted, and efforts to alleviate the problems blossomed. Beginning in the 1970s, pressure from black students led to the offering of African American courses and studies.

One university that was addressing its racial tension was the University of Massachusetts, Amherst. The Dean of the School of Education, Dwight Allen, was committed to putting racism and sexism on the school's agenda. Under his leadership, the School of Education decided to admit a student population that was half white and half people of color and to bring the issues of racism and sexism into the curriculum. Judith H. Katz, an early activist and a graduate student at the time, was hired as a human resource coordinator for 14 predominantly white residence halls. She developed and led groups for white students that focused on their own role in racism and on taking responsibility for it.

Rather than viewing racism as a "black problem," as had traditionally been done, Katz began viewing racism as a problem that whites had responsibility for creating and for changing. She also viewed racism as a systemic problem, with cultural, structural, and institutional components. Recalling her book *White Awareness* (1978), Katz said, "I wanted to reframe the conversation so that whites could understand that they have a role in maintaining racism and must take responsibility for change."

In 1972, Elsie Cross and others were using organizational-development methodologies and small-group educational activities with the Pennsylvania State College system. She recalled:

> My work went beyond awareness and training. I created an intervention with the presidents and their executive teams—organizational development—to supplement and support the work we were doing with students and administrators. The focus of the intervention was on analyzing policies, procedures, and practices that discriminated against employees and students and on creating mechanisms to remove barriers.

In 1973, employees at AT&T won a landmark class-action suit about pay discrimination. AT&T was the largest employer in the United States at the time, but among its 1 million employees, 56 percent of whom were women, there were no women officers. The $50 million consent decree included more than $38 million in higher wages and back pay for 13,000 women employees and 2,000 men of color.[17] AT&T thus became the first company to enter into agreement with the EEOC on affirmative action issues. The company agreed to train managers and ultimately ran for 10 years Men and Women in the Work Environment workshops. Two of the consultants involved were Edith Whitfield Seashore and Hal Kellner. Over time, they brought in a dozen or so other consultants.

At New York Telephone, at the time an AT&T operating company, Marilyn Loden—then an organization development specialist and now a corporate-change consultant and writer on diversity issues—had the responsibility for its gender awareness training. She recalled:

> Initially, I thought the issue was what to do for women managers who came into the role with fewer skills than the men. However, I discovered that the problem for most women was *not* an issue of lack of skills or knowledge, but rather an issue of opportunity and perception.

Loden hired Kellner and Seashore to start training the top-level employees at New York Telephone. Loden described their efforts:

> Initially, we looked at the impact of bringing more women managers into the executive suite and at male attitudes toward this change. We ran programs for both men and women addressing competition, collusion, and gender bias and took a deeper look at socialization. Within two or three years after the programs began, women's progress accelerated in the company. Many realized they could be more successful if they joined with other women as allies, resources, networks, and support systems. In the awareness training, we asked participants to talk about their feelings regarding men and women working together as peers. Interestingly, we found it was harder for the men, many of whom focused on their loss of influence, whereas the women focused on the upside potential.

During the 1970s, many other corporations, warned by the $50 million consent decree against AT&T, were concerned about the possibility of being sued for discrimination. They called in consultants to educate managers about nontraditional workers—that is, people of color and white women, who were beginning to enter the work force as a result of equal employment opportunity and affirmative action. At some of these corporations, the focus was on awareness training and the preparation of white women and minorities for the time when they would gain entrance into the higher levels of management.

Beginning in 1978, Elsie Y. Cross started working with Exxon's refinery in Linden, New Jersey, to address racism and sexism. The intervention was called "Managing and Working in a Diverse Workplace Environment." The intervention, which spanned six years, focused on the organization and its policies and practices and engaged management in providing the leadership for organizational change and renewal. Cross recalled:

> The significance of the Exxon intervention is that it went beyond individual understanding of bias and prejudice and engaged the organization in an analysis and diagnosis of problems that were built into the organization itself

and that created barriers for some and advantages for others. It included educational and awareness-training components and systems change work around policies and structure . . . We looked at recruiting practices and performance appraisal ratings and determined how and where the "discretionary powers" influence these factors. We engaged the management board to explore policies, practices, and organizational structures.

Work also began at Digital Equipment Corporation in 1979. Managers didn't like affirmative action because it was government mandated. In keeping with its innovative computer design technology, Digital Equipment wanted to design a more creative approach to affirmative action. Out of this came many "Core Groups," brought together to discuss differences and to learn experentially about race and gender.

Digital Equipment and Barbara Walker, the first person with the title Manager of Valuing Differences, shifted the frame of this work from assimilation and trying to minimize differences to one of valuing differences. Walker characterized this as a breakthrough:

> Through the work of valuing differences, we discovered valuing diversity. This was the product of many people's work. We were trying to make it part of the fabric of the company. We took a broader approach to affirmative action and equal opportunity. By 1985, each major part of Digital had a Manager of Affirmative Action/Equal Employment Opportunity/Valuing Differences. We also did a workshop called "Understanding the Dynamics of Diversity," which addressed other issues besides race and gender, such as ethnic groups, and the differences between Digital organizations. We took this international, too.

The U.S. Defense Department also took action to eliminate discrimination during the 1970s. The military had the same issues to deal with as the nation did. But what differs in the military is that mandates permeate down through the organization by the chain of command. The major issues the military was dealing with were how to prevent shipboard riots, how to increase the number of people of color in upper ranks, and how to deal with stress, turnover, attrition, and intergroup relations and tension.

In the early 1970s, the first significant efforts were made to promote people of color to senior ranks, and serious debate began about the role of women in the military. In the mid-1970s, the Office of Naval Research—under the direction of Robert Hayles, who managed research on diversity—funded important studies on a host of issues and technologies to achieve equity among people.

In 1975, the U.S. Naval Academy hired Edith Whitfield Seashore to assist them in going co-ed. Seashore recalled that "Through this work, I began to understand things that were masked in other organizations—

for example, the importance of bringing women together and building support systems."

Other organizations where this work was going on during the 1970s
included Procter and Gamble, Cummins Engine Company, IBM, Union
Carbide, Xerox Corporation, the National Education Association, the
National Institutes of Health, the U.S. Department of Agriculture, the
U.S. Department of Labor, the U.S. Department of State, and the
University of California at Berkeley, among other universities.

TRENDS IN THE 1970s

Organizations addressing diversity tried to include more people of
color and white women in their organizations and to train everyone
already there about differences and about the legal requirements of
equal opportunity. Some organizations pursued these goals because
they genuinely believed it was the right thing to do for both the
organization and its employees. Others did so in response to or to
avoid legal pressure. Increasing numbers of people were learning
about racism and beginning to deal with sexism. White women and
people of color were experiencing and exploring what it meant to be
among the first of their groups to hold managerial positions; white
men were experiencing and exploring what it meant to be working
with these pioneers.

Race awareness programs were often confrontational, with the focus
on "people having to feel the pain," as Judith Palmer recalls. As the
decade progressed, programs shifted from the aggressive approach to
one of encouraging people to share their feelings. However, only in a
few places were systemic actions taken for organizational change.

As the 1970s unfolded, things did not go as most had expected. It
became apparent that people of color and white women were not
progressing in most organizations as had been anticipated. The
"revolving door" appeared, with people of color and white women
leaving organizations much sooner and faster than white men. The
"glass ceiling" was identified: an invisible, but virtually concrete,
barrier that keeps white women and people of color from the top
executive ranks in organizations. It became clear to leaders in the
field that (1) hiring people of color and white women in an organization was not enough to eliminate discrimination, and (2) awareness
alone was not sufficient to create an environment where everyone
could succeed. Judith Katz summarized her impressions of this era:

> Those of us working in this field had a conception of the need for systems
> change, but many people didn't have the tools yet to accomplish it. In

addition, most organizations were unwilling to make the commitment of time and resources to make change fully sustainable.

Mark Chesler added:

> Another issue, from my perspective, that continued through the mid-1970s was: Once desegregation occurs and you have "more bodies," what do you have to do to integrate? What do you have to do to change the pedagogy, the culture, the systems of organizations?

It also became painfully apparent that the organizational systems themselves were working *against* change. For the pioneers in the field, as well as others, the question became: How can we build organizations that support the desire for change that occurs in workshop sessions?

More and more people began to see the need to bring an organizational-systems perspective to their efforts. In 1978, Kaleel Jamison wrote an article for the *OD Practitioner* called "Affirmative Action Program: Springboard for a Total Organizational Change Effort," in which she said:

> What many organizations don't always see is that an Affirmative Action program, if properly managed, can be the springboard for a total organizational change effort that will upgrade all of their management skills and processes and enable them to reap rich benefits of productivity from the resulting multicultural organization.[18]

This article, along with the work, presentations, and writings of others helped to shift and expand interventions into client systems. First, it changed the focus from individuals to organizational systems. Second, it switched the approach from education and training to systems change. And third, it moved the strategy away from affirmative action to valuing diversity.

Some of the people not mentioned in this article who were facilitating, consulting, and writing on these issues were Clay Alderfer, Eliot Aronson, Pat Bidol-Padva, Michael Broom, Ron Boyer, Nancy Brown, Ron Brown, Barbara Benedict Bunker, June Caldwell, Allan Drexler, Janice Eddy, Jane Elliot, Delyte Frost, Darya Funches, Len Goodstein, Raggle Hayes, Chip Henderson, Stan Hinckley, Bev Hinckley-Brown, Rosabeth Moss Kanter, Hal Kellner, Kate Kirkham, Donald C. Klein, Jonathan Kozol, Len Lanski, Jane Moosbruker, Rod Napler, Carol Pierce, Merlin Pope, Irv Robinson, Santiago Rodriguez, Alice Sargent, Eva Schindler-Rainman, Walter Sikes, Kenneth Sole, Larry Waller, Leon West, and Robert Wood. In addition, many of the people working in this field were influenced by Saul Alinsky, Bob Chin, Kurt Lewin, and Herbert Shepherd.

MAJOR TRENDS OF THE 1980s AND THE 1990s

The 1980s saw a host of changes in the arena of the work to eliminate discrimination and support diversity in organizations. As business conditions tightened, the rationale to do diversity work because "it is the right thing to do" lessened. The imperative to comply with EEO laws and affirmative action efforts also declined under Presidents Reagan and Bush, even as the Hudson Institute report *Workforce 2000* identified and projected a more diverse work force. Global competition increased. White women and people of color were not rising in the organizations as they and others thought they should. Organizational development involving diversity evolved to include systems-change work, not just education.

Regarding diversity itself, a new focus came into being. Replacing the melting-pot paradigm of the 1950s were the "salad bowl," "stew pot," and "mosaic" analogies. These concepts recognized that assimilation was not such a worthy goal, that groups did not want to give up their individual characteristics, and that the country might be better off if they didn't.

By the end of the 1980s, people had begun to reframe the work of eliminating discrimination in organizations toward creating an organizational work culture, environment, system, and infrastructure so that each person could offer her or his full potential in the work place. Evidence was found that organizations that could fully use and value the diverse talent and perspectives of their people could gain competitive advantage in the increasingly complex world of a more diverse work force and a diversely targeted marketplace. Many of these points were driven home by R. Roosevelt Thomas, Jr., in his article "From Affirmative Action to Affirming Diversity," published in the *Harvard Business Review* in 1990.[19]

To understand these shifts in the work to eliminate discrimination and encourage diversity in organizations, it is helpful to look in more detail at the internal and external trends that emerged and how they influenced how organizations and practitioners did this work.

First of all, many other groups, in addition to white women and African Americans, entered the work force in larger numbers. These included both recent immigrants to the United States and Asian, Latino, and African American U.S. citizens. The changing work force increased the complexity of dealing with people, as groups tried to maintain some aspects of their own cultures, values, and styles. It was no longer possible merely to conduct oneself according to a set of memorized rules for dealing with all people the same way. Rather, people needed to develop skills that helped them interact with and learn from others who were different from themselves.

Second, the publication of *Workforce 2000* had caught the attention of leaders and managers with its projections of the demographic, racial, and cultural makeup of the work force in the year 2000. For companies to prosper in their competitive arenas, they would need to utilize the talents of a more diverse work force.

Third, for many reasons—including ongoing individual and systemic discrimination—white women and people of color had not progressed as far or as fast as previously expected. The U.S. Department of Labor completed a study called "The Glass Ceiling Report" that proved the existence of an invisible barrier preventing white women and people of color from reaching the top echelons of organizations. Concurrently, backlash and cries of reverse discrimination occurred.

Fourth, global competition increased. This helped change the prevailing view of diversity from a legal or moral imperative to a business rationale offering an opportunity for competitive advantage.

Fifth, advanced technology permitted more precise target marketing. Having employees who understood the needs and desires of various customer groups became a recognized organizational asset.

Utilizing these five trends, sometimes referred to as the "business case for diversity," more and more organizations could point to fundamental business reasons to harness the power of diversity. Some organizations became much more committed to diversity efforts once they analyzed the costs of employee turnover, competition for employees, opportunities lost to competitors who had capitalized on diversity for market or product advantage, and a host of other business challenges.

Women continued to struggle and to make progress. Rosabeth Kanter's *Men and Women of the Corporation* (1979) and Alice Sargent's *The Androgynous Manager* (1983) took women's issues further, informing women and men about the realities of the organizational world and about strategies for change.

During the 1980s, additional groups demanded better treatment and equality of rights. For example, the Americans with Disabilities Act (1990) mandated efforts to stop discrimination against people with disabilities and required public buildings to provide physical access for everyone. It is considered to be the most sweeping piece of civil rights legislation since 1964. A handful of organizations—including Apple Computer, Ben and Jerry's Ice Cream, Lotus Development Corporation, Levi Strauss, and Stanford University—instituted employee benefits for gay and lesbian partners similar to those available for married couples. Many organizations developed policies in response to the needs of a more diverse work force, such as flex-time, on-site day care, maternity and paternity leave, leave to care for elderly parents, and part-time or shared work. Sexual harassment moved to the forefront as an issue with some widely publicized cases, including the Clarence Thomas hearings.

ENDING DISCRIMINATION AND SUPPORTING DIVERSITY

Many organizations initially tried to improve the working relationships and performance of small, diverse groups. As the years progressed, however, more organizations saw the need to make system-wide changes if diversity was to be successful and add value to the organization. To do this required changing norms, structures, belief systems, policies, and procedures and developing new ways of thinking about organizations. Issues were raised about who "owns the system." A vision of inclusion was being developed where all would be valued for all they bring to the table. Leaders in diversity began to ask what it would be like to have organizations that did not oppress people and fully included everyone.

In commenting on these topics, Evangelina Holvino, researcher and consultant, described a view she shares with many colleagues:

> We saw limitations in affirmative action educational programs. In trying to apply traditional theories of sociology (which have dealt with race and class), we had to transform the theories. We found we had to integrate material from many fields.

Clearly, during the past 30 years, important progress has been made against discrimination in organizations. The changes that have occurred have made the work environment better for everyone. However, there is still much more work to do. In the words of Orian Worden, "The higher in organizations you go, the more male and the more pale it gets."

Thus, we see that by the end of the 1980s there was a decline in legal incentives for organizations to end discrimination and support diversity. Simultaneously, the business rationale for ending discrimination and supporting diversity gained momentum. The technologies to eliminate discrimination involved not only individual education and awareness training but systems change to align the policies, practices, and structures of organizations to support inclusion. Debate within the organizational-development community continued about the degree of emphasis to place on ameliorating oppression as compared to understanding diversity.

The 1990s is sometimes referred to as the "decade of diversity." Whether history will prove this true will depend on how strongly current legislation is enforced and how dedicated and consistent we are in our efforts to end discrimination and support diversity.

NOTES

1. *Workforce 2000* (Hudson Institute, 1987).

2. Peter B. Vaill, *Managing as a Performing Art* (San Francisco: Jossey-Bass, 1989), p. 1.

3. Sumner and Rosen, "The CIO Era, 1935–1955," in J. Jacobsen, editor, *The Negro and the American Labor Movement* (1968).

4. *Steele* v. *Louisville & Nashville Railroad Co.*, 323 U.S. 192 (1944).

5. Theodore Eisenberg, *Civil Rights Legislation, Case and Materials*, 3rd ed. (Charlottesville, Va.: Michie Co., 1991).

6. *Brown* v. *Board of Education*, 347 U.S. 483 (1954).

7. *Plessy* v. *Ferguson*, 163 U.S. 537 (1896).

8. *Brown* v. *Board of Education*, 329 U.S. 294 (1955) (widely known as *Brown II*).

9. A. Leon Higginbotham, Jr., "An Open Letter to Justice Clarence Thomas from a Federal Judicial Colleague," *Racing Justice, Engendering Power: Essays on Anita Hill*, Toni Morrison, editor (New York: Random House, 1992), p. 16.

10. Kenneth C. Davis, *Don't Know Much about History: Everything You Need to Know about American History but Never Learned* (New York: Avon, 1990), p. 387.

11. Milton Viorst, *Fire in the Streets: America in the 1960s* (New York: Simon & Schuster, 1979), pp. 337, 436.

12. *Ibid.*, p. 341.

13. *Ibid.*

14. Kanowitz, "Sex-Based Discrimination in American Law III: Title VII of the 1964 Civil Rights Act and the Equal Pay Act of 1963," *Hastings Law Review*, 20 (1968), pp. 305, 310–12.

15. Flora Davis, *Moving the Mountain: The Women's Movement in America Since 1960* (New York: Simon & Schuster, 1991), p. 45.

16. *Ibid.*, p. 54.

17. *Ibid.*, p. 336.

18. Kaleel Jamison, "Affirmative Action Program: Springboard for a Total Organizational Change Effort," *OD Practitioner* 10, no. 4 (Dec. 1978), p. 1.

19. R. Roosevelt Thomas, Jr., "From Affirmative Action to Affirming Diversity," *Harvard Business Review*, March–April 1990, vol. 68, no. 2, p. 107.

II

VOICES OF CHALLENGE AND OPPORTUNITY

VOICES OF CHALLENGE AND OPPORTUNITY

Oppression often comes cloaked in privilege, position, or organizational culture. Sometimes it's not so well camouflaged—for instance, when it looks like a glass ceiling or a sticky floor. Sometimes it's as shockingly blatant as ethnic cleansing.

The challenge is to recognize and ameliorate oppression no matter what its disguise. And once we do, we can discover the opportunity to benefit and profit from, even celebrate, the diversity of human life.

Chapter Two

Price M. Cobbs

The Challenge and Opportunities of Diversity

Price M. Cobbs

■

Price M. Cobbs, MD, is an internationally recognized management consultant. His clients range from Fortune 500 companies to inner-city businesses and government and community agencies. His company, Pacific Management Systems, consults with global organizations on executive development, achieving a diverse work force, effective communications, and the psychology of networking. Among his writings, the best known are Black Rage *and* The Jesus Bag, *coauthored with William Grier.*

T he United States of America is, and will continue to be, a heterogeneous society. While other nations may find creative genius in their homogeneity, the creative genius of the American experience has always been our diversity. Whatever our stops and starts and detours, the American impulse has always been to expand rather than contract—to include more diversity rather than less.

The world is increasingly interdependent and diverse. In some ways, it will be to the United States and its institutions that other nations will look to learn how to achieve diversity—what succeeds and what fails. Clearly, there will be other models, but ours will be a major model.

I submit that those of us who aspire to leadership in helping people of different values create a world community must understand and influence ourselves and our families before we will be able to influence our colleagues, our clients, our communities, and our organizations.

MODEL FOR VALUING DIVERSITY

My model for unraveling and more deeply understanding the many critical perspectives on the psychology of race is to focus at three levels: personal, interpersonal, and global. At the personal level, each person needs to actively examine one's values, particularly values about differences. Probing at the interpersonal level involves a thorough and more minute analysis of what goes on between people, particularly where there are racial, gender, or cultural differences. At the societal or global level, one needs to comprehend the role of race and difference in the world. Let's look at each of these in more detail.

Personal

All of us must begin a process of identifying and examining the underlying thoughts, feelings, attitudes, and assumptions that block our understanding and embracing of diversity. We have got to understand that none of us is immune from ethnocentrism, chauvinism, racism, sexism. Studies show that we are all capable of prejudice. But most people are unaware of their prejudices. What's interesting is that oppression affects the oppressor as well as the oppressed. I believe that people have a preconscious knowledge that the world out there is not as equal as they might have thought. Part of understanding our own prejudices is the ability to introspect and to begin to understand one's own attitudes and assumptions. Only by having a core value of diversity that transcends tribalism can any individual hope to banish the demons of superiority and inferiority, of exclusion and inclusion.

People must also get in touch with their personal power. As Lord Acton said, "Power corrupts," but the converse is also true: Powerlessness is not a virtue; it, too, corrupts. To get in touch with one's personal power requires getting in touch with one's personal history, examining it, acknowledging one's feelings, and discarding the elements that do not serve oneself. It is also important to incorporate the aspects of oneself that contribute to personal power—for example, owning one's intelligence and capabilities. I refer to this process as "ethnotherapy: the search for discovery." It is an identification, a claiming of a major part of oneself that has been denied and devalued. This leads to a healthy pride, but it is a difficult process for people who have been oppressed. It is a lifelong process, and often starts with another person, such as a teacher, therapist, or friend. It helps people to become internally driven to broaden their personal stage.

Interpersonal

At the interpersonal level, we need to understand and move beyond the timidness and intellectual laziness that make us see people who are different in terms of categories and stereotypes. We must all realize that the ultimate aim of valuing diversity is to be able to individualize each and every person we encounter, taking into account all facets of his or her identity. The people themselves become the category rather than having to fit into categories we assign them.

To do this, we need techniques to look beyond words and see the dynamics of what creates "old-boy clubs" and "glass ceilings." On all sides, we need to address the conscious and unconscious factors that create oppression, that pull some people in and keep others out. And we need to identify what people on both sides of the organizational walls need to know to remove obstacles.

In a multicultural way, individuals should ask themselves with whom are they most comfortable and least comfortable. Although most people are most comfortable with people like themselves, this doesn't necessarily mean that everyone is racist. The problem is how to relate to people different from oneself, how to be more candid and achieve better understanding.

True diversity is reflected in people's ability to bond across areas of difference. It's the bonding that helps people become more predictable to one another. We need to begin to set up processes to bring people together in teams and to work together; this is the essence of managing differences. And we need to acknowledge the differences. We live in an era that celebrates differences, but we each must acknowledge that we don't know much about these differences.

As we begin to celebrate our differences, we can expand our stage. Through workshops, seminars, and T-groups, we can explore the unspoken hot buttons and "encounter" one another. We must be able to talk about more things so that we're not waiting for the other shoe to drop. People perceive the same situation differently because of different filters. We need to share some reality with others—for example, the reality that we will not always agree. And we need to engage in this dialogue with a motivation to really understand the other person.

Organizational

In our organizations, we must fight to make valuing diversity a bedrock value and not something that is optional or somehow outside the parameters of how business is conducted. We have the opportunity to help leaders set core organizational values of diversity. In this way, diversity can be as basic a value as productivity, efficiency, quality, and excellence.

Only when valuing diversity is a core value of our organizations will we begin to be uncomfortable when we do not see diversity.

Once diversity gets in your gut, you begin to feel uncomfortable when you don't see it. "If this is supposed to be a diverse organization, then why are all of us here men . . . or black men . . . or Jewish . . . or women?"

This clearly does not obviate the occasional need for support groups, for bonding with people who understand our pain, our victimization, or our life situation. The ultimate aim of our journey is to value diversity and expand our humanity so that we can include more.

The bottom-line benefit of celebrating differences is that it adds value. In the banking industry, for example, 65 percent of the entry-level employees are women. But they have to figure out how to be like Chairman Joe in order to succeed. At what point do we push organizations to stretch? We need to celebrate differences first among groups and then among individuals. People need to see that it is in their self-interest to identify and demystify success factors in organizations. White men, for example, are as much a part of diversity as anyone. Diversity will help us all get in touch with our humanity. When I can celebrate differences with others, I don't have to oppress or be oppressed.

Cultural habits of organizations are instinctual. Our communities, our organizations need to learn more: How do we attain more efficiency? How do we help workers feel more valued and empowered? How do we attain more collaboration, more consensus, more teamwork?

What Organizations Can Do

A key dynamic in organizations revolves around the following questions:

> Is it the task of people who come into the organization to conform to the organization in order to succeed?
>
> Or is it the task of the organization to broaden itself to include others?

The progress to date has been the acknowledgment of diversity around demographics. In reality, we've barely begun this work. There is no state-of-the-art in organizations concerning diversity. You can't buy my bag of tricks and be over all this in five years because we're dealing with every person's core. There is no quick fix in diversity. The reality is that we ameliorate oppression in organizations by figuring out what makes people angry and what to do about it. You don't ameliorate oppression by asking the oppressor to stop.

Elements for Achieving a High-Performance, World Class, Diverse Organization

The mindset of diversity. The mindset of diversity flows out of an understanding of who you are and then an openness to the experiences of others. You do not need a checklist of how people act or a compilation of group characteristics. The mindset is aimed at trying to individualize each person. It is not the clinical sterility of color blindness and gender blindness. It is the ability to be additive rather than reductive in understanding a whole person.

Skills and competencies. First and foremost, we must help everyone, particularly managers, know that we interact with and manage *people*. All else is secondary.

It is important to develop competency as an active, nonjudgmental listener, to learn to stretch one's values to hear and experience someone who is different, and to learn how to accept and give feedback. It is also important to learn how to focus on talent and make style secondary. It is much easier to adjust to a person's style than to find talent. People should also learn how to discuss perceived barriers, whatever they are, without feeling guilty or intimidated.

Accountabilities. People are accountable for knowing how to mutually educate, participate in developmental processes, coach, and mentor. People are accountable for making diverse "pools," whether they are for hiring, promotion, or successor planning.

Commitment. The organization must be committed to diversity in all its forms as a core value of the organization. Understanding and doing this will then dictate needs, what is defined as a problem, how problems are solved, and expectations for behavior.

Leadership. Successful leadership involves doing all of the above and then collaboratively creating and defining an ongoing vision. Leaders will see themselves as taking risks and will know that their legacy will be institutionalized, permanent workplace diversity.

Facilities locations. Organizations must locate their facilities in cities, which helps energize small businesses. Organizations must also establish partnerships between themselves and the people, in particular hooking up disenchanted people with businesses.

MELTING POT TO MULTICULTURAL SOCIETY

We must acknowledge and understand that we are undergoing a monumental paradigm shift from America as a melting pot to America as a multicultural society.

The melting-pot paradigm, at its height in the 1950s, held that newcomers and people of difference would, and should, assimilate into the mainstream of Western European–based U.S. culture. But all of us didn't melt, and we lost something if we had to change our name or drop cultural attributes that were uplifting and healthy.

The struggle to change the paradigm occurred in the 1980s. Political correctness is one major signal of the paradigm shift. The term *colored* was an imposed designation. It evolved to *Negro,* then to *black,* and now to African American. African American is an American identity with different facets. People today are much better able to talk about such different facets of themselves. Such discussions are encouraged now, whereas they were punished previously.

WHERE WE ARE TODAY, WITH A LOOK TOWARD THE FUTURE

We are only in the first stages of achieving diversity. The work will go on for generations, and there will be many more questions along the way.

At this time, we are struggling with what it means to be a multicultural society. We consider ourselves good if we stop stereotyping, and all too often that leads us merely to color and gender blindness. We need to develop a vocabulary of difference, to describe and define that which is different in ways that are individual and nonstereotypical.

We're on a path that will continue to involve peeling "layers of the onion" to get closer to our humanity. The United States, whatever its flaws, is in the best position to lead the world through this process. Within organizations, we need to set up systems and processes to encourage everyone to be intellectually curious about those who are different. What's interesting is that in organizations that are more actively working toward diversity, you see more things of a personal nature being discussed.

I believe that we will have continued progress *and* we will continue to scare one another. Today, one important aspect of leadership is to demonstrate that as we reveal ourselves we don't have to frighten others. A big fear I have is about how to realistically write about what's going on, give accolades where they are due, and also let folks know that we're a long, long way from where we want to be.

Some of the key issues of our times have clearly been racism, sexism, homophobia, anti-Semitism, and an increasing amount of anti-Arabism. If we are going to stay the course, we must constantly expand the scope of what we are looking at so that we do not, in our liberation, allow other people to be victimized.

Along with much of the global village, our nation is once again at a critical juncture. With breathtaking speed, significant parts of the world have reordered themselves. In the United States, long-awaited structural change has begun to occur. In this country, the era of color and gender blindness, of conformity to narrow models and limited vision, mercifully, has begun to pass.

There are immense challenges in understanding these changes and managing this reordering. Most importantly, individuals, groups, and nations are in a volatile period of redefinition. Because of this, danger and fragmentation lurk everywhere. However, for those willing to assume the risk of leadership, a golden psychological moment has arisen. We can acquire and model a new vision of inclusion or watch a retreat back into a deadly, all-consuming tribalism. Therein lies the challenge: to overcome that tenuous and volatile interface between danger and opportunity, between risk taking and restlessness. We must seize the moment.

Chapter Three

Elsie Y. Cross

Truth—or Consequences?

Elsie Y. Cross

■

Elsie Y. Cross is founder and president of Elsie Y. Cross Associates, Inc., an organization development consulting firm in Philadelphia and publisher of The Diversity Factor, *a quarterly journal. Since 1970, she has consulted to organizations in Europe, Africa, and the Caribbean, as well as to U.S. corporations and national, state, and local governmental agencies. The firm consults on organization development, managing diversity, team building, strategic planning, and conflict resolution. She is one of the coeditors of this book.*

I magine you are the CEO of a major U.S. corporation and employees tell you that:

- Racial jokes are common in their work environment, and work-related information is routinely denied them because of their race or gender.
- Sexual harassment is commonplace and covered up, and women feel their expertise is ignored.
- People from many different groups—African American men and women, Hispanic/Latino women and men, white women, gay and lesbian people, Asian men and women—believe their chances for development and advancement are limited because of their identities, and their turnover rate is much higher than that of white male employees.
- Customers who are not white men have had bad experiences with your organization.
- Morale and productivity have suffered.
- Managers in your organization feel uncomfortable about giving—or even unable to give—feedback and career development assistance to people of color and white women.
- Even the white men are complaining: They want better solutions for their work and family issues and more guidance for working effectively with their colleagues.

While you are being pelted with all these messages, your Human Resources Department is delivering more bad news. The workplace you joined many years ago is startlingly different now; by the year 2000, less than 20 percent of the incoming work force will be white and male.

What would you do? Some organizations choose to do nothing. Some focus on "fixing" white women and people of color to make them behave like white men. This may mean sending African American employees off to "finishing school" or sending some employees to accent reduction classes so that they will "fit in" better.

Some organizations begin a frenzy of activity: They plan a cultural diversity day, create ethnic menus in the company cafeteria, import a speaker to talk about multiculturalism, organize a diversity council, or issue an affirmative-action or diversity vision statement.

Smart organizations recognize that they have a problem and set about addressing it intelligently and systematically. First, they commit themselves to understanding the problem and how their situation evolved.

LOOKING AT THE FACTS

Twenty-five years ago, nearly all American businesses, universities, and other organizations were led and managed by white men. White women and minorities in these organizations were either "exceptions"—professionals who were hired because of the cynical response to affirmative-action and equal employment opportunity laws—or employees at the lower levels of the hierarchy. Today, the situation is radically different. In some companies, as many as 75 percent of the workers are women, and 20 percent are people of color.

Twenty-five years ago, it was assumed that nearly all business, university, and other organizational leaders were heterosexual. Today, we know that many of these leaders are *not* heterosexual; but we still do not know how many gay men and lesbian women are in our work force because they fear for their careers—and even their personal safety—if they acknowledge their sexual orientation.

The social history of these issues includes the legacy of slavery, segregation, and resegregation of African Americans; the stereotyping of people of Latino, Asian, Hispanic, or Native American ancestry as inferior to whites; widespread and largely unquestioned homophobia; and socialization patterns that say men are naturally dominant and women are naturally subordinate.

We don't even know how to talk about these issues, much less how to work on them effectively. In many organizations, racism, sexism, xenophobia, and heterosexism are so deeply and invisibly embedded in the organization's culture that there is no way to dig down to them—and little desire to change.

GETTING STARTED

In the midst of all these considerations, corporations still have products to produce, services to render, and profits to make. Customers must be satisfied, and a highly skilled, cohesive work force must be developed to serve their needs. The CEO and senior managers have a choice: either learn how to manage an organization that can confront the changes with courage and competence or manage an organization that will become increasingly contentious and expensively litigious.

The first step any organization must take is to admit that the changes are real. They are permanent, and the challenges they present must be addressed seriously.

There are common elements in the goals of organizations committed to meeting these changes. The need to meet the legal requirements of equal employment opportunity and affirmative action and avoid expensive litigation is a universal impetus, but that alone is insufficient to launch an effort and keep it going.

More promising for the long-term success of the effort are such factors as the recognition of the diversity of the customer/client base, the threatened loss of "employer of choice" status, the opportunities for improved teamwork, the additional creativity that results from the application of disparate viewpoints during problem resolution, and the increase in productivity that results from improved employee satisfaction and loyalty to the company.

Corporations with successful programs also have other similarities:

- Top management's commitment to the effort.
- Willingness to hold employees accountable for success and to reward them for positive results.
- Tenacious determination to

  make sure that the work goes beyond individual behavior and bias,

  examine patterns of discrimination caused by organizational policies and practices,

  change aspects of the organization's culture that create advantages for certain kinds of people and erect barriers for others.

- The fortitude to "hang in" against charges of reverse discrimination, quotas, "political correctness," and the other guises of resistance to change.

- Recognition that correcting the course of a large, complicated organization incurs enormous cost, the least of which is the time commitment required of its managers.

STRATEGIES

If your organization needs to change in order to provide equal opportunity and access to men and women of color and white women, the strategies to create that change will have become evident:

- You must educate your employees. Not just a few. Not just those in the Human Resources Department. Not just middle managers. You must begin with yourself and your management board. You must commit the organization's resources to the education of a large number of employees, with the goal of creating a critical mass of educated managers and others. In this way, your organization can move toward a culture that values, supports, and develops white women and people of color as well as white men.

- You must create managerial processes and structures that will maintain the change effort. At this point, it is important to create groups charged with the ongoing maintenance of the culture-change process: diversity councils, task forces, and management development programs. You will need to look at every aspect of your business, including recruiting and hiring, performance appraisal, succession planning, and so forth.

- Management of diversity, quality, employee development, and other initiatives must be integrated under a single umbrella in order to guard against the possibility (or strong likelihood!) that racism and sexism will come creeping back into your business practices.

- You must engage your entire organization in a process that makes visible the unwritten, informal aspects of your culture. You must find the sources of racism, sexism, and other discriminatory attitudes and behaviors and replace them with attitudes and behaviors that will create a new, vigorous, more open, and more productive organization. You must recognize that just as biodiversity creates healthier natural environments, human diversity creates stronger organizational environments.

BENEFITS

Why bother to do all this? Are you facing the prospect of risking hard-won earnings on a gamble with no way of assessing the payoff?

Organizations that engage in this process receive payoffs right from the start. Visible changes occur at the individual level, at the group level, and, gradually, throughout the organization. You must expect an ongoing struggle between the forces for change and the forces supporting the status quo. But if you are clear about your vision and consistent in supporting the institutionalization of that vision, you'll begin to see and feel the changes sooner than you might expect.

Individuals in organizations undergoing such change report the following:

> "I have achieved greater control and power over events in my own life."

> "I have recognized attitudes and biases that I never dreamed I had—and I have learned I don't have to hold onto them."

> "I used to wonder if I had a persecution complex. I no longer have to take each incident personally."

> "I now have the language to talk about issues of diversity."

In addition to enjoying improved work relationships, men and women often report that they have better relationships with their spouses and children. Husbands have attributed their new attitudes to the "managing diversity" work.

There are also benefits that occur at the group level:

> "In our organization, we see people of color and white women becoming more hopeful that things will really change."

> "We feel proud to be Asian Americans."

> "I no longer feel bogged down in guilt. I recognize that white men are empowered to make choices and that we have important contributions to make."

> "We see payoffs beyond what we expected. At a recent meeting in the South, we noticed that white people in our organization were comfortably appreciative of black culture. We also saw folks from the North and the West being appreciative of Southern culture in general."

There are also numerous payoffs at the organizational level:

> "We were facing an EEOC investigation; they've looked at what we're doing and have backed off."

> "In the last two years, turnover has been minimal."

> "We are more customer-focused because we are not as individually competitive; we are more confident within ourselves."

> "We've found that the heavy up-front costs are being offset by the decrease in legal actions and in turnover; we now have a net gain on the bottom line."

> "This year three people of color and one woman were promoted to vice president."

"At a recent national sales meeting, a comedian told a sexist joke and *no one laughed!* All 400 people in the room were stunned."

"We have developed a corps of 'champions' of the new culture. Our champions help us avoid becoming too complacent and comfortable."

"We have learned how to build new coalitions, aligning across race and gender and levels."

"We are increasing our internal capability to manage change. Learning to work together across race and gender has helped us be more creative in approaching all kinds of challenges."

"This is becoming a fun place to be. I look forward to coming to work every day."

"We are building a place where everybody is recognized and rewarded for contributions, whether they are white men or men of color, women of color or white women."

"We're replacing the 'myth of meritocracy' with a system where individual contribution is actually solicited and honored."

One organization that had spent years on diversity work experienced a time of economic stress that required downsizing. During this period—and without the help of consultants—the company was able to continue its diversity efforts. It made sure the procedures that resulted in the necessary layoffs or firings did not revert to the old business-as-usual processes favoring white men and putting men and women of color and white women at the top of the list of those to be let go. There was certainly pain and anger and resentment, but it was not the *same* pain and anger and resentment. Management emerged from the experience exhausted, but confident that they had done the right thing and knew how to do it better in the future.

Chapter Four

Frederick A. Miller

Forks in the Road
Critical Issues on the Path to Diversity

Frederick A. Miller

■

Frederick A. Miller is president of The Kaleel Jamison Consulting Group, Inc., a leading management consulting and strategic cultural change firm. He was formerly a manager with Connecticut General Life Insurance Company (now CIGNA), where he was responsible for its pioneering diversity effort, which started in 1972. He serves on the boards of directors of Ben & Jerry's Homemade, Inc., The National OD Network, and the Institute of Development Research. He is the managing editor of this book.

E mbracing diversity requires a major shift in the way we see the world. Learning to think, act, and work productively in partnership with people of different cultures, styles, abilities, classes, nationalities, races, sexual orientations, and genders means more than just acquiring new skills and new attitudes. It also means giving up the old familiar identities, expectations, roles, and operating patterns with which we have grown so comfortable.

After more than 20 years of helping organizations prepare for, cope with, and profit from diversity, I feel justified in making a sweeping generalization: *People don't understand the magnitude of the changes involved.*

The road to diversity is a bumpy one. It's full of potholes, speed traps, and unmarked detours. Here are some of the areas where organizations often go astray.

INCLUSION VERSUS EXCLUSION

Accepting the concept of inclusion requires a great deal of rethinking for most organizations—and for each of us individually. For thousands of years, human beings have been trained to be suspicious of people who are different, to avoid strangers, and to "stick with our own kind." *Exclusive* has come to mean *desirable* and *comfortable,* as in exclusive clubs, exclusive schools, exclusive neighborhoods.

t exclusion breeds sameness. Members of exclusive groups tend alike, dress alike, even walk alike. They agree on virtually all important issues. Their norms and values are static. Monocultural groups resist change. *Inclusion* turns *comfortable* upside out and inside down. Inclusive groups thrive on difference. They seek out different points of view so they can assess situations from every angle. They see cultural diversity not as something to be avoided or tolerated but as a necessity for success.

Inclusive groups encourage disagreement because they realize it leads to more-effective solutions and more-successful adaptations to a changing environment. Instead of pressuring members to leave their individual and cultural differences outside, inclusive groups ask everyone to contribute to the full extent of their being. It's a fundamental shift: from *e pluribus unum* to *e pluribus magnificentia*.

REVOLUTION VERSUS EVOLUTION

In today's rapidly changing world, monoculturalism has become obsolete. It is simply too costly, wasteful, and limiting.

The assembly-line, mass-production manufacturing methods of the early twentieth century fostered monoculturalism, and vice versa. Today's trends toward microproduction, product customization, and niche marketing *demand* diversity.

"Any color you want, as long as it's black"—the saying associated with the Ford Model T—has given way to "Any color you want, when you want it, in any size or shape you want it in." Diversity in the marketplace requires diversity of the work force, both to perceive the differing demands of niche groups and to supply the energetic creativity required to meet all the various demands.

Diversity creates a far more challenging existence than monoculturalism. Instead of business as usual, it means constant expansion—not necessarily in size but in vision—to include a broader range of people, customers, stakeholders, suppliers, profit centers, products, services, and business partners.

Diversity asks organizations to adapt to radically changing market conditions, to move at high speed, to learn to service a highly diverse global marketplace, and to innovate more rapidly than ever before. And it challenges the members of the organization to bring more to the table than ever before, to achieve an undefined maximum rather than some standardized minimum.

These trends exert evolutionary forces on organizations, promising growth to those that can adapt while threatening with extinction those that cannot. But *within* organizations trying to adapt, evolution doesn't begin to describe the kinds of changes taking place. Considering the magnitude and scope of the changes required by diversity, and the time frame required to implement them, the process can only be described as a *revolution.*

INVESTMENT VERSUS HANDOUTS

How important is a successful cultural change process for an organization? How much is it worth?

When cultural diversity/change looks like affirmative action or a handout for disadvantaged groups, it looks expensive. The bottom-line value-to-cost ratio may make the effort hard to justify. But when change is seen as critical for future organizational success, it's much more likely to be perceived as a worthwhile investment.

The cost of people leaving a corporation can far exceed the cost of any organizational change effort. In many large companies, it costs about $100,000 per person to recruit and train middle- and upper-level managers. One company had 70 people leave in the course of a year—a loss of $7,000,000 in recruiting and training expenses. No company can afford to spend that kind of money and end up with people who feel underutilized, who cannot give a full contribution, or who want out. That's a very good way to a bad bottom line.

The question becomes: How much is it worth to an organization to make it possible for its people to stay and contribute to the best of their abilities? Considering training and recruitment costs, productivity, continuity, quality of customer service, and value of innovation, the answer can be a great deal indeed.

INTEGRATION VERSUS ISOLATION

To gain the maximum benefit from diversity, an organization must establish a comprehensive, integrated strategy of inclusive policies, procedures, and systems. Addressing isolated areas with isolated policies keeps both the change effort and the people isolated.

Revising a company's recruitment and hiring practices may actually compound its problems unless the company also addresses its cultural biases. Working on the cultural biases will not create inclusiveness unless the company also updates its systems of benefits, rewards, bonuses, and incentives.

A comprehensive strategic cultural change effort must do more than raise awareness. It must prepare people for changes in procedures, systems, structures, and leadership approach. It must teach skills in communication, conflict resolution, advocacy, and problem

solving. It must address fears about inclusion of many cultures. It must insist on behavioral change.

Short-term, single-issue training courses simply can't address the entire interrelated spectrum of areas affected by creating an inclusive organization. Unless tied together with an integrated, systemic strategy, these courses just waste the participants' time and the organization's resources.

POCKETS OF READINESS VERSUS KEEPING EVERYONE TOGETHER

To implement change in large organizations, management often thinks everyone in the organization must move ahead together. This thinking is admirable, but it is often counterproductive. There are going to be parts of the organization—business units or functional areas—that can move a lot faster than the rest of the organization. These *pockets of readiness and opportunity* can be very advantageous to the change effort because they can model the change and its benefits for the rest of the organization. Create a pull process (I want that) versus a push process (You must take this).

When people try to do the same thing in every part of the organization at the same time, they're sure to have difficulty. What's appropriate for one unit may cause resentment and backlash in another. It's far better to recognize the diversity of the different units. Each may need a different type of intervention or an individualized variation on an overall theme.

You're far more likely to achieve success if you have a successful unit to hold up as a model to show people that diversity can work. Success lies in getting people to see the value of the change so that they buy into the effort and eventually take the initiative themselves.

AGREEING TO DISAGREE VERSUS KEEPING A LOW PROFILE

Aggressive communication is a key characteristic of successfully inclusive organizations. Because of their different cultural perspectives, members of inclusive groups disagree on many issues, which ensures consideration of more than one side of those issues. Different points of view are required for a group to be able to see all aspects of the landscape.

In monocultural groups, members who disagree with the prevailing view learn to keep a low profile. They don't want to be labeled malcontents. In inclusive groups, members are valued specifically *for* their differing points of view. Not only are they expected to have differences, they're expected to *express* them.

FOCUS GROUPS VERSUS ASSUMPTIONS

"Just do what you did for XYZ Corporation." I hear that request probably 20 times a year. Then I explain that each organization is like a safe with a seven-digit combination lock. Experience will probably help us guess the first three digits. The next three digits will be unique to that organization, and we use focus groups to reveal them. The last digit only comes with time and engagement with the organization. Operating simply on assumptions is like trying to open the lock knowing only the first three digits. Unless you're extremely lucky, you end up either quitting the job before the payoff or having to blow up the safe.

Without a well-structured cultural assessment to use as a guide, cultural-change interventions can cause backlash reactions, deep resentments, mistrust of management, and increased internal conflict. Focus groups provide the key for developing effective interventions that defuse tensions and bring people together. Focus groups help sort out where an organization is along the path from monoculturalism to inclusiveness.[1] They provide a fairly clear picture of the organizational landscape: the key issues, the underlying concerns, the communication styles, the problem-solving methods, and the way the people of the organization see themselves and how they fit in.

LOCAL VERSUS GLOBAL

In some organizations, there is a tendency to want to become internationally diverse without first achieving a culture that is inclusive of all the local members. Perhaps it's more glamorous to learn to appreciate Japanese family values or the Korean work ethic than those of Latinos or African Americans. Perhaps it's less threatening to accept the differences of people across the ocean than those of the people across the hall.

For diversity to work, an organization must start by including and embracing the diversity it has *now*—with the people in this building, this corridor, the next cubicle; with the shipping department as well as the sales department; among the maintenance crew as well as management.

Whatever we learn about the person in the next cubicle—her individuality, her culture, his identity group, his nationality—will help us work better with that person and appreciate what that person has to offer. We can build from there; everything we gain from knowing the current members of the organization will help us learn to appreciate new members who join us later.

Addressing the international agenda before working on including the people in your local area can cause resentment and backlash: "Why are you so interested in people outside our area when you don't seem concerned about the people right here?" "Why are we offering full acceptance to *that* group when *my* group still isn't fully accepted?"

LEVELING THE PLAYING FIELD

It can be very hard for a dominant cultural group to realize it has stacked the deck in favor of itself. It's hard enough for it to realize it might even *have* a culture. When you're inside it, it looks normal. It doesn't look like a culture; it looks like what is. As a friend says, only a flying fish could have discovered water.

The U.S. white-male culture is one example. The values of rugged individualism, pragmatism, stoicism, and competitiveness seem absolutely natural to those who share them. Many fail to see the unfairness of policies based solely on those values.

One of the most common examples of cultural bias creating an unlevel playing field occurs in organizations' benefits plans. Many organizations still seem to use "Ozzie and Harriet" as the model for determining benefits. To derive full advantage, employees' families must fit a mythical mold of working man, homemaker wife, healthy children, and nonexistent (or healthy and self-sufficient) parents. Unfortunately, such benefits plans don't work for the majority of today's work force. They put barriers in the way of peak performance by dual-income family members, single parents, gays, lesbians, people with disabilities, and many others.

The first step in leveling the playing field is accepting that biases exist and understanding that the "new" people bump up against them every day.

By exposing and rooting out biases, you widen the bandwidth of acceptable behavior to allow more people to contribute more completely. The goal is to make the organization as inclusive as possible without undermining the behaviors that produce success in the organization. In fact, widening the bandwidth actually increases the number of behaviors that produce success by encouraging new ways of thinking, seeing, and problem solving.

CAMPSITES ON THE JOURNEY

In the United States, we tend to make laws, establish policies, and build structures as if they're permanent, as if the reasons for building them won't change. That has left us with a lot of awkward laws, embarrassing policies, and empty buildings.

Coping successfully with diversity, and thriving because of it, requires acceptance of constant change. A successful, diverse, inclusive organization recognizes that its composition and capabilities (and therefore its opportunities and vision of what can be) will have to change and adapt constantly. A successful organization continually seeks to *increase* its diversity—to expand its ability to see the landscape, broaden its range of perception, enhance its creativity, and improve its problem-solving abilities.

With acceptance of constant change comes the possibility of strategic planning based on moving targets, changing vehicles, shifting goals, and even a moving starting point.

Instead of building permanent structures based on today's vision, a successful organization must build temporary structures that offer the best means for *both* dealing with today's needs and moving on toward tomorrow's new challenges. It must be ready to break camp tomorrow and leave behind everything of no use on the next leg of the journey.

Campsites, with their connotation of being movable and improvable, provide an outstanding metaphor for today's strategic thinking. If we commit to permanent structures—or fall in love with today's solutions, buildings, equipment, or policies—we will be forced to respond to tomorrow's needs with yesterday's solutions.

POSITIONING THE ORGANIZATION FOR THE TWENTY-FIRST CENTURY

The times require speed, adaptability, and the ability to see as much of the landscape as possible. Diversity gives organizations a greater probability of achieving those capabilities than does monoculturalism. An organizational culture biased toward maximum diversity and inclusion offers the greatest potential for 360-degree vision and the broadest resource base for adaptability, growth, creativity, productivity, and high performance—exactly the attributes organizations will need to survive and thrive amid the rapid and unforeseeable changes of the twenty-first century.

NOTE

1. This concept of a continuum from monoculturalism to inclusiveness is based on a model developed by Bailey Jackson, Rita Hardiman, and Mark Chesler in 1981. A comprehensive discussion of this continuum can be found in "Cultural Diversity as a Developmental Process: The Path from Monocultural Club to Inclusive Organization," by Judith H. Katz and Frederick A. Miller (1993: The Kaleel Jamison Consulting Group).

Chapter Five

Judith H. Katz

White Women's Collusion
Caught Between Oppression, Power, and Privilege[1]

Judith H. Katz

■

Judith H. Katz, EdD, senior vice president, The Kaleel Jamison Consulting Group, Inc., has focused her 20-year career in organizational development on linking strategic initiatives with diversity efforts. Her book, White Awareness: Handbook for Anti-Racism Training *(1978), was one of the first works to address racism from a white perspective. A respected educator, consultant, and writer, she is also the author of* No Fairy Godmothers, No Magic Wands: The Healing Process After Rape *(1984) and numerous articles on diversity, oppression, and empowerment. She is one of the coeditors of this book.*

T oday, white women still face very real issues of discrimination and oppression in our society and organizations. We still face the very real issues of glass-ceilinged management structures, gender-based salary and benefit inequities, widespread sexual harassment that continues to be winked at, and pandemic violence against us (about which we continue to be accused of "asking for it"). And even in the most enlightened dual-income families, women still end up with primary responsibility for child care and virtually all of the housework.

Most of the playing fields onto which we venture remain steeply slanted against us. We still have much to do to eliminate the oppressions we face every day. But in looking for the oppressors we need to confront, we often neglect to look within. Living with our feelings of anger, pain and frustration, it is difficult to imagine that we might be causing the same feelings in others. By concentrating our attention on identifying those who have oppressed us, we too easily and too often avoid looking at how we oppress others.

LET SHE WHO IS WITHOUT SIN. . .

We see clearly how white men have oppressed us in society and in our organizations. We are quick to ally ourselves with women of color in identifying the violence as well as the systemic oppression visited upon women by men of all races and cultures. But we are puzzled when the women of color in our organizations don't rush to join us and help carry our banners as we lobby for more representation in senior management.

Somehow we don't notice that, while women may be excluded from the top echelons of the organization, women *of color* are often excluded from all but the lowest positions. And if we do notice, we don't consider the possibility that we could have contributed to the stratification of the organization's workforce along racial lines.

When we identify ourselves as victims of oppression because of our gender, we tend to absolve ourselves of any possible involvement in the oppression of anyone else. After all, oppression requires power plus prejudice,[2] and as an oppressed group ourselves, we don't admit to possessing the power to oppress others. Looking through the lens of our gender, we remain blind to the very real differences of experience and opportunity that exist among women, not only across racial lines, but including class, age, religion, and sexual orientation.

The truth is not flattering. As whites, we have enjoyed a lifetime of privilege based on our membership in the dominant racial identity group. Our privilege is virtually invisible to us. We don't see the countless benefits we receive. We don't see the built-in advantages that give white women an edge in competition with women of color. While we focus on the glass ceiling, we don't notice those who are struggling to free themselves from the sticky floor.[3]

One of our greatest advantages comes from our relationships with white men, often the same white men who oppress us. They see us as their wives, daughters and mothers, and they often feel they have to protect and provide for us. They give us the benefit of the doubt on questions of competency, trustworthiness, intelligence, character, reliability, and commitment to the organization. They also feel more comfortable with us than with people of other races. Though they may not be especially comfortable with women in general, they're a lot more comfortable with white women than with our African-American, Asian, Native American, or Hispanic sisters. And when these men make the decisions about who gets hired and promoted, you know who they're more likely to hire and promote.

OWNING OUR PREJUDICE

Looking inward, we must examine our feelings, beliefs and perspectives about people who are different from ourselves, not just people of color, but also people not born in the United States, people with disabilities, people with nonheterosexual orientations, small people, large people, people with foreign accents, people from different socioeconomic classes. Is our discomfort prejudice? And if we possess power in addition to that prejudice, what do we do with it and what does that make us?

Consciously or unconsciously, we accept our more senior positions in our organizations as part of the natural order. We assume we gained our status strictly on our own merit and believe we're just more deserving than others, without noticing that those others are often from other racial identity groups. We may be crystal clear about how, as women, our talents are diminished, overlooked and unheard. But we rarely see how we maintain those same beliefs and behaviors toward others. Understanding our power and our prejudice can help us identify how we are part of the systems that oppress us and how we collude with those systems.

COLLUSION OF SILENCE

Collusion is one of the ways we support and maintain our privilege and power. Make no mistake about it, our unwillingness to speak out against the systemic and casual expressions of discrimination we encounter every day is collusion. Our silence contributes to the continuation of that discrimination. When we fail to object to injustice, stereotypes, racist language, sexist jokes and elitist behavior, we help it flourish.

One way we collude is to see issues as individually focused and deny that they exist on a systemic level. We avoid raising questions of how our racial differences contribute to our being heard differently and treated differently in our organizations. We continue the collusion when we don't talk about how oppression, power and privilege have shaped us differently, nor challenge ourselves to see the impact on each of our lives, nor admit to responsibility for how things are, nor take responsibility for changing them.

It takes courage to break the code of silence. We often collude out of fear. We distance ourselves from controversy so we do not have to confront enmity, ridicule or retaliation. Sometimes, we simply fear change. But sometimes what we fear is loss of the power and privilege the system confers upon us.

DISOWNING OUR PRIVILEGE

Admitting to our position of privilege is difficult. As Peggy McIntosh says, "For me, white privilege has turned out to be an elusive and fugitive subject. The pressure to avoid it is great, for in facing it I must give up the myth of the meritocracy."[4] But owning our privilege is an important step. It allows us as white women to understand that we do possess power. And if we possess the power to oppress, we also have the power to create change.

Many of us who are in professional roles do indeed speak out and advocate for change in regard to issues important to women. But all too often, these are primarily middle class white women's issues. We ask for "flex-time" so we can spend more quality time with our families, yet we fail to support flex-time for the many women in the organization who are in hourly classifications. We may even get upset when inconvenienced because people on our support staff need time off for their own family issues.

When we seek coalition with other women in our organizations to address our common issues of oppression, our narrow-viewed agendas often fail to address issues that are of greatest concern to those who are most marginalized. They may not be as interested in *equal* wages as they are in *living* wages. They may not be as concerned about breaking through into upper management as they are about whether they'll still have jobs tomorrow.

Often we are blind to how these different priorities cause resentment of us and the gains we make because of our privilege. Perhaps our unquestioned acceptance of our privilege makes it hard for others to accept us as partners against an oppression of which we seem so much a part.

A major challenge in addressing this resentment is in specifying the shape of our privilege. Privilege tends to be invisible to those who have it. As members of the privileged racial identity group, white women don't bump up against racial barriers, and may not notice how pervasively issues of race affect our daily activities. We don't notice the preferential service we receive in the shops where we buy our business clothes. We don't have to drive to a different part of town where we don't feel very comfortable to get to those shops, or worry about being welcomed or attended to as customers. We don't experience the same difficulties in finding housing convenient to our jobs, or in obtaining financing for it. We don't experience the same covert or overt hostility from our new neighbors when we move in. And so on into the night and over the horizon. It is virtually impossible for us to appreciate how deeply race affects the daily lives of women of color. Nonetheless, we also must try to appreciate its impact.

Issues of privilege don't stop with race. There are many differences among us, and many different kinds of privilege that set us apart and keep us apart:

- A single woman can accept a job transfer to another city without worrying about her partner finding a job there.
- A heterosexual woman can bring her lover to an office party without fear of losing her job.
- A childless woman needn't worry about arranging child care during school holidays.

In addition, there are other sets of privilege that are harder to see. To move ahead, we must make the effort to see all of them and their interrelationships.

ESTABLISHING TRUE SISTERHOOD

To form coalitions with people from other identity groups, we must first own and acknowledge our privilege. Understanding the advantages we have over others will make it easier for us to see how their needs are not being met. It will give us the opportunity to advocate for those needs, and in so doing to forge coalitions that can work to address our own issues as well.

In our search for common ground, it's tempting to single out child care as a critical issue for all working women. But white women often forget that, for many of us, our child care has traditionally been handled by women of color. And while they were taking care of our children, did we show any concern about who was taking care of theirs?

Another point at which we often try to connect is how white women and women of color are inextricably tied together as victims of violence. After all, the experience of sexual and physical abuse cuts across all lines of race, class and color. But perhaps because the experience is so pervasive, it's also so difficult to talk about. Many women don't want to admit that it can happen, or has happened, to them. We often fall back on the denial-based belief that those who are raped, or harassed at work, or physically abused by their husbands have somehow brought it upon themselves. Like the experience of being a victim of violence, the denial-based blaming of the victim also cuts across all lines of race, class and ethnicity.

For white women and women of color to be able to work together more effectively on issues of common interest, we have to explore actively what our common interests truly are. This means that white women must stop setting the agendas and start listening to, understanding and supporting the issues impacting women of color and other groups of women.

Our work as white women begins with accepting that racism is just as important an issue as sexism. We must be willing to see ourselves as women *and* as white. We must be willing to address, confront and take responsibility for the ways we maintain racism in ourselves and in our interactions with other whites. We must speak up when we notice ourselves and others referring to *women* but really meaning *white women*. Our sisterhood must be built on a foundation that empowers us all.

WORKING TOGETHER, DIFFERENCES AND ALL

To support each other effectively, and to understand what really are our areas of common interest, white women and women of color must establish a broad and rich dialogue in which we can explore and appreciate our differences as well as our connections.

This requires a commitment to accept, trust, listen to and learn from each other. We'll need to help each other to do it, because it's easier for *you* to see how I oppress you than it is for *me* to see how I oppress you. We'll also need the patience, perseverance and grace to hang in with each other despite our disagreements, mistakes and flaws. After all, coalition is not about perfection, it's about cooperation. And with real commitment to each other, we can get there—differences and all.

NOTES

1. A special thank-you to Cathy Royal. This article was inspired by an interview with her addressing issues that emerge when white women and women of color work together in groups.

2. Judith Katz, *White Awareness: Handbook for Anti-Racism Training* (Norman, Oklahoma: University of Oklahoma Press, 1978).

3. I first heard the term "sticky floor" used in this context by my colleague and friend, Fred Miller, president of The Kaleel Jamison Consulting Group, Inc.

4. Peggy McIntosh, "White Privilege: Unpacking the Invisible Knapsack," *Peace and Freedom*, July/August 1989.

Chapter Six

Evangelina Holvino

Women of Color in Organizations
Revising Our Models of Gender at Work

Evangelina Holvino

■

Evangelina Holvino, EdD, is an organization development trainer and consultant who has worked in Puerto Rico, the United States, Europe, Southeast Asia, West Africa, Latin America, and the Caribbean since 1975. Her work focuses on improving management systems and organizational interfaces with the environment using applied behavioral science technology. She is vice president of the Boston Center of the A. K. Rice Institute and a member of NTL Institute.

I n the work force of the United States of America, 49 million people—47 percent of the work force—are women. They are still paid 26 percent less than men as full-time workers and are highly disadvantaged in terms of low pay, job segregation, workplace harassment, and inequitable family responsibilities. Only 14 percent are covered by union contracts, although women union membership has doubled in the past three decades.

Women of color constitute 20 percent of the women's work force. In 1987, the median yearly wage distribution of full-time year-round workers was: white men—$27,468; black men—$19,385; white women—$17,775; black women—$16,211; Hispanic men—$17,872; and Hispanic women—$14,893.

Although the study of gender in organizations has changed during recent decades from an individual-centered approach to a systems approach,[1,2] the interaction of system and individual, and how they influence each other, is still a relegated perspective in our work on "managing diversity." Our dominant approaches to differences in the workplace treat issues of women and minorities in organizations as if the problem lies in the system (outside of the individual) or in the person (as if the system did not have any relation to how people experience and behave in organizations), not in the *interaction of system and person* and how they constitute and socially construct each other in a mutually reinforcing relation.

In the last decade, feminist and organizational theorists have shifted the study of women in organizations to studying how people in organizations constitute a gendered workplace, which means they create the workplace. The question of women in organizations has been transformed from *What are the differences between men and women affecting their behavior in organizations?* to *How do our current forms of organizing work affect men's and women's behavior in organizations?* In other words, how are organizations-as-systems and the individuals in them part of a web of gender, race, and class relations that produce and reproduce each other?

The problem I want to address is one of theory *and* practice. How can we enrich the models we have for understanding differences in organizations in order to intervene more effectively? And what other perspectives do we need to bring organizational theory, feminist theories, and the intersection of race, gender, and class into our analysis of organizational life in order to enhance our ways of thinking about and doing "diversity work."

I begin by providing a definition of *gender* and an explanation of gender processes in organizations. This reflects the contributions of feminist theories to the analysis of organizations. Next, I explore examples of how these gender processes interact with race and class and how they operate in organizations. Finally, I discuss the implications of using an approach that integrates gender, race, and class to understand and intervene in organizations on issues of social diversity and justice.

GENDER IN ORGANIZATIONS

Gender is the social organization of the relationship between the sexes. In our culture, gender is the meaning socially attributed to the differences between women and men. Gender is a relation and a category of analysis as opposed to a static and essential property of being.[3] So, in our culture, gay politics on the one hand and the return to "family values" on the other exemplify the contested meaning of gender. Gailey illustrates how gender is socially constructed by contrasting the two-gender cultural model in the United States to cultures in which there are four sets of gender relations: children, women of reproductive age, men of reproductive age, and elders.[4]

Feminist theory has introduced the term *gender processes:* what people do and say and how they think (or do not think) about what they do and say. Gender processes are organized in terms of hierarchical differences between men and women where men are privileged and women are subordinated. This process of favoring one side in the male–female dichotomy involves both the material and the symbolic.

There are four key gender processes that are an integral part of organizational life: gender divisions, gender symbols and identity, gender interactions, and gendered structures.

1. *Gender divisions:* Organizations construct divisions along gender lines. These gender divisions are produced in organizations through internal wage differentials and job segregation. For example, women constitute 96 percent of all secretaries, while 90 percent of partners in the largest law firms are white males.

2. *Gender symbols and identities:* Symbols, images, and internalized forms of consciousness underlie and support gender divisions—for example, pinups of naked women and the images of the rational-male manager and the bitchy-emotional-female manager. Organizational activities and symbols "construct" organizational members' subjectivities in the sense that males are seen as (and believe themselves to be) aggressive and rational, while women managers are seen as (and believe themselves to be) bitchy and emotional. These reproduced internalized gender expectations and images come to form part of our work identities and self-perceptions.

3. *Gender interactions:* Organizational interactions enact patterns of dominance and subordination between men and women, women and women, and men and men. These interactions create gender alliances and exclusions, as exemplified by sexual harassment in the workplace, the secretary's role as "office-wife," and the "queen-bee syndrome."

4. *Gendered structures:* The above gender processes work together to build upon and to help reproduce gendered social structures inside and outside organizations. They are both processes *and* effects, in that they *reproduce* at the same time that they *reflect* the gender structure of society. For example, 52 percent of U.S. working women have preschool children; 20 percent of women in the labor force would work and 25 percent of part-time workers would work more hours if child care were available.[5] These data reflect and reproduce one gender(ed) arrangement in society where women are disproportionately responsible for taking care of children at home as well as in such work organizations as schools, hospitals, and day-care centers.

Gender symbols, processes of gender identity, gender interactions, and structurally defined material inequalities between men and women are manifest in such organizational variables as the structure of the labor market (i.e., job stratification), internal wage differentials (i.e., salary inequalities), and job segregation.[6] For example, if we wanted to end job segregation, more than 60 percent of the women (or men) in the labor force would have to change jobs.

But gender processes do not occur in isolation from other social processes. Gender processes intersect with race and class as elements of our identity and in the social structures and processes of organizations and society. The intersection of these processes creates specific effects and links that the experiences of women of color help make apparent. However, by not paying attention to this intersection, women of color are made invisible, which profoundly hinders our ability to understand and change social relations in organizations.

AT THE INTERSECTION OF GENDER, RACE, AND CLASS

How does the intersection of gender, race, and class manifest itself in organizations? Third-world feminists criticize the ways in which white feminists have treated gender as *the* category of analysis in isolation of other social categories and processes like race, culture, and class. The data reflect the lower earnings of women of color in organizations compared to that of white women. But in addition, the *quality* of their experience is different. As the following examples will show, studying gender in isolation of race and class provides, at best, a very incomplete understanding of the social relations of race, gender, and class in the workplace.[7] It also leads to inappropriate change interventions.

The Structure of Work and Gender

Kanter demonstrates how one's position in the organizational hierarchy constitutes the behaviors of power and powerlessness observed in men and women respectively in organizations.[8] She aptly documents examples of four stereotypic roles taken or given to "the token woman" in skewed organizations: the "iron maid," the "seductress," the "mascot," and the "mother." What is important to understand is that these roles are not intrinsic to women, but reflect a dynamic of structural dominance in which women, because they are relatively few in parts of the organization, come to be seen and behave in these structurally shaped ways.

A more recent description of the hierarchy of work, in an electronics firm in Silicon Valley, reflects the gender, race, and class structure of the postindustrial world:

> At the top was an unusually high proportion (25%) of the most highly educated and highly paid salaried employees in any industry—the engineers and professionals employed in research and design. The vast majority were white males (89% males, 89% non-Hispanic whites). At the bottom, were the [Hispanic] women, three-fourths of the very poorly paid assembly workers and operatives who performed the tedious, often health-threatening work assigned to 45% of the employees.[9]

Though there may be nothing intrinsically wrong with organizational hierarchies, these examples show that when these hierarchies sort themselves out by race, gender, and class, the implications for organizational equality and change are enormous.

The Public and Private Division of Work

The public–private division refers to the gendered dichotomy that assigns women to the sphere of the private and men to the sphere of the public. This division is the basis for the "organization of production," which separates productive work (i.e., remunerated) from unproductive labor (i.e., unpaid and unrecognized household and informal sector).[10] This differentiation favors productive over reproductive labor and is a basic aspect of gender domination.[11] This division between the public and the private manifests itself in daily organizational interactions. For example, a Chicana worker speaks about her experience of this artificial division:

> The boss tells us not to bring our "women's problems" with us to work if we want to be treated equal. What does he mean by that? I am working here because of my "women's problems"—because I am a woman. Working here *creates* my "women's problems." I need this job because I am a woman and have children to feed. And I'll probably get fired because I am a woman and need to spend more time with my children. I am only one person—and I bring my whole self to work with me. So what does he mean, don't bring my "women's problem" here?[12]

By using the label *women's problems*, we avoid questioning arbitrary gendered arrangements in organizations and instead continue to reinforce these gender divisions. In addition, by not paying attention to how public–private gender divisions interact with race and class, we fail to appreciate that the professional advancement and organizational mobility of working class women and women of color is not the same as the career track of affluent white men or white women.[13]

Managerial Symbols, Images, and Identity

Acker analyzes how masculinity in the workplace is currently typified by "the image of the strong, technically competent, authoritative leader who is sexually potent and attractive, has a family, and has his emotions under control."[14] In contrast, women's bodies, sexuality, and emotions have been denied and treated as problematic in organizations. A certain kind of "hegemonic masculinity," formed around dominance over women and in opposition to other masculinities (e.g., black or Hispanic), is part of the symbolic engendering of organizations. Images of black women, on the other hand, involve stereotypes of strong, castrating, and matriarchal females.[15] White female managers are thought of differently than black women and therefore face different problems in organizations. We have so few studies of Latina or Asian American female managers in the workplace that we lack cultural images to support their managerial roles. Borrowing from Jennings and Wells, we can say that "Hispanic authority is an oxymoron."[16]

But while we may be lacking positive images of female managers of color, the representations of working class women of color are not even considered, and their experiences in organizations remain invisible and irrelevant. What would it do to our understanding of organizations if we paid more attention to other rarely recognized organizational "heroes," like Chicana workers in the electronics industry:

> The youngest of six children, Lupe Collosi was thirty-six years old and from San Jose. Her father was a construction worker and her mother a homemaker . . . Lupe identified herself as "Mexican American," and although she was bilingual, she preferred English. She graduated from high school, had some clerical training, and met her husband, who was a truck driver, in a local nightclub . . . They had two daughters and a son, all between the ages of six and twelve. Lupe's husband did not like the fact that she worked, and they had separated for a while but were recently reconciled.[17]

Bringing in these other images to represent other organizational subjects challenges many taken-for-granted assumptions about organizations and organizational change. Such assumptions include our belief that managers are the principal subjects of organizations and organization change. It also opens the possibility for other kinds of theoretical and practical questions. For example, how do women at the bottom of the organizational hierarchy manage their organizational roles and dignity? And how is this the same or different among Chicanas and African American and Asian American women? How does our emphasis on white women in management limit our understanding of the experience of women of color in organizations, the majority of whom remain concentrated in the lower-paying jobs, with few opportunities for promotion and little job security. And how does our continued emphasis on management (e.g., *managing* diversity) limit the possibilities for understanding and transforming current social relations in organizations, of which managers and the activities of managing are just one form?

REVISIONS TO OUR DIVERSITY THEORY-PRACTICE

I have identified some ways in which gender, race, and class processes occur in our daily organizational life. I have also challenged the approach to differences that compartmentalizes race, gender, and class and treats them as unrelated to each other and have presented analyses of gender that take race and class as interacting processes in organizational life.[18] From these analyses, I derive the following implications:

First, we need to examine organizational life in a broader context, one that includes community and societal relations. This stretches our concepts of "open systems" and "boundary management."[19] It also means that intervening on issues of diversity and differences in organizations requires addressing multiple levels: societal, institutional, organizational, role, and individual.[20]

Second, race, gender, and class cannot continue to be addressed as isolated social phenomena or separate variables that can be studied independently. Rather, they are intertwined *relations* that are codetermining of and with other social processes. Making this theoretical shift will help us envision new types of interventions that simultaneously tackle gender hierarchies, racial hierarchies, and skilled-unskilled organizational (class) divisions.

Finally, by using race and gender to refer to relations of power and elements of subjective identity that affect us all (white women, women of color, white men), we can understand how these relations are also mediated by other social processes, such as class, ethnicity, and culture. Our ways of intervening will change when we recognize that we are all embedded in a social and organizational world of race, gender, and class relations.

NOTES

1. M. Chesler and H. Delgado, "Race Relations Training and Organisational Change," in *Strategies for Improving Race Relations: The Anglo American Experience*, eds. J. W. Shaw, P. G. Nordlie, and R. M. Shapiro (Manchester, England: Manchester University Press, 1987), pp. 182–204.

2. B. W. Jackson and Evangelina Holvino, "Working with Multicultural Organizations: Matching Theory and Practice," in *Proceedings of the OD Network Conference, 1986* (New York: OD Network, 1986), pp. 84–96.

3. D. L. Sheppard, "Organizations, Power and Sexuality: The Image and Self Image of Women Managers," in *The Sexuality of Organizations*, eds. Jeff Hearn, D. L. Sheppard, P. Tancred, and G. Burrell (London: Sage, 1989), p. 140.

4. C. Gailey, "Evolutionary Perspectives on Gender and Hierarchy in *Analyzing Gender: A Handbook of Social Science Research*, eds. Beth B. Hess and Myra M. Ferree (Newbury Park, CA: Sage Publications, 1987), pp. 32–67.

5. G. Spitze, "The Data on Women's Labor Force Participation," in *Women Working: Theories and Facts in Perspective*, 2nd ed., eds. Ann H. Stromberg and S. Harkess (Mountain View, CA: Mayfield Publishing, 1988), pp. 42–60.

6. J. Acker, "Hierarchies, Jobs, Bodies: A Theory of Gendered Organizations," *Gender and Society* 4 (1990), pp. 139–58.

7. E. L. Bell and S. M. Nkomo, "Re-visioning Women Managers' Lives," in *Gendering Organizational Analysis*, eds. A. J. Mills and P. Tancred (Newbury Park, CA: Sage Publications, 1992), pp. 235–47.

8. Rosabeth M. Kanter, *Men and Women of the Corporation* (New York: Basic Books, 1977).

9. J. Stacy, "Sexism by a Subtler Name? Postindustrial Conditions and Post-feminist Consciousness in Silicon Valley," in *Women, Class, and the Feminist Imagination*, eds. Karen V. Hansen and Ilene J. Philipson (Philadelphia: Temple University Press, 1990), pp. 343–4.

10. G. Burrell and Jeff Hearn, "The Sexuality of Organization," in *The Sexuality of Organization*, eds. Jeff Hearn, D. L. Sheppard, P. Tancred-Sheriff, and G. Burrell (Newbury Park, CA: Sage Publications, 1989), pp. 1–28.

11. Nancy Fraser, *Unruly Practices: Power, Discourse and Gender in Contemporary Social Theory* (Minneapolis: University of Minnesota Press, 1989).

12. K. J. Hossfeld, "Their Logic Against Them: Contradictions in Sex, Race, and Class in Silicon Valley," in *Women Workers and Global Restructuring*, ed. Kathryn Ward (Ithaca, NY: ILR Press, 1990), pp. 149–78.

13. E. Higginbotham and L. Weber, "Moving Up with Kin and Community: Upward Social Mobility for Black and White Women," *Gender and Society* 6 (1992), pp. 416–40.

14. J. Acker, "Hierarchies, Jobs, Bodies: A Theory of Gendered Organizations," *Gender and Society* 4 (1990), p. 153.

15. R. G. Dumas, "Dilemmas of Black Females in Leadership," in *Group Relations Reader*, vol. 2, eds. Arthur D. Colman and Marvin H. Geller (Springfield, VA: Goetz, 1985), p. 325.

16. C. L. Jennings and L. Wells, "The Wells-Jennings Analysis: A New Diagnostic Window on Race Relations in American Organizations," in *The Emerging Practice of Organization Development*, eds. Walter Sikes, A. B. Drexler, and J. Gant (Alexandria, VA: NTL Institute/San Diego: University Associates, 1989), pp. 105–18.

17. Patricia Zavella, *Women's Work and Chicano Families: Cannery Workers of the Santa Clara Valley* (Ithaca, NY: Cornell University Press, 1987), p. 77.

18. Evangelina Holvino, "Organizational Development from the Margins: Reading Class, Race, and Gender in OD texts," EdD dissertation, University of Massachusetts–Amherst, 1993.

19. M. Bayes and P. M. Newton, "Women in Authority: A Sociopsychological Analysis," *Journal of Applied Behavioral Science* 14 (1978), pp. 7–20.

20. P. Y. Martin, D. Harrison, and D. Dinitto, "Advancement for Women in Hierarchical Organizations: A Multilevel Analysis of Problems and Prospects, *Journal of Applied Behavioral Science* 19 (1983), pp. 19–33.

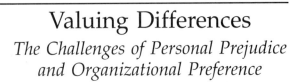

Chapter Seven

Valuing Differences
The Challenges of Personal Prejudice and Organizational Preference

William J. Paul
Ava Albert Schnidman

∎

William J. Paul

William J. Paul, PhD, and Ava Albert Schnidman, PhD, are partners in Deltech Consulting Group, an organization specializing in the management of complex change, strategic thinking, leadership team development, technology introduction, and valuing differences.

Bill Paul has been organization development and planning manager for Exxon Chemical Company and the Raoul de Vitry d'Avancourt Visiting Professor at INSEAD. He is also author of a book and many articles and recipient of the APA Cattell Award for Excellence.

Ava Schnidman was previously with Index Systems, Inc., and Connecticut General Life Insurance Corporation (now CIGNA) and was adjunct professor at the University of Connecticut School of Business and at the University of Hartford School of Business.

Ava Albert Schnidman

T he vast majority of people are well-intentioned in their approach to dealing with those different from themselves. Their motivation isn't malicious, nor is their intention oppressive. Why is it then that individual experience and organizational statistics persistently demonstrate a distribution of attention, rewards, and promotion that is disproportionately in favor of a single category of employee? Why is it that exclusion and harassment persist? Why is it that after these things are brought to people's attention it is still exceedingly difficult to change? Why, in most companies or countries, does one group tend to dominate? Why is there one group that tends to be favored over others?

Years of research and consulting experience suggest that two distinct forces act in parallel to create organizations and communities

FIGURE 7–1

Personal Prejudice versus Organizational Preference

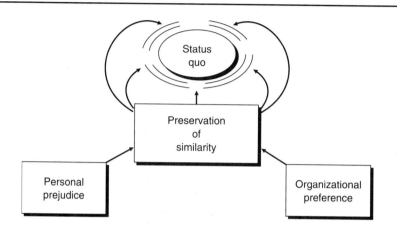

that can be relatively inhospitable to those outside the dominant group. The first of these, and the more widely recognized, is *personal prejudice.* This causes individuals to stereotype, exclude, or even oppress based on differences of nationality, race, gender, ethnicity, style, religion, sexual orientation, physical ableness, etc. Prejudices— or prejudgments—are typically learned early in life, well before our critical faculties are developed, and usually are not reexamined until an event or relationship challenges their validity. The second force is more systemic and less personal: Organizations tend to develop and act on a strong *organizational preference.* Organizations create potent, distinct, and narrowly defined images of what a successful or worth- while person is like. Then they teach and regulate the behavior of their members so that they will be as nearly like the image as possible, and they make choices that favor those most like the image.

These twin forces—personal prejudice and organizational pre- ference—combine to preserve similarity in a manner that is ex- tremely difficult to alter. This preference for similarity is self- perpetuating and tends to act in favor of the sort of people who founded the community or the organization (see Figure 7–1).

PERSONAL PREJUDICE

Groups of people who share a common identity—whether derived from, for example, nationality, race, gender, or religion—tend over time to evolve a unique culture. Each culture is based on a distinctive set of values, beliefs, and behaviors that represent a preferred way of doing things. These preferences result from each group's agreed-upon answers to basic questions as: How do I pass time? How do I judge people? How do I relate to nature? The answers form the bedrock on which cultures are built. They are taught to children, from birth, as a set of right versus wrong ways of thinking and behaving. They are concepts that are necessarily taught by example because they are absorbed as the way things are, not as a set of choices. Behaving differently is usually deemed wrong and punished.

The sense of right and wrong, good and bad, ranges across all of the ideas and behaviors that form our identities. These may be as mundane as ideas about what and how to eat or as abstract as whether time is precious or abundant. Whatever they are, we learn the "right" ideas early and embed them deeply. The questions are lost, but the answers are preserved as the right way to be. Those who are different are wrong—or uneducated—or perverse! Difference itself becomes suspect. Because we experience our way of being as normal, we tend to assume that if others could see clearly or correctly, they would also be like us; only someone less educated, less intelligent, or less moral would be different. Judgments like these are accepted as normal long before we have the ability to recognize that different answers and different behaviors are common and, for those who practice them, equally normal.

For most of us, these judgments govern until the force of circumstance—new neighbors, new work colleagues, a new friend—compels us to reexamine the "one right way."

If the process of examination hasn't occurred during the school years, the prejudgments we make (our personal prejudices) follow us wherever we go, including to work. There they act, typically at an unconscious level, to cause us to view people different from ourselves as less able, less trustworthy, less willing, less motivated, less credible, or having less potential. We experience not so much their difference as we do their "poor" performance or motivation or apparent inability to learn and adapt. From this perspective, it becomes genuinely difficult to promote, mentor, hire, or even accept them as real members of the team.

For a few, these prejudgments go well beyond self-fulfilling prophecies about capabilities or social skills. For some, the prejudgment is tinged with fear or hate and the reaction is strong, often leading to avoidance, oppression, ridicule, or harassment of entire categories of people. If these prejudgments are commonly held by the dominant group—the group with the greatest influence on the choices and judgments being made by the organization—the impact can be systematically oppressive.

The challenge in dealing with personal prejudice is to provide an environment that fosters an open-minded exploration of the cultures of people who are different. For adults to be able to make adult judgments about what people are like and why, the environment must provide, over a long enough period of time, a first-hand experience of people who are different. People need enough first-hand experience of others to be able to appreciate that there are enormous differences among them and that no single judgment is likely to hold true for the whole group. People need to be candid enough to be able to surface and test thoughts that aren't considered polite to talk about. Adults need adequate exploration to be able to understand that almost everyone has something to contribute that would enrich the whole. Dealing with personal prejudice must be a deliberate act. Left to the normal course of events, one's selective perception either blinds her or him to anything but the stereotype held or, worse, causes him or her to see only that which confirms the prejudice.

ORGANIZATIONAL PREFERENCES

The creation of community—whether in a village or a corporate organization—is more than a nice thing to do; it is essential. In order to get on with the business at hand, it is essential to get beyond having to agree about how things will be done, who is a member and who isn't, what assumptions will govern, and what the basic identity or mission of the organization is. These choices become the foundation on which the rest of the structure will be built; and like the foundation for a house, they serve best when they are mainly invisible and rarely tampered with. In a company, it is typically the founders who establish the foundation, and reasonably enough, they make choices, establish core beliefs, declare values, encourage behaviors, and set norms with which they are comfortable. Therefore, they select leaders for the organization who, as nearly as possible, exemplify the basic beliefs and values—who look and seem as much like the founders as possible.

The United States was founded (i.e., its constitution, its governance structure, and its educational system and philosophy were created) by a group of men who were Anglo-Saxon, affluent, well educated, and, most of them, lawyers. The foundation they built was one they could believe in, one they could be confident of, and one that would reflect the values they most cherished. Although many of their choices have universal appeal, many others are most appealing to men who have an Anglo-Saxon heritage and are affluent and well educated. Others who were different from the founding fathers, by reason of their heritage or appearance, had to adapt and accommodate to values, beliefs, and behaviors that were different from their own. Thus, for some, the fact of their birth was nearly enough to assure that they would be accepted into and embraced as exemplars of the nation. For others, the acceptance was much more grudging, if given at all. There were those who were "in" and those whose appearance, gender, heritage, or status left them "out": They were denied the rights of voting, property ownership, citizenship, education, access to public accommodations, etc.[1]

The story is similar in organizations. The founders have intentions, beliefs, and values that are woven into the fabric of the organization. They choose people to work with and people to replace themselves who, they are confident, exemplify their values and intentions. If these people are successful, the organization is preserved and grows and the image of what a successful leader is like becomes clearer and more embedded in the minds of those who work in the organization.

The larger and more complex the organization, the more difficult it is to see a direct or immediate relationship between the activities of an individual and the success of the organization, especially near the top. Still, the decisions about who will lead and who is most deserving have to be made. In these circumstances, dependence on the image of what has been successful in the past becomes much greater. It is reinforced by repeated use and repeated success. The image itself takes on the character of legend or myth. Even though few people, even at the top, fit the description precisely, the description remains largely unchanged and continues to govern whenever choices are made about who is most likely to be successful or who is most deserving. The image becomes the template against which everyone is compared. Those who are the least different, create the least dissonance, "set off the fewest alarm bells," are likely to seem the safest and surest people to entrust with the organization's future. Everyone is encouraged to be as nearly like the image as possible. Those who succeed, win.

In the founding and growth of the United States, with its reliance on successive waves of immigration to provide the work force needed to build its industrial strength, the notion of being like the image came to be known as the melting-pot theory—the idea that over time, we would all let go of our family or national heritage and adopt the language and culture of the founding fathers; we would all be assimilated into a single, homogeneous culture. Although the notion continues, it seems apparent after more than 200 years that cultural heritage is a precious source of identity and strength that some people are not willing to give up. For others, their skin color makes melting impossible. Highlighting our differences rather than seeking ways to obscure them may in fact be a primary source of competitive strength.

In companies, something akin to the melting-pot theory takes place. When people are brought into the organization, they are recruited with the "right" social and educational background and then trained and socialized so that their work and appearance are consistent with the image of success that has evolved from the founders. The processes for teaching and regulating the "right" behavior and appearance are often subtle and are typically very powerful. The degree to which people have been socialized by these processes—taught that there is one right way to be—is typically not appreciated by individuals. If it is detected, it usually comes as a surprise. The success image describes a strong organizational preference and is a powerful force for preserving similarity. Those whose physical appearance precludes fitting the image and those for whom the gap between the way they naturally are and the organization's preferred style is simply too great very often are left out when rewards are given or leaders are chosen. This often leads to feelings of isolation or a decision to leave the company.

CREATING A CULTURE THAT VALUES DIFFERENCE

Relaxing the combined grip of personal prejudice and organizational preference on the tendency to preserve similarity involves changing primary anchors of personal and organizational culture that are rooted in strong feelings that drive quite different behaviors. Eliminating personal prejudice as a force within an organization won't alter the status quo. By the same token, promoting the successful image of the organization won't alter the status quo either. Creating an organization that values differences requires strategies that simultaneously act on these two forces. The prejudice that each of us brings, and many of us share, can only be moved out of the realm of uninformed choice if individuals are willing to learn and are provided with a sustained opportunity to confront and explore untested beliefs about others.

Organizational preferences that are too narrow and too deeply rooted in history flourish when the organization's systems and processes permit the implicit and unchallenged use of a template in making organizational choices. Until the processes become more explicit, the choices more visibly tied to strategic needs, and the debate more public and inclusive, the company myth will persist.

Because the processes that preserve the status quo are self-sustaining and very potent, changing them requires deliberate and sustained change strategies at both the personal and systemic levels.

NOTE

1. Mark Williams, a colleague, originally shared with us the concept that the founding of the United States is a potent example of "organizational" preference.

Chapter Eight

Robert W. Terry

Racism
Multiple Perspectives—One Fear

Robert W. Terry

Robert W. Terry, PhD, is president of Terry Group, consultants and trainers in leadership, quality, and diversity. He recently completed 11 years as senior fellow and founding director of the Reflective Leadership Center at the Hubert H. Humphrey Institute of Public Affairs, University of Minnesota. He is author of For Whites Only *(1970), a study of racism, and* Authentic Leadership: Courage in Action *(1993).*

Racism is a scourge on the earth. It ravages communities, nations, and individuals' lives. It challenges the human community as one of our most persistent problems. It demands our very best thinking about its nature, what keeps it thriving, and what to do about it.

Racism appears in many guises, speaks in many voices, behaves in many ways. Each manifestation suggests a different definition and strategy. Underlying these diverse expressions resides a unified and terrifying primordial fear. When unacknowledged, the fear corrupts, destroys, and separates people from one another. It must be faced and embraced or it will continue to divide and destroy humankind, ultimately undermining the ecological and human foundation necessary to sustain life on earth.

There is broad agreement that racism should be suppressed and eliminated. This agreement vanishes when questions are raised about what it is, why it persists, and how to eliminate it.

At a recent conference on cultural diversity, I was nearing the conclusion of my talk on racism and metaphors when a man raised his hand. He looked agitated.

"When are we going to get to the real issue?" he asked in exasperation.

"What is that?" I asked.

"Racism," he replied.

"What is racism to you?" I asked.

"Oppression," was the rapid reply.

Ironically, I had just covered oppression as one of many perspectives on racism. Later, I thought to myself, "Isn't it odd that we cannot even tolerate diverse perspectives on racism at a diversity conference?"

SIX METAPHORS FOR RACISM

We need multiple perspectives to see and deal with racism's multiple faces, voices, and behaviors. I have found metaphorical analysis a fruitful approach for describing the lenses through which we derive our views on racism. Metaphors help us describe our most profound understandings of the world. They allow us to name our perspectives and thereby understand them as different views of the same reality.

Life as a Gift

All of life is a gift: the good, the bad, the enjoyable, the sad, the joyful, the tragic. It should be embraced, even when not understood.

Proponents of the gift metaphor often perceive life in a spiritual context, affirming creation as good, blessed, and sacred. Their core value is that history is sacred. Not sacred in a particular religious tradition, but sacred as the only history they have.

Racial supremacists utilize the gift metaphor as the underpinning of their world view. While advocating life as a gift, they assume that some gifts are superior to others. They do not consider themselves racist; they believe everyone has a right to exist as long as everyone else stays in a subservient place. To them, it is a simple biological fact that one group is superior to another. Supremacy and inferiority are built into the gene pool through survival of the fittest or the will of God. Their sacred history perceives this as a reality.

Threaten supremacists, and they hate. They commit genocide. They become what they deny they are. They segment the sacred gift into superior and inferior gifts and then try to eliminate the inferior. The irony is that supremacists behave as inferior human beings. Rather than accept all of life as a gift, they refuse all but their own narrow part.

Their underlying fear is death, the destruction of their natural gifts. In fear, they hunker down rather than reach out. Cornered, they revert to their most base nature: They attack because they fear they will be eliminated.

Life as a Market

Life is a continuing series of market-driven decisions. Informed decision makers bargain in the market to reach mutually satisfying agreements or contracts. Some people win, some people lose; but overall, society wins.

Only by bringing some value-added part of oneself to the market can one consummate an exchange. Without developed "marketable" talents or skills, a person is hardly going to be welcomed.

Racism denies access to the market through the use of inaccurate information and arbitrary power: prejudice and discrimination.

A truly free market fosters ingenuity, determination, and the adding of value to each exchange. Barriers to a free and open exchange, such as racism, are antimarket. Bad information distorts trade; monopolies give one set of players undue access and influence. Intrinsically, the market supports equal opportunity.

To eliminate racism, we must have sufficient knowledge of each other so we can make accommodating exchanges in the marketplace that guarantee equal access.

What keeps racism alive? Market ignorance. Not understanding the long-term implications of excluding people from the marketplace and the inability of those already in the market to perceive the value of those trying to get in.

If you threaten market advocates, they will sacrifice market freedom to the expediency of self-protection. They become the monopoly they say they abhor. Opportunity for all becomes opportunity for some.

Their underlying fear is failure, the destruction of their utility in the marketplace, so they surround themselves with material possessions, hoping that an outward accumulation of objects demonstrates success. Through greed, they seek protection from the vicissitudes of the market.

Life as a Body

Life is an interdependent organic system that adapts to external changes in search of equilibrium. When one part becomes ill, the rest of the system will be affected. Bodies go through life cycles, from birth to death. They can be functional or dysfunctional. They reject alien elements unless fooled into believing that the intruder is not hostile. The goal of the body is sustainability.

Racism is dysfunctional, a social disease, an illness that can infect the whole body. It produces abhorrent behavior in many parts of the system. Poor family socialization, absentee fathers, lack of role models, poor self-concept, and lack of teamwork highlight the problems of individuals. Breakdown of the health delivery system, education problems, welfare dysfunctionality, and financial instability highlight the institutionally based sickness.

Systems based on the body metaphor can have a profoundly racist impact on people of color. Typically, society is divided between the healthy and the sick, and the victims of racism or of systems that perpetuate racism are identified as sick. In either case, both sides of the equation need to be healed.

Solutions usually require expert intervention by, for example, government programs, institutional reforms, or subsidies. Affirmative action replaces equal opportunity to correct for past discrimination. Justice overshadows freedom, seeking to redress grievances and guarantee equity—not just equality.

Racism persists because of a lack of or breakdown of inclusion in otherwise healthy systems. When systems don't reach out and nurture people, underlying economic, social, and cultural forces can destroy the social fabric and their social worth. Only by rectifying those root causes can one hope for a healthy body politic.

Body advocates become what they fear when they fail to address system problems, focusing instead on assimilation or victim blame. Instead of promoting health, they perpetuate sickness.

Their underlying fear is isolation, rejection from the body. Their response is to do whatever is necessary to belong. Thus, addicted individuals, families, organizations, and societies perpetuate themselves. Dysfunctional becomes normal; social sickness prevails.

Life as the "Ups" versus the "Downs"

Life is a constant struggle between polar opposites: rich versus poor, old versus young, white people versus people of color, urban versus rural, straight versus gay, able-bodied versus those with disabilities. Either/or thinking predominates. One either wins or loses, accommodates or is accommodated, lives or dies.

Conflict drives history. Differing self-interests drive differing groups into collision. Shared power and full participation are core values. A single center of power is dangerous. Racism is oppression by "ups": unilateral exploitation, domination, and tyranny based on color and ethnic history.

For the most part, the "up-down" metaphor is advocated by "downs." Most whites who use this perspective are antiracists who work with other "ups." In the United States, their key objective is to help whites understand white privilege.

As a consequence of their "upness," whites receive benefits that are undeserved and often unrecognized. When whites understand this system of white privilege, they will be morally outraged and motivated to change to a system of shared power.

In the previous perspectives, racism was not directly linked to power. From this perspective, only ups can be racist. Downs by definition cannot be racists; they have no power. The consequence of this view is that ups are read as bad, downs as good.

The solution is to organize, mobilize, and participate. Downs must take charge of their own destiny. Ups can help, but they must subordinate their natural racist inclinations to the will of the downs.

What keeps racism alive? The rooting of ups' privilege in exploitation, domination, and rigged institutional arrangements.

If you threaten up/down advocates, they will oppress groups below them. Shared power quickly transforms itself into unilateral power. New ups become indistinguishable from those they replaced.

Their underlying fear is victimization. Their response is to victimize downs and to stay up by whatever means necessary.

Life as a Journey

Life is one adventure after another, a continual series of comings and goings, opening new paths of discovery. Only by bumping up against differences can one know oneself as well as others. Our personal histories limit what we can see and know.

In order for the journey to thrive, travelers must attend to one another, listen to one another, care about one another. Without caring or love, the journey implodes upon itself rather than moving out into the world.

Racism expresses itself as ethnocentrism, the belief that one's own journey is the norm for all journeys.

The solution to racism requires deep education of self and other, going beyond the trading of knowledge advocated by the market. It requires one to understand, in a way not made available in other metaphors, that life is paradoxical. Out of pain comes joy; out of giving one's life, one discovers one's life; in the midst of diversity is a profound unity.

Whites can be color conscious and admit to being both racist and antiracist at the same time. People of color can wrestle with the significance of living in a racist world while facing choices about how to take charge of that cultural world without being overwhelmed by it. All human beings are sojourners and travelers. Acknowledging and embracing that fact is the challenge facing all human beings.

What keeps racism alive? Ignorance of self and the world, especially among ups. Ups don't know how they lose from racism and the consequences of that ignorance. As they attend to themselves and others on the journey, they could learn that to be white in the United States is *not to have to think about it.* One who discerns the magnitude of that insight is propelled on a journey of inquiry about racism.

Threaten journey advocates, and they retreat into ethnocentrism, solidifying their own trip as the only trip worth pursuing. In the process, they learn less about themselves and the world.

Their underlying fear is loss of direction—a distortion of the journey. The response is self-righteous surety. Life is simplified into good and evil, right and wrong, black and white.

Life as Art

Art reveals life to us. It takes us into the shadows and the scary places, inviting us to see with new eyes. It helps us understand with fresh insight those aspects of the world and ourselves that we do not want to see. Art connects what other means do not connect—teaching, confronting, cajoling us to interpret a new world on its own terms.

Life does not interpret itself. We are responsible for the interpretation and the actions that follow from that interpretation. This is true for all of life—that which we revere and that which we despise, the debased part of life as well as the grand part of life.

Racism is the denial of our personal and cultural shadows, our sense of superiority and/or inferiority, dangerous feelings, shameful desires and dreams, unethical actions, and generalized fears about life. Our shadows stand in stark contrast to how we want to be perceived. Racism denies one's involvement and distorts one's humanity. It says, "I am not responsible, not connected, not involved."

The solution is to face the shadow in ourselves and in our culture, recognizing that no culture is totally good or bad. Each of us has a shadow side, lurking to quicken our fears, limit our possibilities, and undermine our humanity. To be responsible is to acknowledge, name, and accept our shadow side and to seek to mitigate the negatives while enhancing what is humanly rewarding.

What keeps racism alive? The terror of the shadow being made public. One refuses to deal with the whole culture and thereby lies about what is really going on.

Threaten art advocates, and they abdicate responsibility for their connections and involvements. They refuse to own their shadows, admitting only to their publicly accepted faces and voices. They, too, become what they reject. They become racist on their own terms.

Their underlying fear is disorientation, a destruction of artistic inventiveness. The result is alienation and cynicism. Life flattens an ethical sensibility erodes.

HOPE: FINDING A HOME IN AUTHENTICITY

Those of us who offer leadership against racism face the constant threat of cynicism. We do battle, we try alternative strategies, and still racism persists. What will sustain our hope?

I believe that at the heart of life is authenticity, that which is most true and real in ourselves and in the world. Authenticity is a prerequisite for building a viable human and ecological future. Racism is a sin against authenticity. For those with spiritual inclinations, it is a sin against God.

The spirit of authenticity embraces differences and seeks to build a humane future. Primordial fear that distorts authenticity must be acknowledged, embraced, and, finally, transcended.

Hope comes not just from an anticipated future but in daily encounters with authenticity. It comes in the small conversations with colleagues who have experienced a breakthrough in self-understanding. It comes as a community takes charge of its destiny. It comes when a group affirms the richness of its sacred history. It comes when people join together across barriers of color to find unity without losing identity.

Racism comes in many forms. So does authenticity. Faith suggests that authenticity is constantly on the move, embracing what is unauthentic, what is distorted, what is sinful. Hope undergirds our commitment to face racism head-on in the world, in our community, and in ourselves. Hope inspires us to transcend racism and to live a new reality, not just in the future, but as much as possible today.

Chapter Nine

John Scherer

The Mechanics of Prejudice
What Changes When People Change?*

John Scherer

■

John Scherer has been an innovator in applied behavioral science for over 20 years. A former Navy officer and minister, Scherer has helped numerous organizations master change and conflict to achieve high performance. They include GTE, Polaroid, Marriott, Aetna, the Government Accounting Office, Ford, Northern Telecom, the U.S. Army, and the New York Power Authority. He cofounded the nation's first competency-based graduate program in the field and created the Executive Development and Leadership Development Intensives.

W hen prejudice and negative judgments shift to understanding and respect, what is it exactly that has changed? Is it the way someone *thinks* about others or *feels* about them? Or the way he or she *sees* them? Could it be all of that and more? And once we understand the mechanics of prejudice and its reversal, how can we help such changes come about?

In 20 years of working with corporate executives and their organizations, I have witnessed many clients' experience of fundamental change in the way they viewed a colleague or a group of co-workers. These breakthroughs are usually accompanied by a sense of relief and an increase in productivity and teamwork, as the energy formerly used to maintain the old perception (prejudice) is applied to getting the job done.

CHANGE: OUR TOUCHSTONE TO REALITY

Managers and employees simply *must* become more fluent in the language and process of fundamental change—the key to creating a diverse workplace.

---

*A version of this article appeared in the Fall 1989 issue of *Creative Change,* the journal of the Association for Creative Change.

Alvin Toffler pointed out that ours is an age of exponential change. The organizations that will survive are those than can adapt internally to what's going on around them. For this to happen, individual managers need to be capable not only of overcoming their own resistance to change, but of actually learning to enjoy the process. Change begins at the personal level.

WHERE WE'RE COMING FROM DETERMINES WHERE WE END UP

The change that takes place when things truly change—such as when a prejudice dies—goes beyond thoughts or perceptions or feelings. What changes is where these came from, the source of these thoughts and perceptions: our belief system. *Where we're coming from determines where we end up.* The world we see is that which filters through senses uniquely our own. What we "see" is a product of our own private and instantaneous interpretation.

Each of us operates with a belief system that has traceable origins. Its roots begin in early family life and evolve into the sense we make of the experiences that come later. Growing up is learning what everything "is." The restless mind can't stand having an experience without knowing what it means. For a fleeting nanosecond, however, each and every experience is just raw data, "sound and fury signifying nothing." But then we label it—say something to ourselves about it—and whatever we say becomes what happened to us.

Just as the objects in the Garden of Eden were without useful reality to Adam until he named them, so it is with the world around us. At the instant of experiencing a stimulus (sight, smell, sound, taste, touch, thought), we *name it.* We convert our experience into a concept: judgments, feelings, reactions, associations, reflections, labels. So long as those labels remain in place, experience lives for us not as raw experience but as the cluster of concepts that replaced the experience. Once we know (say to ourselves) what an experience means, we tend to go out and find it again and again. And lo and behold, it always "means" what we named it in the beginning. We can always count on finding data to support our interpretation.

X IS YET ANOTHER EXAMPLE OF Y

A formula that individuals—and even systems—carry unconsciously goes like this: "X is yet another example of Y." Whenever something happens, X, we know what it means: It's yet another example of Y (what we all know to be the case around here).

In the realm of diversity, for example, this labeling/naming process goes something like this: The hard-working, effective, and productive woman or minority employee is seen as a great support person. The hard-working, effective, and productive white male is an executive-in-the-making.

REALITY AS "MISTAKE"

Before we can change this pattern, it is crucial to understand how all human behavior is an act of faith based on things that are "not true." What we believe results from the naming and patterning of experience into bit-size conclusions. The Italian psychiatrist Edward deBono has pointed out that the most efficient way for the mind to function is to create quickly recognizable information patterns. "It does not matter whether the patterns are right or wrong," he says, "so long as they are definite. Since the patterns are always artificial ones created by the mind, it could be said that the function of the mind is mistake [reality]." This "mistake" is what we operate on.

Using this principle, we can see that we are prejudging everyone and everything all the time. Even when we like or respect someone, our conclusion is still based on the same "mistake" we call reality.

FROM BELIEF TO ACTION

The following model shows how we create the belief world in which we live. It also shows those "pressure points" that occur in the process of moving from experience to action, where fundamental change (e.g., reversal of prejudice) can be created.

Perceptual map. What we believe about ourselves and the world is usually invisible to us. This explains why we might be inclined to take note of "leadership" behavior where a colleague notices mostly "aggressive" behavior in the same employee.

Field of focus. Our map determines what we see. We tend to notice the leadership or aggressiveness we believe is out there.

Diagnosis. Here's where the mind assesses, makes conscious judgments, determines rightness and wrongness, and answers the question "What's wrong with this picture?"

Strategy.   This is where we form intentions, whether by an elaborate intellectual process, by habit, or by hunch. It's the basis for action and possibility.

Alternatives.   With intention in place, we select from a field of possibilities artificially funneled down through the above process.

Action.   We do what we do.

This model offers an interesting insight into human history by showing just how reflexive most of our actions are, based on a world that exists only in our heads. So long as we navigate by the psychological autopilot of our perceptual map, getting "outside the box," expanding our galaxy of the possible, seeing someone in a new way, is essentially impossible.

THE WAY OUT OF THE PREJUDICE BOX

The alternative to living this knee-jerk, unconscious life is to constantly examine our perceptual maps, or core beliefs. This, of course, is one of the most difficult of all human acts because when we examine our beliefs, we do it *through* the very beliefs we are seeking to examine. It usually takes a significant emotional experience to unstick the label we applied earlier. When this happens, there is a breakdown of the formula we've been operating on. It doesn't work anymore. Some piece of evidence crashes in that doesn't fit with the map we've been using, and this time we are unable—or unwilling— to force the data to fit the theory.

It is in this context that we can see how breakdowns serve as a blessing. Breakdowns, of course, do not guarantee breakthroughs. They merely introduce the possibility of making a breakthrough by creating an environment of new openness. But breakthroughs by definition go beyond mental frameworks. By asking questions like these, you can open the door to sidestep your normal interpretive pattern:

- Who is this person in front of me, really?
- What is happening here that I'm not seeing?
- What am I saying to myself about what is happening, and what is another interpretation that could be just as valid?
- Where is my judgment coming from?

This line of inquiry stretches that nanosecond before our experience is labeled, creating the possibility that another interpretation might enter our closed belief system. Letting go of our labels takes what I would call faith. But there is a big difference between the conscious, awake, alert faith that allows us to live as if new worlds forever await our discovery and the dead faith that tells us that what we see before us at any given moment is all there is.

REVERSING PREJUDICE

In all likelihood, managers can't cause breakthroughs in people's belief systems, at least not in the way they can cause new products or markets to come into existence. What they can do, first of all, is develop their own capacity and tendency to "listen to themselves think," to catch themselves in the act of judging and inquire about the source of that judgment. Being open with those being judged is another way to open the door of prejudice even wider. By modeling this new behavior, they can also create the kind of environment or space in which getting outside the box becomes more likely.

Fundamental change or breakthroughs leading to true egalitarianism in the workplace will only happen when we all (1) wake up to the ongoing presence of prejudice in our perceptions, (2) create an intention to see things the way they are ("around our glasses"), and (3) actively allow our old, continuously outdated systems of belief to be changed by contact with corrective experiences. The best news: Because every perception represents a "mistake," then *any* moment can be a corrective experience. The more powerful the feelings associated with our perception, the more dramatic the possibility of change.

Chapter Ten

Kate Kirkham

Daily Diversity
Individual Experience and Group Identity

Kate Kirkham

■

For over two decades, Kate Kirkham, PhD, has focused her work, teaching, research, and consulting on the integration of organizational behavior and race and gender issues. She is a member of the faculty of the Graduate School of Management at Brigham Young University's Department of Organizational Behavior and is an associate of Elsie Y. Cross and Associates. Her research and consulting have involved volunteer, government, business, and educational organizations such as Corning Inc., American Express, and others.

W*ho gets to determine how one is individual?* When asked to describe who they are, people select different dimensions of their being and experience to create their identity.[1] Some dimensions of who we are never change, though their meanings in our daily interactions may vary. Rosner and Loden refer to these as *primary* aspects of identity. Other dimensions—those that can and do change— they label as *secondary*.[2] Race and gender are primary dimensions of diversity.

I will explore three core implications of primary group identity that affect individuals in a diverse workforce:

1. The meaning of group identity—the dynamics of power and preference.
2. Identity implications for different groups.
3. Strategic assumptions.

THE MEANING OF GROUP IDENTITY

At the beginning of a workshop I once ran, a participant wandered over and looked at the roster I was holding. The names of all participants and their group identities (race or gender) were listed there. This person was surprised to see how the organization had identified him.

A staff member of another organization I worked with advised me that one of the participants in an event was black, but that others in the meeting would not know that. She wanted me to be aware that on other occasions, when the individual had identified herself as black, those present had responded with "Oh, no, you're not!"

Forms used to collect data about students or employees often have a number of group categories followed by the general category "other."

Why does it seem that a great deal of tension persists in organizations over who determines an individual's primary group identity? Who decides what language will be used to describe the primary identity of individuals?

Underneath organizational discussions about "politically correct" (PC) labels are two consistent themes that predate the term *politically correct* and that I suspect will still be a source of tension after PC.

One concern that has come from all groups is about the use of any label other than *individual* or *human being*. Embedded in this concern about usage is a concern about double standards in the use of labels for members of some primary identity groups.

I have rarely heard an employee say, "You need to talk to that white manager over there," when identifying someone I should meet. And I can count on one hand the number of times a white employee has used the racial identity of another white person as a way to identify her or him. The news-reporting practice of not using racial identity for whites while using it for all others is changing somewhat. Still, I frequently hear terms such as "the woman VP," "the new black VP," or "the Asian who is now a VP."

Members of all groups have argued that the use of labels associated with an individual's primary identity limits that person's opportunities, that the real issues that shape experience are economic in nature, not racial. From this perspective, references to race or gender identity are seen as implying that an experience was obtained *because* of that identity.

What determines when a primary group label is used to identify individuals?

The second ongoing concern is almost always heard from members of the traditional U.S. majority group—whites—when discussing racial issues and from men when discussing gender issues. Boiled down to the vernacular, it sounds like this: "Hey, what you want to be called is different from what she or he wants to be called. What am I supposed to do? This discussion is just making me more uncomfortable and dividing us!"

At whose level of comfort or discomfort are issues of diversity managed in organizations and why? What determines the overall paradigm for how difference is viewed in a society?

In developing a framework for participants in diversity meetings, differences can have negative and positive dimensions: stereotyping and valuing differences, respectively. Stereotyping is now generally seen as a negative and dysfunctional way of thinking and is specifically viewed as inappropriate in the workplace. But there is less clarity on what the positive side of difference really means on a day-to-day basis in organizations. Positive definitions of group-level differences in our society are typically mentioned only in efforts to increase cross-cultural awareness.

Politicians and others who regulate racial and gender terminology have supported terms such as *color-blind* or *gender-blind*, implying policies or experiences that are neutral and independent of an individual's primary identity. Unfortunately, we have daily evidence that there is no neutral zone associated with group identity heard in such statements as "She just happens to be _____," "I'm not trying to speak for all _____," "If I come to that meeting, I'll be viewed as having an agenda based on my being a _____, and I want to be valued for my own contribution," even "I don't think of myself as a _____" and "You can't put me in a group; I'm an individual first."

As a white person, I find that the "neutral ground" seems only to have existed for me and other majority-group members as a place where we do not have to think about our racial identity nor be confronted with the data that indicate racism is a factor in how we see others. As a woman, I marvel that I could be seen as anything other than a woman. If gender-blind means "I don't think of you as a woman," then as what else am I to be thought of? And here is the vortex of dual identity (which will differ for each of us): My being a woman is much more in the daily breath of who I am in organizations than my being white is (in U.S. society).

Ironically, as a group, white women can be comfortable with the macrodefinition that positions gender issues as "ours" and racial issues as "theirs." We can then focus change efforts on those things that *others* do that are sexist, but not those things that *we do* that are racist. At the same time, if as a white I believe a policy is color-blind, then I might not look for racism. But the failure to investigate is as serious as the defensive response "You're making a racial issue out of this," which is frequently heard from white people who are pushed to examine a policy beyond an initial acceptance that it is color-blind.

IMPLICATIONS OF GROUP IDENTITY

The politics of meaning is the most critical dimension of group identity in organizations. In many ways, it is difficult for individuals to pinpoint the exact incident that demonstrates the totality of their experience of group identity as an asset or liability. But there are several tangible implications of group identity in organizations.

Visibility

Rosabeth Kanter discusses issues of visibility, along with the other tensions, such as being a token or one of the few O's in a group of X's.[3]

We are discovering new implications of visibility as the interaction of organizational culture and diversity is investigated. In an organization whose culture is based on the fundamental assumption that employees do not call attention to themselves, but work to demonstrate solid competency before generating visibility, those who are by group identity different from traditional employees have already "violated" basic cultural assumptions. The irony is that while others have an individual choice about creating visibility or not, different (in many cases, black) employees' identities have created visibility beyond their personal choice. Yet many "majority" employees believe such a person's high visibility is an intentional act to get attention and is evidence that he or she is not willing to be a team player.

Positive and Negative Group Identity

In a recent study of culture and diversity, the data from 16 focus groups revealed a pattern of very specific positive and negative dimensions of group identity in the organization.

Positive outcomes of focusing on employee group identity include the following:

- Knowledge that role models exist.
- The presence of a different group is seen as evidence that diversity efforts are succeeding.
- The group data are useful in monitoring progress in employee categories.
- Help in identifying patterns not available at the individual level of analysis.
- Demonstrates that differences are valuable.

Negative outcomes of focus on employee group identity include the following:

- Attention focused on difference is seen as divisive.
- White males frequently associate attention to group-level identity as a form of preferential treatment for members of that group; hence, they are not treating all employees as individuals.

The focus group data indicate that very different patterns of "sense making" about group identity occur both within groups (for individuals) and between groups. Analysis also indicates different *group-level* patterns of response. In one particular organization, for instance, the experience of employees who are people of color other than black (e.g., Indian, Pakistani, Asian) stand out. At times, respondents in these groups identified with the experiences of the traditional (white, male) majority group; at other times, they identified with the experiences of black employees.[4]

How Race or Gender Identity Determines Individual Action

Members of traditional majority groups show a proclivity to act out of individual prerogative. Not every member of a group will exhibit this behavior, but the pattern is well established.

The most tenacious behavior pattern shows up in office meetings or conversations. Members of majority groups do not use their awareness of group-level dynamics to regulate their individual behavior. They hold onto a prerogative about what determines their individual behavior. For example, in a diversity committee meeting discussing racial issues, white members asked questions of the people of color and raised concerns about the organization's readiness, but they did not make statements expressing their commitment. When asked later if they observed the imbalance of contributions between white people and people of color, some said no (they do not pay attention to the group-level implications of the discussion), and others said yes, but didn't think it meant that they *individually* should have done anything different in the meeting. They assessed the group-level implications, but they did not think that awareness should change their actions in the meeting.

Another example: I asked a man who had spoken up on gender issues in a meeting when only women had previously spoken why he had made a comment. He replied, "I looked around the room and realized that only women had spoken on the issue and that your experience of the men in the room could include me in a way that I didn't want to be included, so I acted to both differentiate myself from the other men and to contribute my individual comments."

It is imperative that employees of all groups learn to assess group-level contribution and to adjust their individual actions correspondingly, exercising or choosing not to exercise their individual prerogative. Managers should coach their employees about what they contribute to the work group, and should do so as actively concerning issues of diversity as they do concerning issues of quality.

Managing and Living with Diversity

Managing diversity does not mean managing the employee who is different from traditional majority-group employees. It means managing everyone effectively—managing employees who collectively represent a wide range of primary identities. And a major criterion for assessing effectiveness will be how differences in the meaning of group identity are managed.[5]

In true diversity, the historical prerogative of the "majority" group to label or refuse labels is gone. All primary identity groups within an organization—black, white, and Hispanic groups, and women as a group—have the same two tasks:

1. Reporting the experience associated with their group membership.
2. Responding to the way that others outside the group experience them.

However, not all groups or group members are willing or able to engage in these tasks. While willingness is an individual expression of motivation, it is affected by the experience that individuals have accumulated because of their group membership and its meaning. For example, as a woman my willingness to talk about terminology or report my experiences associated with being a woman may be affected by my past efforts at doing so with men. And as a white, my willingness to talk about racism may be inhibited by a fear that I will inadvertently cause problems—say or do something inappropriate— or that I will discover, or others will see, racism in my behavior.

To achieve a truly diverse workplace, organizational personnel must create work environments in which the meaning of difference is discussed as often as needed to manage both the legacy of racism and sexism and the contemporary diverse experience of primary group membership in the organization. Clearly, the discussion must preserve individual choices and yet investigate patterns of experience that accumulate for some members of the organization, whether or not they individually value their group identity.

The discussions must include the following:

- Perspectives on terminology and language.
- Opportunities to learn about the meaning of group identity and to discuss perceptions of others outside the group.
- Analysis of the negative and positive implications of group identity given the organization's culture, policy, or work practices.

These are critical ingredients in discussions that a manager or employee can generate within her or his own area of an organization.

Managing diversity must be seen as a daily skill and not just a program or workshop.

We also need national-level discussions that shed light on the tension between individual performance and group identity. If managers address group identity only in terms of meeting affirmative action goals or eliminating stereotyping, then we have failed to generate the insight necessary to talk about the value and contributions of each group's primary identity.

Failure to maintain a dialogue on racial or gender issues makes it more difficult to develop authentic relationships that strengthen our analysis of group-level identity. If I cannot talk about the basic dimensions of experience associated with race (for example, what is racism?), then I cannot contribute much to a more sophisticated analysis of such issues as the use and abuse of group-level identity by change agents in organizations.

The more important the aspects of group-level identity (confronting oppression—racism, sexism, and other "isms"; correcting current patterns of inequity; and affirming the value of diversity), the more sophisticated our conversation will become.

STRATEGIC ASSUMPTIONS

Every employee contributes to the climate of an organization. The following are some assumptions that promote effective behavior:

- Discussion of the meaning of group identity is important, and opportunities for such discussions can be created.

- Diversity requires continuous learning and discussion of different perspectives. One discussion of an issue associated with group identity doesn't mean that the issue has been resolved. Racism, sexism, and other "isms" that negatively affect individuals because of their identities are not just rational checklist items.

- The discussion of difference will create discomfort for some individuals in *all* groups; often discussions are at the expense of one group's comfort over another's.

- Group-level awareness and behavior can be an indicator of individual performance. (I am not saying that group identity must be uniformly valued but that understanding and the ability to use group-level diagnosis and potential action is a skill organizations can and must value.)

- People at all levels of an organization should be able to manage the interaction of individual and group-level identity effectively. Such skills don't belong just to human resource personnel or members of some race or gender groups.

NOTES

1. Kate Kirkham, "Dimensions of Diversity," paper presented at the Institute for Women and Organizations Conference, 1988, Long Beach, CA.

2. Marilyn Loden and Judy Rosener, *Work Force America* (New York: Business One–Irwin, 1992), p. 18.

3. Rosabeth Kanter, *Men and Women of the Corporation* (New York: Basic Books, 1977), pp. 206–242.

4. Kate Kirkham, "Organizational Culture and Diversity," *in preparation.*

5. Clayton Alderfer, "Problems of Changing White Males: Behavior and Beliefs Concerning Race Relations," in *Change in Organizations*, ed. P. Goodman and Associates (San Francisco: Jossey-Bass, 1982), pp 122–164.

Chapter Eleven

Oron South

All Culture Change Is Not the Same

Oron South

■

Oron South, PhD, was director of the Midwest Group for Human Resources when it was the Midwest Division of the NTL Institute for Applied Behavioral Science. He was also on the faculty of the School of Engineering, Vanderbilt University, and the College of Education, Florida State University. For the past 25 years, he has consulted regarding organization change. His last extended consultation was as resident consultant and OD team leader in the IRS. He now edits The Diversity Factor.

I n approaching organizational culture change, it is important to distinguish between national-level culture change and organizational-level culture change.[1,2] Their socialization processes are quite different.

Focusing culture change on race and gender involves dealing with the national culture as it exists in different organizations and institutions and in society at large. This can amplify and support internal resistance to change. It is necessary to address both national-level and organizational-level cultural differences when the objective is to focus change on race and gender. Working on these two cultural levels, it is clear that not all cultural change is the same.

SOCIALIZATION IN THE NATIONAL CULTURE'S RACE AND GENDER SYSTEM

We learn traditional race and gender roles at an early age. By the time we are 10, they are fully internalized. We know what the roles are for men and women, and we know how to feel and act toward someone of a different race or gender.

In working with teenagers, Paul Kivel,[3] cofounder of the Oakland Men's Project, uses a role-play of a confrontation between a father and son that ends with the father pushing his son out of his chair saying, "When are you going to grow up and act like a man around here?" After discussing the role-play, Kivel asks the youths to tell what it means to be a man. Typical responses include: having no emotions, yelling at people, not crying, not making mistakes, knowing about sex, not backing down, pushing people around, being able to take it, and so on. Kivel puts a line around these responses and labels this the Act-Like-a-Man box. The young people are quite aware of how risky it is to step out of this box.

Similar boxes can be constructed for other groups. In fact, our traditional role system has four boxes: the Act-Like-a-White-Man box, the Act-Like-a-White-Woman box, the Act-Like-a-Man-of-Color box, and the Act-Like-a-Woman-of-Color box. (We can now add the Gay Box, the Lesbian Box, the Disabled Box, etc.) Assuming the role for each of the traditional boxes leads, unfortunately, to systematic social inequality for white women and people of color because each generation is trained to reproduce the roles that lead to inequality.

The persistence of inequality obviously is no accident; it was designed into the social system many centuries ago. The basic elements in the design go back to the early Greeks. Saxonhouse points to the fear of diversity, a fear that differences lead to chaos and unpredictability.[4] To achieve order and unity, the Greeks tried to assimilate differences, a common strategy in our time. When assimilation attempts failed, the Greeks turned to other devices, such as classification. This was supposed to reflect the natural order of things, leading to the conclusion that nature ought to be as it is because it cannot be otherwise. Thus, if women and people of color by nature are inferior, they cannot be otherwise.

Another device was hierarchy. Aristotle said that hierarchy is the principle by which the parts are organized. From birth, it is established that certain people are meant to be ruled and others are meant to rule. Those meant to be ruled are put at the bottom of the hierarchy, while those meant to rule are placed at the top. Although Aristotle conceded it is impossible to distinguish between the slave-by-nature and the ruler-by-nature, he felt the principle still held: certain individuals are free by nature, and certain individuals are slaves; and for the latter, slavery is beneficial and just.

The key ideas and assumptions held by the Greeks were accepted and endorsed by our founding fathers. By taking a backward look, it is possible to see how deeply ideas about race and gender roles are buried in the national memory and American psyche. We can also see that the same ideas have been the basis for public policy—that is, the principles and assumptions underlying individual role behavior have been built into public and private organizations, leading to what we now call institutional racism and sexism. This helps to maintain economic and social advantage for whites. And every day, we can see the Greek strategies of hierarchy, nature, and assimilation at work to keep women and people of color "in their place."

Built-In Resistance to Learning

At the same time children learn role content and behavior, they also learn not to question the role system and its effects. Name calling, social ostracism, and economic reprisals are only a few of the devices used to discourage the exploration of roles other than those found in the traditional boxes. The public schools and universities reinforce the nonlearning system, as they provide little or no learning about race and gender issues. Too controversial, they say.

The prohibition against learning is very powerful, especially among white men. Self-starters in race and gender learning are hard to find, and the literature of self-starters is almost nonexistent. In corporations, white men expect to be taught by people of color what life is like for them in the corporation.

The lack of personal learning and personal self-reflection shows the strength of the role and gender system internalized when one is young. Such a lack, along with the original roles laid out, makes for a self-sealing system, one that is difficult to change. Added to this are the defenses against change built into the system. Many of these revolve around the notion that the roles fit "nature"—that is, "Women by nature are _____ ," and "People of color by nature are _____ ." In many cases, the nature charge has been supplemented with supposedly scientific studies that purport to show women and people of color to be inferior.[5]

Schein examines the origins of organizational culture by going back to the corporation's founders when possible and looking at changes and additions as he works forward.[6] This approach in race and gender change is stoutly resisted. Examining national behavior from the viewpoint of slavery, or interactions with Native Americans, with Mexicans, with the Japanese in World War II, etc., is difficult.

Marilyn Geewax, an editorial writer for the *Atlanta Constitution*, with eight other journalists, was invited by Atlantic Bridge, a non-profit group, to take part in a study tour of Germany. Contrary to the journalists' expectations, they found that at every turn they were confronted with the brutal truth about the Nazi past. Throughout the country, they found government-supported memorials to Nazi victims. The memorials and the willingness of the tour guides to accept the consequences of past national actions led Geewax to wonder what she could show a group of Germans coming to this country to learn about our nation's past. "Where would I go," she asks, "to explain how some 10 million human beings were shackled and shipped from Africa to the Americas in the horrifying 'Middle Passage' across the Atlantic Ocean?" And where could she go to show visitors the whips and guns used to keep slaves working? And where could she go to show other aspects of slavery, such as the breakup of families? She concludes by saying that the Germans she met made it a habit to speak frankly about the past and to find a way to live with collective guilt without becoming dispirited. "In America, we have made a habit of pretending that slavery was just a brief and tragic error, a flaw at the edges of our otherwise noble history."[7]

ORGANIZATIONAL SOCIALIZATION

Socialization for technical, specialist, and managerial roles in corporations takes place much later in life, so such roles are not as deeply embedded as those involving race and gender. Furthermore, they do not carry the antilearning precept found in race and gender roles, nor the built-in defensive routines. Although functions may be strongly defended in turf battles, they nevertheless are more accessible to study and critical analysis. And those white men outside the turf being defended are not prevented from taking part in the examination and analysis, as they would be with race and gender issues.

ORGANIZATIONAL ISSUES

Race and Gender Issues Have No Boundaries

Race and gender issues cut across functional boundaries, hierarchical levels, and organizational boundaries. Systemic in operation, they are not clearly defined systems or processes like accounting, manufacturing, and marketing. And they are not "owned" by any function or level. This means that establishing ownership of culture change is a major issue for top management. Establishing the credibility to lead a change effort is also an issue.

What makes the credibility task doubly difficult is the game-playing that takes place concerning issues of race and gender. This has, to use an old expression, poisoned the well. Whatever top managers say has been taken to be code for "You know I have to say this, but you also know what we actually will do." Cutting through the deliberate evasions and circumlocutions that have marked communication from top management to the rest of the organization, and within the organization, to create conditions for honest dialogue is a difficult task.

At one point in their book *Corporate Culture*, Deal and Kennedy say, "Now is the time to put all of these factors together—values, heroes, rites and rituals—and see how they actually work in the corporation."[8] Although it may be true that a corporation has heroes who have tried to change the race and gender system, it is more likely that for white men the heroes, the rites, and the rituals reflect those who are defending the status quo. Although the heroes, rites, and rituals may be useful in many types of corporate culture change, they may not be available in race- and gender-centered culture change.

Lack of a defined system for race and gender change and of assigned functional responsibility means that no one knows what resources for change the organization has nor where the most resistance will be encountered. These will have to be discovered. And given the built-in resistance of white men to launching inquiries into race and gender issues, it is necessary to develop leadership and the credibility to lead among top managers (who tend for the most part to be white men).

Top management also has to develop a frame of reference for leading and managing culture change, as the normal frames of reference available may not be useful. This frame will identify what is in and out of the frame and what the boundaries of the change effort are. The frame makes it easier to set up a management structure and process. In other forms of culture change, it is often possible to assign some of the major tasks to existing systems.

In *The Critical Path to Corporate Renewal*, Beer, Eisenstat, and Spector assert that it is not essential that top management consistently practice what it preaches in the early stages of a renewal.[9] The opposite is true with race- and gender-centered culture change. The record shows that top management must "walk its talk" and demonstrate early-on the change in behavior it advocates for the organization. Kotter and Heskett say, "The most visible factor that distinguishes major cultural changes that succeed from those that fail is competent leadership at the top."[10]

Distinguishing Between Danger and Defenses

When issues such as backlash, white-male bashing, emotionalism, and the danger of separate cultures are raised, how does the CEO tell the difference between danger ahead and new forms of resistance? CEOs are quite familiar with defenses around turf, but chances are they will not be equally familiar with the defense dynamics around race and gender change. Further, many of those shouting "Danger ahead" may not themselves be aware of the use of "backlash" as a defensive strategy.

Changing the Interpretive Context

Organizational values, goals, structures, and processes direct attention toward certain information and affect how top managers interpret or understand that information. This interpretive context determines which organizational issues are considered legitimate and motivates managers to frame the issues and information they confront in particular ways.

When organizations undertake to promote and perpetuate the traditional culture of race and gender, this leads them to ignore people who look, talk, and think differently. White women and people of color are invisible in this interpretive context. For culture change to take place, it is necessary for different ways of knowing, being, and acting to become part of the interpretive context and to influence how both external and internal environments are scanned, framed, and acted on. This will align the race and gender domain with strategic objectives. Making this kind of change is a different business than increasing the number of white women and people of color in corporations and moving them into managerial positions. Further, it is a different kind of change than is envisioned in other kinds of transformations, as they start with an assumption, usually unstated, that the prevailing mindset and interpretive context will be continued unchanged.

What makes this kind of change so difficult is that it involves changing habits of attending and thinking developed over a lifetime. Many white men, for example, simply are not aware that white women and people of color are invisible to them in meetings and business social gatherings. Similarly, many white women are not aware that a black woman in their midst is invisible to them.

What we have now are various different subcultures produced by different life-experience and socialization processes: the white subculture, the black subculture, the Mexican subculture, the Japanese subculture, the Native American subculture, and so on, each of which has important individual differences. To bring these subcultures into work force effectiveness, the following tasks must be addressed:

1. Make the invisible visible—getting people to "see" those from other subcultures and to acknowledge them.
2. Develop the ability to understand what those in other subcultures are saying and not saying.

3. Understand what significant events and situations will mean to those in the other subcultures; when such understanding is not present, communication is difficult.

4. Learn how to think like those in another subculture. Many of those who live in border towns in Europe and Asia are able to speak and think in two or more languages. This ability to switch to different modes of perception and thinking is very useful in teamwork and in being able to build on what others are saying and doing.

In short, culture change involving race and gender calls for a difficult kind of cognitive and emotional change, one that requires dealing with what Argyris calls "skilled incompetence,"[11] and for promoting double-loop learning (going outside the normal frame of reference to examine mental models and basic assumptions). Meeting this requirement is not easy.

NOTES

1. Geert Hofstede, *Cultures and Organizations: Software of the Mind* (London, England: McGraw-Hill, 1991).

2. Edgar H. Schein, *Organizational Culture and Leadership*, 2nd ed. (San Francisco: Jossey-Bass, 1992).

3. Paul Kivel, *Men's Work: How to Stop the Violence That Tears Our Lives Apart* (New York: Ballantine, 1992).

4. Arlene W. Saxonhouse, *Fear of Diversity: The Birth of Political Science in Ancient Greek Thought* (Chicago: University of Chicago Press, 1992).

5. Nancy Leys Stepan, "Race and Gender: The Role of Analogy in Science," in *Anatomy of Racism*, ed. David Theo Goldberg (Minneapolis: University of Minnesota Press, 1990), pp 38–57.

6. Edgar H. Schein, *Organizational Culture and Leadership*, 2nd ed. (San Francisco: Jossey-Bass, 1992).

7. Marilyn Geewax, "The Shadow of Slavery," *The Atlanta Journal/The Atlanta Constitution*, July 25, 1993, pp. G1 ff.

8. Terence E. Deal and Allen A. Kennedy, *Corporate Cultures: The Rites and Rituals of Corporate Life* (Reading, MA: Addison-Wesley, 1982), p. 107.

9. Michael Beer, Russell A. Eisenstat, and Bert Spector, *The Critical Path to Corporate Renewal* (Cambridge: Harvard Business School Press, 1990).

10. John P. Kotter and James L. Heskett, *Corporate Culture and Performance* (New York: Free Press, 1992).

11. Chris Argyris, *Overcoming Organizational Defenses* (Boston: Allyn and Bacon, 1990).

Chapter Twelve

Harold Bridger

Interdependence
The Elusive Factor in Working with Diversity and Oppression

Harold Bridger

■

Harold Bridger, TD, is one of the founding members and senior consultant of the Tavistock Institute of Human Relations. During World War II, he served as a battery commander and later as a member of the group (including Bion and Trist) that introduced new forms of officer selection. After the war, he helped to set up the institute itself. His working conferences are designed to further the capability of people at all levels to deal with the accelerating transitions in today's and tomorrow's open sociotechnical systems.

The main problem today is that people want to arrive without the experience of getting there.

The tragedy occurring in Yugoslavia as this is being written strikingly illustrates the critical importance of the title chosen for this article. Nor is that sad region an isolated example of how impotent other countries and the United Nations are in their endeavors to resolve conflicts. Indeed, the would-be peacemakers demonstrate the same group dynamics as the warring factions, albeit without the lethal results.

To some extent, diversity and oppression occur in all group situations with different degrees of strength and intensity. Furthermore, the dynamics are not contained, but affect all within or in contact with the environments involved. The forces that are produced in turn create an "open system" by which attempts to resolve internal difficulties are externalized. For example, Edward Albee wrote in *A Delicate Balance* of a mother who refers to her daughter as "having the divorces for all of us." And the reverse may also occur. When conditions in an environment become complex, turbulent, uncertain, or even explosive, systems within the environment may become more open and internalize corresponding dynamics in an effort to cope and to control events.

Examples of the latter situation are common today. Increasingly, the information explosion—combined with the technological one—has made many aspects of life very complex and turbulent, and the effects are felt within all communities and organizations that attempt to maintain themselves or to develop and grow. The individual or family can attempt to react or interact. In either case, the effects are radically different from what would occur in a relatively stable environment. But to pretend that a stable environment exists today is to deny reality.

Still, as T. S. Eliot wrote, "Humankind cannot bear much reality." And rationalizations are not uncommon in governmental—and in personal and institutional—decision-making, policies, and actions.

It is understandable and no accident, therefore, that social scientists and politicians tend to deal with increasing complexity, turbulence, and uncertainty by encapsulating problems in terms that focus attention on what appears to be the key issue and thus giving the impression that they know how to solve them. From time to time, these terms change, depending on the dynamics of the time, and the history of applied social science provides many examples. In politics today, we have market forces, subsidiarity, and political correctness; in social science, we have moved through human relations, action-research, participation, OD, sociotechnical systems, and now diversity and oppression—for which I am postulating the need for interdependence. This process of naming and renaming is not to be derided, though some may use such terms as buzzwords and try to create the impression that all one has to do to solve the problems at hand is adopt the technique or program of a certain professor, specialist, consultant, or executive.

NATURE AND CHARACTERISTICS

It was said earlier that diversity and oppression will occur in all groups, communities, and organizations, albeit to different degrees at different times. The possibility that diversity will affect any given oppression may also depend less on its nature than on strategies, policies, purposes, and environmental conditions and forces that impinge on the group in question. In today's world, the one-to-one relationship of diversity and oppression is beset by many other factors. We have to acknowledge that in many countries diversity has intensified elements of oppression, which can take the form of laws and regulations and not just physical actions.

We must therefore rely on the *promise* offered by diversity rather than on its nature. And this reliance must be tempered by attention to the dangers of diversity if we are not to be misled into the kind of "positive thinking" that has led to disastrous results in religious, societal, and political endeavors (e.g., the Crusades, fundamentalism, and Thatcherism). Unity of values, of culture, of purpose, etc., demands much more attention in diverse settings. And to achieve that unity, individuals of varied cultures, specialties, personalities, may well be prepared to suffer a degree of oppression. This is not playing the devil's advocate, but recognizing that both diversity and oppression can be experienced in other than the expected sense.

A few years ago, the director of the Brookings Institute pointed out to me the range of research studies that had been commissioned and had made important recommendations but had not been implemented. Important decisions and precepts in that wide field known as "the need for change" often meet a similar fate. And certainly, where diversity is concerned, multiple sets of forces are set in a train within and between the individuals, specialists, or groups involved.

From my point of view, just focusing on change itself—the need for it and even the benefits—is counterproductive because we are part not only of a rotating world in a largely mysterious galaxy, but also of a *Weltanschauung*. Our lives and times are complex and could settle anywhere—if they settle at all! But fortunately, we can hope because the world has settled in phases throughout history and prehistory. One might also be encouraged by a comment by Antoine St. Exupery (author of *The Little Prince*) in his book *The Wind and the Rain*. "Our task is not to foretell the future but to enable it," he wrote.

In today's world of organized multicultural communities and managed institutions, intensive multitechnological and multifunctional systems interact more and more with environmental forces and conditions so that diversity, as well as oppression, will only be minimally affected by concentrating on interpersonal and intrapersonal methods. These, like the T-group and the A. K. Rice (Leicester) models, can undoubtedly contribute to personal and social insights, but they are of only limited use in the tasks, responsibilities, and working relationships demanded of purpose-oriented organizations.

It is beneficial to recognize that even the household (as distinct from the family) has become an open sociotechnical system, with "operational friendships" frequently added to and even replacing extended-family connections. It is not that family and personal relationships have disappeared, but that they are embedded in intensive patterns of role and functional/specialist relationships, which introduce force fields quite different from those of relationships based in the family or social interaction.

Thus, diversity and oppression, both of which have also become more complex and prevalent today, will require quite different approaches to be understood and treated. In particular, the promise of diversity as a weapon against oppression will only be fulfilled if the basis of learning is related to accepting what might be called a double-helix approach to the dynamics of groups and organizations. This approach must address the demands of both overt and purposeful objectives, activities, and operational interdependencies and the unrecognized system of tensions inherent in the endeavor. This tension system is itself a related but different set of interdependencies.

The relationship between these sets of interdependencies, when confronted and worked through, offers that promise by which diversity and greater acceptance of differences have the opportunity to remedy oppression against or within a group or organization.

Efforts to apply directly the insights about personal, interpersonal, and group relations to real organizational issues and problems will, on the other hand, be an inadequate approach based on inappropriate premises.

INTERDEPENDENCE: ITS PROMISE AND DEMANDS

Andrew Clements recently reviewed *Diversity of Life* by Edward O. Wilson in the *Financial Times* (London). In his article, he noted that "Species diversity, the range of living organisms to be formed in a single habitat, is at its most luxuriant in the rain forest; there the niches into which animals and plants can adapt themselves are narrower and more ingenious than anywhere else on earth." He added later, "In the fact of this unaccountable profusion, man has set about winnowing it with an effectiveness unparalleled in the history of life on earth." He does not, however, comment on the struggles for life and space within that habitat, within and between those species— the "oppressions" of various kinds. However, one might assume that the promise of that diversity had enabled a relative balance to be struck that the modern, turbulent, voracious environment was destroying.

In the case of our human endeavors, we also have environments and contexts that offer both opportunities and threats, and our habitats are working (and not just social) systems increasingly open to those environments. Similarly, our diversities can only show promise if the memberships accept differentiation—that is, recognition of roles, functions, outlooks, and cultures, as well as, and not just, personal relationships. We also need to test out and work through the demands that corresponding and conflicting purposes impose upon us. Differentiation is no easy task. Individuals and subgroups, specialties, and entities of various kinds have "aspirations, hopes and fears which they have to reconcile"[1] with demands of many different kinds—primarily with the immediate system, but also with others in the environment of that system.

This is not the place to go into detail about the dynamics of working groups and organizations, but if we are to indicate some hope for our complex and potentially promising and dangerous diversity, some reference must be made to Bion and his seminal work on groups.[1] Briefly, he postulated the basic assumptions by which the group-as-a-whole purports to fulfill a purpose effectively, but may actually modify or negate that purpose to suit the subtle "group-sensed" interaction of individuals' and subgroups' private intrapersonal concerns. Two common examples will suffice to give force to these points. When groups are prepared to achieve key objectives or steps that everyone knows should be taken in light of a given situation, it is common for those very objectives or steps to be sacrificed to keep the peace between members who cannot agree about how they should be done. Again, we have all seen or heard about a group of sane, humane people that decided upon and carried out a mad or irresponsible action.

Bion was also quite precise in recognizing the need for the overt task or purpose to be clearly evident, because it provides the basis upon which the unrecognized (and unconscious) forces operate. In one sense, the overt purpose acts as a "cover," but it also provides the counterpart to the "hidden diversity" and basic assumption(s) by which the group actually performs.

FULFILLING THE PROMISE

My contention is that institutions of all kinds—professional, public, and private organizations—have not yet come to terms with the paradigm shift that subjects their boundaries, both internally and externally, to what might be called an "osmosis" of factors and forces that affect all aspects of their work. In addition, if one includes in an accounting of oppressions the unrecognized as well as the overt restrictions and impositions that derive from the very nature of responsibilities and accountabilities in fulfilling purposes, strategies, and objectives, then the task facing diversity demands much more than "sweet reason" or even good leadership. Today, those who hold authority and stand accountable have to learn to live and work at the boundaries of their domains. They thus will be accountable, while their "diverse memberships" will be responsible for fulfilling immediate objectives.

It will be impossible to develop the necessary interdependencies within those spheres of accountability unless those in authority are ready to reorganize, understand, and promote the capacities necessary to face the many implications of working with *interwoven* aspects of the organization or community. The emphasis on *interwoven* is critical, because attempting to resolve each aspect separately will lead to erroneous or confused conclusions.

In this context, it will be recognized that while earlier forms of group relations training and development—A. K. Rice groups, T-groups, and even sociotechnical approaches—can contribute insights, they cannot provide answers to our current stress-laden, open-system world. Indeed, they are just as likely to mislead in any context but that of a small group pursuing a limited objective.

Returning to the situation in Yugoslavia, we can see that the bewildering array of agreements and ceasefires—all of which so far have failed—and the Vance-Owen plan demonstrate all too painfully a world-size example of this analysis. Nor is this example unique; many others—such as the difficulty of unifying East and West Germany and the influx of refugees—indicate how strife and oppression will exist so long as a society does not recognize an interdependence with which to replace earlier structures and their cultures.

When the need for transitional processes is overlooked or bypassed, the results can be tragic. The statement at the head of this article attempts to sum up the current malaise. But the transition to interdependence can be made if and when we can confront and learn to accept those psychodynamics in the context of our ultimate purpose. The unlearning in that development can be painful, but the reward can fulfill the promise.[2]

NOTES

1. Wilfred R. Bion, *Experiences in Groups and Other Papers* (London: Tavistock Publications, 1961).

2. Harold Bridger, "Courses and Working Conferences as Transitional Learning Institutions," in *Training, Theory and Practice*, eds. W. B. Reddy and C. C. Henderson (NTL and University Associates, 1987).

Chapter Thirteen

Kevin Boyle

An Injury to One Is an Injury to All

How Unions Can Reemerge as Forces for Social Progress

Kevin Boyle

■

Kevin Boyle is an organization development professional with key accomplishments in cooperative labor–management efforts, participative management, and strategic planning in unions and jointly between labor and management. He has also been involved in the joint approach to workplace design and redesign. Kevin recently sat on a panel moderated by President Bill Clinton to discuss workplace and structural changes needed for business, labor, and government in the future of the American workplace.

L ess than a century ago, joining a union was an act of desperate courage. The oppression of working men, women, and children was the common thread that bonded people as they struggled against the inhuman conditions of American industry. Oppression of all kinds is linked by a common origin: economic power and control. During the past century, American labor has played a central role in elevating the American standard of living and limiting this control on peoples' lives. As organizations, unions continue to serve as a system of checks and balances against the power of American capitalism.

The ultimate, timeless goal of labor so eloquently put by Samuel Gompers 100 years ago is still true today. What does labor want? Gompers answered, "More."

> We want more school houses and less jails, more books and less arsenals, more learning, less vice, more constant work and less crime, more leisure and less greed, more justice and less revenge.

In order for unions to generate a consensus on "What does labor want?" they must generate shared values from throughout the organization and within the external community. They must learn from everyone about different realities, create a means for networking among the membership and their communities, and create a feedback and mentoring process for ongoing development of all people within the union.

Through the decades, the labor movement has constantly changed and adapted to reach out to people in American society striving for their share of opportunity and reward. This must continue to be the goal of unions today. But instead of focusing on industry or trades, unions must look at the needs of the community of workers who are feeling the impact of today's changing economics. This community of workers is more diverse than ever. In fact, by the year 2000 only 15 percent of new entrants in the labor market will be native white males. The remaining 85 percent of the new workers will be women, minorities, and immigrants. This rapidly accelerating change in the American labor market poses new challenges for unions and their leaders.

As the nation is faced with awesome economic, demographic, and technological change, unions can still provide the organization for workplace and societal progress. But today's issues demand a new model for unions as organizations for change, a model that will recognize the changing expectations of a diverse membership and a diverse community.

Some of the more progressive local and international unions are turning away from focusing on the occupational and cultural differences within their organizations. Instead, through organizational assessments, they are maximizing their strengths as organizations of multiskilled members within multicultural communities. This change of focus has raised debate about some of the unions' long-held beliefs, such as the system of seniority and functionalized technical and clerical wage scales.

In a letter to the local leadership and the district staff outlining a strategic planning process, the Communications Workers of America— District 7 International Vice President Sue Pisha said, "It is going to be essential that we identify and act upon common ground, involve a more diverse group in our decision-making than we are used to, and take a much broader view of the issues facing us . . . We each have pieces of a very complex puzzle known as the future of our Union. As we begin to plan, we need to create a shared view of what is going on in the world, talk of our hopes for the future, and gain a consensus of what we want to do about it." This planning process was designed to go beyond getting to know one another and different cultures better; it was about getting to know the broader world environment and then identifying the union's relationship to it.

CONFRONTING THE NEED FOR CHANGE

To begin this change process, unions must come to realize and face up to the issues of oppression that are alive and well within their own union halls. An awareness must be created of behaviors based on stereotypes such as attitudes toward people with disabilities, sexism, racism, homophobia, and others. This can be achieved by seeking a more diverse membership to assess and debate the issues and barriers that exist for all. It is essential that union leaders begin to educate their membership to achieve better understanding of the different characteristics, values, and behaviors that diversity brings to the union.

In creating this environment, leaders will have to confront some very basic assumptions about how the union interacts in the community. One example is that the locations of union halls tend to exclude participation of many of today's members. Unions traditionally were organized within industries, and the places to meet were centered in neighborhoods close to where the members worked. These were the neighborhoods of the white, male heads of the household who were working-class union members.

Today's union membership is much more diverse, and members tend not to live in the same neighborhood in which they work. The pressures on working families today—with many single parents and women as head of household—do not allow for the same kind of participation in the union as was the norm in the past. The challenge for unions today is to safeguard their democratic nature by communicating quickly and effectively with a diverse membership. The increasing number of people of color and women and the acknowledging of gays and lesbians in the workplace are forcing changes in some deeply rooted attitudes within the union movement about who will participate and how. Greater awareness and understanding of the value of diversity will be the beginning of changing and revitalizing the union organization.

LEADERSHIP AND PARTICIPATION

Leadership must begin to make an effort to educate and mentor a broader base of people in the union and to expand the agenda from wage negotiations to include union participation in many different business and community areas. Local leaders must become more active in recruiting and organizing new members. In doing so, leaders should use multiple resources to gain an understanding of the values of these potential members. This will enable union leaders to discuss issues with which the new members can readily identify. Furthermore, it is imperative for labor to enhance its image to the entire community in order for its message to be heard and ultimately attract a more representative membership.

In order to represent effectively the needs of a more diverse membership, union representatives need to be aware of differences with respect to age, race, ethnic background, gender, religion, physical ability, and so forth. Equally important, union leaders must understand and acknowledge their own prejudices. Oppression and stereotypes do not occur in a vacuum, but are reinforced behaviors of both prejudiced people and their targets. Until these differences are understood, it will be very difficult for the union to meet the various needs of its membership.

Some local and international unions are participating in diversity training for their members and leaders. Because members are expecting a higher level of participation and representation for their dues, they want to be a part of the decision-making process. To enjoy solidarity, labor leaders are including diversity in their agenda and enhancing people's ability to participate in this agenda.

As the goals of the union expand and diversity is integrated into the operation of the organization, union leaders will face extraordinary challenges. Diversity is a potential source of innovation for the union, but it also brings the risk of increased racial, ethnic, and gender conflict. The union can enhance creativity and participation by accepting the risk and providing the skills necessary to deal with inevitable confrontations. New skills are prerequisites for participation. Skills development can range from interpersonal problem solving, communications skills, and running more-effective meetings to more-complex education in technical, business, and self-management skills. All these skills will be required to participate in recognizing the diverse needs of the members and also to meet the demands of changing technology and workplace design.

The union can be the leader in developing new systems of learning with employers and with educational institutions within the community. An additional role the union can play is marketing the skills of its members to various companies within the community to increase employment opportunities.

One of the greatest challenges unions will face is diversifying the elected leadership. The most evident form of power within the union lies in the election process. Individuals, groups, and organizations tend to replicate themselves or others close to them. Unconscious though it may be, this is the colonial effect in action. The membership elects those who look and act the most like them. In order for the union to fulfill its values of equity, solidarity, and justice, the leadership must bring both the minority and majority cultures into the process, no matter how politically risky it might be to individuals in power today.

Thomas C. Kohler points out that "Individuals and societies alike become and remain self-governing only by repeatedly and regularly engaging in acts of self-government. It is the habit that sustains the condition." Kohler goes on to say, "Unions can act as schools for democracy, where habits of self-governance, direct responsibility, tolerance and mutual respect are instilled." Unions have a very important role to play in developing democracy and fighting oppression, but the reality is that the environment and the needs of society have changed and the structures and processes of the union remain stuck in the past.

Some of these structures and processes must change, and union leadership needs to become more proficient at monitoring changes in the environment and more flexible in its response to changes. As with any democracy, structural changes will demand energetic debate in order for change to be realized. Union leaders who have developed their own potential for intercultural awareness will be better able to lead and respond in ever-changing, multicultural communities. This type of awareness and debate will help bring about the changes needed for labor to reinvent itself for the twenty-first century.

UNIONS AND ORGANIZATIONAL DEVELOPMENT

Contemporary union leaders will need to learn sound organizational development principles, know how to use the structure to the union's advantage rather than only to their own political advantage, and be able to enhance the unions' response to a diverse membership as well as to its environment. To change the union as an organization, it will be necessary to clarify and understand the union's purpose and goals and the systems developed to implement and support them. These include systems for making decisions, holding people accountable, communicating information, establishing relationships between people and expectations of behaviors within the organization, and rewarding expected outcomes.

The norm for managing change in the union today is to build small coalitions focusing on equity issues or working to change the power group. For the most part, these efforts are entirely internally focused. This approach results in further splintering of the union and prohibits intercultural participation in proactive, strategic change efforts.

The systems and structures of the union should be explored and modified as a whole and inclusive process. A whole-system, concerted effort for change would modify the structures to support and develop all people in leadership, decision-making, communication, personal power, organizing, and other skills that will support and strengthen the union. Recognizing people as individuals and blending individual skills with cultural traits creates a strong, interwoven community. Through this assessment and development, unions and their leaders can begin to develop their purpose, goals, and structures to meet the needs of diverse memberships and communities. By successfully managing this process, unions can increase their membership base, operate with greater strength in the workplace, and gain new insight into the possibilities of forging cooperative relationships with employers and the broader community.

By using the tools of organizational development (OD), unions are, indeed, recognizing their strengths and emerging as catalysts for new organizational design principles in the workplace. Through proactive involvement in labor–management efforts, unions have the opportunity to strengthen themselves as organizations. Participation in work site meetings and training offers the chance for educating the broader membership about union goals and for hearing from more members about their needs and outlooks. This form of "proactive militancy" can allow unions to actively listen to members and respond to their needs and concerns before they become demands. Once issues become demands, they are usually dealt with in the traditional process of grievance or collective bargaining. These processes serve a greater purpose when they are used as a long-term strategic approach instead of a short-term problem-solving process. Workplace participation also creates structures for members to be involved in ongoing decisions and provides all members with opportunities for active involvement in fulfilling the union's purpose. This proactive approach has placed some unions in the forefront of social and economic change.

CONCLUSION

Obviously, change is going to continue into the twenty-first century. Unions are going to have to take on new responsibilities, and the organizational structure that served the members for 100 years is going to need to change. Some unions are changing their organizational systems using the skills and processes of organization development. These processes must develop a relationship between labor's values and goals and the development and implementation of new technology, the public education system, national health care, community development, civil rights, employment equity, and a collection of other issues important to multicultural communities.

This change process has no end. There is no end to wanting more dignity and less oppression. But change has a beginning, and that beginning dates back to the birth of a labor movement that gave a voice and vehicle for change to working people of many cultures. American labor's responsibility into the next century is to adjust to the new conditions so that unions may achieve an optimum ability to represent their members, create a balance for greater freedom and a measure of human dignity for all working people, and contribute to the evolutionary progress of American democratic society. As long as there is injury to one—regardless of one's color, gender, physical or mental ability, sexual orientation, or cultural or economic background— the work of labor is not complete.

SOURCES

L. Be, K. Boyle, P. Coppoletti, D. Hutchinson, J. Perich-Anderson, J. Prantil, and G. Storms, "An Organizational Approach for Managing Change: Employee Involvement as an Example," *unpublished paper,* 1990.

L. Be, K. Boyle, D. Hutchinson, J. Perich-Anderson, and K. Wilson, *The Joint Process: A Workbook for Union Representatives,* Communications Workers of America, Seattle, 1988.

D. Bell, *Faces at the Bottom of the Well: The Permanence of Racism* (New York: Basic Books, 1992), pp. 7–10.

Joseph A. Bierne, *Challenge to Labor: New Roles for American Trade Unions* (Englewood Cliffs, NJ: Prentice-Hall, 1969), pp. 198–201.

Kevin Boyle, "Whole Systems Consulting in Unionized Organizations," in *Proceedings of the Organization Development Network National Conference,* (Portland, OR: Organization Development Network, 1991), pp. 332–343.

Richard B. Freeman and James L. Medoff, *What Do Unions Do?* (New York: Basic Books, 1983), pp. 134–135.

John E. Jones, "The Organizational Universe," in *Annual Handbook for Group Facilitators,* eds. John E. Jones and J. William Pfeiffer (San Diego: University Associates, 1981), pp. 155–64.

T. Kohler, "Unions Declined as Our Institutions Unraveled," *editorial, Detroit Free Press,* Sept. 6, 1992.

G. Lapid-Bogda and S. Bradford, "Diverse Approaches to Diversity: What, When, Why," in *Proceedings of the Organization Development Network National Conference,* 1991, Long Beach, CA, pp. 119–25.

R. Marshall and M. Tucker, *Thinking for a Living: Education and the Wealth of Nations* (New York: Basic Books, 1992), pp. 89–90.

S. Myers, "Balancing the Organizational Responsibility and Individual Potential," in *Proceedings of the Organization Development Network National Conference,* 1991, Long Beach, CA, pp. 131–3.

Suzanne Pharr, *Homophobia: A Weapon of Sexism.* (Inverness, CA: Chardon Press, 1988), p. 1.

Sue Pisha, "Strategic Planning for CWA—District 7," speech to Communications Workers of America, St. Paul, MN, 1993.

M. Sheahan, "Keep It Complicated: What Unions Owe Local Leaders to Prepare Them for Their Role in Joint Programs and Work Restructuring" (Detroit: UAW Region 1A Labor-Management Council for Economic Renewal).

M. Tyson, "The Future of Unions," *Proceedings of Ethics at Work: A Symposium on the Worker and the Workplace,* 1992, Cedar Falls, IA.

VISIONS OF OUR HUMAN POTENTIAL

VISIONS OF OUR HUMAN POTENTIAL

Perceptions of our potential as humans are often limited to discussions of our nature. Human nature is blamed for the existence and continuation of much of the misery in this world. Domination of the weak by the strong, victimization of the minority by the majority, scapegoating, war, genocide, and even rape have all been excused at various times as inevitabilities of the human condition.

To create a world in which the norms, values, and systems favor inclusion of all people and the utilization of their individual and identity-group differences, we need a new view of human nature—a more ambitious vision of what *can* be.

Here are six images of a world that can be . . .

Chapter Fourteen

Toward Creativity, Cooperation, Community

Marilyn Loden

■

Marilyn Loden

Marilyn Loden is president of Loden Associates, Inc., a San Francisco–based management consulting firm. Her work in public and private institutions focuses on managing organizational change and valuing employee diversity. She is the author of Feminine Leadership, or How to Succeed in Business Without Being One of the Boys *(Times Books, 1985) and coauthor of* Workforce America! Managing Employee Diversity as a Vital Resource *(Business One Irwin, 1991).*

A s we approach the third millennium, it seems timely to reflect on the valuing-diversity movement, both where it has been in the recent past and what it can offer in the future. Looking back at the last decade, it is clear that diversity moved from the background to the foreground in the United States and in other parts of the world. Globalization, shifting work-force demographics, immigration, political instability, and the basic human yearnings for autonomy, dignity, and respect all helped to heighten interest in the value of diversity.

As a result, there is now growing public consciousness in our society regarding the role that culture plays in shaping people's values and lives. There is also greater recognition of the importance of a multicultural perspective in developing new ideas and creating common ground. Yet, despite increased awareness, social fragmentation, intolerance, and oppression still abound.

Now we must rededicate ourselves to the difficult work of building a community that crosses multicultural lines. To optimize the promise of diversity—as men and women; gays and straights; whites and people of color; young and old; able-bodied and disabled; Buddhists, Hindus, Jews, Muslims, Christians, and citizens of the world—we must move from serving only our particular constituencies, based on our core identities, to understanding issues from the perspectives of *others*. And as we learn more about the world from *others*, we must use this new learning to shape our hopes, plans, and vision for a better tomorrow.

In the future, as ambassadors for diversity, we will need a multicultural yardstick to measure everything, including our impact as change agents. As such, we cannot hope to be effective by serving only our core constituencies. Instead, we must be passionate about issues of fairness and justice for *others* as well as for ourselves. This work will be difficult. It will demand that we challenge traditions, manage ambiguity, and take risks. It will create discomfort and self-doubt. It will test our real commitment to diversity as never before and require deeper levels of humility, patience, and forgiveness. But it will also repay us with a new sense of hope, connectedness, and joy.

What can derail our efforts as we move ahead are the human tendencies to become complacent about injustice directed at *others*, defensive about our own biases, and morally superior about our right to define and control the multicultural movement. If we succeed in overcoming these frailties, then we will be positioned to add our unique perspectives to the collective vision of diversity and to realize its great promise: creativity, cooperation, and true community for us all.

Chapter Fifteen

Robert W. Terry

Authenticity
Unity Without Uniformity

Robert W. Terry

■

Robert W. Terry, PhD, is president of Terry Group, consultants and trainers in leadership, quality, and diversity. He recently completed 11 years as senior fellow and founding director of the Reflective Leadership Center at the Hubert H. Humphrey Institute of Public Affairs, University of Minnesota. He is the author of For Whites Only *(1970), a study of racism, and* Authentic Leadership: Courage in Action *(Jossey-Bass, 1993).*

The theoretical problem of the "one and the many" has long intrigued philosophers. Theoretical no longer, this philosophical issue now frames the problems of everyday life. How much unity, how much diversity is the right mix to build a creative and long-term viable future in neighborhoods, communities, the nation, and the globe? The temptations and pressures to err in either direction are enormous. Yet the challenge confronts us: Build a unified society without uniformity. Assimilation and exclusion (even elimination) mark the outer poles of the debate. In between bubble all the policy and personal issues bedeviling the United States and the globe.

My vision and my answers are threefold. First, a seemingly paradoxical answer: Only *in* unity can there *be* diversity. Second, on underlying confidence: Only by being authentic can we build the credibility with each other that sets the foundation for both agreement and disagreement. And third, a commitment and belief: We must have the courage to face our fears to free ourselves to stand side-by-side in a continuing partnership.

Six ethical principles are necessary to affirm and support diversity: dwelling, freedom, justice, participation, love, and responsibility. To deny them will result in genocide, discrimination, double standards, oppression, apathy, and abdication. Only by living, not just affirming, these principles in policy and in our everyday actions will we have the strength to embrace differences and let them thrive.

Tragically, we have exhausted authenticity credits with each other. No more benefit of the doubt, no more opportunity to make mistakes and mature in our understanding of others and ourselves—thus, no possibility for profound dialogue. That leaves us with accusations, defensive denials, rationalization, and counter-accusations.

Yet, I know from 25 years of experience that it *is* possible to build authenticity credits with each other across color, class, gender, religion, disability, sexual orientation, and other seemingly unbridgeable chasms.

Beginning in Detroit in 1968 with PACT (People Acting for Change Together) and now with the Minneapolis Initiative Against Racism in 1994, we have demonstrated that real and abiding partnerships are not only possible but can enhance the well-being of all the partners in the dialogue and consequent shared actions.

What, then, does it take to be authentic? What it requires is the courage to face our fears of the "stranger," admit those fears, own our own history—both its good parts and its destructive parts—and discover the hope that arises when living a caring truth. I worry about trivial diversity in which we only share safe aspects of our respective cultures. My food doesn't threaten your food; my dress doesn't threaten your dress. Imagine, in contrast, an exploration of exploitation and domination within all cultures as well as honoring our glorious histories. And imagine doing it without fear that what is reported and admitted will be used against the group sharing the hard truth. I know it's possible because I've experienced it firsthand. Yet we are a long way from feeling safe enough to do it nationally and in our own communities.

Our past may be prologue; it is not necessarily our destiny. Focusing on our current realities can be difficult, if we are honest with ourselves and with others. Yet as we tell our stories, reporting what we abhor in our inheritance and in what we rejoice, we will make an astonishing discovery. We will indeed find out that our life journeys overlap in surprising ways. And as we listen, share, and care, we will discover a wonderful fact: We can unify without marching in lockstep. We can join in common cause to resist the negatives and build on the positives of all of our cultures. And amazingly, the gift of differences helps all of us see more clearly not only others but ourselves as well. And even if we do not like what we see, we will be encouraged to connect at deeper levels as we forge authentic bonds of unity without requiring uniformity.

Chapter Sixteen

When Diversity Means Added Value

Frederick A. Miller

■

Frederick A. Miller

Frederick A. Miller, president of The Kaleel Jamison Consulting Group, Inc., was formerly a manager with Connecticut General Life Insurance Company (now CIGNA), where he was responsible for its pioneering diversity effort, which started in 1972. He serves on the boards of directors of Ben & Jerry's Homemade, Inc., The National Organization Development Network, and the Institute of Development Research. He is a member and former board member of NTL Institute. He is the managing editor of this book.

M y vision for the future is a day when diversity *isn't* something that people have to remember or plan for, develop strategies for, be surprised about, see as something different, see as something to be added to the plate, or can forget—but rather as something they see as adding value to their organizations, their communities, their individual lives.

My vision of the future is a day when a critical mass of people realizes that there is no value without diversity—that, in fact, without diversity, you have minus value. I envision a day when a critical mass realizes that people and their diversity, uniqueness, and identity-group memberships *are* the plate—that without people, we have nothing, and that once you add people, by definition, you add diversity.

My vision eliminates both blatant and passive oppression. It challenges the stubborn notion that one-up, one-down is the only way people can interact and organizations can be constructed. I envision *different* to mean not one being better and one being worse, not one being superior and another inferior, but simply meaning not the same, having a variety of characteristics that can result in a dazzling myriad of looks, styles, approaches, and outcomes.

In my vision, we enter interactions showing grace toward each other and with the capacity to develop mutual respect, caring, and love.

My vision is of a time when perfection is no longer the goal. Instead the goals are continuous learning and an aggressive desire to enhance ourselves and to bring our uniqueness to our partnerships with others.

Finally, I envision a future when humankind will show faith in our differences and no longer fear our differences.

Chapter Seventeen

Bailey Jackson

Coming to a Vision of a Multicultural System

Bailey Jackson

■

Bailey Jackson, EdD, is a professor of education and the dean of the School of Education at the University of Massachusetts. He was a founding faculty member of the Social Justice Education Program at the School of Education, Amherst, Massachusetts. He is also a founding partner of New Perspectives Inc., a firm that specializes in training and consultation services related to social diversity and social justice in organizational settings.

M y attempts to construct a vision of a multicultural system were extremely frustrating until I realized it is impossible for me or any other single person to construct such a vision of a multicultural organization, community, society, or other social system. It is impossible because the criteria that would have to be satisfied would make it virtually impossible for any one person to complete the task. To develop the right vision, as much attention would have to be paid to the process of creating the vision and the perspectives that must be reflected in it as to the words that are used to convey it.

To create a vision of a multicultural system, a diversity of perspectives must be represented in a group of people who are engaged in a dialogical process such as that put forth by Paulo Freire as *Praxis*. Praxis—or, by Freire's definition, the process of naming, reflecting, and transforming—best describes the type of dialogue that I believe must take place to get to this vision. The people involved in this process are as important as the process itself.

What became extremely clear for me as I contemplated this essay was that one person cannot conceive a vision of a multicultural system. My notion of what it takes to develop a multicultural vision requires a diversity of perspectives not available to me or any other single person. While I believe that I have considerable experience and knowledge in the area of multicultural systems development and the development of theoretical constructs that serve that work, there are a number of perspectives and experiences that I believe this task requires, but that I do not have and will probably never have. It would take a great deal of arrogance or a great lack of understanding about the demands of this task for one person to think that he or she could succeed in fully developing such a vision.

The people who could develop a vision of a multicultural system would be, yes, some people like me—that is, people who have a lifelong commitment to social justice and social diversity. People who are thoughtful about how that can be manifested in social systems. People who are skilled at facilitating change in social systems. But in addition to those people, and others who share my experience and perspectives, the task requires people with a spiritual perspective. And it requires those from a revolutionary, tear-the-system-down-and-rebuild-it perspective. But there should also be those who believe in being able to work within the existing system.

There must be those who can call upon their personal experiences with the worst forms of social injustice and those who have experienced some of the best of our social systems in "walking toward the multicultural talk." There must be an economic perspective and a psychological perspective. And the perspectives, experiences, and hopes of diverse social and cultural groups must be fully involved in this process.

As I list some of the perspectives that I believe should be represented in this process, I am aware that I might overlook perspectives that ought to be included. All this leads me to realize that the process of constructing the group could be an extremely powerful experience in and of itself. This all sounds both scary and exciting.

A group of people with these perspectives engaged in this process would come up with the right words. The process might take a long, long time, but I believe that while it is happening, we will all learn by either observing or participating in the process.

Chapter Eighteen

One of Many

Kate Kirkham

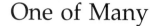

Kate Kirkham

Kate Kirkham, PhD, has focused her work, teaching, research, and consulting on the integration of organizational behavior and race and gender issues. She is a member of the faculty of the Graduate School of Management at Brigham Young University's Department of Organizational Behavior and an associate of Elsie Y. Cross and Associates. Her research and consulting have involved volunteer, government, business, and educational organizations such as Corning Inc., American Express, and others.

B ecause I have studied the traditional race and gender "majority" groups in U.S. corporations, I will focus on their contributions to a diverse work force.

Whites' and men's behavior in the United States has been governed by a majority/minority paradigm. The pattern of their reported perceptions was to be "one of many *individuals*." The collective behavior of their own group was not a focal point, even though correcting conditions caused by racism and sexism and working to include women and minorities may have been. To acknowledge that being white and/or being male is to be a member of one of the many groups that now both own the workplace and regulate a global economy is a paradigm shift. Whites and men who acknowledge the changing paradigm will see the following implications.

PERSPECTIVE ON COLLECTIVE IDENTITY

"Majority" group members operating under the old paradigm act as if they would be willing to look at racist and/or sexist issues if they were individually aware of the oppressive behavior in their organizations. Many frequently attribute their lack of attention to (1) failure of the "other" group to bring concerns to their attention and (2) lack of sufficient proof of the existence or magnitude of racism, sexism, or other forms of oppression.

With a paradigm shift, many whites and men see themselves as co-contributors and co-competitors in a diverse workplace and seek to recognize the individual and group dimension as needed. Under this paradigm, whites and men will expect to learn about oppression, including how they can improve their contribution to authentic work relationships, and take direction from a variety of leaders. They will be driven by a desire to contribute to (not dominate) the creation of new models of organizations in which policies, practices, and values are not based on racism or sexism.

INVESTIGATING INTERACTION PATTERNS

Members of the majority groups have been observed as (1) failing to initiate critical feedback with people of color and white women and (2) avoiding risk-taking in a public setting on issues of racism and sexism. As one of many groups in a work force, whites and men will look for opportunities to improve their ability to publicly discuss with colleagues the racist and nonracist (or sexist and nonsexist) aspects of work styles, feedback, and organizational strategies. As they more frequently watch the behavior of others like them, whites and men will identify ways to differentiate themselves from the stereotypical responses of members of their groups. They will learn to read the race and gender implications of group dynamics.

PREPARATION TO CONTRIBUTE

Traditional majority groups will expect to see career systems, work time, and holiday celebrations demonstrate diversity without subordination based on race or gender or other dimensions of identity.

The process of managing diversity will be shared. Ownership will not rest on those who are victimized, nor on the passion of advocates. Competency will be expected from all. Diversity will be measured not only by the populations present in an organization but by how those present respect differences and value the contributions of the many in the work world.

Men and whites will "do their homework." Under the paradigm of co-contributors, in general, they will seek to understand *the dynamics of oppression* and to acquire *specific knowledge* about individuals and groups. The process of sorting through positive and negative implications will be valued as a skill. Individually and collectively, as one of many, each of us will identify changes and celebrate that which we can jointly achieve.

Chapter Nineteen

Edith Whitfield Seashore

Save the Dream for Everyone

Edith Whitfield Seashore

■

Edith Whitfield Seashore has consulted to industrial, military, educational, and voluntary organizations for 25 years. She is a social psychologist concerned with organizational change, team building, strategic planning, and multicultural organizations. In addition to her consulting practice, from 1974 to 1979 she was president of the NTL Institute for Applied Behavioral Sciences. In 1979, with Morley Segal, she founded the American University/NTL Master's Program in Human Resource Development. She is a coeditor of this book.

We've lost it! Lost it all! Our passion, our beliefs, our values, our dreams. We've forgotten what we've struggled for: to live in freedom, with dignity; to be everything we dreamed to be, never letting biases or prejudices stifle our opportunities.

Harry Belafonte was quoted recently as saying, "We're in a struggle for the soul of this country. We're in a struggle for America's moral center. And unless that can be made straight, I'm not sure any of the other battles are winnable." He added that in this country there is a mass movement for change, waiting for some accident of history to ignite it. My vision is that this explosion will happen and that this country and the world will regain the dream of democracy.

In the words of Langston Hughes:

> There is a dream in the land with its back against the wall . . .
> The dream knows no frontier or tongue,
> The dream no class or race:
> The dream cannot be kept secure in any one locked place.
> This dream today embattled with its back against the wall,
> To save the dream for one, it must be saved for all.

IV

VOICES OF EXPERIENCE

VOICES OF EXPERIENCE

Oppression is so enmeshed in the warp and weft of our daily lives that we sometimes forget how much it hurts—economically, socially, and personally. Whenever people are left out or singled out and prevented from making contributions, not only do the individuals suffer, but so does the organization and society.

No matter how we feel, only by listening to one another can we understand our common experience. Our investment in listening will help ensure that all people are heard and will bring us closer to the day when all of us will be appreciated for our contributions.

Chapter Twenty

Deborah Yarborough

Reflections on the Not-So-Level Playing Field

Deborah Yarborough

■

Deborah Yarborough is manager of strategic cultural initiatives at Sun Microsystems in Mountain View, California. Before joining Sun in 1991, she founded and managed Bridge-to-Jobs, a nonprofit consulting firm that provides job placement assistance to persons with disabilities.

Achieving corporate objectives with an increasingly diverse work force requires a commitment to diversity.

The charter of any diversity program, when one exists and is called such, is essentially to be the catalyst for creating strategic cultural initiatives among the members of an increasingly diverse work force. This includes minimizing friction between individuals and groups that interferes with productivity and optimizing individual and group performance to achieve corporate objectives.

THE BUSINESS RATIONALE FOR DIVERSITY

In companies whose customers represent a broadly defined cross-section of the population, the motivation for addressing diversity issues is already closely tied to profitability. An increasingly diverse customer base is looking for marketing, service, and sales of products that suit individual tastes, needs, and styles. If these customers don't feel respected and listened to, they will take their business elsewhere. It is no great mystery why businesses that produce food products, clothing, and other consumable goods are enthusiastically embracing diversity as an integral part of their business strategy.

On the other hand, manufacturers of high-end products predominantly purchased by consumers with advanced educations and big budgets are not similarly motivated. Their customers do not yet reflect the diversity of the general population, and, in most cases, the people they are doing business with look like and want to be treated like the executives of the corporation.

How do businesses that sell high-end high-tech products get motivated to undertake cultural change if not by customer demand? Sometimes, the push comes from employees.

Workforce 2000, a study published by the Hudson Institute and widely distributed a few years ago, was going to provide such an impetus. The study indicated that 85 percent of all new entrants to the work force by the year 2000 would be women and people of color and that there would not be enough new entrants to the work force overall to satisfy all of the labor needs in the United States. But then there was a recession. New words got added to American corporate vocabularies, such as *right-sizing, redeployment, restructuring,* and the like. Although the makeup of the work force has in fact begun to change, the change has not been as radical as predicted because of a weak economy. The unspoken message to employees who expressed concerns about diversity issues was, "If you don't like working here, you are welcome to leave. There are a lot of people who need a job out there waiting for your spot."

The next most likely source of motivation for corporate cultural change is our government. However, during the 12 years of Republican dominance, companies did not worry too much about compliance with EEO/affirmative action requirements. Most executives were confident that all they had to do was direct their human resources staff to give these regulations a little lip service now and then. There was very little concern that federal contracts would be lost if they did not address these issues too seriously.

The Clinton administration is a different story. From the campaign rhetoric to the first months in office, this president has made it clear that diversity is a priority for his administration. He has also talked about building up the nation's infrastructure. For companies that derive significant revenue from the U.S. government and would welcome the opportunity to support any infrastructure projects, the new administration's passion for diversity has provided a certain impetus for adopting greater enthusiasm for EEO/AA requirements, even if they might require changes in the corporate culture.

DIVERSITY IS NOT EGALITARIANISM

For most, executive diversity translates to egalitarianism. Adoption of this paradigm in a company does not usually represent a corporate cultural change, but the articulation of perhaps unspoken rules that already exist. These rules worked well when the work force was very homogeneous and the "golden rule" was the best way to approach human interaction. Popular phrases like *level playing field, color-blind,* or *gender-blind* are often used by corporate executives who subscribe to this paradigm. When executives use these expressions, they are generally sincere. They believe that anyone can be successful at the company as long as she or he puts enough effort into the work. No discrimination exists. Everyone is treated exactly the same. In most cases, managers are genuinely convinced that it is unnecessary—and furthermore, a bad business practice—to treat anybody in a manner that is tailored to unique or "special" needs.

People who believe there is a level playing field have usually been viewing that field from box seats. Their life experiences have not given them any reason to think there are big potholes in the field. A little crabgrass maybe, but no ankle-breaking potholes.

Diversity advocates often find themselves looking for ways to show corporate executives what the field looks like when you have a closer view. A variety of methodologies have been employed: asking executives to speak to minority organizations; inviting experts on diversity to speak to management at seminars and workshops; and various role-plays and simulations. Out of all of the possible interventions that have been tried, one has proven to be the most effective: giving executives the opportunity to experience a relationship with someone very different from themselves, someone who can provide them with a different view of the world, a view that is far from the box seats and close to the potholes.

ON BEING DIVERSE

In my case, the pothole I'm standing in is pretty deep. At 4 feet, 2 inches, there are few people over the age of six whom I don't look up to. Being short-statured (yes, that is the politically correct term) has afforded me a unique vantage point. While I'm looking up, the person looking down also has an unusual circumstance to think about. What people are thinking when they see me is often quite transparent. Poker faces are rare. Reactions range from those who seem delighted to see me, as if they had discovered a leprechaun who might lead them to a pot of gold, to people who are intimidated and afraid, believing me to be a gnomelike being who has jinxed their path. Finally, there are those who experience an insatiable thirst to satisfy their curiosity about the most mundane aspects of my life, as if I were an extraterrestrial who had just stepped off a space ship. ("Where do you buy your clothes? What size shoes do you wear? Do you drive a car?")

In describing these interactions, I purposely chose descriptors of myself that have been frequently used throughout our cultural folklore to depict people who are short-statured. Leprechauns, gnomes, and extraterrestrials are just some of the many bizarre beings that have crept into literature, plays, and television to represent "little people." Those of us who are under 4 feet, 8 inches tall are rarely, if ever, portrayed as the girl next door, the loving parent, the gifted teacher, or the dedicated worker. There are roughly eight million people in the world who are short-statured, representing every possible ethnicity and cultural heritage and, to my knowledge, there isn't a leprechaun, gnome, or ET among us. How is it, then, that our culture attributes these fantastic mythologies to us?

Lack of integration. Lack of exposure. Protected, segregated, and shunned by society in subtle and not-so-subtle ways, like most "minorities," people who are short-statured have developed unique coping skills in order to survive in a less-than-hospitable environment. A common characteristic shared by minorities is their adaptive skills. What it looks like on the outside is assimilation into the dominant culture. Short-statured people dress like average-sized people even though they cannot buy their clothes to fit off the rack; they use pedal extensions and seat cushions to drive their cars; and they live in homes with multiple step stools strategically placed to reach appliances and other modern "conveniences." There are not enough of us to create a demand for custom-designed clothing, cars, and homes. So we dress, drive, work, and live in the environment as it is, with as much dignity as we can muster as we stretch and strain to meet challenges presented by a tall world.

It takes a lot of energy to participate, much less compete, when you have to adapt chameleonlike to an awkward environment—energy that takes away from productivity. An example of where my energy was spent less productively than it might have been occurred when I represented my company at a recent conference in Washington, D.C.:

- Baggage is a major headache when I travel. Weighing only 75 pounds means that moving luggage from point A to point B is no small feat.

- Sitting in an airplane seat designed for an average-sized person means that the circulation to the back of my legs will be cut off and my head will be pushed forward for the duration of the flight.

- Having arrived in the baggage claim area, I must take great care not to get knocked down or run over by other passengers zealously grabbing their luggage and dashing for ground transportation.

- When the hotel van arrives to pick me up, I must endure the indignity of crawling up into the van because my legs are not long enough to step up into the vehicle.

- When I check in the hotel, I must stand back a couple of feet from the registration desk for the clerk to see me, and I sign my name on the counter's vertical surface.

- Having safely arrived and wanting to freshen up before joining the reception for conference attendees, I balance myself precariously on my overnight case to reach the sink in the hotel bathroom.

- As I join the cocktail hour, I am greeted by a moving forest of people with lighted cigarettes and sloshing drink glasses, creating a hazardous maze at my eye level. Conversation is nearly impossible unless I can find a chair to ask someone to be seated in so that we may hear each other.

- Later, at the banquet table, I find myself sitting at about chin level with my plate. Once settled, I notice which of my table partners sees me as a leprechaun, a gnome, or ET.

- In conversation, I attempt to be gregarious by employing humor, intellect, and geniality to help people feel more comfortable interacting with me.

- Having enjoyed the banquet keynote speaker, my mind is filled with questions during the Q&A. As I raise my hand, I notice it is especially quiet as the people around the room strain to hear my inquiry. The speaker listens intently as well, appearing wary of what I might ask. Once the question is understood, relief spills out. "That was an *excellent* question, young lady!" Sometimes I don't hear the rest of their answer. I am too busy asking myself, was it really a terrific question, or was it remarkable only in that a short-statured person was the one to pose it?

- When the evening is over, I gratefully return to my room. Part of me longs to be home, with my strategically placed step stools. Another part of me feels a heady exhilaration at having once again risen to the challenge of fully participating in a world that is not very accommodating with some measure of dignity and self-respect. I note for the millionth time that I was the only person in the room with a disability, and I wonder how long it will be before I can check my perceptions with someone who shares a similar experience.

I do not think that my experiences while traveling to conferences are unique. Although the reactions would be altered in some regards, those who find themselves in the position of being a very visible minority are likely to have the spotlight on them and feel a good deal of stress and anxiety as they try to assimilate. Emotional ups and downs in the not-so-level playing field can and do affect productivity.

HOW BEING DIVERSE HELPS TEACH DIVERSITY

Does it help or hinder your work to represent the diversity you are attempting to teach as a diversity manager? Unquestionably, this is one effective way to achieve change. Getting to know a person with a different point of view provides a safe opportunity to experience what it looks and feels like to be in the minority. For executives, interacting with me—or with other people who represent the diversity of the human race—gives them an opportunity to test their mythology without a lot of personal risk. When a sense of safety is created in an interaction between the dominant and minority cultures, it is quite likely that things will be said and done initially that have the effect of increasing the stress and anxiety experienced by a person who is different. And yet, the more we interact with one another, the more comfortable and natural it will become.

Not everyone who is "diverse" is willing to make—nor should she or he be coerced into making—this kind of a contribution. All too often, employees who represent minority cultures are "conscripted" into this role by their company. Volunteers make much more effective change agents than draftees in this role.

Volunteers from the so-called dominant culture have an important role in corporate strategic cultural initiatives as well: to understand and own their cultural identity. The unprecedented scrutiny this group is now undergoing is at times quite painful. Stereotypes that describe dominant-culture members as arrogant, privileged, and self-absorbed are just as untrue and unfair as the discriminatory generalizations that have previously been ascribed to members of various other cultural groups.

WHERE DO WE GO FROM HERE?

Perhaps the simplest way to think about this enormously complex issue is to return to a childhood rule and modify it a little. The Golden Rule: Do unto others as you would have done unto you. The problem is, we can't assume everyone wants to be treated exactly as we would like to be treated in all situations. When welcoming people into a new group, regardless of how different or alike they seem to be, call to mind a time and place where you felt out of sync (e.g., being the new kid in school; your first day on the job; being the only white person at an African American, Latino, or Asian community event). Ask yourself from this frame of reference what you needed then: a welcoming smile, a little humor, polite and sincere acknowledgment without a lot of attention drawn to you, some gentle guidance and support, a sense that you were not being judged or ostracized. Not a one-up, one-down "I'm being generous for your sake," but a genuine connection. Allow yourself to notice how much you have in common as opposed to how different your styles or approaches are—instead of judging the other person as being too out of place and walking away. Take advantage of your opportunity to see your surroundings with new eyes, with the aid of someone who can afford you a view from a different perspective.

When you are able to get to this neutral point, it won't matter whether you are being politically correct in the words you choose. When people are being sincere and respectful with each other, the social nuances work themselves out naturally.

CONCLUSION

Throughout recorded history, human beings have struggled with unresolved issues between cultural identity and integration. The fact that we are talking about these issues more openly is an important first step toward cultural harmony in corporations and in the world in general. The good news is that more and more people are realizing that in our collective future our world will be very small and very diverse. If we can make that future world a place where individual shortcomings are minimized and individual potential is maximized, it will be a better place for all of us. The companies that create corporate cultures that model this future state sooner rather than later will enjoy not only the humanistic rewards of greater intercultural harmony but also, undoubtedly, the capitalistic rewards of greater revenues.

The job of the diversity manager is to facilitate and expedite the metamorphosis of strategic cultural initiatives within the corporate culture. Should a core competency for this change agent be that he or she represent some visible "minority" culture? No, it is not necessarily the diversity of someone's outward appearance that uniquely qualifies that person to successfully model and evangelize the changes you wish to facilitate in your organization. What you need is someone—or better yet; several someones—willing to risk and share something of her- or himself, thereby giving people a chance to relearn and practice the modified Golden Rule.

Chapter Twenty-One

Jean Kim

The Limits of a Cultural Enlightenment Approach to Multiculturalism

Jean Kim

■

Jean Kim, EdD, is vice president for student affairs and dean of students at the University of Hartford, Hartford, Connecticut. Kim is also a consultant working with organizations in the areas of managing a multicultural work force, valuing diversity, cross-cultural communications, organizational development, and other fields.

Multiculturalism is very popular these days. I don't want to call it a fad, but it's definitely the "in" thing for organizations. Many practitioners are approaching it from a purely "cultural enlightenment" point of view. The assumption of the cultural enlightenment approach to multiculturalism is that if we understand each other's culture better, we'll get along with each other better, and this will create a harmonious, multicultural environment.

Cultural understanding does play an important role in some situations. People need to have accurate information so that they can understand the reactions and realities of people who are different from them. European-Americans, who are going to work in Korea, for example, need to understand the Korean language, food, customs, holidays, and so forth, so that they can interact effectively with Koreans. In this country as well, such cultural sensitivity and understanding will help to reduce some misunderstandings between people of different backgrounds. However, learning about another culture in order to live or work in another country is quite different from creating a multicultural society in this country.

Cultural enlightenment alone is an insufficient base for creating a truly multicultural environment that values people *because* of the differences they bring rather than *in spite* of them. This is because cultural understanding alone does nothing to change the power equation. Who's in charge? How is power used? Who are the losers in the sociopolitical power game?

In addition to understanding other cultures, people need to understand how the "isms" like racism, sexism, heterosexism, ageism, and all the rest are maintained in our society and what role each person plays in keeping the status quo. Unless we are willing to look at these hard and discomforting issues, multicultural programs may serve as yet another detour on our road to establishing equitable organizations.

My experience of racial prejudice and oppression began when I came to Springfield, Massachusetts, from Seoul, Korea, at the age of 12. I was sent for by my mother, who is Korean, and my stepfather, an American who had served in the U.S. Army in Korea. I spent my first weeks here crying and praying and fantasizing about going back to Korea. I didn't speak any English, I had no friends, and the only person I could communicate with was my mother.

By the end of that year, I had learned to speak English, I could read, and I had made some friends, but I also realized that being Korean in this country meant that I was "less than" European Americans, and I was often the object of ridicule from other children. I suffered from the kinds of racist taunting that anyone who is not European American in this culture experiences. For African Americans, the taunts primarily involve their skin color. For us Asians, the insults focus on other physical features, such as the shape of the eyes or nose. For some reason, it seems that most Asian Americans, including me, are nearsighted—and that became another target of ridicule. I was so sensitive about it that I wouldn't wear glasses. Most of those years went by in a literal blur.

Because I knew I was here to stay, my survival depended on becoming fully assimilated and acting more American than Americans. In my attempt to be acceptable, I did a lot of denying about who I was. I gradually lost the ability to speak my own language, for one thing. I went through a major life detour from the time I arrived here until I was about 23. In graduate school, I began to figure out what all this meant. With the help of a strong support network and knowledge of how racism and sexism operate, I was able to develop a positive identity as an Asian American and regain my self-confidence.

As part of my comprehensive exam for a counseling psychology degree, I analyzed my experiences dealing with racism, what it had done to me, and the psychological price I had paid. That led me to explore what other Asian Americans may experience, in terms of living with a negative self-concept and denial of one's racial identity and eventually regaining positive self-esteem. For my doctoral dissertation, I did research on how Japanese American women perceive their struggle to achieve positive identities in the United States.

THE MAIN FACES OF RACISM

All of that research and the many hours of conversations with other Asian Americans—mostly women, but some men as well—helped to reaffirm my racial identity and gave me insights into the subtleties of how racism and oppression affect Asian Americans. All Asian Americans share this experience of racial discrimination, regardless of our diverse ethnic and generational backgrounds. The ties that bind us together are those of pain and suffering.

However, the ways in which we respond to racism seem to vary. For one thing, the experiences of Asians who are born in the United States or who come here as children are very different from the experiences of Asians who come to this country as adults. It is easier for folks like me, who experienced racism during their formative years, to internalize the racist messages about us and other people of color. We get steeped in the American ideas of the superiority of one race over another and of men over women.

Those Asians who come after they have established themselves in their home country are much better defended against these racist messages. They are less apt to internalize racist attitudes and less apt to go through a painful period of denial, as I did. They tend to be more assertive, more vocal, and more successful in business. Of course, this applies more often to Asian men than to Asian women. Asian American women, like other women of color, experience the double bind: first racism and then sexism.

We also should not overlook the fact that those who come here from Asia, whether as children or adults, bring with them antiblack racist attitudes from exposure in their own countries to American culture in movies, television, the print media, and so forth. The fact that Asian Americans are discriminated against and experience subtle forms of racism does not automatically help us to understand the oppression experiences of other minorities. Asian-Americans need to come to terms with their own prejudices and ignorance about other racial groups.

In the corporate world, these lessons of racism and sexism, and the various ways we internalize or react to them, produce stereotyped expectations. Common stereotypes of Asian Americans include the beliefs that we are inarticulate, submissive, quiet, unassertive, hardworking, and technically adept, but not very creative. In short, Asian Americans are not expected to be "uppity." This partially explains why Asian Americans in corporations have had greater access to professional opportunities than African Americans or Latinos. Asian Americans are not stereotyped as lazy or stupid—a view that is too often held of African Americans and Latinos.

Stereotypes have many negative consequences. For example, when I am assertive, my actions are often perceived as being aggressive because people have stereotypical expectations of the Asian American female as being quiet and submissive. So when I behave outside their expectations, my actions are amplified in their minds. And then there are new labels. An Asian American woman who doesn't fit the passive stereotype is given a new stereotype: She may be called a "dragon queen" or some other derogatory term.

DIVIDE AND CONQUER

In spite of all the stereotypes about us and the reality of our experiences in this country, some Asian Americans believe there is no racism in the United States. Because many Asian Americans have been successful academically or in the professions or in business, there is a tendency for some people to feel that if other people of color are less successful, it's their own fault. Sometimes it is difficult for Asian Americans to even think of themselves as people of color, because that means identifying with people who are looked down on in mainstream American culture.

For Asians who have come here as adults, it is understandable that they do not want to be identified with those who are the objects of scorn in this culture. For those who were born in this country or came as children, this reluctance to identify with other people of color derives mainly from their internalization of the racism they have experienced and the subsequent denial of their own racial identity. When people are in the midst of denial and internalizing oppression, they spend most of their energy trying to avoid acknowledging their feelings about racist slurs that come their way. So there is little energy left to defend or sympathize with other people who may be in the same boat. The fear is that the more you associate with others in the despised group(s), the more pain you will bring on yourself. It is only when people begin to emerge from denial and begin to understand how racism works that they can identify with others in the same situation. Asian Americans have to come to terms with their own feelings about being discriminated against and their own racial prejudices before they can see that they have much in common with other people of color in this society.

Of course, there are also some good historical reasons for the way various groups of Asian Americans have adapted. Japanese Americans who went through the experience of internment later opted to be as invisible and as American as possible; they are more likely to distance themselves from other Asian ethnic groups.

Asian Americans are also sometimes used as pawns in the power games of racism. We are often held up as model minorities to keep other minorities in line. One outcome of this has been to place Asian Americans at odds with other people of color who question the legitimacy of our minority status.

THE UNITED STATES PARADOX

The interesting thing about the United States is that equality is part of our credo—even though the reality is far from it. At some level, though, we really do believe that equality is our national goal. The most racist or sexist people in this country may still say they believe in equality, albeit conditionally. Equality is part of our heritage; without it, there's no possibility of a moral push.

On the other hand, very few U.S. corporations tackle multiculturalism or valuing diversity for moral reasons. Often they get involved because they see the business benefit of trying to make diversity work. But still, the values of fairness and equality are somewhere underneath their efforts.

In Asian countries, the ideal of equality among races and genders does not exist, but respect for authority does. If you tell an Asian American man that the right thing to do in this organization is to treat women as equal, he's going to try as hard as he can to do that. One cultural value outweighs another. He may not believe that women are equal to men, but he may well have a strong respect for a visible authority.

My perception is that African Americans and white women have a much stronger sense of entitlement than Asian Americans. Once they have really brought the realities of racism and sexism into conscious thought (as opposed to just being angry or depressed without knowing why), they tend to be more demanding and say, "We deserve an equal deal, and we deserve to get it without being hassled." Asian Americans as a group need to be reassured that it's acceptable to demand their rights.

Approaching the development of a diverse work force based on these concepts of cultural enlightenment and awareness of oppression requires a great deal of time, training, and money. Too often, a corporation will prefer the cultural-enlightenment-only route because it is a short-term effort and less conflict oriented. But it won't do the job. Getting the job done requires training, reinforcing the training with follow-up activities, creating networks, changing policies and practices—in short, it is a total organizational change and development process. It demands more time, but in the long run it is more cost effective to take the slow route. The quick-fix version of cultural-enlightenment-only may start out with a bang, but unless supported by ongoing, structural changes, the investment may prove to be money down the drain.

Chapter Twenty-Two

Sexual Orientation
A Work-Force Diversity Issue

Mark G. Kaplan and Jay H. Lucas

■

Mark G. Kaplan

Mark Kaplan and Jay Lucas are diversity consultants who focus on sexual orientation as a work-force diversity issue.

Mark Kaplan has been a training and organizational development consultant for six years. His work includes professional and management training with individuals and groups.

Jay Lucas, who began consulting in 1984, confronts the challenges faced by gay professionals in the recently published The Corporate Closet (1993), *coauthored by James D. Woods.*

Jay H. Lucas

C ontemporary organizations have recently undertaken efforts to improve themselves by attempting to create conditions of empowerment and inclusion for women and people of color. The goal is to remove barriers so that all members of the organization have the opportunity to be successful. Although some organizations have worked on issues of race and gender for the last 20 years, the issue of gays and lesbians in the workplace is only now becoming a topic of concern.

The gay liberation movement began more than 20 years ago, but it is only recently that gay men and lesbians have started to become visible in organizations. Historically, invisibility has been maintained by gay men and lesbians who perceived too much risk in coming out and heterosexuals who have been prevented from seeing or acknowledging the impact of homophobia and heterosexism. Gays and lesbians have suffered in silence, and their straight co-workers—and the organization—have suffered in ignorance. But workplace invisibility by gays and lesbians is a thing of the past.

"Sexual orientation is about what you do at home behind closed doors" goes the refrain. "What does it have to do with the workplace?" "It's too controversial." There are numerous reasons given for not dealing directly with sexual orientation as a work-force diversity issue and for ignoring the reality that a significant group of people, as many as 10 percent of employees, live with the daily fear that an accidental slip—revealing the "wrong" information—could lead to the collapse of their careers. Knowledge of their sexual orientation could mean loss of access, credibility, and, in some cases, employment. *Of the roughly 10 percent of the workforce that is gay or lesbian, very few come out of the closet.* The fact that so many gay men and lesbians remain secretive and closeted is itself evidence that a deep-seated oppression exists, an oppression so powerful that gays and lesbians go to incredible lengths to avoid disclosing a basic, core part of their human identity.

This article will attempt to bring some visibility to the experiences of gay men and lesbians in organizations and the issues they face. It is based on our experiences as gay men inside and outside American organizations, our research and work with gay men and lesbians, and our work with colleagues in the field of diversity management and organizational development.

SOME PERSPECTIVE: A SHORT COMPARISON TO RACE AND GENDER

Women and people of color are generally visible and identifiable, and their presence is tracked in organizations. Because race and gender are usually obvious physical characteristics, a person of color or a woman is forced to deal with the impact of personal identity in the workplace; they will always be identified as a woman or person of color by others and will likely be subject to barriers on an individual, group, and organizational level.

A gay man or lesbian in a corporate environment has a different experience: most can choose whether, when, and how to disclose their sexual orientation. Because most gay and lesbian employees hide their sexual orientation at work, there is often little evidence of corporate discrimination, with the result that many nongay people believe that gays and lesbians aren't oppressed in organizational settings. Often an assumption is made that discrimination against gays and lesbians is not a significant problem—and even if it were, gays and lesbians could always avoid discrimination by choosing to stay in the closet. Our own experiences and our research with hundreds of gay men and lesbians in corporate settings make it clear that this is a myth—there really is no good choice available, and each of the available choices has significant negative consequences.

Every day, gay men and lesbians are forced to deal with homophobia and heterosexism. This happens whether they are closeted or not. Homophobia is the irrational fear of homosexuals and homosexuality. It takes the form of harassment, discrimination, and discomfort in developing trusting work relationships with gay and lesbian co-workers. A more subtle example would be neglecting gay and lesbian employee associations while engaging in productive dialogues with networks for women and people of color.

Heterosexism is the belief that heterosexuality is superior to homosexuality—the presumption that everyone is straight, and if not, they should be. In organizations, it often takes the form of denial, such as human resource managers acknowledging that a significant percentage of their work force is gay and lesbian, but then behaving as though none are. It is present in benefit inequities. It is present when departments have office parties and include spouses, but only those of the opposite sex. Heterosexism and homophobia clearly affect gay men and lesbians in organizations, whether they are in or out of the closet.

Thus, the choice to stay closeted does not eliminate inequities based on sexual orientation. It reduces direct targeting, but it increases other pressures: ethical dilemmas such as lying for self-protection, psychological stress, and the diversion of significant energy from productive work. When these forced choices are made to mitigate the overt oppression that would result from disclosure in a homophobic and heterosexual work culture, *presumptive oppression is created*.

Presumptive oppression occurs when gay men and lesbians presume that others will be uncomfortable or will behave in a biased way if they are honest about their sexual orientation. When this assumption is at work—as it is in most cases for gay men and lesbians in organizations—great effort is put forth to manage information so that one's true sexual orientation will not be revealed. However, the penalties for "passing" are substantial. Far from being a safe haven, closets are cramped, dark places that negatively affect the ability of gay men and lesbians to contribute to their organizations. By not doing anything other than sending signals to pass or stay in the closet, the organization may not seem to be oppressing a closeted gay man or lesbian, but gay men and lesbians perceive an oppressive reaction and, in self-protection, stay closeted, which is itself a form of oppression.

THE CASE OF LAUREN

Lauren is a senior marketing analyst for a midsize company. She has risen quickly and is on the cusp of management. Her career is at a crucial crossroads as she feels professionally ready to make that next career step. However, Lauren is finding the step onto the management team very difficult—so difficult that she is unsure whether she wants to take it.

In a perfect world, there would be no doubt that she would want to reach the next level—she has always put her career first. However, for Lauren there are other considerations. Lauren is a lesbian and has not shared this information with anyone in her company. She is aware that her company's nondiscrimination policy includes sexual orientation, but she has never heard it discussed. As a woman, she is all too familiar with nondiscrimination provisions that aren't well enforced or are completely ignored. She knows of only three other gays and lesbians at the company, one of whom is the butt of jokes she has overheard. Most of the other managers are married or have straight significant others who are often included in social activities.

Lauren faces a dilemma that millions of gays and lesbians face in organizations. Because Lauren is one of several strong performers at her level, she fears that if her sexual orientation were known, she would no longer be considered a candidate for the management team. A logical response is for her to stay closeted—and she has.

Staying closeted has taken a great psychological toll on Lauren: the daily insults and jokes from co-workers who presume she is heterosexual and the constant battle to manage information about her personal life, making sure that she is prepared to handle questions about what she did over the weekend, whom she lives with, when she's going to get married, etc. She's tired of forcing such a strict boundary between her personal and professional lives. She feels horrible about hiding the fact that she has been in a long-term relationship while co-workers proudly display pictures of spouses and children in their offices. Because she has been closeted for so long, it is likely that management and her co-workers have not developed enough comfort or trust with her, as they know very little about her life outside of work. She has observed the informal camaraderie between co-workers and managers, the way they socialize together, and the trust that has developed because they know each other so well.

Lauren faces a dilemma shared by many in her situation: she is likely to be negatively affected if she comes out of the closet, and she is negatively affected by staying in the closet. Recently, Lauren has begun to focus her attention outside her company and is considering leaving to go somewhere where she won't have to be closeted.

EXPERIENCES OF GAY MEN AND LESBIANS IN ORGANIZATIONS

Lauren's case exemplifies the situation faced by gay men and lesbians in corporations today. Their situation is inherently problematic because of the risks involved in both coming out and staying closeted. Quite often, the choice of coping strategy—or how to deal with managing one's personal identity at work on a day-to-day basis—represents something midway between coming out and staying in the closet. We call this middle-of-the road strategy *avoiding.*

Avoiding falls along the middle of the continuum of coping strategies that gay men and lesbians use to manage their sexual identity at work. On one end is being totally out of the closet. We call this *integrating:* the presentation of information about sexual orientation in the same way heterosexuals present such information. On the other end of the continuum is being in the closet. We call this *hiding:* the presentation of information that encourages the listener to presume a heterosexual orientation. Integrating is the least common choice of strategy. Among gay men and lesbians in the workplace, avoiding is probably the most common strategy.

Gay men and lesbians are affected in many ways by their choice of coping strategy. No matter what the choice, the decision will be difficult. For hiders, providing untrue or misleading information may give them an easy out, but the psychological price of having to lie or live a double life will be high. For integrators, there will always be the risk of confronting prejudice and the strain of always being aware that the impact of who you are may be difficult for others to deal with. This choice can be undertaken, however, with the heavy weight of deceit and avoidance off one's shoulders and the likelihood that eventually the stress will decrease, that the "game" will be over.

Avoiding is the attempt to capture the best (or worst) of both worlds: being vague ("They don't know about me, and I don't have to lie"). The price of avoiding is high, however, to both the individual and the organization. In an attempt to balance personal integrity with pragmatic career concerns, an avoider may be more concerned about what a co-worker knows about him or her than whether a productive working relationship is developing. For women in the workplace, there is a glass ceiling; for gays and lesbians who are avoiding, there is a glass wall—between them and their straight co-workers. By managing these boundaries closely, the avoider loses countless opportunities to access the informal organization, to develop networks and mentors.

For Lauren and many other gays and lesbians, this situation manifests itself on a day-to-day basis when they isolate themselves in organizations where teamwork, personal commitment, and trust are important, thus damaging both their careers and the organization's performance. This should compel an organization to be proactive.

Companies have a great deal invested in Lauren and many other gay and lesbian employees. Without knowing it, companies are creating and sustaining an organizational environment that is inhibiting to gay men and lesbians, giving them an incentive to leave to find a more accepting work environment.

SOME KEYS TO CREATING CHANGE

Organizations that tolerate or foster a hostile work environment for their gay and lesbian employees are in a lose-lose situation. The employees lose as they experience stress in managing their personal identity. The organization loses as creativity, loyalty, commitment, and trust are reduced. To turn work environments into win-win situations will require a strong effort from straight and gay employees alike:

1. *Replace misinformation with real information.* The best way to provide real information to your organization and change attitudes is for gay men and lesbians to come out of the closet voluntarily. Research shows that when "straights" know a gay or lesbian, their degree of homophobia is significantly reduced. It is, however, unrealistic to expect gay men and lesbians to come out of the closet unless there is a commitment from the organization to support them. It is incumbent upon the organization to contribute to this effort. There are a number of ways to do this, including publicizing the organization's nondiscrimination policy (if it includes sexual orientation—and changing it, if it doesn't), making sexual orientation a part of diversity interventions, using inclusive language (such as *significant other*), and featuring an openly gay or lesbian employee in company literature.

2. *Properly position sexual orientation as a business issue.* Much of the resistance in organizations to this subject is based on the belief that by including it as a legitimate issue of diversity the organization is endorsing a set of moral beliefs that may be contrary to those of some employees. There is also often a fear that sexual orientation is equivalent to sexual behavior. Talking about what one did over the weekend, putting a picture of a loved one on the desk, or disclosing one's sexual orientation is not about sexual behavior, for homosexual people *or* heterosexual people. It is critically important to focus on appropriate workplace behavior. Heterosexist and homophobic behaviors hurt gay and lesbian employees and the organization. While

individual employees may hold any beliefs they wish, they cannot translate those beliefs into discriminatory behaviors against anyone, including gay men and lesbians.

By failing to view their treatment of gay and lesbian employees as a business issue, companies run the risk of losing good employees. If you were a highly skilled gay computer technician considering a position in the high-tech industry, would you choose to work for Lotus or Apple, both of which offer domestic partner benefits and take other supportive actions regarding gays and lesbians in their companies, or a company with an indifferent or intolerant attitude toward gays and lesbians?

3. *Break the cycle of invisibility by starting with you.* Breaking the cycle of invisibility that keeps gay men and lesbians behind the glass wall and their often well-intentioned co-workers uninformed is the key that will open the door for gay men and lesbians in American organizations. To break this cycle, organizational members and change agents must look at their own behaviors and attitudes. When sexual orientation is being discussed in the context of diversity management, is it fully discussed or is it hidden under the table? Does the first show of resistance end the conversation? When faced with resistance, do change agents run up against their own lack of information and discomfort? Is this discomfort projected onto clients? Is including sexual orientation on a long list of aspects of diversity without any serious discussion considered good enough?

Change agents in organizations have the opportunity to create a good choice for both their gay and lesbian employees and their organizations. They can create an accepting, nurturing environment, where gays and lesbians can choose to be themselves. They need to help their organizations to start looking at the fact that most of their gay and lesbian employees are closeted and are wondering why. They should set a goal to create an environment that is supportive of all employees, one where Lauren and people like her can come to work and bring all that they have to offer: their skills, energy, creativity, and commitment. It is time to end denial and invisibility and deal with the reality of gay men and lesbians in our organizations.

Chapter Twenty-Three

AndréAnna Jovan

The Invisible Minority
Emancipating Gays and Lesbians in the Workplace

AndréAnna Jovan

∎

AndréAnna Jovan, PhD, is a consultant and professor in the field of organization development and leadership. She specializes in helping organizations improve interpersonal communications and relationships, focusing on shared decision making in diverse work groups. As a lesbian, she assists organizations in developing strategies for effectively reintegrating gays and lesbians into the workplace.

M arie listens in silent embarrassment as her co-worker Derek criticizes their boss, "She's so pushy; she must think she's a man . . . probably some lesbo! I can't stand queers." Marie laughs aloud with the others, appearing to agree and trying not to show her fear. She must maintain her relationship with her co-workers, whatever the cost, and for Marie, a lesbian, the cost is high.

Oscar joined his company a year ago because its nondiscrimination policy includes homosexuals. However, people have always avoided him, snickered at him behind his back, and withheld work-related information. Lately, he's been getting hate mail and threatening telephone calls. Oscar's boss tells him to "just lay low."

BEING HOMOSEXUAL IN CORPORATE AMERICA

Ignorance is the enemy.

These stories demonstrate what it is like being a member of the "invisible minority" in the workplace. Fear and confusion, distrust and degradation threaten lesbians and gay men every day of their working lives. Their deeply embedded fear is sustained by the culture of the American workplace and society, as demonstrated by state and local initiatives to deny equal employment to homosexuals and increased violent incidents of "gay bashing" across the United States.

Unlike most other minorities, we homosexuals can be invisible. We have the option of blending into the mainstream work force, spending our entire working lives undetected, unrecognized. As a result, the magnitude of this oppression is often overlooked and underestimated.

Invisibility, however, comes at a high personal cost. Homosexuals suffer a lonely, isolated existence, our identities concealed in fabricated lifestyles. Fear of exposure thwarts our full participation as equal members of the organization. We would rather spend our workplace life outside the corporate closet—if we would be safe, if we would not be harassed, if we would receive unbiased consideration for promotion and career development, if we would be treated equitably. These conditions do not yet exist in most workplaces.

CORPORATE COSTS OF INVISIBILITY

We don't need affirmative action—we're already here.
We need the freedom to be visible.[1]

John Wofford, attorney

Marketing research among openly gay men and lesbians suggests we are highly educated, commanding above-average salaries with a higher disposable income than the average heterosexual. A 1991 survey indicates that "more homosexuals work in science and engineering than in social services; 40% more are employed in finance and insurance than in entertainment and the arts; and ten times as many work in computers as in fashion."[2] This well-educated and affluent group is becoming a desirable target for marketing efforts of many large corporations.

Companies are recognizing homosexuals as a considerable portion of their customers. Nationally, the market is estimated to be worth $514 billion a year.[3] Homophobic practices within corporations are placing that customer base at risk. Corporations that have "liberated" their workplace, openly supported the lesbian and gay employees, and even targeted their advertising to the gay market are being financially rewarded. Many companies are getting the message: equal rights for homosexuals just makes good business sense.

Discrimination based on sexual orientation costs companies, and our nation, dearly. In financial terms, there are expensive lawsuits costing businesses millions of dollars in settlements and litigation expenses. Colorado recently discovered the high cost of discriminatory legislation passed in the state. Boycotts by gays, lesbians, and their supporters—including canceled convention plans by major cities such as San Francisco—stung the economy, dramatically affecting the winter tourist trade.

A more subtle cost to business is the loss of productivity due to a segregated workplace. The negative environment spawned by secrecy and nonparticipation in the corporate community weakens the cultural fabric that holds organizations together, reducing their efficiency and effectiveness. Equally detrimental are losses due to untapped creativity and mental health problems and stress-related illnesses experienced by individuals forced to constantly live a lie. Perhaps the most significant loss, though, is that of highly qualified employees who leave, seeking more emancipating environments in more accepting companies.

The actual cost in dollars of lost productivity for organizations is difficult to measure for several reasons. Perhaps the most obvious reason is that gays and lesbians are invisible, and most choose to remain so today. Additionally, there is the problem of measuring the effect of attitude on the bottom line of organizations. This is the same difficulty faced in attempting to measure the effect of downsizing on the productivity of remaining employees who fear they will be next. Efforts are under way to address this issue. A national group, comprised of members of gay and lesbian organizations within corporations, is working to determine more concretely the value of uncloaking the invisible minority at work.

Changing attitudes about the value of lesbians and gays are being recognized by more-progressive companies across the United States— for example, AT&T, 3M, Chevron Corporation, Levi Strauss & Co., and Stanford University. New human-resource principles are being developed to recognize individuals' unique qualities, regardless of sexual orientation. Gay/lesbian/bisexual employee organizations are being formed, some with company sanction, to address this group's concerns and needs. Many organizations are extending company benefits to include homosexual partners. "These benefits are rapidly becoming a competitive advantage to companies that offer them, particularly in the high-tech industry."[4]

The desire by business to attract and retain highly talented employees, the potential economic benefits of the vast gay market, the elimination of costly discrimination lawsuits, and the improved productivity of a fully integrated workplace are strong arguments for elimination of discrimination against gays and lesbians in the workplace.

The closet door is opening a crack, and a small trickle of light is filtering through. It's a beginning, but much work remains to be done to eliminate this oppression. Cultural change does not occur overnight, and it does not occur without awareness of the needs of the oppressed and commitment to meeting them.

OPENING THE CORPORATE CLOSET

Heterosexism: the assumption that everyone is straight, or ought to be.

Brian McNaught, author and trainer

Leaders are responsible for demonstrating acceptance of lesbians and gay men as equals in the workplace. Unless leadership is clearly demonstrated, efforts to change will not succeed

Too often, companies focus only on developing policy statements—which cannot succeed without well-thought-out action plans. A major software company added the words *sexual orientation* to its nondiscrimination policy, but this did not stop the discriminatory treatment experienced by one openly lesbian employee. As she indicated, "There is a 'non-stand' [lack of action] by the company that enables groups to continue to discriminate in sectors within the company." Prying open the corporate closet, and keeping it open, requires appropriate and consistent strategic actions.

Appropriate and consistent actions also help create the level of trust required for lesbians and gay men to face the uncertainties awaiting them once they have "come out" at work. Trust is very important because once homosexuals step out of the closet, they cannot turn back. Closeted employees must trust that policies will be upheld, consistent practices will prevail throughout the company, opportunities will not be withheld, and support systems (such as mentorship, professional development, and leadership opportunities) will not be withdrawn.

As in any situation, it is the responsibility of each individual employee to strongly take a stand against discrimination. Avoiding offensive comments and challenging those made by others, eliminating prejudice from business decisions, and communicating acceptance of homosexuals are significant actions for heterosexuals to take. These actions create a supportive environment in which closeted gays can safely reveal themselves.

THE LEADERS MUST LEAD THE WAY TOWARD UNDERSTANDING

Recognize and work to change your own homophobic and heterosexist biases.[5]

Plans for eliminating discrimination will no doubt be different for individual companies, but they must include very tangible actions taken with direct involvement of the leadership team.

Leaders who start by developing their understanding of the culture, experiences, needs, issues, hopes, and fears of lesbians and gay men are better prepared to support development and implementation of successful action plans. There are several initial steps that leaders can take to accomplish this.

Talking to consultants who understand the culture is extremely helpful. Consultants who are openly homosexual can explain the language and general concerns and which actions would be most appropriate. They can also provide valuable information regarding resources available to assist them in eliminating this discrimination. These preparations will help leaders and those they meet feel more comfortable. Most important is an openness to the difficulties experienced by homosexuals and a sincere desire to work with them in overcoming their alienation.

Next, meetings with openly homosexual employees or representatives of the lesbian and gay community within the company will orient leaders toward the experiences of gays and lesbians at work and provide the opportunity for both groups to explore issues more deeply.

COLLABORATION SUCCEEDS WHERE DIRECTIVES FAIL

Collaboration is a less prescriptive and systematic approach than traditional methods used in solving most issues within organizations. It is, however, most effective when dealing with issues involving the needs of diverse groups within organizations. Because the solutions, procedures, and directions emerge from the combined efforts of those directly involved, the procedures cannot be predetermined. Nevertheless, participative processes result in immediate change that is highly effective and lasting. The following highlights key aspects of a participative approach.

The best results occur when a collaborative process fully engages homosexual and heterosexual employees in identifying the issues, determining the implications, exploring the options, discerning the course of action, implementing the plan, and monitoring progress. Leaders' close involvement provides guidance and offers ongoing support to the employee group. To the extent leaders inspire rather than direct the group, the outcomes will be more satisfactory. Shared power among group members will also be essential in assuring the highest quality strategic action plan.

During the collaborative phase, the group of employees will be interacting with other employees to gather the information required to determine the appropriate actions to be taken. They will encounter a wide range of reactions inside as well as outside their group. They will more than likely require strong support, perhaps group facilitation, in dealing effectively and appropriately with these strong emotions and issues.

Their recommendations will become the collaborative basis for organizational strategies and specific action plans. During this phase, they will examine existing policies and make changes and additions that support equal treatment of homosexuals in all aspects of the workplace. This is necessary and an important indicator to all employees. However, it will not stop discriminatory practices, and it does not supersede local, state, and federal laws. Thus, policy must be reinforced by other actions taken within the company.

Training, perhaps the most easily identified approach, presents a unique dilemma: Is training to be mandatory or voluntary? At Bell Labs, the programs are mandatory because there was concern that otherwise no one would attend. In the rest of AT&T, where training is voluntary, only 3,000 of the 300,000 employees attended "homophobia workshops" in the four-year period from 1987 to 1991.[6]

Whatever the recommendations of the group, their focus must be on actions that communicate trust and commitment to all employees, with the focus on cultural changes.

CONSISTENCY IS ESSENTIAL

Employees will watch for strong positions and actions to be taken by leaders early in the process. Openly discussing the new company view regarding the value of homosexuals in the workplace sends a clear message consistent with the policies and other actions being initiated. Consistency becomes critical at this point. In the balance will be the environment of trust that is still very fragile this early in the process.

Leaders at a major computer software company, with offices in Oregon and Utah, were willing to send letters opposing antihomosexual state measures to the governors. These were even signed by the vice president of legal and public affairs. However, when lesbian and gay employees asked to have something in the newsletter about these actions, that was not agreed to. "They seemed willing to support it in a quiet way, but not vocally," says Jeff, one of the gay employees. This communicated a message of secrecy and avoidance.

In contrast, Apple's former CEO and Chairman John Scully, before stepping down, met for two hours with lesbian and gay employees regarding adding same-sex partner coverage. After the meeting, in a rare personal note, Scully publicly commented, "I am personally delighted by this decision."[7]

Media coverage regarding the work of the group, actions being taken both inside and outside the company, and the policies being established can help provide and demonstrate consistency. Internal statements underlining leadership's commitment to homosexual employees is very important. External press coverage solidifies the company's message within the homosexual community at large.

The right actions, in the right way, at the right time can make the difference between success and failure of this undertaking. AT&T, which adopted a statement of nondiscrimination on sexual orientation back in 1975, uses a variety of approaches to communicate the message. They even invest in a Gay Awareness Week that includes speakers from various gay and lesbian organizations. Yet, their "valuing diversity" calendar depicting holidays, events, and people from a variety of traditions, omitted gays and lesbians. An additional indicator of inconsistency at AT&T is the pending lawsuit regarding partner benefits. The lawsuit claims that denial of survivor pension benefits violates AT&T's own policy of nondiscrimination.[8] Consistency throughout the company is a key success factor.

KEEPING THE CLOSET DOOR OPEN

Prejudice and fear are not eliminated, nor even slightly altered, overnight. People who have spent most of their lives, and particularly all of their working lives, concealing their sexual orientation do not find it easy to make such a significant change. People who have developed attitudes of heterosexism will find it difficult to suddenly abandon their fears and preconceived ideas about homosexuals. Thus, a long-term commitment with regular checkups is in order.

Helping the original employee group shift from development to ongoing monitoring and problem solving can assure successful integration of homosexuals back into the workplace. Through established networks, the group can explore issues, needs, and concerns as they arise, working collaboratively with the employee body and leadership to find equitable resolutions. As members of the organization, they are well positioned to determine new strategies and actions that recognize the rights and contributions made by all employees. Through continued vigilance, the organization or company will find itself better positioned as it enters a new era of equality for all humans, regardless of race, creed, or sexual orientation.

NOTES

1. T. Stewart, "Gay in Corporate America," *Fortune* 124, no. 14 (Dec 16, 1991), pp. 43.

2. *Ibid.*

3. C. Rauber, "Gay, Straight Businesses Finally Come to the Table," *San Francisco Business Times* 7, no. 26 (1993), p. 1.

4. *Ibid.*, p. 20.

5. K. Morgan and L. Brown, "Lesbian Career Development, Work Behavior, and Vocational Counseling," *The Counseling Psychologist* 19, no. 2 (April 1991), pp. 287.

6. T. Stewart, *op. cit.*, p. 50.

7. C. Rauber, *op. cit.*, p. 20.

8. E. Mickens, "AT&T, and the Trouble with Paradise," *Working It Out* 1, no. 2 (Summer 1992), pp. 4–5.

Chapter Twenty-Four

Lucia Edmonds

Understanding Black Identity
A Primer for Whites in Corporate America

Lucia Edmonds

■

Lucia Edmonds, PhD, is a cofounder of Partners and the Diversity Group, both companies that specialize in increasing the effective utilization of human resources in public, private, and not-for-profit organizations. Her specialties include managing diversity, building high-performance teams, conflict utilization, and strategic planning. She also teaches graduate-level courses at American University and the University of the West Indies.

> *None of us is free, empowered, or whole while any of us is denigrated.*

I begin this article with a story about a very important personal experience. I end it with a theory of black identity development and a challenge for whites to reexamine the costs of living in a society where superiority and inferiority are defined along racial lines.[1] The theory is offered as a special case of black identity development, yet it is more than that. Other racial/ethnic groups who live in the United States, white women, and gays will find themselves in this model. White men who feel pain but often do not identify it as the pain of oppression will come to recognize the ways in which they, too, are oppressed by living in a society that teaches that *different* means *inferior*.

THE STORY

This story, a lifetime in the making, took form while I participated in an 18-month postgraduate course in organization and systems development. Of the 36 people enrolled in the course, 10 were black. This was the first time in the history of the course that blacks were so solidly represented.

The course structure required work both as a class "community" and in smaller groups. At our first meeting, one black participant proposed that a black learning group meet regularly within the context of the program. In this way, we could apply course learnings to better understand our societal experiences as black Americans. In the face of much resistance from the white members of the community and the faculty, we ultimately negotiated a one-hour time period for different subgroup meetings.

Against the backdrop of black subgroup formation and white resistance, I experienced new levels of racial awareness. I captured my thoughts from time to time during the eighteen months in my journal:

> When the black group formed, I did not see myself as having a choice of whether to join. I was black. Therefore, I was a part of the black group. But living inside of me was my assimilationist drive not to separate myself out, not to be a "visible" black.

I was stunned as these words came off my pen. I continued:

> That's a heavy statement. Let's think about it for a moment. Not to be a *visible black* is to be *invisible, not seen.* It is *to give up presence.* For what am I if I am not black? And who am I if I am not a black woman? Fortunately, I had no choice. At least I saw myself as having no choice but to be a part of the black group and, by so doing, to be a visible black woman.

There is something very powerful about standing with one's group and publicly announcing one's presence as a member of that group. As with all forms of "speaking out," it is a transforming process through which we become more fully what we speak out for. Publicly announcing my blackness removed ambiguity for myself and my white classmates (many of whom probably would have said, "I never thought of you as black").

Public announcements of this sort are at once frightening and freeing. Taking a visible and public stand invites reactions. The visible black becomes vulnerable, a target for anger, and a receptacle for assumptions and projections. This coming out of hiding also releases the energy formerly tied up with pretending sameness and leaves open the possibility for direct and honest communication.

> I did not know the gift the black group held for me when first I left the room as a part of the black collective. I do remember when the gift first found expression. The subject of the day was identity development, that is, the movement from infancy to adulthood, from dependence to independence. I listened to one of our white faculty members with mild interest as she talked about identity formation. She displayed a diagram with a series of four circles. Inside of each circle was a smaller circle that became increasingly black as it differentiated itself over time from its background.

Later that day, the topic of the black group came up again, as it often did. The faculty member talked about her awareness that she was accustomed to having her way, to having power and influence. The confrontation with the black group was the first time she found that what she wanted did not matter, and she didn't like it.

> A chord was struck in me that impelled me to talk about what being a member of the black group meant for me. I found myself out of my chair, "Remember your diagram?" I asked. "When I started this program, I was like your first circle, undifferentiated from you and the other white people in this community. Now, as a result of being in the black group, I have become that black dot, clearly differentiated from you. Now we can talk. You from your position of clarity and me from mine." A saying comes to mind, "We are caught in a web of mutuality. You cannot be all that you ought to be until I am all that I can be."

I remember appreciating the faculty member's honesty. From the beginning, I had suspected that the dynamic at the bottom of white resistance was one of power and the question of who determines what happens. I believe that the whites in the course wanted to experience a harmonious, integrated community. However, they operated under two assumptions, both rooted in their accustomed position of power. First, they assumed that their readiness for relationship signaled our readiness. In doing so, they acted out of their privilege to choose the time and place for engagement without consideration for the impact of a lifetime of rejection by whites on our desire to engage. In fact, we questioned why it was that we (the blacks) were suddenly so indispensable to their sense of community when they (the whites) had the opportunity to build relationships with blacks every day of their lives.

Their second assumption was that they alone could decide the nature of the relationship with the black group. When we refused to reciprocate their longing for camaraderie and contact without a separate space for self, they interpreted our behavior as hostile. They saw our affirmation of self as a rejection of them. A quote from Audre Lorde captures our community dynamic: "The supposition that one group needs the other's acquiescence in order to exist prevents both from moving together as self-defined groups toward a common goal."[2]

The black group/white group dynamics formed the ground out of which my theory of black identity development emerged. As members of our black group moved away from the implied expectation of assimilationist behaviors and toward a definition of self that required that relationships be based on mutual choice and negotiation, we created a gap that could not be bridged without whites redefining their assumed position of superiority.

THEORY OF BLACK IDENTITY DEVELOPMENT[3]

Two things should be noted about the theory. First, it is most applicable to middle-class blacks and less applicable to blacks who have had few opportunities and have never perceived that the United States held a promise for them. Second, the stages, though sequential, are not discrete. Although one stage predominates, traces of prior or future stages are always present.

Stage 1: Assimilation

Assimilationist behavior means going along with the status quo. This ranges from doing just enough to ensure survival and security to striving to do more than expected in the hope of gaining acceptance. It also means devaluing one's own abilities and potential and according greater knowledge and expertise to others (e.g., whites, usually men). Much energy is spent being tuned into "the other"[4] so as to gauge one's own behavior. Feelings of fear, vulnerability, and self-doubt predominate. The fear takes many forms, such as an inability to cope with the consequences of not going along: being fired or facing anger, punishment, or rejection. During this stage, one perceives a lack of control over one's own destiny and doubts one's sanity as others question the reality of these injustices.

Stage 2: Anger

Anger is the ultimate refusal to accept that one is crazy and imagining things. This stage is characterized by protest, blaming, rejection of the other's espoused standards. Frequent references are made to the way things should be. Disparities between policies and practices become particularly apparent. Feelings of anger and hurt come from the recognition that the perceived *quid pro quo* for conformance has not been forthcoming. Feelings of victimization grow out of this sense of injury. Powerlessness emerges from the perception that the other is in control and that things can get better only if the other changes.

Stage 3: Letting Go

Letting go means giving up the hope for acceptance—that is, accepting nonacceptance. This letting go of one's expectation of the other leaves space for another way of being. The focus of attention shifts from a preoccupation with the other to a shared consideration of self and other. At this stage, one becomes a witness. This brings an

never will be become angry—accept yourself

objectivity that enables one to see oppression as a process in which the oppressor is addicted to the exercise of power and privilege and the oppressed is codependent.

Stage 4: Becoming Whole

Moving from undifferentiated to differentiated is a restructuring process. In the undifferentiated state, there is a lack of clarity about boundaries between me and the other. With clarity about the me emerges an ability to interact with the other from a point of wholeness and choice. Becoming whole requires claiming, reclaiming, relinquishing, and realizing. *Claiming* is publicly announcing one's presence as a member of the black group. It requires owning all parts of one's group identity: the good, the bad, and the indifferent. *Reclaiming* means taking back the positive qualities of beauty, power, knowledge, and leadership that one has projected onto whites and denied as part of oneself. *Relinquishing* is giving back the negative projections of violence, thievery, inferiority, and laziness that whites have projected onto blacks and denied as a part of themselves. *Realizing* means acknowledging one's own oppressive behaviors and the ways in which one colludes with the white oppressor through these behaviors.

Stage 5: Transformation/Reframing

In this stage, one reframes the course of one's life from that of a "pilgrimage of suffering and pain" to that of a "heroic journey" and celebrates that one has moved from invisibility to visibility. The challenge of this stage is to move from voicelessness to voice, to be articulate and to speak out against oppression of all forms—to become a radicalizing presence. In the early stages of development, the objective was to survive. The objective in this stage is to honor one's survival by using it as an opportunity to live one's life with meaning.

Stage 6: Transcendence

Transcendence means operating from a point of universal wholeness, living as creator, and providing a vision of healing.

CONCLUSION

It would be inappropriate to conclude that the solution to today's racial problems is for blacks to go through a six-step transformative process. This would be to condemn every black child of current and future generations to the same dehumanizing struggle that generated the theory. Rather, whites with power, compassion, and concern must ask, "What is it about us as a nation that requires one group of people to go to such extraordinary means just to survive?" The answer is that we exist in a white-dominated system. This means that the political, economic, psychological, and social arrangements are configured to maintain white superiority and black inferiority.

Both for blacks who accept an inferior designation and for those who don't, the struggle is murderous. Blacks who accept the inferior designation are psychologically beaten and die of broken hearts. Blacks who do not accept the inferior designation are often killed by the struggle, literally or figuratively. A preadolescent black male summed up his fears: "If you try to help black people, you will be killed. Look at Martin Luther King, Malcolm X, and George Jackson. I don't want to die."[5] At the figurative level, the daily struggle against the "package" of oppressive assaults wears away the soul.

The second question should be, "What is the cost to us as a nation of adhering to the political, economic, psychological, and social arrangements that perpetuate the dynamic where blacks must struggle so mightily for survival?" There are many answers to this complex question. The one I put forth here is the cost to the nation of the institutional practice of projecting onto blacks all of the major societal problems. Here are several examples:

- *Drugs.* Although the same percentage of whites and blacks use drugs, blacks are four times more likely to be arrested on drug charges and four times more likely to be pictured on network news stories about drug abuse.[6]

- *Poverty.* Traditionally, poverty has been portrayed as a black problem. However, the Center on Budget and Policy Priorities reports that from 1989 to 1991, non-Hispanic white unemployment rates increased somewhat faster than minority unemployment rates, leading to faster poverty growth among non-Hispanic whites.[7]

- *Single-parent families.* The white out-of-wedlock rate more than quadrupled, from just over 4 percent in 1965 to 17.8 percent in 1988. Senator Daniel Moynihan recently stated, "Illegitimacy levels that were viewed as an aberration of a particular subculture [the black] 25 years ago have become the norm for the entire culture."[8]

- *Education.* For many years, poor educational skills were seen as a black problem. We now confront illiteracy and poor educational preparation as a national problem.

"My future just passed," might be the theme of the dynamic described above. Maladies that show up first in the black community are symptomatic of broader societal problems. The white process of denial and projection allows these problems to go unattended until they reach a crisis. Only when the problem is clearly visible in the white community can it no longer be denied. Left unattended, these problems snowball and the resources once available to deal with them are either no longer available or are insufficient.

The third question for whites is, "What can we do to bring about social change?" Clearly, white supremacy is a lose/lose situation. A new paradigm is required, for blacks cannot be truly integrated at a level of parity in a white-dominated system. The challenge for whites, whose primary identity has been tied to their socially constructed superiority over nonwhites, will be to redefine themselves in terms of their intrinsic self-worth.

From a systems perspective, a redefinition of blackness requires a redefinition of whiteness.

NOTES

1. I choose to use the designation "black" rather than "African-American" because the negative messages that came to me were about the skin color of my group rather than about our historical or geographical origins.

2. Audre Lorde, *Sister Outsider: Essays and Speeches* (Freedom, CA: The Crossing, 1984), p. 51.

3. For seminal writings on Black Identity Development see W.S. Hall, W.E. Cross, and R. Freedle, "Stages in the Development of Black Awareness: An Exploratory Investigation," in R.L. Jones, ed., *Black Psychology* (NY: Harper and Row, 1972), pp. 156–165; W.E. Cross, "Discovering the Black Referent: The Psychology of Black Liberation," in J. Dixon and B. Foster (eds.), *Beyond Black or White* (Boston: Little, Brown, 1971), pp. 95–110; and B.W. Jackson and R. Hardiman, "Racial Identity Development: Implications for Managing the Multi-Racial Work Force," in R. Ritvo and A. Sargent (eds.), *The NTL Managers' Handbook* (Arlington, VA: NTL Institute, 1983), pp. 107–119.

4. A term commonly used in anthropological writing, *the other* refers to how one's self-definition or identity, whether as an individual or part of a group, often develops out of what one sees that one is not. Thus "the other" is something one sees as fundamentally unlike oneself—an opposite.

5. Frances Cress Welsing, "Black Fear and the Failure of the Black Analytical (Ideological) Commitment," *The Isis Papers: The Keys to the Colors* (Chicago: Third World Press, 1991), p. 156.

6. *USA Today*, July 23, 1993, Sam Vincent Meddis, page 6A.

7. *The Washington Post*, October 9, 1992, p. A4, Spencer Rich. Writer.

8. *The Washington Post*, January 22, 1991, p. A3, Paul Taylor.

Chapter Twenty-Five

Charles N. Seashore

The White Male Category at the Intersection of Race and Gender

Charles N. Seashore and Beverly R. Fletcher

Beverly R. Fletcher

Charles N. Seashore, PhD, works with a large number of team and organization development programs in government and health care. His practice also includes a variety of private industrial organizations as well as nonprofit community groups and organizations.

Beverly N. Fletcher, EdD, received her doctorate degree from the University of Massachusetts at Amherst. She teaches master's-level courses emphasizing various aspects of organization change, development, and transformation at the University of Oklahoma.

A category should not be confused with a stereotype. Unlike a stereotype, a category is a way of describing a group of people according to the most commonly held characteristics of a significant number of its members. On the other hand, a stereotype is a fixed supposition or belief about a group of people that may not be true of the majority of people in that group. Categories are a sociological concept, much like "national character" and can be used to describe, predict, or understand group, community, or societal behavior.

PERSON TALK VERSUS CATEGORY TALK

Category talk does not necessarily apply to all individuals in a category in that the concept may not always be useful for predicting a particular individual's behavior.

White males do not believe that there is a white male category. If they think of it at all, they seem to treat it like an optional religious concept—"Maybe I'll belong this week if I feel like it." Although they conceptualize other groups of people in terms of categories, they do

157

not think of themselves as belonging to a category. This may be because white men in their historic position of privilege, power, and dominance have only focused outward in their efforts to understand people and have developed a rather myopic vision when it comes to themselves. In contrast, most other people acknowledge that they themselves and others (including white men) belong to categories.

Try to imagine the reactions of white men to requests to participate in sessions where they are asked to think about themselves as a category and have the pleasure of hearing other people describe them in category language. The feelings that white men have described experiencing at the beginning of such sessions range from stress, fear, and dread, to feelings of being attacked and being subjected to "white-male bashing."

As shown in Table 25-1, category talk is different from person talk. When engaging in person talk, it is important to be quite specific, to discuss the uniqueness of the person involved, to be descriptive and accurate, and to point to specific things that are either currently happening or happened in the past about the individual's behavior. On the other hand, category talk is very general, discusses common characteristics rather than unique characteristics, and is frequently exaggerated talk in that it refers to "all" instead of "some." These characteristics are at times taken out of context by women and people of color and treated as fact. Many white men find this practice exasperating. Women and people of color often discuss patterns of white male behavior that they perceive as facts because of their experiences. On the other hand, the white male concept of a fact is a specific event that has occurred within the current experience or present context.

The following is a typical example of the misunderstanding that can occur:

African American woman:

"Well, I'll tell you, Ralph. If I were up there on that podium, instead of you, discussing white males, I wouldn't be getting the same respect that you're getting."

White male:

"What the hell are you talking about, Clare? You're not up here. You're gonna be up here tomorrow. Why don't you wait and see whether you will or won't get any respect?"

The problem is that Clare knows how it's going to work out for her because she has experienced and witnessed this pattern a hundred times in a hundred different contexts. She treats the pattern as a reality, a fact. And even if her presentation goes well tomorrow and she somehow manages to gain the respect of her audience, she will

TABLE 25–1
Person Talk Versus Category Talk

Person Talk	Category
Personal	Impersonal
Specific	General, often exaggerated
Unique characteristics	Common characteristics
Descriptive of individual behavior	Descriptive of probable behavior based on common characteristics
In context	Often out of context
Past and present events	Past and future patterns

continue to believe in the "fact" of a negative response pattern toward women of color. In contrast, Ralph reacted to the discussion from a personal and individual perspective. He did not understand that Clare was talking in category language, and he did not comprehend that a fact is different when you talk category talk than when you talk person talk.

RACISM AND SEXISM

When we discuss racism and sexism, we are not talking about harmless attitudes. Racism and sexism are pervasive throughout our culture and have staggering effects on everyone. One way of describing these phenomena in total is *oppression:* acts of power that inflict gross injustices, deep, long-lasting pain, even violence and death. Racism and sexism are acts of oppression. We define *racism* as racial prejudice plus the power to deny personal liberties and educational, social, career, and financial options based on race. Similarly, we define *sexism* as gender bias plus the power to deny personal liberties and educational, social, career, and financial options based on gender. With these definitions, there is an obvious difference between racial prejudice and racism and between gender bias and sexism.

The common white male response to these "isms" is: "These topics are kind of interesting, but they don't really apply to me." White males often have difficulty understanding why white women and people of color react to them in various ways. They do not understand the mechanics of racism and sexism, and they do not believe in the reality of their category.

White men want to be seen first for who they are individually. That sounds good. It even sounds like something Carl Rogers or Abraham

Maslow or other humanistic psychologists would say. There's one problem, however: Not only do white men want to be seen as persons first, they want to be seen as persons second and do not want to be seen as a category at all. They will go to great lengths to differentiate themselves from anybody else of their "type." They say, in effect, "As a white man, I distinguish between myself and Bob in some very important ways that make it impossible for us to be in the same category." White men build a world for themselves in which all they believe in is individual white-male personhood. What they fail to realize is that everybody in all of the other categories would like to have the same privilege.

It is not an irrelevant desire to want to be seen for ourselves. Most of us want to be seen for ourselves. However, the fact is (speaking in category language) that everyone other than white males knows that they will always be seen as a category first, and they may not ever be seen for who they are as individuals.

An African American man in a diversity group made the following comment. "You'll never understand what it's like when I get into an elevator with a white woman. She will always clutch her handbag tighter in a predictable way. That always happens to me." This is an illustration of what it means to be seen as a category first.

Over the last 30 years, the civil rights movement and the feminist movement have attempted to help white women, African American men, and African American women to think of themselves and talk about themselves positively. This has been necessary because so many women and people of color have internalized negative stereotypes that have been attributed to the categories they are locked into. In contrast, over the same period of time, white men have increased their power to forcefully deny that negatives even exist when it comes to looking at themselves.

Continuing our discussion of racism and sexism, we refer to institutional forces rather than individual forces. It is essential to realize that individuals in all categories may be prejudiced. However, racism and sexism require prejudice plus power to live and breathe. Racism and sexism are often institutionalized phenomena that are so deeply woven into the fabrics of our organizations that they are out of the conscious awareness of those in power. (We use the term *out of awareness* instead of *unconscious* in order to avoid discussions about whether there is such a thing as the unconscious.)

When women and people of color bring up how an organization's rules, processes, or norms negatively impact them, white men hear these complaints as personal attacks on themselves, and they respond accordingly: "I am not racist/sexist," "Here we go again with another round of white-male bashing," "Couldn't find a volleyball, so you've decided to do this instead!"

The energy it takes for women and people of color to be heard by white men is enormous. It is very frustrating to women and people of color to constantly have to deal with the personal reaction of white men who are looking at the discussion from a personal perspective. The difficulty lies in getting white men to see and acknowledge their institutional sexism and racism. Their typical response is: "This organization (or country, society, etc.) was created by people before my time (or before I was born). I am not responsible for what they did." One of the first questions white men ask is "Who are you talking about?" When women or people of color refer to them (white men as a category) as being sexist or racist, white men look over their shoulders, as if "they" must be out there. They do not recognize that sexism and racism are rampant in their institutional processes, procedures, norms, and conceptual perspectives.

HOW WHITE MEN, WHITE WOMEN, MEN OF COLOR, AND WOMEN OF COLOR INTERACT

In one group composed of white men and women and African American men and women, a discussion took place about the relationship between white women and African American women. The issue of feminism came up between the two groups, and it was discovered that major problems develop between white women and women of color because an unspoken contract between them is never fully played out. The contract goes something like this: African American women agree, "We will show up to support work regarding sexism, if you agree to show up for work on racism." But when the time comes to do work on racism, only women of color show up. The abandonment of the issue of racism by white women is a serious problem that causes a lot of women of color to wonder whether they can trust this concept of working with white women.

Another problem exists between African American men and women. Conversation is extremely difficult between the two groups, and this has something to do with the fact that many African American women perceive African American men to be a scarce resource. Most of the tension occurs around the tendency of many heterosexual black men to seek white female partners. The perceived abandonment of the African American community by black men—leaving black families without male role models—is a serious point of contention. There is also resentment between women of color and white women over the same issue.

What happens between white men and women of color is something that we are just beginning to explore, but some concepts have emerged. One of these has to do with sexuality. The idea that white men might see and experience women of color as more sexual than white women was a notion that was revealed through the questioning of white men. The idea was also revealed that white men might see women of color as objects and targets—things that don't have to be treated as individual people. Another white male attitude experiences women of color as caretakers—someone remembered as being a cleaning woman, cook, or nanny. Of all the categories, including their own, white men probably feel least threatened by women of color.

Interrelationships among white men and white women are quite interesting. White men may have a problem when they perceive that white women prefer nonwhite men. White women may prefer others they perceive as more passionate, more direct, and more honest than white men. On the other hand, some white women are willing to make extraordinary compromises to overcome the shortcomings of white men. In order to have access to the white males' power, dominance, and other "goodies," some white women may make compromises about their self-esteem and self-worth. They may also make compromises about opportunities, about careers, and about geographical location in order to access power. Along with making such compromises, white women may feel a fair amount of resentment toward white men because of what they feel they must put up with in order to feel secure.

Between white men and men of color, there is probably a lot of fear and resentment. White men sometimes resent men of color because some white women are attracted to them. Men of color resent white men because they withhold access to economic power and security. There is probably a lot of fear between the two categories, fear of violence, fear of competition, and perhaps even fear among white men of being "found out" by men of color because they have a lot in common as men.

WHITE MEN'S DISADVANTAGE

Despite having reaped the benefits of their dominant position throughout history, white men today face a disadvantage: Most have no eyes or ears to perceive the rampant oppression around them; and if they do perceive it, they cannot and perhaps even should not take responsibility for it. But what they *can* do is look at all the issues described here, from category talk versus person talk to the subtle complexities of relationships between and among people who are different. When white men are able to view themselves as a category as well as part of the human continuum, they will begin to contribute to the struggle against oppression.

SOURCES

Robert L. Bogomolny, ed., *Human Experimentation* (Dallas: Southern Methodist University Press, 1976).

Paul Bohannan and Philip Curtin, *Africa and Africans*, 3rd ed. (Prospect Heights, IL: Waveland Press, 1988).

John D. Brewer, *After Soweto: An Unfinished Journey* (New York: Oxford University Press, 1986).

Committee for the Compilation of Materials on Damage Caused by the Atomic Bombs in Hiroshima and Nagasaki, *Hiroshima and Nagasaki: The Physical, Medical, and Social Effects of the Atomic Bombings*, trans. E. Ishikawa and D. L. Swain (New York: Basic Books, 1981).

Vine Deloria, Jr., and Clifford M. Lytle, *American Indians, American Justice* (Austin, TX: University of Texas Press, 1983).

John Ehle, *Trail of Tears: The Rise and Fall of the Cherokee Nation* (New York: Anchor Books, 1988).

Helen Fein, *Accounting for Genocide: National Responses and Jewish Victimization During the Holocaust* (New York: Free Press, 1979).

Gustav Henningsen, *The Witches' Advocate: Basque Witchcraft and the Spanish Inquisition, 1609–1614* (Reno, NV: University of Nevada Press, 1980).

Alton Hornsby, Jr., ed., *Chronology of African-American History: Significant Events and People from 1619 to the Present* (Detroit: Gale Research, 1991).

C. P. Horton and J. C. Smith, *Statistical Record of Black America* (Detroit: Gale Research, 1990).

Susan K. Kinnell, ed., *Military History of the United States: An Annotated Bibliography* (Santa Barbara, CA: ABC-Clio, 1986).

David Mechanic, *From Advocacy to Allocation: The Evolving American Health Care System* (New York: Free Press, 1986).

Richard H. Minear, trans. and ed., *Hiroshima: Three Witnesses* (Princeton, NJ: Princeton University Press, 1990).

Robert O'Brien and H. H. Martin, eds., *The Encyclopedia of the South* (New York: Facts on File, 1985).

Carl C. Pegels, *Health Care and the Elderly* (Rockville, MD: Aspen Publications, 1980).

M. E. Perry and A. J. Cruz, *Cultural Encounters: The Impact of the Inquisition in Spain and the New World* (Berkeley: University of California Press, 1991).

J. P. Robinson, *The Effects of Weapons on Ecosystems* (Oxford, England: Pergamon, 1979).

Frank L. Schick and R. Schick, eds., *Statistical Handbook on U.S. Hispanics* (Phoenix: Oryx, 1991).

Kyoko Selden and Mark Selden, eds., *The Atomic Bomb: Voices from Hiroshima and Nagasaki* (Armonk, NY: M. E. Sharpe, 1989).

Thomas M. Shapiro, *Population Control Politics: Women, Sterilization, and Reproductive Choice* (Philadelphia: Temple University Press, 1985).

Arthur L. Smith, Jr., *Hitler's Gold: The Story of Nazi War Loot* (New York: St. Martin's, 1989).

W. H. Smith, *Air Pollution and Forests: Interactions Between Air Contaminants and Forest Ecosystems* (New York: Springer-Verlag, 1981).

J. Tivy and G. O'Hare, *Human Impact on the Ecosystem* (New York: Oliver and Boyd, 1981).

Michi Weglyn, *Years of Infamy: The Untold Story of America's Concentration Camps* (New York: Morrow, 1976).

Patricia Whelehan, et al., *Women and Health: Cross-Cultural Perspectives* (Granby, MA: Bergin and Garvey, 1988).

Chapter Twenty-Six

Joseph Potts

White Men Can Help—But It's Hard

Joseph Potts

■

Joseph Potts, PhD, is an organization development consultant and an associate of Elsie Y. Cross Associates. Previous positions include president/executive director of NTL Institute and director of product development for G.D. Searle Co. He has worked with a number of clients on issues of diversity. They include Johnson Wax, Kodak, Exxon, Bank of America, Arthur Andersen, Ortho Pharmaceutical, the University of Pennsylvania, and CIGNA. He now lives in Canada.

W hy should a white man like me be writing about fighting racism, sexism, and other forms of oppression? The answer is that I know the part of the oppressor. I am an expert on this part of the dynamic of racism and sexism. And I know about the unearned benefits and privileges that I have received just because I am a middle-class white man.

I grew up in the Midwest, in the upper middle class. I had all of the privileges that being a middle-class white boy can bring. About the only things that set me apart from my friends were that my mother was a professional nurse and that my father died when I was 13 years old.

I remember thinking as a kid that I was "lucky" that my mom could work and support us. I was incapable of seeing as an achievement her ability to earn a nursing degree in an era when most people in our town did not go to university. I was blinded by the belief that women were subservient to men, in spite of the evidence to the contrary.

In spite of information I had first-hand about white women, African Americans, and Japanese and Indian people, I maintained a belief in their inferiority through college, graduate school, and the first 10 years of my corporate career.

During the last 10 years I worked in a corporation, I began to see the horrible effect of oppression on friends and colleagues who were not white and male. I was appalled by the other white men who were doing this awful deed. Eventually, I saw that it was me and others like me who were the real problem.

What stops us from fixing the problems of sexual and racial inequity? There are lots of things, but in this article I want to concentrate on what stops most white men from acting and what makes a few take serious action.

Most white men face a major dilemma. We were rewarded in life for being good at problem solving. We were also told that taking action was a good thing to do. We were not told to acknowledge our feelings or nurture others. When problems are too big or too difficult to resolve, the only choices we white men have are to ignore them or pretend they do not exist. A more sophisticated version of this is to develop "Band-Aid" solutions just to feel we have done something, because any action is better than no action. Whether it helps or not is beside the point. After all, most of us were not taught to nurture or worry about the feelings of others.

Although this summary of the socialization of white men is no doubt overgeneralized and oversimplified, it reflects my experience and that of many of my white male friends, colleagues, and clients.

Applying this perhaps somewhat overgeneralized principle to race and gender oppression means many white men assume that racism and sexism do not exist in our organizations. Of course, part of the defense is not to look for these problems in our work or home environment. We are too busy to delve into the details of the treatment of Rodney King by the Los Angeles police, the Central Park attacks on women, the pay inequity for women at Harvard, the discrimination against Asian students at Stanford, the denial of basic legal rights of Native American people at Wounded Knee, and so on.

When a person of color or a white woman brings issues of oppression to our attention in such a way that we can no longer avoid acknowledging them, we usually move to denial. It is at this stage that we tell the complaining person that he or she is oversensitive. We also hasten to explain that our boss is really a good person, and we are sure he did not mean it.

It is not true that we believe the person is too sensitive or that we are convinced the accused is a good person. Rather, we feel irritated about having the issue brought to our attention. It diverts us from problems that we can resolve and that make us feel valued (e.g., decreasing costs, increasing sales, implementing new systems).

The net impact is that many white men avoid even acknowledging there is a problem. The motivation for their avoidance is fear of impotence.

Top-level managers are even more reluctant to open up these issues. But they do know how to take action. The issue is referred to the human resources (HR) department or to some task force. They are asked to look at the recruiting policies to make sure the organization is getting the "best" minorities and women to develop better communication about the seriousness of harassment or to do an in-depth analysis of the most recent company questionnaire.

Assignment of responsibility to a task force or to HR puts the onus on another group. The idea is to appear to act without having to do anything out of the ordinary. But there is no direct attempt by the white men in leadership to understand the problem. They are insulated from the pain white women and people of color feel in the same organization where they feel comfortable.

There are many variations on this general theme of avoidance:

1. "If it ain't broke, don't fix it—and don't go asking if it's broke, either." The assumption in this case is that if there are no complaints, there is no problem. The saddest part of this scenario is that many people of color and white women do their work in a system they know is broken. They perform their jobs in spite of this knowledge. They feel angry and frustrated that they cannot get the white male leader's attention. They know they could do better work if they felt welcomed and valued by the organization. They want to contribute. But very few white men in authority want to hear about their issues because there is no easy resolution.

2. Bootstraps. Many white men in leadership positions believe that they have worked hard to get where they are. They subscribe to the notion that success requires that individuals pull themselves up by their bootstraps. This stance assumes that "my way is the best/only way." When told about problems that others encounter, these white men say that these things happened to them, too. There is no exploration of the different impact these problems have on others, the number of times these events occur, or the absence of such privileges as mentoring and networking. Discussion is stopped because they only want to avoid feeling impotent.

3. Elitism. First, nearly all white men grew up believing that white is better than black and that men are superior to women. We may have had parents who us differently, but the media, our teachers, the church, and our schoolbooks all told us otherwise. We learned that our country had "founding fathers," that whites were responsible for the salvation of the black savages in Africa, that Native Americans were childlike and easily duped in trading, that women were supposed to have babies and care for children. In short, we learned that those who are not white men are inferior.

Second, most of us grew up with very strong value of equality. We learned to be proud of the United States because it was founded on the principles of liberty and justice for all. The discovery that groups of people have been deprived of their rights and are still being treated unjustly generates overwhelming feelings of dissonance and discomfort. We feel powerless dealing with these strong feelings.

So we white men have mixed messages. We believe in equality, and we have been taught that we are the best. Our feelings of elitism are buried under our belief that all of us should be treated equally. Not only is it difficult to access our feelings because of how we were socialized, but the sense of elitism is accompanied by feelings of guilt. The consequence is that we avoid looking too deeply at our beliefs.

All of this seems pretty overwhelming and partly explains why many white men take no action. What is different for those who do take action? There are several factors that influence some white men to act:

1. The business case. Some executives realize that costs in their organizations are too high. Closer inspection reveals that the turnover for people of color and white women is much higher than that of white men. One executive discovered that the loss in sales while a new recruit was being trained was over $100,000. He felt the turnover rate was too high for the white men, but he was extremely upset to find that the turnover rate was twice as high for white women and three times as high for people of color.

In my experience, the business case provides a rationale for engaging issues of racism and sexism. Action taken from the business platform is limited to exploration of the issues. By itself, it is not enough to gain commitment.

2. Quality. In some organizations, the concept of quality has been integrated into the culture. The discovery that white women and people of color do not feel welcomed or included is alarming in these types of organizations because the years invested in quality and the progress made through implementation of quality concepts are at risk if all employees are not committed.

Managers who have a lot invested in the success of the quality effort often become advocates for diversity and take effective action from this platform. The efforts to support diversity are more emotionally laden than the efforts to achieve quality, but the underlying issues of involvement and commitment are similar.

Top-level executives can see that they need to act differently if they want to implement quality programs. There is little emotional "baggage" that accompanies this type of learning. But learning about racism and sexism is emotionally loaded. Learning that we are contributing to racism and sexism unless we are actively fighting against them is deadening.

In my experience, understanding quality concepts helps managers see why diversity is important. It helps managers think about these difficult issues in manageable chunks. But managers need a great deal of support to grapple with the intense emotions that lie along the path toward achieving diversity.

3. Relationships. Some white men have developed more spontaneous relationships with people of color or women that are enriching and based on "equal power."

Several white men have told me they have had—and I myself have also had—the experience of being excluded as children and then finding a friend who was a different race or gender or physical ability. The quality of the new friendship seems to be critical in that it was based on mutual respect or power equity.

If important cross-racial or cross-gender relationships are part of our experience and we find out that people we care about are having bad experiences in "our" organization, we find it intolerable. When we hear the problem is caused by our own race or gender, it is despicable. Action must be taken. This is a very powerful platform for action.

White men who take this approach are sometimes disliked by their white male peers. They are seen as radical. White men who care this much are often excluded from some of the social events that kept them on the "inside" and are excluded from casual conversations among insiders. Sometimes, they are perceived as zealots.

White men who are motivated by relationships with people who are different by race or gender often live in two worlds and do not feel at home in either. They are always suspect by the different others because they can choose to be silent on oppression issues. Other white men are suspicious because they have relationships that are unusual and their loyalty to their own kind is not certain.

Unconsciously, we are socialized to avoid dealing with emotionally loaded issues. It takes an exceptional set of events to motivate us to take action to ameliorate racism and sexism in our organizations.

The business case may be sufficient motivation to explore issues of oppression, but it is not adequate to take serious action. It is insufficient because the business case deals with oppression as if it were a typical business issue. There is an attempt by top-level executives to delegate the problem rather than understand their responsiblity as leaders and their need to change.

Commitment to quality or concern for relationships are important factors for action. Each of these has its own set of consequences, which have to be managed: accepting the deep emotions on the one hand and not belonging on the other.

Taking action on issues of racism or sexism or other types of oppression requires white men to delve into their emotions. It is not easy for most of us, but it is possible. The rewards are personal. Letting go of undeserved privilege is worthwhile.

Chapter Twenty-Seven

Senior Executive Women, Power, and the American Business Organization

Barbara Benedict Bunker

■

Barbara Benedict Bunker

Barbara Benedict Bunker, PhD, is associate professor of psychology at the State University of New York at Buffalo and a partner in the Portsmouth Consulting Group. Her recent research and writing have included studies of Japanese senior executive women, commuting couples in the United States, a new model for training effectiveness in organizations, and large-systems interventions. Among Bunker's recent clients are Corning, Inc., Exxon U.S.A., Scott Paper Co., First Tennessee Bank, Canisius College, and the University of Miami Business School.

W e are all aware of the way the media feature women who have "made it." *Business Week* and *Fortune* publish portraits of successful female executives as well as studies of groups of women who are near the top. Everyone wants to know why there are so few women in top executive jobs in the United States. *Fortune* reports that less than one-half of 1 percent of the highest-paid officers and directors of the Fortune 1,000 largest U.S. industries and service companies are women.[1] The national discussion about the bottleneck, or "glass ceiling," at the top has picked up momentum.

Former Labor Department Secretary Lynn Martin completed a study to diagnose and address the problem.[2] But what is the problem? It is complex, with causal factors at several levels: individual, organizational, and cultural. The problem is so complicated that we are apt to find proponents of a particular explanation overly focused on one aspect to the exclusion of others.

INDIVIDUAL CHARACTERISTICS

Generally, the average age of women in senior executives roles is in the early to mid-40s.[3] They are highly educated, many with master's degrees in business administration.

A substantial number of these women never married (19.4–33 percent). In 1982, just over half of these women indicated that they were currently married (50.9–51.4 percent). More recently, the percentages of married women senior executives have varied widely, from 33 percent to 68 percent.

In the 1982 studies, close to two-thirds of the women who were married had no children (61–70 percent). By the late 1980s, the percentages were closer to 50 percent (51.3–53.7 percent), with the exception of the *Business Week* study, where only one-third of married women had children. Thus, there is a suggestion in these data that some women who have achieved executive success may have chosen not to marry or not to have children.

Morrison and her colleagues[4] investigated specific factors that are critical for success in senior executive women. In this study, a selected group of highly placed executives who had long experience promoting key executives were interviewed and asked what factors led to the advancement of men and women to executive status. After the data were analyzed, it was possible to compare the most important promotion factors for successful men and women.

On the women's list, the top factor was help from above—that is, a good relationship with someone at the top of the corporation. Second was a proven track record of achievement (89 percent); third, desire/drive to succeed (84 percent). The next three factors were ability to manage subordinates (74 percent), willingness to take career risks (74 percent), and the ability to be tough, decisive, and demanding (68 percent).

For men, the top factor was a proven track record (75 percent). Second and third for men tied for seventh among women: smart (70 percent) and works through others (60 percent). The next three factors for men were help from above (55 percent), can manage subordinates (50 percent) and desire to succeed (45 percent). Thus, factors concerning individual job competence are high for both men and women, but an organizational factor, support from above, is especially important for women.

ORGANIZATIONAL FACTORS

The preceding discussion suggests that both individual characteristics and organizational factors affect success. Are there particular companies where women have a better chance of rising to executive status? If there are, women with high career aspirations would do well to target them for their employment.

Over the last 10 years, the popular press has featured companies where women are making progress in management. The paucity of women in heavy industry and the greater numbers in other companies has been easy to notice. Zeitz and Dusky used three types of criteria to select their 50 top companies in *The Best Companies for Women*.[5] First, they looked at the number of women in middle and senior management; then at affirmative-action, promotion, and development policies. Second, they assessed sexual harassment policies and a positive company culture. Third, they evaluated benefits, pay equity, and working arrangements that enabled women to meet both their job and family responsibilities.

Do these "good companies" appear more often in some industry groupings? Using a slightly modified version of the categories used by Levering et al.,[6] I grouped the 50 best companies for women under 10 industry types to see whether there were some types of industry that had higher numbers of best companies. Seventy-eight percent of the companies were in five industry groups: media and publishing, high-tech firms, retailing (apparel and cosmetics), banking and finance, and communications.

The types of companies that appear among *Business Week's* Top 50 Women Executives and *Business Month's* Top 100 support the idea that there is more going on in traditional manufacturing organizations than is sometimes credited. Manufacturing was the top category in both surveys (24 percent in *Business Week,* 39 percent *Business Month*). Other categories over 10 percent in both surveys were high-tech companies and financial institutions. This does not necessarily mean these companies are woman-friendly because some women described themselves as having had to "claw their way to the top."

Organization policies about pregnancy, child care, and flexible working conditions are critical to women who have families. I believe they are a necessary but not sufficient criterion of a good company. They can support corporate willingness to train and advance women. There is, however, some danger that flexible hours, benefits, and child care arrangements can lull women into a false sense of confidence. Rosener, for example, appropriately raises questions about the tendency to assume a relationship between these things and access to powerful roles.[7]

WOMEN IN POWER: LEADERSHIP STYLES

Any discussion of women in power or women's preferred style of using power must take account of individual characteristics, of the organizational setting in which she acts, and of environmental opportunities and constraints. There is a natural tendency to compare people in the same role (e.g., managers), especially when obvious gender differences have been heightened by cultural biases about appropriate roles for men and women.[8]

In their discussion of why some women on the executive track "derail," Morrison et al.[9] present a very useful discussion of the very narrow band of acceptable behaviors that are available to women executives as compared with their male counterparts. They propose that some of the difficulties that women face in enacting their executive role come from the subtle requirements that they do so within a narrower range of behaviors than is allowed for men. They are expected to "take risks, but be consistently outstanding. Be tough, but don't be macho. Be ambitious, but don't expect equal treatment. Take responsibility, but follow others' advice."[10]

In terms of the traditional sex roles, men are less apt to be sanctioned for the more extreme masculine—that is, aggressive—behaviors and are rewarded for moving into traditionally feminine spheres as long as the masculine behaviors are in place. "Isn't it wonderful that he is so good with his children—and such a decisive executive, too!" Women are stereotyped if they are too masculine or if they are too feminine. Thus, women walk a more difficult tightrope to behave acceptably in corporate America.

This perspective on why there is a glass ceiling is an argument not at the level of gender differences but from the framework of roles. Yet it does not explain why there has been so much energy in the debate about whether men and women behave in the same or different ways as managers.

In their landmark review and meta-analysis of gender and leadership styles, Eagly and Johnson[11] point out that differences in style between men and women do not emerge in organizational settings. Men and women were only different in laboratory and assessment studies—that is, men were more task oriented and women were more interpersonally oriented. They suggest that organizational roles require behaviors from both men and women that overwhelm any sex-role preference. Even more interesting, they found that women had a tendency to lead more democratically and men more autocratically across all three types of studies. These differences begin young, as seen in Maccoby and her colleagues' studies of interaction patterns among young children.[12] Boys below the age of five have been shown to have a dominance-oriented interaction style that girls seem to find distasteful. Girls tend to prefer their own sex, where they have more opportunity to influence.

Recently, there have been several articles about the way powerful women at the top of an organization choose to use their power. These accounts support the Eagly and Johnson conclusions. Grace Pastiak's style of running her Tellabs plant, for example, was featured in the business section of *The New York Times* (May 5, 1991). She shares decision-making power and information in a collaborative way with workers at the plant and has motivated them to meet tough challenges. Often such profiles of women leaders are supported by quotations from writers who propose that women have special skills to contribute at a management level.[13,14] It leaves one wondering whether the role constraints described by Morrison[15] may operate primarily on women on their way to the top, but may be much less of a problem for women who have arrived.

Eagly and Johnson also comment on the emergence of two different approaches to understanding whether there are male and female leadership differences.[16] During the 1980s, social scientists in psychology departments and schools of management who reviewed the considerable research on gender and leadership styles concluded that there were no reliable differences between men and women.[17,18,19] At the same time, there have been repeated attempts in the management literature to support a view that men and women do indeed behave differently as managers in the workplace. The two most substantial attempts in the 1980s were Alice Sargent's book *The Androgynous Manager*[20] and Marilyn Loden's *Feminine Leadership*.[21]

Sargent and Loden, who are referred to by Eagly and Johnson as management experts, are not part of the academic management establishment, but rather management consultants with roots in the applied behavioral science tradition of the National Training Laboratories (NTL Institute). They have a great deal of experience consulting on the integration of women into the workplace. Sargent's proposal that both men and women would be more effective leaders if they used both the appropriate male-type behaviors and the best female ones, was a direct translation of Sandra Bem's work on sex roles.[22] Bem moved the field forward a giant step when she changed the behavior scaling procedure from a unidimensional masculine/feminine scale to two scales, one for masculine behavior and one for feminine behavior, and rated all subjects on both scales. The message was that both feminine and masculine behaviors could be exhibited by both genders. This was highly congruent with the participative leadership model endorsed by NTL Institute, which had its roots in early social psychological studies.[23] The model proposes that effective group members are those with a wide range of behaviors who are able to vary their behavior as group needs change. Effective leaders are those who enable others to join in taking responsibility for the group and who have a wide range of behaviors allowing them to supplement behaviors in other members. In other words, leaders are skilled and flexible. Sargent's proposal for androgynous managers put men and women on equal footing. Each had something by dint of gender and sex-role socialization, and each could expand that to become even more effective by learning new behaviors and using them appropriately.

Sargent's work can also be seen as yet another rung in the ladder attempting to challenge the hierarchical organizational model of control and command as a management principle. Her work suggests, as has the work of others before her, that developing commitment through participation in the people working for you may be much more effective than managing by controlling them.

Control has been the major management paradigm throughout the twentieth century.[24] It was challenged in the 1950s and 1960s by applied behavioral scientists. It is being challenged again in this argument about male and female leadership styles. I believe that what is really at issue here is power and the best way to use it.

Loden's proposal can also be seen as a second major effort to challenge the control paradigm via this discussion of male and female management styles.[25] It proposes that women have a special contribution to make to the workplace that is much needed to moderate the predominant style of leadership that emphasizes role power. She contrasts role power and personal power and sees men as more oriented to role power and women as more oriented to personal power. The leadership model she suggests has as its key characteristics lower control, empathy, collaboration, and high performance standards. It sounds very much like other proposals in the management literature for a more participative style of leadership—for example, Bradford and Cohen[26] and Cohen and Bradford[27]—except that it is labeled as the special contribution of women.

Rosener's study of the International Women's Federation in which she compared women executives with male counterparts was the source of data from which she proposes that "transactional leadership" is more characteristic of women.[28] Responses to her study level a number of legitimate criticisms and point out that some of her ideas are old ones with new labels. They also point out that most of her samples came from settings where they were more likely to have been able to use a more participative style—that is, medium-sized, nontraditional organizations. If some or even most women do have a preference to lead more democratically, they could find their behavior treated as unacceptable in some settings and as innovative and useful in others. If, indeed, we are changing paradigms, then it is little wonder that there is fire and energy around these issues. The reason they won't go away is that the underlying question is not "Do men and women manage differently?" but "What is the most effective way to manage?"

To the degree that women are seen as symbols of a transition from the more traditional control-focused leadership model to one, whatever its label, where power is used differently, resistance should be expected from those comfortable and committed to the old model. Men who are corporate officers and who make the decisions about promoting women into their ranks are probably more likely to have some affinity for this traditional model compared with their juniors and are less likely to have experience with a more participative model.

Whatever barriers women encounter on their way to the top executive ranks, they can be sure that because there are so few women at the top, their climb will—for the time being, at least—be lonelier and lonelier the higher they climb. And they will arrive as top executives—and just as much pioneers.

NOTES

1. J. Fierman, "Why Women Still Don't Hit the Top," *Fortune*, 1990, pp. 40–62.

2. U.S. Department of Labor, *A Report on the Glass Ceiling Initiative* (Washington, DC: U.S. Department of Labor, 1991).

3. L. Baum, "Corporate Women," *Business Week*, June 22, 1987, pp. 72–88; Heidrick and Struggles, *The Corporate Woman Officer* (New York: Heidrick and Struggles, 1986); Korn Ferry International, *Korn Ferry International's Profile of Women Senior Executives* (New York: Korn Ferry International, 1982); A. M. Morrison, R. P. White, E. Van Velsorn, and the Center for Creative Leadership, *Breaking the Glass Ceiling* (Reading, MA: Addison-Wesley, 1987).

4. A. M. Morrison, R. P. White, E. Van Velsorn, and the Center for Creative Leadership, *Breaking the Glass Ceiling* (Reading, MA: Addison-Wesley, 1987).

5. Baila Zeitz and Lorraine Dusky, *The Best Companies for Women* (New York: Simon and Schuster, 1988).

6. Robert Levering, M. Moskowitz, and M. Karz, *The Best Companies to Work for in America* (Reading, MA: Addison-Wesley, 1989).

7. J. B. Rosener, "Ways Women Lead," *Harvard Business Review,* Nov.–Dec. 1990, pp. 119–25.

8. I. K. Broverman, D. M. Broverman, F. E. Clarkson, P. Rosenkrantz, and S. R. Vogel, "Sex Role Stereotypes and Clinical Judgments of Mental Health," *Journal of Consulting and Clinical Psychology* 34 (1970), pp. 1–7.

9. A. M. Morrison, R. P. White, E. Van Velsorn, and the Center for Creative Leadership, *Breaking the Glass Ceiling* (Reading, MA: Addison-Wesley, 1987).

10. A. M. Morrison, R. P. White, E. Van Velsorn, and the Center for Creative Leadership, *Breaking the Glass Ceiling* (Reading, MA: Addison-Wesley, 1987).

11. A. H. Eagly and B. T. Johnson, "Gender and Leadership Style: A Meta-Analysis," *Psychological Bulletin* 108, no. 2 (1990), pp. 233–56.

12. T. De Angelis, "Men's Interaction Style Can Be Tough on Women," *APA Monitor*, Nov. 1989, p. 12.

13. J. B. Rosener, "Ways Women Lead," *Harvard Business Review*, Nov.-Dec. 1990, pp. 119–25.

14. Sally Helgesen, *The Female Advantage: Women's Ways of Leadership* (Garden City, NY: Doubleday, 1990).

15. A. M. Morrison, R. P. White, E. Van Velsorn, and the Center for Creative Leadership, *Breaking the Glass Ceiling* (Reading, MA: Addison-Wesley, 1987).

16. A. H. Eagly and B. T. Johnson, *op. cit.,* pp.

17. Bernard M. Bass, *Stogdill's Handbook of Leadership: A Survey of Theory and Research*, rev. ed. (New York: Free Press, 1981).

18. Veronica F. Nieva and Barbara A. Gutek, *Women and Work: A Psychological Perspective* (New York: Praeger, 1981).

19. K. M. Bartol and D. C. Martin, "Women and Men in Task Groups," in *The Social Psychology of Female-Male Relations: A Critical Analysis of Central Concepts*, eds. Richard D. Ashmore and Frances K. Del Boca (Academic Press, 1985), pp. 259–310.

20. Alice G. Sargent, *The Androgynous Manager* (New York: AMACOM, 1981).

21. Marilyn Loden, *Feminine Leadership, or How to Succeed in Business Without Being One of the Boys* (Times Books, 1985).

22. S. L. Bem, "The Measurement of Psychological Androgyny," *Journal of Consulting and Clinical Psychology* 42, no. 2 (1974), pp. 155–62.

23. K. Lewin, R. Lippett, and R. White, "Patterns of Aggressive Behavior in Experimentally Creative Social Climates," *Journal of Social Psychology* 10 (1939), pp. 271–99.

24. R. E. Walton, "From Control to Commitment: Transforming Work Management in the United States," in *The Uneasy Alliance: Managing the Productivity-Technology Dilemma*, eds. Kim B. Clark, R. H. Hayes, and C. Lorenz (Boston: Harvard Business School Press, 1985).

25. Marilyn Loden, *Feminine Leadership, or How to Succeed in Business Without Being One of the Boys* Times Books, (1985).

26. David L. Bradford and Allan R. Cohen, *Managing for Excellence: The Guide to Developing High Performance in Contemporary Organizations* (New York: Wiley, 1988).

27. Allan R. Cohen and David L. Bradford, *Influence Without Authority* (New York: Wiley, 1980).

28. J. B. Rosener, D. J. McAllister, and G. K. Stephens, "Leadership Study: International Women's Forum," unpublished ms., University of California—Irvine, Graduate School of Management, 1990.

SOURCES

A. B. Fisher, "Where Women Are Succeeding," *Fortune,* Aug. 3, 1987, pp. 78–86.

L. R. Gallese, "Corporate Women on the Move," *Business Month,* April 1989, pp. 31–56.

M. Hennig, "Career Development for Women Executives," PhD dissertation, Harvard University, 1970.

H. W. Hidebrandt, "Learning from Top Women Executives: Their Perceptions on Business Communications; Careers; and Education," unpublished ms., University of Michigan, School of Business, 1984.

Kane, Parsons and Associates, *A Survey of Women Officers of America's Largest Corporation: Reporting of Findings* (New York: Kane, Parsons and Associates, 1982.

Korn Ferry International, *Korn Ferry International's Executive Profile: Change in Corporate Leadership* Korn Ferry International, 1982).

Chapter Twenty-Eight

Judith C. Hoy

Women in Organizations
The Struggle for Equity Continues

Judith C. Hoy

Judith C. Hoy, EdD, consults to executives on managing change in both not-for-profit and profit organizations: Bell Labs, Coopers and Lybrand, IBM, New England Telephone, NYNEX Science and Technology, Pfizer, TRW, Winston and Strawn (law firm), and Union Carbide. Her doctoral work at Columbia University Teachers College focused on how executive women learn. She currently is adjunct professor in the Business School of the University of Connecticut.

W hite women have moved into the labor force steadily and in increasing numbers over the past 15 years, and most current management literature and practice related to "women's issues" has evolved from the Anglo-American perspective. These issues include salary inequities, questions about equal pay, and the small number of women in executive suites. Although many of the issues and problems raised may be similar to those faced by women of color, the research cited usually does not distinguish between white women and women of color. In an excellent article detailing the differences between Anglo, African American, and Hispanic women managers, Betters-Reed and Moore identified this problem as the "whitewash dilemma."[1] The research cited in this article focuses on issues faced by Anglo women and uses *women* to refer to Anglo women and *men* to refer to Anglo men. However, the three-pronged approach to assuring that women will be able to contribute fully to organizational success is designed to apply to all women—white women and women of color alike.

WOMEN AND MEN AS MANAGERS

Research done on differences between men and women managers leads to one very clear point: In terms of managerial skills, there is little difference between men and women.

Two studies focused specifically on the differences between men and women managers. Donnell and Hall found no significant differences between the men and women in their study. Women managers performed as effectively as men did on a wide range of managerial behaviors.[2] Schmidt and Posner, in examining managerial *values,* found women to be more career-oriented than their male counterparts. Further, they found that women view relationships with other managers, employees, co-workers, and bosses as more important than do their male colleagues. They conclude that even with those differences, the profiles of men and women managers are strikingly similar.[3] Other studies comparing men and women in such skills as leadership show little difference between women and men in skill level.[4]

UNDERSTANDING SUBTLE DIFFERENCES

Although examining managerial and leadership skills yields little in identifying differences between men and women, there are subtle differences in how Anglo women and men reason that are important in examining women's behavior in organizations. Two important contributions to understanding women's approaches to relationships that have implications for women at work are the writing of Carol Gilligan in *In a Different Voice* and research done by Mary F. Belenky, Blythe M. Clinchy, Nancy R. Goldberger, and Jill M. Tarule described in *Women's Ways of Knowing.*

Gilligan found that women placed importance on relationships, not on rules or absolutes.[5] She showed that women value not hurting others and that they wrestle with the dilemma of being true to themselves when doing so may hurt others. One can easily see how these values relate to the processes of organizational life. Women would be concerned about the relationships of their subordinates to one another, about the myriad relationships inside and outside of the organization.

In *Women's Ways of Knowing,* Belenky and her colleagues describe a framework that characterizes how women learn.[6] Theirs is a model of the various ways in which women receive, question, digest, and use information and knowledge. These are key skills for survival in any organization, where both women and men, in order to be successful, must learn about their work, about the culture of the organization, and about themselves and their own skills.

Two of the ways of knowing are especially characteristic of women in organizations. The first is described by the writers as "the official voice of the academy." It is the method of analysis; it is impersonal and authoritative. It is the voice of the manager saying, "It won't work," "Prove it to me," "Show me," "What if . . . and then what if?" The second way is looking for what is right, finding where there is agreement. It's an active use of intellectual empathy, where one imagines oneself in the other person's position, sees her or his world view. It starts with an appreciation, an attachment to the other's view. Here, the manager says, "Let me see if I understand you," "I see what you mean," "Let me understand how you think about this and how you came to do it this way." Belenky and her colleagues believe that women have a proclivity for this kind of knowing, that women would rather think *with* someone than *against* someone.

A common theme throughout these studies is the importance of collaboration and collegiality in women's interactions. Contrast this with the not uncommon view that competition is a key ingredient in managerial success. Loden, in *Feminine Leadership*, describes masculinism in corporations as a valuing of competitive behavior, assertiveness or aggressive behavior, analytic or strategic thinking, maintaining control, exercising objectivity, and adopting an unemotional attitude.[7] Looking again at Gilligan's research, we find that women perceive danger in achievement and competitive success because of the threat such success poses on relationships.[8] Therefore, aggression must be contained; otherwise, it could lead to the destruction of the relationship and isolation.

HOW WOMEN MANAGERS ARE PERCEIVED

Many of the studies documenting differences between women and men managers came from research focused on women in nontraditional careers in the late 1970s and the 1980s. These studies are important in that they identify what attitudes toward women were and remind us that changes as far-reaching as role changes take time. *The Harvard Business Review* published a study in 1965 that examined attitudes toward women in business. It was replicated in 1985 with dramatic results.[9] Respondents expressing an unfavorable attitude toward women as managers dropped from 41 percent in 1965 to 5 percent in 1985.

In 1965, half of the men and women surveyed agreed that women rarely want or expect positions of authority. In 1985, less than 10 percent of the respondents held that view. Additionally, 60 percent of women and 54 percent of men didn't believe that men are more competitive than women. When asked to respond to the statement "Almost everyone dislikes a competitive female," both men and women expressed agreement in 1965. However, in 1985 only 17 percent of men and 31 percent of the women agreed. Although these changes in attitude signal change, all of the evidence suggests that behavior has yet to catch up to the described attitudinal changes.

WHAT DO WOMEN WANT? WHAT MUST ORGANIZATIONS DO?

Given that within the next decade women and African Americans, Asians, and Hispanics will outnumber Anglo men, organizations that plan to become or remain competitive have little choice but to address the following issues. First, women experience discrimination in not being able to get the kinds of jobs they are capable of doing. Second, they report discrimination, including sexual harassment, in interpersonal relationships once they get the jobs. Third, they are kept from peak performance by a variety of subtle—sometimes obvious—messages from organization cultures and systems about how they should behave.

Getting the Job

First, women have difficulty getting the kinds of jobs they may aspire to. Gary Powell describes the difficulties of personnel officers and managers in hiring.[10] Recruiters who are responsible for screening many applicants for jobs often receive only minimal information about candidates (usually a one-page résumé). With such scant information, they are more likely to fall back on gender stereotypes in evaluating the candidates. Not only gender stereotypes, but stereotypes about age, race, ethnic group, religion, and geographical region of origin are likely to influence decisions as well.

Powell cites a study that examined how candidates are evaluated. Men were more positively evaluated for what are considered male-intensive jobs (such as engineer, physician, security guard), and women were seen more positively when evaluated for female-intensive jobs (such as nurse, sales person, or secretary).[11] He notes, "This effect has particular relevance for hiring for managerial positions. The job of manager at any level has been male-intensive until recently (and in many organizations still is), and the job of manager at upper levels is highly male-intensive ... In fact, most studies of hiring for managerial jobs have found a preference for male applicants."[12]

Other problems in fair hiring occur because of recruiter characteristics, such as degree of authoritarianism. Highly authoritarian employers prefer male applicants. And when it comes to appearance, attractive men are preferred over unattractive men, and unattractive women are preferred over attractive women for managerial positions.[13]

Appropriate Interpersonal Behavior

The second way in which women face discrimination involves behavior from men (and occasionally from women in positions of power). Women are told, directly and indirectly, that their job is to assimilate into the white male culture. These messages come in casual comments about what is appropriate office attire (usually a tailored suit, never a flowered silk dress) or about how to behave at meetings. Women are coached to walk a fine line between aggressiveness and assertiveness, expected to speak the organization's language, and expected to ignore inappropriate sexual innuendo and advances.

Many women describe situations in which conversation among their male colleagues is dominated by sports. Kanter described the phenomenon as a way men subtly exclude women, noting that if the woman is able to join in the conversation about sports, men will increase the level of detail needed to keep up with the conversation, perhaps moving from a general discussion of the current status of teams to the history of the team, trades made in the past decade, and other intricacies that exclude all but the most knowledgeable.[14]

Sexual harassment ranges from the obvious "Your promotion [or continued employment] depends on your having sex with me," to more subtle references about appearance or, as in the case of the fire fighters in Los Angeles, pornographic pictures of women hanging in lockers. If these behaviors are acceptable in the organization, women receive a clear message about what and who is important. In addition to deterring effective individual job performance, such behaviors isolate and decrease the likelihood of teamwork. One can hardly work on a team with people one cannot trust. Disparaging comments about women, ignoring women's comments at meetings, and raising one's voice to talk over women's comments are all part of the fabric of harassment. And, to add insult to injury, women are offered assertiveness courses so that they can learn to overcome the limits of their "less assertive" behavior. Rather, men could be taught to respond positively and respectfully to differences in styles rather than expecting conformity.

Changes in Organization Culture and Systems

Lastly, many organizational systems, regardless of their training programs in valuing differences or attempts to hire x number of women, do not encourage women's full participation. While removing pornographic pictures is an obvious statement that women will not be overtly considered sex objects, more-subtle cues hint at the "proper" role for women. For example, one of the leading high-tech companies recently instituted a family leave policy for families with new babies. The policy is for women only. Men cannot apply. Message: The proper person to give child care is the woman. Women are not offered the same opportunities for job assignments, often because "women don't want to leave their families." Message: Husbands should never give up their jobs or change locations because of their wives' employment opportunities. Men's work is more important.

CHANGES TO CREATE EQUITY

Three actions are critical for organizations that want women and others who are not white men to become full partners. R. Roosevelt Thomas has described three approaches organizations typically take: *affirmative action, valuing differences,* and *managing diversity.*[15] Although only managing diversity offers the organization long-term change that welcomes all members who are not Anglo men, each of the other two has advantages if used in conjunction with the broader approach to change.

Affirmative Action

First, organizations must adopt an affirmative-action approach. Simply put, women must be hired into significant positions in significant numbers. There is no question that qualified women are available. The question is whether the organization will take the time to find them. Executives and managers must be rewarded for their efforts and their success both in finding talented women to fill positions and in promoting them as opportunities occur. Young women MBA students frequently discuss the importance of having female role models. Women need each other to strengthen what they bring to the workplace that is different from what men bring, whether that is in decision making or in developing interpersonal relationships.

Valuing Differences

Second, organizations must teach people what behavior is acceptable and what is unacceptable in a workplace that values and honors differences. Workshops, training programs, and discussions about ways in which women and men differ and are the same, what language is appropriate, and what behaviors are appropriate should be offered. The orientation must be toward honoring differences rather than implying the need for assimilation. The challenge is in the creation of new ways of working together. Anglo men are concerned about how to treat women now that they are more aware of the possibilities of sexual harassment charges. As one young manager pointed out, "The accusation is the conviction as far as management is concerned." The awkwardness felt over trying to arrange dinner meetings between men and women doing business and the struggle over who should open the door or carry the sample case are examples of issues women and men can discuss and, in so doing, learn from each other.

Managing Diversity

Third, beginning a process of culture change that honors diversity is the only strategy for long-term success. In fact, the previously described strategies are doomed to failure if they are the only ones used. Examining how decisions are made, how systems operate, and who is rewarded for what kind of behavior and scrutinizing the numbers of women in management positions are part of understanding what the organizational system is doing to discourage or encourage the full participation of women at all levels. If there are no women in the boardroom, it must be found out why. It is surely not for lack of qualifications. The group of Anglo men seated there must ask themselves why and commit themselves to finding the answer—likewise for every system that favors or is not used by or discourages one gender over another. Are norms for hours of work impossible if one has a child in day care? Can fathers *and* mothers leave early for appointments with doctors or teachers? Complete understanding of the system is required in order that the changes can be made with full participation of those whom the system affects and currently disenfranchises.

FINAL THOUGHTS

There can be little disagreement over the many changes our society and its organizations have experienced in the last 20 years. Many still look to the notion of assimilation—the melting pot—as the appropriate metaphor for how Americans should try to get along. But what is needed now as we re-create ourselves and our society and its organizations is a new model, one yet to be named. Some think of it as a salad bowl, where ingredients keep their unique flavor and shape. Others will suggest different ways to describe how we can value differences and work together.

Whatever the new metaphor is, it will emerge from the work of women and men in organizations looking for the best ways to use their talents and creativity. Finding such a theory begins with an acceptance of the current reality. The population of organizations is changing. We need all the help we can get to improve our economy and productivity. To misuse resources is foolish. We need the bright, capable, creative, motivated members of our society—all of them.

Organizational change that begins by looking at the parts of the organizational system and their impact on women, helping employees learn about diversity and develop respect for differences, and ensuring that the numbers of women match the intent to use human resources wisely is a way to make our organizations more effective. These are the things we must do. We have no choice.

NOTES

1. B. L. Betters-Reed and L. L. Moore, "Managing Diversity: Focusing on Women and the Whitewash Dilemma," in *Womanpower: Managing in Times of Demographic Turbulence,* Uma Sekaran and Frederick T. L. Leong, eds. (Newbury Park, CA: Sage Publications, 1992).

2. S. M. Donnell and J. Hall, "Men and Women Managers: A Significant Case of No Significant Differences," *Organizational Dynamics* 8, no. 4 (Spring 1980), pp. 60–77.

3. W. H. Schmidt and B. Z. Posner, "Managerial Values in Perspective," American Management Association Survey Report (American Management Association, 1983).

4. H. S. Astin and C. Leland, *Women of Influence, Women of Vision* (San Francisco: Jossey-Bass, 1991).

5. Carol Gilligan, *In a Different Voice: Psychological Theory and Women's Development* (Cambridge: Harvard University Press, 1982).

6. Mary F. Belenky, B. M. Clinchy, N. R. Goldberger, and J. M. Tarule, *Women's Ways of Knowing: The Development of Self, Voice, and Mind* (New York: Basic Books, 1986).

7. Marilyn Loden, *Feminine Leadership, or How to Succeed in Business Without Being One of the Boys* (New York: Times Books, 1985).

8. Carol Gilligan, *op. cit.*

9. "Executive Women—20 Years Later," *Harvard Business Review* 63, no. 5 (September-October 1985), 42–60.

10. Gary Powell, Women and Men in Management (Newbury Park, CA: Sage Publications, 1991).

11. *Ibid.*, p. 92.
12. *Ibid.*
13. *Ibid.*, p. 93.
14. Rosabeth M. Kanter, *Men and Women of the Corporation* (New York: Basic Books, 1977).
15. R. Roosevelt Thomas, *Beyond Race and Gender* (New York: AMACOM, 1991).

SOURCES

E. A. Ashburn, "Motivation, Personality and Work-Related Characteristics of Women in Male-Dominated Professions" Ruth Strang Award Monograph Series, no. 2 (Washington, DC: National Association for Women Deans, Administrators, and Counselors, 1977).

B. R. Crump and H. M. Handley, "Factors in Self Concept Discriminating Between Women in Traditional and Non-Traditional Areas in Business," *Journal of Vocational Education* 8, no. 1 (Winter 1983), pp. 1–19.

L. R. Gomez-Mejia, "Sex Differences During Occupational Socialization," *Academy of Management Journal* 26, no. 3 (1983), pp. 492–9.

M. Hennig and A. Jardim, *The Managerial Woman* (New York: Doubleday, 1976).

J. A. Hochschartner, "A Comparative Study of Father–Daughter Relationships in a Group of Non-Traditionally and Traditionally Professionally Employed Young Adult Women," PhD dissertation, Boston University, 1984.

L. Kohlberg and C. Gilligan, "The Adolescent as Philosopher: The Discovery of Self in a Post-Conventional World," *Daedalus* 100 (1971), 1051–1056.

J. P. Lemkau, "Personality and Background Characteristics of Women in Male Dominated Occupations: A Review," *Psychology of Women Quarterly* 4, no. 2 (1979), pp. 221–39.

H. H. Solomons and A. Cramer, "When the Differences Don't Make a Difference: Women and Men as Colleagues," *Management Education and Development* 16, no. 2 (1985), pp. 155–68.

Chapter Twenty-Nine

Elizabeth Hostetler

Leadership
The Silencing of the Feminine

Elizabeth Hostetler

■

Elizabeth Hostetler, PhD, director of organizational development at American University, has over 10 years' experience helping leaders and teams develop, move through change, and explore how power, dependency, and diversity influence the flow of work. She has a background in psychology and counseling and writes about leadership and other human processes.

In the realm of leadership, we have long applauded masculine characteristics. We have asked leaders to be strong and assertive, to take charge and protect us. But have we depended, in silence, on the essential feminine characteristics? Have we unconsciously participated in a conspiracy of silence?

This is an exploration of leadership styles in the context of sex-role socialization. It is built on the work of Bem,[1] Singer,[2] Sargent,[3] Loden,[4] Strandberg,[5] Korabik and Ayman,[6] Powell[7] and others; and much of this article is based on dissertation research and unpublished work by Hostetler.[8] This study provides a quantitative measure of what some have known intuitively for a long time: how the beliefs that leaders hold about what it means to be a woman or a man influence their work.

In this article, *feminine* and *masculine* do not refer to the characteristics of females and males, but rather to the inner qualities or characteristics that all humans possess and are capable of developing. The term *feminine* refers to characteristics that have traditionally been considered by American society as the ideal for females; *masculine,* the ideal for males.

The results of my original research will show the relationship between leadership styles and sex roles. Then, additional research will be used to examine the silencing of the feminine characteristics in leadership. The conditions that make this possible—sexism, adaptation, and stereotyping—will be explored. The article ends by providing strategies that leaders, both men and women, can use to move from silence into recognition of the feminine within themselves and others—to move from fragmented to whole leaders.

SITUATIONAL LEADERSHIP STYLES

The situational leadership model suggests that individuals are effective when they attend to both task and relationship, depending on the readiness and needs of the follower. Leadership effectiveness is driven by the requirements of the situation, rather than based on a static set of traits or static set of behaviors that leaders carry out.[9] Task and relationship behaviors are the key elements used by leaders in this model to influence followers. The styles that emerge are: high direction/low support (Style 1), high direction/high support (Style 2), low direction/high support (Style 3), and low direction/low support (Style 4).[10] A match between leader style and follower readiness on a given task is what determines leader effectiveness.

SEX ROLES

The masculine ideal has traditionally been defined as autonomous, directive, logical, action oriented, and attending to task; the feminine ideal, as communal, supportive, expressive, receptive, and attending to relationship.[11] Before 1974, sex roles were generally considered to be dichotomous: femininity and masculinity were considered polar opposites. To have a high degree of one meant, by definition, to have a low degree of the other.[12] Those who scored midway between the two were in an ambiguous position. The midpoint seemed to suggest sex role ambivalence, deviance, or maladjustment.[13]

In 1974, Sandra L. Bem published the Bem Sex-Role Inventory (BSRI), the first to measure masculinity and femininity as independent dimensions. She believed that they were not mutually exclusive, that individuals could assess themselves as high on both masculinity or femininity or low on both, as well as differentiating between the two. Bem's work transformed the measurement of sex roles and opened the door for the exploration of a new concept called androgyny.[14] Androgyny is the presence within one individual of characteristics that are considered to be more culturally desirable for males as well as characteristics considered to be more culturally desirable for females.[15]

THE RELATIONSHIP BETWEEN LEADERSHIP STYLES AND SEX ROLES

Research was conducted to determine the relationship between sex roles and leadership styles in a sample of 135 leaders in business organizations.[16] It was based on the work of Sargent,[17] who wrote *The Androgynous Manager*, and Strandberg.[18] The Bem Sex-Role Inventory was used by managers to categorize themselves into sex roles, and the Leader Behavior Analysis II Other (LBAII Other), by Blanchard, Zigarmi, Forsyth, and Hamilton, was used to measure subordinates' perceptions of their leaders' styles. While much of the previous research in the field used leaders' self-reports of effectiveness and other measures, this study used subordinate ratings to gain a more objective picture.

It was hypothesized that there would be a significant relationship between styles and sex roles and that specific sex roles would be related to specific styles:

- High direction/low support would be related to masculinity
- High direction/high support would be related to androgyny.
- Low direction/high support would be related to femininity.
- Low direction/low support would be related to undifferentiated.

The results showed that a significant relationship exists between leadership style and sex roles in specific cases. Leaders, male or female, who categorized themselves as masculine on the BSRI were seen as using a high direction style on the situational leadership model significantly more often than others ($p < .01$), and feminine leaders, male or female, were seen as using this style significantly less often than others ($p < .05$), as predicted. In addition, androgynous leaders were seen as using a high direction/high support leadership style more often than others; and a low direction/low support style less often than others, in findings that approached, but did not reach, significance.

These findings do not, of course, show causation; one cannot conclude that beliefs about sex roles influence leader style or vice versa. One can conclude that a relationship exists between them in specific cases.[19]

THE SILENCING OF THE FEMININE

Research conducted in the 1970s using the Bem Sex-Role Inventory consistently found that the "good manager" was perceived to be masculine. In the late 1980s and early 1990s, another flurry of research was generated to learn what, if any, changes in perceptions had taken place as a result of the passage of time and changes in sex roles.[20,21,22] Surprisingly, these studies found that overall, little had changed.[23]

"If 'good managers' are masculine, what are 'bad managers'?" This is the question Powell and Butterfield asked nearly 1,400 management students from two universities in the Northeast.[24] They learned that these students viewed the bad manager as one "low in both masculinity and femininity, or in nonstereotypical terms."[25] "Good managers were not described as androgynous (they were masculine, as before), but bad managers were viewed as the opposite of androgynous."[26]

The absence of the feminine characteristics was considered to be bad management, yet the feminine was not identified as important to good management. Its importance was apparently assumed but not voiced. This is a profound omission.

IMPLICATIONS FOR LEADERS

If effective leadership means choosing the right style for the demands of the situation and specific leadership styles are related to beliefs about sex roles, then expanding limiting beliefs about sex roles may improve leadership effectiveness. Moving beyond the grip of the limitations of prescribed sex roles may allow leaders to discover internal resources they have not yet acknowledged or tapped. This could enhance their ability to lead.

SILENCE IN THE ORGANIZATION

The feminine characteristics of both female and male leaders are silenced when intuition and connection work are devalued or ignored. It happens when resources of time and money are allocated to task production, but the resources necessary to building a team are not allocated. When someone is rewarded for taking charge by playing the expert role more than she or he is rewarded for listening with deep receptivity, the feminine is silenced. If acts of separation, or "cutting our losses," are acknowledged more frequently than demonstrations of continued support, the feminine is silenced. According to Glennon, when there is sole reliance on quantitative over qualitative analysis—crunching numbers of things that can be counted (linear thinking) versus recognizing things that cannot (nonlinear perception)—the feminine is silenced.[27]

HOW THE FEMININE IS SILENCED

Sexism is a powerful and deadly force silencing the expression of the feminine in management. It is the pattern of discriminating against people, especially women, on the basis of gender. Sexism, an outgrowth of patriarchal society, has profoundly molded the culture of the American workplace. Adaptation and stereotyping are two of the forms that it takes.

Adaptation to male norms has been a critical coping mechanism for women managers. "From the late sixties on, adaptation has been a major requirement of women in nontraditional careers, including management."[28] Since the passage of the Civil Rights Act in 1964, which opened the doors to women by making employment discrimination illegal, women have had no viable alternative but to conform, Loden suggests. Many women learned the traditionally masculine style of decision making and communicating so that they could fit in. Men, too, adapted to a male stereotype that limited the expression of the feminine within themselves.

Stereotyping—a willingness to assume that an individual feels, thinks, or acts like other members of the group to which they belong—is another powerful force that limits the expression of the feminine in management circles. Institutionalized sexism results in stereotyping of both women and men; it is often assumed that each will play out the roles that have been traditionally assigned to them. Although the definition of appropriate behavior for the sexes has changed over time, one thing has remained constant: The prescribed roles have been distinct for each gender.[29]

THE COST OF SILENCE

The failure to recognize the feminine within themselves is costly to both women and men and to the organization. Women leaders, in particular, have been put in a double bind: They are socialized to cultivate the feminine characteristics to a greater degree than other possibilities, and then they are devalued for expressing them at work. It is clear that the contributions of women leaders, more than those of men, have been devalued or completely ignored. The cost of this is impossible to estimate, but it is clear that the cost is too high.

MOVING FROM SILENCE TO VOICE

The feminine characteristics of leaders, male and female, must be acknowledged, nurtured, and respected. Giving voice to the feminine will require that the organizational culture change.

The first step is to acknowledge and confront sexist practices, from subtle microinequities to blatant offenses. Sexism is the glue that holds the limiting beliefs of the current culture together. Sexist practices must be eradicated.

The second step is for leaders to examine their beliefs about sex roles and experiment with expanding the options they have chosen. In spite of training to behave according to the rules that were written for them, many leaders, both women and men, are taking courageous risks to find a way, as Carl Rogers put it, to be more fully who they really are.[30] These efforts must be supported and rewarded. Organizational culture will begin to value the feminine only when leaders begin to value it in themselves.

Women in leadership roles may find that they want to reclaim the feminine qualities they have known at a deep level but blocked from expression. They have been trained by society to express the feminine, yet as leaders they have been taught to adapt to and express masculine characteristics. The opportunity for women now is to set aside the external directives about how they should be and seek what is natural and real for them. Adaptation should no longer be the first job requirement for women.

Men may find that use of the masculine ideal of power, based on either/or, right/wrong logic, has prevented them from getting what they really want. In their search for alternatives, they may find that they have limited access to their inner resources. Their task is to nurture the development of the feminine within themselves.

Accordingly, the path to becoming whole leaders is to integrate the masculine and feminine within. Each gender has been defined in part by the absence of characteristics of the other. To become whole again, new definitions of gender are needed.[31]

STRATEGIES TO DEVELOP AND HONOR THE FEMININE

The following are strategies that leaders, both women and men, can use to develop and honor the feminine as leaders.

Be Still

We have been trained to have a bias for action. Constant action is a trap, with quick payoff and long-term bankruptcy. Being still is the first step to receptivity, where real creativity begins. If silence is new for you, tolerate the discomfort it creates.

Focus on the Whole

Everything is connected. We can ignore this, and we have, but the costs are killing us. Focus first on yourself as a whole being, and move out from there.

Come into Balance

Listen to both the feminine and masculine voices within. The feminine has been ignored. You will need to nurture it if it is to be heard. It is essential to wholeness. The masculine may want to take over. Give it permission to rest.

Become a Learner

Learning is all there is. When everything is in flux, the notion of mastery or control is an illusion. Nurture the attitude that there is no right or wrong and that play and experimentation are appropriate responses to life.

Join with Others

Those who are different from you are not competitors; they are another part of the whole that you share with them. Together, you can create what is needed.

Ask for Help

You are no more fully human than when you are vulnerable. As leaders, that is not what you were taught to be, but it is what you are.

Discover Rather than Decide

Sit in a circle with others and take the time to discover the truth about the situations. You may be able to avoid making an unnecessary compromise if you take time to discover the truth.

Move Incrementally, Unless It's Time to Leap

Some kinds of learning need time for experimentation before understanding can develop. A gentle, playful pace is called for. Other kinds of learning, like the shift to a new paradigm, can happen only if you leap.

Tell the Story

It is the only way to move from silence to voice.

PARTNERSHIPS WITHIN AND BETWEEN

This work is about tapping the internal resources all leaders have available to them and that all leaders need. Allowing the masculine and feminine to work in partnership within, to come into balance, creates the necessary conditions for partnerships between people.

NOTES

1. S. L. Bem, "The Measurement of Psychological Androgyny," *Journal of Consulting and Clinical Psychology* 42, no. 2 (1974), pp. 155–62.

2. June Singer, *Androgyny: Toward a New Theory of Sexuality*, 2nd ed. (Garden City, NY: Anchor Books, 1977).

3. Alice G. Sargent, *The Androgynous Manager: Blending Male and Female Management Styles for Today's Organization* (New York: American Management Association, 1983).

4. Marilyn Loden, *Feminine Leadership, or How to Succeed in Business Without Being One of the Boys* (New York: Times Books, 1985).

5. K. A. Strandberg, "The Relationship of Psychological Androgyny to Leader Style Adaptability, Style Range, Openness, and Effectiveness," PhD dissertation, U.S. International University, 1986.

6. K. Korabik and R. Ayman, "Should Women Managers Have to Act Like Men?" *Journal of Management Development* (England) 8, no. 6 (1989), pp. 23–32.

7. Gary N. Powell, *Women and Men in Management: The Dynamic of Interaction* (Newbury Park, CA: Sage Publications, 1988).

8. Elizabeth Hostetler, "A Study of the Relationship Between Sex-Role and Leadership Effectiveness, Flexibility and Style in Selected Managers in Business Organizations," PhD dissertation, American University, 1993.

9. Paul Hersey and Kenneth H. Blanchard, *Management of Organizational Behavior: Utilizing Human Resources*, 5th ed. (Englewood Cliffs, NJ: Prentice-Hall, 1988).

10. Drea Zigarmi, C. Edeburn, and Kenneth H. Blanchard, *Research on the LBAII: A Validity and Reliability Study* (Escondido, CA: Blanchard Training and Development, 1991), p. 2.

11. S. L. Bem, *op. cit.*

12. A. Constantinople, "Masculinity-Femininity: An Exception to a Famous Dictum?" *Psychological Bulletin* 80, no. 5 (1973), pp. 389–407.

13. J. I. Berzins, M. A. Welling, and R. E. Wetter, "A New Measure of Psychological Androgyny Based on the Personality Research Form, *Journal of Consulting and Clinical Psychology* 46, no. 1 (1978), pp. 126–38.

14. S. L. Bem, *op. cit.*

15. S. L. Bem, *Bem Sex-Role Inventory Professional Manual* (Palo Alto, CA: Consulting Psychologists Press, 1981).

16. Elizabeth Hostetler, *op. cit.*

17. Alice G. Sargent, 1983, *op. cit.*

18. K. A. Strandberg, *op. cit.*

19. Elizabeth Hostetler, *op. cit.*

20. Gary N. Powell and D. A. Butterfield, "Sex, Attributions, and Leadership: A Brief Review," *Psychological Reports* 51 (1982), pp. 1171–4; and "The 'Good Manager': Did Androgyny Fare Better in the 1980's?" *Group and Organization Studies* 14, no. 2 (1989), pp. 216–33.

21. V. E. Schein, "The Relationship Between Sex Role Stereotypes and Requisite Management Characteristics, *Journal of Applied Psychology* 57, no. 2 (1973), pp. 95–100.

22. V. E. Schein, R. Mueller, and C. Jacobson, "The Relationship Between Sex Role Stereotypes and Requisite Management Characteristics Among College Students," *Sex Roles* 20, no. 1–2 (1989), pp. 103–10.

23. M. E. Heilman, C. J. Block, R. R. Martell, and M. C. Simon, "Has Anything Changed? Current Characterizations of Men, Women, and Managers," *Journal of Applied Psychology* 74, no. 6 (1989), pp. 935–42.

24. Gary N. Powell and D. A. Butterfield, "If 'Good Managers' Are Masculine, What Are 'Bad Managers'?" *Sex Roles* 10 (1984), pp. 477–84.

25. *Ibid.*, p. 477.

26. *Ibid.*, p. 482.

27. L. M. Glennon, "Synthesism: A Case of Feminist Methodology," in *Beyond Method: Strategies for Social Research*, 7th ed., ed. Gareth Morgan (Newbury Park, CA: Sage Publications, 1990), pp. 260–71.

28. Marilyn Loden, *op. cit.*

29. S. L. Bem, 1981; Marilyn Loden, 1985; Alice G. Sargent, 1983.

30. Carl R. Rogers, *On Becoming a Person* (Boston: Houghton Mifflin, 1961).

31. Carol S. Pearson, *Awakening the Heros Within: Twelve Archetypes to Help Us Find Ourselves and Transform Our World* (San Francisco: Harper and Row, 1991).

SOURCES

Mary F. Belenky, B. M. Clinchy, N. R. Goldberger, and J. M. Tarule, *Women's Ways of Knowing: The Development of Self, Voice, and Mind* (New York: Basic Books, 1986).

Kenneth H. Blanchard and Alice G. Sargent, "The One Minute Manager Is an Androgynous Manager," *Training and Development Journal* 3 (1984), pp. 83–5.

Jean S. Bolen, *Goddesses in Everywoman: A New Psychology of Women* (New York: Harper and Row, 1984).

A. H. Eagly and B. T. Johnson, "Gender and Leadership Style: A Meta-Analysis," *Psychological Bulletin* 108, no. 2 (1990), pp. 233–56.

Riane Eisler, *The Chalice and the Blade: Our History, Our Future* (San Francisco: Harper and Row, 1987).

Riane Eisler, "Women, Men and Management: Redesigning Our Future," *Futures* (England) 23 (1991), pp. 3–18.

Riane Eisler and David Loye, *The Partnership Way: New Tools for Living* (San Francisco: Harper and Row, 1990).

C. F. Epstein, "Ways Men and Women Lead," *Harvard Business Review* 69, no. 1 (1991), pp. 150–1.

Carol Gilligan, *In a Different Voice: Psychological Theory and Women's Development* (Cambridge: Harvard University Press, 1982).

Elizabeth Dodson Gray, *Patriarchy as a Conceptual Trap* (Wellesley, MA: Roundtable, 1982).

G. P. Haddon, "The Personal and Cultural Emergence of Yang-Femininity," in *To Be a Woman*, ed. Connie Zweig (Los Angeles: Jeremy P. Tarcher, 1990), pp. 245–57.

John Heider, *The Tao of Leadership* (Atlanta: Humanics New Age, 1985).

Sally Helgesen, *The Female Advantage: Women's Ways of Leadership* (New York: Doubleday, 1990).

Ruthellen Josselson, *The Space Between Us: Exploring the Dimensions of Human Relationships* (San Francisco: Jossey-Bass, 1992).

J. V. Jordan, A. G. Kaplan, J. B. Miller, R. P. Stiver, and J. L. Surrey, *Women's Growth in Connection* (New York: Guilford Press, 1991).

Rosabeth M. Kanter, *Men and Women of the Corporation* (New York: Basic Books, 1977).

K. Korabik, "Androgyny and Leadership Style," *Journal of Business Ethics* 9 (1990), pp. 283–92.

Marilyn Loden and Judy Rosener, *Workforce America! Managing Employee Diversity as a Vital Resource* (Homewood, IL: Business One Irwin, 1991).

S. Nelton, "Men, Women and Leadership," *Nation's Business*, May 1991, pp. 2–8.

Harrison Owen, *Leadership Is* (Potomac, MD: Abbott Publishing, 1990).

Carol S. Pearson, *The Hero Within: Six Archetypes We Live By*, 2nd ed. (San Francisco: Harper and Row, 1989).

Judy Rosener, "Ways Women Lead," *Harvard Business Review* 68, no. 6 (1990), pp. 119–25.

Alice G. Sargent, *Beyond Sex Roles* (St. Paul: West Publishing, 1977).

M. Segal, *The Personality Theory and Human Resource Development Contributions of Sigmund Freud, Carl Jung, and Carl Rogers* (Annapolis: BDR Learning Products, 1983).

M. Ray and A. Rinzler, eds., *The New Paradigm in Business* (New York: Jeremy P. Tarcher/Perigee, 1993).

R. Tannenbaum and W. H. Schmidt, "How to Choose a Leadership Pattern," in *Classics of Organizational Behavior*, ed. Walter E. Natemeyer (Oak Park, IL: Moore Publishing, 1978), pp. 188–97.

Chapter Thirty

Thomas Kochman

Black and White Cultural Styles in Pluralistic Perspective

Thomas Kochman

■

Thomas Kochman, Ph.D., is professor emeritus of communication at the University of Illinois at Chicago and president of Kochman Communication Consultants, Ltd. He is the author of Black and White Styles in Conflict *and editor of* Rappin' and Stylin' Out: Communication in Urban Black America. *Mr. Kochman is internationally recognized as an expert in African American and Anglo cross-cultural communication.*

American society is changing from a structurally pluralistic society to a culturally pluralistic one. In structural pluralism, the socially subordinate culture, person, or group unilaterally accommodates itself to the dominant cultural group (currently the Anglo-American male) on the latter's terms. This pattern of accommodation has long constituted American policy regarding the integration of immigrants, indigenous peoples, and other minorities.

Equity within structural pluralism is seen as treating everyone the same. This serves both the social interest of cultural assimilation to Anglo-American male norms—to benefit equally from the same treatment, one has to become like the person for whom that treatment was designed—and the social interest of economy and efficiency. Those in power need only choose the one "best" way, and individuals are then held responsible for adapting themselves as well as they can to that same "best" treatment.

Equity within cultural pluralism moves from treating everyone the same—an equality of input (comparable to giving every flower in a garden the same amount of sunshine, fertilizer, and water, which guarantees that only certain flowers will fully grow)—to an equality of effect. This allows variable treatments so long as they are or can be demonstrated to be equivalent.

In cultural pluralism, the Golden Rule of "Do unto others as you would have done unto you" (which assumes that others want for themselves what you want for yourself) needs to be refashioned to "Do unto others as they would want done unto them."

Cultural pluralism, more than structural pluralism, provides both the organization and the larger society with a richer cultural mix from which to draw and a greater flexibility to adapt to changing circumstances.

DIFFERENCES IN BEING AND DOING

Traditionally, mainstream white Americans (especially men) are taught to see themselves as individuals rather than as members of a group. Yet when they become members of an organization or team, they frequently must subordinate themselves to the group's hierarchy and role requirements. In the areas of organized work and play, the mainstream white American cultural style is serious, methodical, and systematic. The more distinctive aspects of mainstream white American male individuality (self and identity) are more often realized in isolation, outside the context of a work group.

Black cultural style in work and play evolves out of a conception that sees change as a constant aspect of cosmic and social order. The cultural style blacks have developed to serve "going through changes" is improvisation, an adapting behavior, an attempt to master one's environment with a resourceful and fluid attitude. Black individuality emphasizes unique character and style, more-personalized and idiosyncratic expressions as opposed to the more routine, uniform, and impersonal forms characteristic within mainstream white organizational culture.

CONFLICT AND CONFLUENCE

Individuality and Functionality

The white mainstream functional rule of work and play, governed by the principles of economy and efficiency, promotes the uniform, impersonal, minimalist, and instrumental (role-oriented) style. The functional rule for blacks is "so long as the moves that are made do not interfere with getting the job done, they should be allowed." These cultural rules clash in the workplace and in the playground with great regularity.[1]

In white mainstream organizational culture, stylistic self-expression, when it occurs at all, tends to be a function of rank. In black culture, however, stylistic self-expression is an individual entitlement. Consequently, one does not have to be the president of the company to drive an expensive top-of-the-line car or wear fashionable clothes. White mainstream organizations interpret such individual stylistic self-expression as a presumption, a laying of claim to greater rank or title.

Role and Function of Competition

In organized work and play within white mainstream culture, competition provides a climate and context to determine who can dominate whom. Within black culture, however, competition has a twofold purpose: to determine who is dominant and to allow opponents to show off their skills in the process. The black goal, therefore, is divided between winning and showboating.

Whites bring work-related values into organized competitive play, making play resemble work, while blacks bring competitive, play-related values into organized work, making work resemble play. The result is that blacks are sometimes regarded by whites as not sufficiently serious or interested in getting the job done.

CONCENTRATION

For white mainstreamers, *concentration* means undivided attention—focusing upon one thing. For blacks, it means divided attention: attending to task accomplishment while simultaneously concentrating on doing it with flair or expressive style. This injecting of "play" values into the workplace may ultimately revitalize and be an important contribution to mainstream American organized work and play culture.

EXPENDITURE OF ENERGY

The white mainstream concept of "hustle" describes a work or play pattern of energy expenditure often greater than is actually needed. The black approach is based on a principle of conservation of energy: to expend only as much energy as it takes to accomplish the task effectively.

To whites, the conservation-of-energy principle often communicates lack of dedication. This is so even when blacks actually accomplish the same amount of work with their "energy-efficient" method that white workers accomplish through hustling.[2]

STYLES OF DISCOURSE

Truth-Creating Processes

For blacks, the appropriate truth-creating process is "sincere argument" (as opposed to quarreling, which blacks also do). For mainstream whites, discussion rather than argument is the ideal.

Black argument as a cultural style is confrontational, personal, advocatory, and issue-oriented. White discussion style is nonconfrontational, impersonal, representational, and peace- or process-oriented—the latter expressed by such concepts as "compromise" and "agreeing to disagree." In the context of truth seeking, contentiousness is unifying for blacks, polarizing for whites.

Another way of characterizing black and white attitudes toward contentiousness is that blacks put truth before peace, whereas whites put peace before truth. In the mainstream American political arena, to be peace-oriented ultimately means to accommodate established political arrangements before which truth is sacrificed in the form of compromise. The black orientation in the political arena is, as with interpersonal disagreements and disputes, to put truth before peace, which is to say, to keep the truth intact and politicize on its behalf.

Reason and Emotion, Truth and Belief

Mainstream American culture believes that truth is objective, which is to say, external to the self; consequently, it is something to be discovered rather than possessed. This assumption has led mainstream Americans to view themselves instrumentally as objective truth seekers, using rational means to produce a rational result.

This has led them to see emotion and belief as contaminants that undermine the objective stance that defines and regulates rational (scientific) engagement and inquiry. People consider themselves and others rational to the extent that they are *not* emotional. Therefore, people socialized to value rational self-presentations are often, in reality, socialized to value unemotional self-presentations.

Strongly held beliefs have also come to be seen as polarizing and therefore counter to the kind of interactional cooperation individuals need for the truth-seeking process to work. For this reason, personnel forms test for mental "rigidity" or its converse, "flexibility," by rating individuals on whether they are "respectful and accepting of others," insofar as they adapt their thinking "to allow for other persons' points of view." Individuals who are less able to adapt their thinking to allow for other points of view are presumably rated less respectful of others.[3]

Some Functions of Neutrality

Neutrality has taken on a new social character. It now works to serve mainstream American social and political interests. For example, neutrality as a generalized public posture easily translates into indifference, thereby enabling mainstream Americans to serve their own goals and interests.

Neutrality also does not compel ownership of a point of view. I call it involvement without commitment (that is, conviction). Thus, individuals can engage in "discussion," but not in "sincere argument," without having a point of view or predisposition to an outcome.

Students, for instance, are given credit on exams and papers for representing the "authoritative" points of view of others, but not for cultivating or developing their own view of things, even when such an explicit formulation might be very helpful and relevant. Later on, when individuals are asked to become team players in organizations, they are also asked to represent the "official" point of view.

In generating indifference and disassociation from one's original roots and loyalties, neutrality also facilitates a greater acceptance of authority.[4] It allows individuals to sacrifice truth in the interest of truce (peace), to regard compromise as the morally sanctioned solution to ideological or political conflict, and to rationalize the accommodation to established political interests as simply being "realistic."[5]

The goal of black presentations is not rationality but consciousness. Truth is not separated from belief, but rather it is expressed in terms of belief and processed (in truth seeking) through the crucible of argument.

Evaluations of Behavioral Meanings

Blacks have also characterized the white discussion style as "devious," perhaps a more severe indictment even than "insincere." This characterization stems from whites frequently not owning the positions they represent nor seeing such ownership as a requirement when engaging in disagreement or debate. From the black standpoint, however, only those views that an individual takes ownership of are admissible when engaging in disagreement or debate.

Finally, the black characterization of white presentation style here as devious derives from its similarity to the pattern of self-presentation blacks adopt when they are "lying," as one black woman put it. This is the style blacks adopt when "they do not care enough about the person or issue to want to waste the energy on it" or when it is too dangerous to say what they believe.

Emotional *self-control* in white mainstream culture is characterized and practiced as suppression of feelings or inhibition. Consequently, when emotions are "out," they are perceived by whites as "out of control." For blacks, self-control is characterized and practiced by "being cool." Being cool does not mean realizing a state of emotional self-denial or restrained emotional expression, but rather being in control of one's emotional heat and intensity (whether laughter, joy, or anger).

The white view of black emotional behavior as "threatening" also stems from blacks and whites having different conceptions of what constitutes a threat. A threat for whites begins when someone says he or she is going to do something. A threat for blacks begins when a person actually *makes a move* to do something. Verbal threats, from the black standpoint, are still "only talk."

COGNITIVE CONSTRUCTS AND PERFORMANCE ASSESSMENTS

Work and play contexts often provide the behavioral "data" from which various official assessments of individual performance are made, whether done informally by supervisors in the workplace or teachers in the classroom or more formally by interviewers in interview or counseling situations.[6]

Black and white raters are equally likely to bring their cultural perspectives with them when they assess worker performance. Objective or impartial performance evaluations are possible only to the extent that raters are successful in factoring out their personal biases. But this depends upon raters' self-awareness and their ability to control their biases.

If raters became aware that culture plays a role in their assessments, they would be hard-pressed to discover the exact nature of that influence. This is because cultural learning itself becomes internalized at the subconscious level, giving it an essentially implicit character.

Compounding matters is the way individuals habitually view behavior, which is not to respond to behavior, per se, but to *what that behavior means.* And the meaning that individuals assign to such behavior comes from their own culture.

The solution to these problems is for observers and raters to have other cultural perspectives than just their own to draw upon. This would enable them to identify the distinctive parameters and character of their own culture—the distinctiveness of one's own culture really becomes apparent only when seen through the perspective of another culture.

It may be necessary to acknowledge the difficulty of this effort and even the improbability that raters will be able to free themselves entirely from personal bias. Perhaps the only reasonable approach is to recognize that while objectivity is something to strive for, individuals might be capable only of understanding (1) the range of subjective factors that are likely to have a bearing on the assessment process, (2) the depth of their commitment to a particular point of view, and (3) their limitations in either factoring out their personal biases or properly assessing their cultures' influence on the performance assessments they make.

Overall, a presumption that raters have not been able to free themselves from personal bias may be the best approach to equity and fairness in performance assessments. Whether the goal is objectivity or honesty about the nature and extent of personal bias, one thing is clear: Raters will have to factor in their biases before they can begin to factor them out. To take their personal biases into account, they must first identify their biases and become aware of their potentially contaminating effects.

NOTES

1. Thomas Kochman, *Black and White Styles in Conflict* (Chicago: University of Chicago Press, 1981).

2. *Ibid*

3. Note that being "objective" is equated here with being open to other people's viewpoints *regardless of how those other viewpoints were arrived at*. The effect of only one individual being "open minded" and/or "neutrally objective" does not necessarily promote objective truth. It may simply weaken the self by allowing for a unilateral *adaptation to another person's* "closed-minded," nonnegotiable assertions.

4. Chester I. Barnhard, *The Functions of the Executive* (Cambridge, MA: Harvard University Press, 1954).

5. Thomas Kochman, "Crosscultural Communication," *Florida FL Reporter* 9 (1971), 53–54.

6. Frederick Erickson and Jeffrey Shultz, *The Counselor as Gatekeeper* (New York: Academic Press, 1982).

VISIONS OF OUR ORGANIZATIONAL POTENTIAL

VISIONS OF OUR ORGANIZATIONAL POTENTIAL

As advocates for social change, we may be very clear about what things need changing in our organizations and in ourselves. But we can never successfully eliminate discrimination and oppression until we can describe the new behaviors, norms, and values with which we want to replace them.

Organizations are even more bound by their experiences than are individuals. Few are willing to experiment with untested systems and modes of operation, no matter how many problems there are with the status quo.

We need to be able to describe in realistic detail what it will be like to live in a world that doesn't punish those who are different, unfamiliar, or less fortunate. We need models for organizations that tap the added value of differences and give all their stakeholders the means to contribute.

Here are eight views of the *other* side of change.

Chapter Thirty-One

Walking Toward Our Talk*

Judith H. Katz

■

Judith H. Katz

Judith H. Katz, EdD, has focused her 20-year career in organizational development on linking strategic initiatives with diversity efforts. Her book, White Awareness: Handbook for Anti-Racism Training *(1978) was one of the first works to address racism from a white perspective. A respected educator, consultant and writer, she is also the author of* No Fairy Godmothers, No Magic Wands: The Healing Process After Rape *(1984) and numerous articles on diversity, oppression, and empowerment. She is a vice president of The Kaleel Jamison Consulting Group, Inc. and a coeditor of this book.*

U nless we can imagine a world without oppression, we can't create one. Not a Pollyanna world of milk, honey, and overflowing human kindness, but a dirt-and-asphalt, nuts-and-bolts world where real people sweat to earn a living and feed their families.

It can't be a fantasy world. It has to deal with real information and real issues so that real people can find commonality and increased benefit by maximizing the contributions that come from their diversity. It has to be a world that *works*.

Most of us are in favor of eradicating oppression. But many of us doubt that it is possible and have only a hazy idea of what might replace it. We may be in favor of equal opportunity, but we don't see our own privileges of race, gender, and/or class as part of what keeps opportunity *un*equal.

We may suspect that there's something wrong with traditional structures of power and privilege based on one-up and one-down relationships (dominant-subordinate), but we can't imagine alternatives. We're stuck in a conceptual trap. The traditional structures are the only ones we know, and we can't imagine anything different. A

---

*This essay is an excerpt from Katz's forthcoming book, tentatively titled *Learnings From the Journey.*

ranked hierarchy and force-fit factory uniformity are what seem to work. Classism, racism, and sexism seem to have been endemic throughout recorded history. Unless we can imagine something new, even those of us who have studied history will be condemned to repeat it.

That's our challenge then: To imagine the unimaginable. To believe that a world (or a nation, a community, a family or a business) without oppression is possible. To envision what it would look like and feel like. To imagine how it can work.

We have to start by imagining a positive, not a negative. Not the absence of oppression but the presence of appreciation. Not the absence of exclusion and exploitation but the presence of inclusion and contribution. Not what we might lose, but what we might gain. We need to know where we want to go, not just what we want to leave behind. We must see the advantage of the journey. We have to envision not just something that works, but something that works *better.*

We have to see a multicultural, diverse, inclusive world not as an unattainable ideal but as a practical solution that serves *everyone's* interests. Unless we have a clear vision of how our self-interest is best served by change, we will stick with what we know, with what we're comfortable with, with what has "always worked"—even if it means that "a few" unfortunate people have to continue suffering. (Whether their misfortune is probably their own doing is another story.)

It's easy to say we need a new model to replace the old oppressive, hierarchical model of power and privilege. And it's easy to describe the model: one in which differences are recognized as value-added instead of problematic, where people cooperate instead of compete, where power is derived from and shared by the many instead of held closely by the few.

But saying isn't doing. More than a new conceptual model, what we really need is a new *working* model. Many of them, in fact. As many as possible.

In my 20 years of working to eliminate oppression and create inclusive organizations, it has become clear to me that to be successful, any change effort must be grounded in creating better options, not simply those that are more politically correct. An organization cannot be bullied into sustainable change. Such change occurs only if it serves the overall self-interest of the system. Shown that inclusive values and practices can lead to higher performance, organizations won't have to be bullied into embracing them.

How to begin? One step at a time. A few small groups or teams equipped with the skills to tap the added value of diversity can serve as role models for an entire organization. They can help show what's possible and thereby help others imagine it. And by showing what's possible now, they can help themselves and others imagine what might be possible with a little more work, a little more resources, a little more knowledge, a little more time.

That's how to create a working model not just for inclusion but for continuous improvement. By imagining how things *could be* and taking the first steps to get there. And with each step, imagining a little further and walking a little bit closer to the vision. It's a continuous process of talking bigger than you are and walking toward your talk; of imagining the unimaginable and constantly working toward that image; of reformulating your goals as you go along, always keeping them just beyond your grasp. This requires a willingness to experiment, take risks, make mistakes, look foolish, and remain open to learning. It's not a pass-fail test but an ongoing journey of discovery and renewal.

I believe we can achieve a world without oppression. We can get there by walking toward our talk. But before we can even begin the journey, we must escape the conceptual trap of oppression's inevitability. We have to imagine a model that actually works. We have to dream it to do it, and we have to create it together.

Chapter Thirty-Two

A Look Back, Twenty Years From Now

Marvin R. Weisbord

■

Marvin R. Weisbord

Marvin R. Weisbord is author of Diagnosing Your Organization *(1978) and* Productive Workplaces *(1987) and coauthor/editor of* Discovering Common Ground *(1992). He was a manager and consultant for more than 30 years. He is a partner in Block Petrella Weisbord, a firm that consults to self-managed organizations, and Blue Sky Productions, a video documenter of innovative workplaces. In 1992, he started Search-Net, a nonprofit, grass-roots, self-help program to support people serving their own communities.*

L ooking back from the year 2014, here is one view from my corner of our global village. Our town is still stuck, I must report, with folks who have an incredible capacity for stereotypes, prejudices, and misconceptions. We are still prone to create oppressive workplaces and polarized communities. To some of us, this comes as naturally as breathing. Others consider our tendency to put each other down, literally and figuratively, as a form of pollution—to our own spirit. But a lot of us are learning to watch ourselves. So there's less of this stuff going around than in 1994.

The big difference between now and 20 years ago is that fewer of us treat *our* better selves as normal and *other* people's worst selves as a toxic-waste cleanup project. Instead, more of us are learning to accept our own natures—good, bad, wise, foolish, tolerant, narrow-minded, rational, and nutty—as a reality to be acknowledged. We respect, even cooperate with, people we have stereotyped or people we disagree with. Instead of trying to change each other, we are more intent on changing those conditions of a world we have made that suit none of us.

More corporations and communities are bringing folks together across vast gulfs of ethnicity, sex, race, status, and hierarchy to listen to each other, pool information, and do business they can't do alone.

More people meet regularly to improve their own workplaces and neighborhoods. Back in 1994, they spent more time trying to control each other while technology controlled them. Now they are sharing economic information that will help everybody take responsibility. As a consequence, they get along better with each other.

My learning laboratory is still a 48-hour "future-search conference." For 30 years now (it *is* 2014, remember), I have seen strangers, even adversaries, reach consensus on their preferred futures on issues many folks considered hopeless, intractable, or unthinkable. I have seen them own up to their denials, tone down their mutual stereotypes, take responsibility for their world. They are saving jobs, improving schools, sharing scarce resources like water and land, getting together on day care, creating better work and affordable housing, and a hundred other action steps, large and small, that make our lives better. They do it by listening to one another and owning up to what is *actually* going on and what they *really want*. They have agreed not to "work" their problems and conflicts, but only to discover what common ground exists among them. (You can't chew gum and whistle, and it's hard to find common ground when fighting.)

In 2014, many organizations regularly bring folks together across all the lines, especially power, status, and hierarchy, to plan on common ground. That is the radical act: deciding that everybody with a stake ought to be there. Doing this task together—for this department, neighborhood, corporation, school, hospital, hotel, summer camp, cruise ship, shopping center, court, church, or political party—we transform our thinking *and* our relationships in "real time." The important thing is that those of us with a stake do the planning *ourselves*, instead of abdicating to bosses, experts, politicians, or consultants.

And what is this (future) work? It is not about reconciling our differences. It is about *listening* to our differences without having to do anything about them. As a result, we are implementing policies, programs, systems, and structures considered unthinkable in 1994.

We have built on the 1940s and 1950s consensus experiments of the social psychologist Solomon Asch and translated by Fred Emery into procedures that "work."[1] Until the 1990s, this knowledge had little impact on bureaucracies caught up in fantasies that science-based technologies (including the behavioral kind) blessed all who embraced them.

In 2014 we have made three major discoveries:

Discovery 1 is that we all live on the same planet, subject to the same laws of nature. My "facts" and your "facts"—whether actually true or false—are inescapably *our* facts. Whether we like it or not does not change *this* fact.

Discovery 2 is that when we face the chaos of our world together, instead of denying it, running away from it, or fighting over whose fault it is, "it" always becomes "us." We discover that psychologically we are pretty much alike. When we own up rather than avoid, deny, finger-point, problem-solve or breast-beat, we become more willing to act together.

Discovery 3 is that we are likely to share an extraordinary consensus with others in our organization, or neighborhood, or region on many features of the future we want, regardless of our differences and despite our polarities. We could never find this so long as we spent our time problem solving, conflict managing, or forcing our standards on others.

Now, because we meet often and acknowledge each other's stakes, we have fewer problems to solve than in the early 1990s. Back then, the "problem" of oppression in our society was out of control, along with economic decline and runaway technology. We were out of control because, fearful of losing control, we isolated ourselves and blamed the other guys. Now those of us who do joint planning *with* the other guys are coming to our senses. We are gaining more control. We learn that there are some conditions we *can* fix because other folks, however different from us, have the capacity to be with us when they can listen to *us* and feel heard. It is impossible to put a price on that kind of learning. So in 2014, the "bottom line," rather than just a number, now means a decision to do the right thing.

NOTE

1. See *Discovering Common Ground,* by Marvin R. Wiesbord, et al. (San Francisco: Berett-Koehler, 1992), if you want to learn more about Asch and Emery.

Chapter Thirty-Three

Jack McGrory

Discard the Melting Pot
Diversity Is Strength

Jack McGrory

■

Jack McGrory has worked for the City of San Diego since 1974. He has been city manager since 1991. Jack has managed the city's Recruitment and Selection Program and Equal Opportunity Program, as well as acted as the city's labor negotiator with employee organizations. Mr. McGrory served in the United States Marine Corps and earned a BA from Colgate University. He also earned a Master of Public Administration degree from San Diego State University and a law degree from the University of San Diego Law School.

A s we enter the next century, no social issues will dominate the American landscape more than the diversity of our culture, ethnicity, and race.

The United States is the most diverse country in the world and has become a mecca for people seeking to be part of a great democracy.

Historically, we have been proud of the multicultural euphemism we call the melting pot. But this image may have planted the seed of our multicultural discord. It implies that each new arriving culture will somehow give up its individual identity to be immersed in our transcendent North American culture. We have largely ignored the arrival of significant numbers of Asians, the inclusion of Native Americans and African Americans, and the continuing influx of Latino immigrants. Other groups have also emerged with a strong voice: citizens with disabilities, gays and lesbians, and older citizens, all with special needs.

The melting pot no longer gives us a vision to deal with the increasing multiculturalism of the United States. Instead, we need to identify a new paradigm that enables all of our cultures to be proud of and celebrate their uniqueness and maintain their traditions, history, and art, and yet, at the same time, share a common vision of our future.

Celebrating our diversity should be the norm. Allowing and encouraging each community to acknowledge, recognize, and en-courage celebration of its unique cultural identity is paramount.

This does not in any way diminish the history of this great country. Instead, it recognizes that the United States is the most diverse country in the world and that this diversity is a strength, a tremendous asset as the global village evolves in the next century and becomes increasingly interconnected.

We must now develop a vision that we all can share and participate in. This vision must be inclusion. This vision must involve a true partnership between communities, business, and education. This vision must be based fundamentally on valuing diversity and treating each other with dignity and respect. But most importantly, this vision must be based on the belief that diversity is a strength.

Chapter Thirty-Four

Evangelina Holvino

A Vision
The Agitated Organization

Evangelina Holvino

■

Evangelina Holvino, EdD, is an organization development trainer and consultant, working in Puerto Rico, the United States, Europe, Southeast Asia, West Africa, Latin America, and the Caribbean since 1975. Her work focuses on improving management systems and organizational interfaces with the environment using applied behavioral science technology.

M y vision of the future of diversity is not so much about increasing diversity in organizations so that we may make them more productive, or about effectively managing diversity so that we may meet the challenges of *Workforce 2000*, or of ameliorating oppression in organizations so that we might preserve the status quo. What I propose instead is that we use "managing diversity" as a form of analysis to destabilize and question what is taken for granted in organizational life. I would like us to use diversity work to push the limits of what can be said, what cannot be said, and what is not even thinkable because of our usual ways of thinking about what is and what is not possible in organizations. With this as a purpose, the constructs and social relations of race, gender, and class become the basis for questions. We must question our assumptions and taken-for-granted beliefs about organizations, change, and the subjects and objects of organizational knowledge and life.

Placing race, class, and gender at the center of our analyses helps us talk and think in new ways and produces a new critical discourse, one that is badly needed in the organizational sciences.[1] It encourages us, for example, to go beyond the traditional criteria of productivity and effectiveness that we use to "judge" organizational health and to consider other factors such as justice, social equality, and social responsibility as part of a new set of criteria for organizational "health."

I envision, then, diversity work as creating spaces from which a different kind of organizational theory-practice can take place. As a Latina feminist who believes that knowledge is power and organizational work a kind of practice, I find that the following ways of creating new spaces seem promising.

Reframe the problem of diversity in organizations by offering other ways of conceptualizing the issues of social differences in the workplace. The problem is not "the better management of human resources," a familiar discourse that privileges managers over the rest of us other organizational subjects, but about finding and understanding ways of producing equality and justice in organizations. Ask, for instance, who governs the organization? Who owns the organization and is entitled to its proceeds? And who has access to either of these?

This approach suggests a different managerial and consulting task, that of creating other visions of organizations and of thinking about and running organizations in radically different ways. For example, explore how other forms of organizing work, such as flextime, self-managed work teams, and hierarchies might lead to more equality in the workplace. Develop new organizational goals and criteria for organizational effectiveness, such as social diversity, shared power, and the maximization of community well-being. Apply knowledge and learning from other disciplines and perspectives to enrich our understanding and visions, such as feminist critiques of organizations, workplace-democracy principles, and Third World theories of change.

If we want to uphold values of democracy, participation, freedom, action, and learning, we need to reflect on how we are implicated in the discourses of power and domination of our time. Attending to diversity as a way of addressing differences, equality, and justice in organizations can help us uphold these values. In the space created between critique and action, between self-reflexivity and intervening, between understanding and changing, lies the possibility for changing the discourse and envisioning possibilities for organization change. This must be the focus for a new sort of organization: the constantly agitated one.

NOTE

1. M. Alvesson and H. Willmott, "On the Idea of Emancipation in Management and Organization Studies," *Academy of Management Review* 17 (1992), pp. 432–64.

Chapter Thirty-Five

America at the Crossroads

Elsie Y. Cross

■

Elsie Y. Cross

Elsie Y. Cross is a member of the NTL Institute and a former chair of the NTL board of directors. She holds a BS degree in business administration and master's degrees in business and in psychoeducational processes from Temple University. She is president of Elsie Y. Cross Associates, Inc. and is a coeditor of this book.

Elsie and her associates have pioneered an approach to the amelioration of racism and sexism that is unique in the field.

The road that will take us from the twentieth to the twenty-first century is moving toward a crossroads. One turning leads to great possibilities and a bright new future. The other bends back toward the past, a course defined by inequality, economic stagnation, and despair.

The road of return is the one most visible from our vantage point in 1994. While corporations and their consultants are learning valuable lessons about the amelioration of racism, sexism, and other forms of oppression, the country as a whole is moving steadily toward an apartheid based on both race and class. As a society, we obstinately refuse to see the work of women of all races as equal to the work of men.

Our economic system is riddled with structural inadequacies, and the political system that should be providing democratic solutions to the problems is itself stubbornly resistant to reform. Our environment continues to erode and our natural resources to decline. Our educational system reflects a profound refusal to truly educate all our children.

Much of the resistance to change is rooted in our national racism toward African Americans, native peoples, and other people of color. But it is also massively evident in our treatment of poor people of any race, whether in Appalachia, urban America, or suburbia. Even though we are jeopardizing the future of all children, we are forcing an ever increasing number of children to grow up in poverty and many millions of women to work two or three jobs but never to rise out of economic despair.

The business organizations that are taking the lead on issues of diversity in the 1990s will have little success unless they can see that their self-interest must also be linked to the overall health of the nation. Unless we make real progress in opening doors to all our people—in the corporate world and beyond—we will find that all of us are increasingly trapped in a prison of our own making.

But the road that returns to the past is not the only way. If we have the will, we can choose a route that leads to a brighter, fairer, and more productive future.

There are some signposts that are beginning to mark out this new direction. Corporations are shifting their thinking, slowly and often fitfully, from the old paradigms based on homogeneity and individualism to models based on heterogeneity and teamwork. Faced with the realities of changing demographics, leaders in both the public and private sectors are beginning to change the terms of the debates around racism and sexism. We are beginning to realize that we must not only tolerate one another's differences, we *need* the full contributions of all our people.

It is possible, then, to look down the second road and see a different scene. White people will have grown tired of the old arguments claiming racial superiority. Men will finally give up their attempts to dominate and subordinate women. We will all have worked together long enough and with sufficiently adequate leadership to have learned that merit and qualifications really are distributed throughout the human population and that it is in our self-interest to accept this fact.

When we have reached this point, it will be much easier to glimpse the way of the future. We will be able to understand that policies and practices create homelessness, despair, and antisocial behavior—and that policies and practices can be changed to eliminate them. We will understand that violent behavior results from deprivation and despair, rather than from race. We will understand that the concentration of economic, political, and social power in the hands of the few is contrary to both the ideals of democracy and to the health of the nation and the world.

If we can fulfill the promise of diversity, we will have made major strides toward fulfilling the promises of the American dream—for all our people.

Chapter Thirty-Six

Catherine S. Buntaine

Beyond Smiling Faces

Catherine S. Buntaine

■

Catherine S. Buntaine, vice president of The Kaleel Jamison Consulting Group, Inc., is a lecturer at American University and a member of the NTL Institute and the Organizational Development Network. Catherine holds a master's degree from the Yale University School of Organization and Management. Her current areas of research and interest involve cross-gender workplace partnerships, competencies of High Performing Inclusive^SM organizations and strategic management technologies.

O ur images of a productive, culturally diverse workplace begin with a myriad of smiling faces—faces of different ages, colors, genders, and cultures spread up and down and across the organization. These are the faces of a new generation of workers who find joy and value in their differences. They acknowledge, appreciate, support, and listen to one another. There is little strife or awkwardness. They are people who are equitably developed and rewarded.

In this "Workplace 2000," oppressive organizational practices have been identified and eliminated through systemic, cultural, and behavioral change. The opportunity to *succeed* is there for everyone.

Or is it? The challenge to creating a workplace of smiling and productive faces, each guaranteed the opportunity to succeed, goes beyond what we envision today. Unless we frame diversity as more than a human resources issue, we may miss the greatest opportunity and the greatest barrier that lie before us.

THE OPPORTUNITY: THE REAL BUSINESS CASE FOR DIVERSITY

Many organizations engaged in diversity efforts focus on "soft" programs, such as awareness training, mentoring, or other human resources initiatives. These initiatives are seen as helpful in promot-

219

ing behavioral change and thus facilitating greater inclusion of those who faced barriers in the past.

A different perspective might suggest that diversity efforts are comprised of so-called soft programs because those are the kinds of programs change agents manage. The vast majority of diversity consultants and their primary contacts within client organizations come from human resources and training backgrounds. And as the saying goes, when the only tools you have are hammers, all your problems look like nails.

Currently, the "business case" for diversity is used primarily as a sales tool: a way to convince an organization to commit to a diversity change-effort. Once the "sale" is made and the commitment is given, the business case disappears into the attaché case. Out come the awareness programs.

If diversity change-efforts were tied more fundamentally to an organization's strategic business plan, we might see a strikingly different scenario. Picture this: The diversity leaders are *business* leaders, and diversity is about *all* aspects of doing business, not just about managing people or delivering programs. When we address issues of diversity, the business case stays on the table, and we start with an assessment of the business needs of the organization. We identify how working with an inclusive viewpoint can benefit the organization in key areas:

- *Among the employees:* increasing worker retention, improving individual development, broadening and deepening worker skill levels, and forging a partnership for performance.

- *In the marketplace:* providing the organization with greater understanding and sensitivity toward an increasingly diverse world of customers, business partners, investors, and suppliers and stimulating development of products, technologies, and partnerships that respond to emerging possibilities.

- *In the community:* improving relations with the surrounding community and filling vacuums created by weakening public infrastructures to improve the business climate and living conditions for employees and other stakeholders.

- *In overall performance:* improving the organization's ability to cope with change, increasing its productivity and reaction time and expanding its creativity, problem-solving resources, and ability to transform itself.

Our business case for building a diverse and inclusive work culture prompts a whole new set of strategies and tools, among them:

- Creative product development and marketing ventures to respond to newly perceived competitive opportunities.

- Partnerships with students, parents, and retirees who become flexible workers (and, often, consumers) rather than recipients of public relations-oriented handouts.

- Joint ventures with other companies, government, religious groups, and community organizations to provide improved child care and health care services.

Inclusive and equitable employment practices are only a beginning to the business case. It takes an integrated and sustained effort comprised of *a range* of internal and external strategies and human resource initiatives—*all connected to strengthening business performance*—to demonstrate the full value of thinking and behaving inclusively.

THE HIDDEN CHALLENGE: CREATING MEANINGFUL WORK FOR ALL

The greatest opportunity offered by diversity involves viewing it as a way to do business, not just a way to manage people. When you focus on the business case, you learn to see and capture the business potential of diversity. But that still leaves the challenge of developing meaningful work—not just for those groups seeking inclusion, but also for those already there.

In today's turbulent competitive environment, few organizations have a clear strategic plan of any kind, much less for their diversity efforts. Strategies change rapidly. Missions and values are unclear. Employees, often performing outmoded roles and tasks, don't feel connected to the overall goals of their organization. They don't see how their jobs contribute to achieving security or success. They don't feel *included* because the fundamental nature of the organization's identity is in flux.

In this all-too-common scenario of organizational identity crisis, everyone is marginalized, and those with differences are marginalized the most (their jobs may *always* have lacked content). A prerequisite to any diversity effort *must* be the clarification of organizational identity and direction and the alignment of work with strategy. Then diversity can truly be harnessed in service of the organization's objectives and its members' inclusion.

By establishing your organization's identity, connecting its strategies and work, and building a business case for diversity, you can ensure that each member will have meaningful work—and, just as important, know why that work is meaningful.

Without these steps, *no one* can be fully included. But *with* them, everyone can enjoy the satisfaction and security of meaningful work. Now *that's* a vision worth working for.

Chapter Thirty-Seven

The New Challenge
For the Good of All

Guillermo Cuéllar

▪

Guillermo Cuéllar

Guillermo Cuéllar, EdD, has interest in the field of creativity and innovation and has contributed 15 years of consulting to profit and nonprofit organizations. He has developed and conducted training programs for organizations in the United States, Colombia, Puerto Rico, Iceland, and the former USSR, covering many areas, including multicultural development, managing diversity, and organization culture change. Cuéllar provides professional services in both English and Spanish.

We may think we have progressed a long way from slavery, but significant vestiges of that paradigm still operate in our economy. Cheap labor from a less-educated work force remains a fundamental way of creating wealth in this country. We maintain social inequality and use it to benefit the few. Leading economists say this will no longer work.

The Japanese and the Mondragon cooperatives in Spain are leaders in new paradigms of management. Managers are facilitators of cooperation and equality. The average pay ratio between CEOs and workers in Mondragon cooperatives is 3:1; in Japanese corporations it is 12:1. In contrast, in major U.S. corporations it is 400:1 or higher.

Communism is no longer an external threat to the United States, but the gross unequal distribution of wealth threatens our infrastructure, economic stability, and world-class competitiveness. Managers must learn to manage the real wealth: human creativity.

W. Edwards Deming, the American who taught the Japanese about quality, opened his lecture at the University of Massachusetts in 1992 by saying, "You cannot mismanage people and get away with it any more. You cannot misuse people's performance and expect to have positive results. The idea that people are resources for the company is a misconception based on objectifying people. Only from a materialistic, competitive perspective can we think such a thought. When managers deny their own humanity, spirituality, and creativity, they are mismanaging. People leave their jobs because they are looking for a place to express themselves and their creativity. But to mismanage the human potential, treating people as if they are not creative, hurts us all."

Dr. Deming and his theories of management are responsible for the revolution in the Japanese automotive, electronics, and metallurgic industries. His theories are now welcome in the United States after 40 years of skepticism from American industry.

Lester Thurow, dean of the Sloan School of Management at MIT, says, "In the USA we can no longer afford to leave our neighbor uneducated if we want to participate in the world economy as a powerful country." To be able to compete in the twenty-first century, employees must be able to understand and measure the impact of their contributions to the overall business profits. This new system of management of an educated work force can potentially eliminate the racist, elitist, and sexist biases of management toward its employees. According to Deming, these new management skills will give employees a sense of self-worth and pride.

What we are hearing are the fundamental changes of a new age: linking individual participation and self-worth to the benefit of the whole. What is interesting is that the new world economy and our own demographic changes are forcing the United States to address our divisive and materialistic tendencies to see individuals and groups as adversaries.

Business is on the cusp of a historical shift that will eventually bury the biased practices that have defined corporations since the beginning of the Industrial Revolution.

We are in one of those great historical periods when people don't understand the world anymore, when the past is not sufficient to explain the future. We are entering a "post-capitalist" era in which organizations have to innovate quickly and interact with a global consciousness. There is a massive transfer of authority, and it requires teamwork.

These themes represent an abrupt departure from past manufacturing practices, in which complex processes were broken down into tiny, easily understood, repetitive segments. The new thinking transforms workers from assembly line slaves into decision makers. In many respects, this change is similar to a return to tribal practices that require a down-to-earth relationship among all members and in which individuals proudly own their decisions and contributions.

Economic forces have changed radically in just 20 years, based on the fact that a better educated and more cooperative work force produces higher quality and cheaper products. Many Japanese companies have implemented this change, making them a leader in the world marketplace. Many product innovations come from line workers themselves, and a capable management system sustains and supports this relationship. Cooperation seems to be the way of the future. New products are manufactured at a lower cost, with higher quality, and with better pay and benefits for employees.

The changes in Japan are impressive, but a more radical departure from business-as-usual has been taking place during the past 40 years in the Mondragon cooperatives of Spain. This remarkable industrial and social experiment emerged after the Spanish Civil War in the Basque province in the northeast corner of Spain. Initiated by Padre José Maria Arizmendi, the experiment started with one industrial cooperative producing cooking stoves. The province has gone through the most exciting transformation ever dreamed of in the modern industrial world. Today, there are nearly 300 industrial cooperatives. They have a central bank that funds new cooperatives, along with a health care system that provides total care for all employees. In addition, cooperative housing and food cooperatives are a communal way of life. The Basque experiment is more profitable than the private enterprises in Spain.

In the United States we face major social, demographic, ecological, and economic change. The world is changing and confronting us with the needs for new paradigms that can transform the fundamental beliefs of slavery and create what some dream of deep in their hearts: productive work situations that bring creativity and pride to all.

The new experiment will combine the quality management system of Deming, the Mondragon cooperative structure and philosophy of the Basques, and the American dream of equality and freedom. The new paradigm implies transforming the fundamental driving beliefs that created slavery into creating ways that will benefit all, not just a few. As Padre José Maria Arizmendi would say, "This decision will be made for the good of all."

Chapter Thirty-Eight

Jane Magruder Watkins

The Future Is Now

Jane Magruder Watkins

■

Jane Magruder Watkins is a consultant with over 25 years of experience in organization development and training. She has special expertise in cross-cultural training, long-range and strategic planning, team building, and conflict resolution. She has worked with clients in the private, government, and nonprofit sectors. She is an adjunct faculty member at the American University. Watkins is chair of the board of directors of the NTL Institute for Applied Behavioral Sciences.

One day a year or so ago, I was walking back from dinner in Rome with a group of colleagues who had gathered to talk about development issues and partnership. My strolling companion was B. D. Amoa, a young Ghanian whom I had met in Kenya. "B. D.," I said, "does it ever strike you strange that a white woman from a small town in Mississippi, USA, and a native Ghanian who lives and works in Kenya are walking down a street in Rome in the company of Europeans, Africans, Asians, and Americans, all of whom call each other friend and colleague?"

It is already a multicultural world around us. It is already too late for those who cling to any illusion of "racial purity" and national identity. That may seem to be a brash statement, but it is not said here to shock or upset. It is a statement of fact. And what a splendid fact it is! Imagine a world where people work together across all the lines of race, gender, ethnicity, sexual orientation, and religion. Imagine a world that values difference as a major asset enabling every decision, every product to be the outcome of multiple points of view and intellects.

The evidence is everywhere that such a world is possible, not just at international conferences where the privileged gather, but at all levels of all societies around the world. I have worked in nearly 50 countries with multiple ethnic groups, and it has been a blessing and an education in reality beyond imagining. The images of cooperation and community far outnumber those of dissent and oppression. Yet it is the latter that scream at us from the press and dominate our belief system about how the world is. It is time to change our vision and to create a global community based on the best, most life-giving examples we can find.

There is a group of women in Kenya who call themselves KERA-WOP, the Kenya Rural Area Women's Project. There are 20 of them, and they represent nearly half of the 40 tribes that make up the population of Kenya. They work together across tribal lines, riding the notorious Matatus (rickety minibuses holding twice their maximum capacity) to help each other run leadership training workshops for rural women. And they do this as members of a church that divides along tribal lines.

Between Johannesburg and Soweto, there is a center that has been for 45 years a place of sanctuary and community for people from all the racial groups in that beautiful and troubled country. People gather there from all over the world to work and learn together. It is probably the only place in South Africa that, once a year, has a six-month course in community organizing attended by representatives of all four of the major rival political parties, including whites.

A Honduran woman, director of an economic development project for poor women in San Pedro Sula, sat on the board of a U.S.-based international development agency to assist in a project in Belize. She also sent Honduran trainers to work with a project in Mexico and another in San Antonio, Texas.

The North/South Dialogue conference in Senegal (the third in a series over a two-year span) transcended the hours of debate and the tension that divides North from South, rich from poor, by issuing a statement to affirm that what is needed is a community of people of good will who are committed to alleviating poverty and oppression wherever it exists.

In Darahamsala, nestled in the foothills of the Himalayas in northeast India, the streets look like a perpetual United Nations as people congregate to be near the Tibetan community and the Dalai Lama. This is only one of 30 areas that the Indian government, in an act of extreme generosity, gave to the Tibetans who fled to India in exile from the Chinese. It is here, where the image of peace is present in the air, that a vision of what could be emerges with great clarity.

The time has come for the reign of the cynic to end. Western society has confused cynicism with reality for far too long. While the popular paradigm focuses on wars and apartheid and street violence as if all of humankind is destined to live forever in oppressive and inhumane "reality," people the world over are saying *enough!* This is not to deny the evil that we create. It is, rather, an attempt to create a different, life-affirming, equitable, and compassionate global community.

Organizations can be the instruments and forgers of such a future. If we view organizations not as problems to be solved, but rather as solutions to be embraced,[1] the role is clear. My vision of the future sees organizations valuing diversity as a major asset. As holders of a positive vision, organizations will become creators and implementers for the social good, clearly understanding that diversity—the richness of multifaceted groups and people—is the creative force of the organization.

A decade ago, who could have imagined in the United States, a presidential cabinet like the one we have today? Not only is the world changing by the minute, but as George Land and Beth Jarman write in their book *Breakpoint and Beyond: Mastering the Future Today*, "The surprising fact is that change itself has changed . . . Modification of our thinking patterns will not work. This new era requires a radical rethinking of the most basic and foundational ways we view the world." In their introduction they note, "Today, across the planet, millions of people are creating a future different from the past . . . [I]ndividual efforts are moving us to a time when the world will truly work for everyone."

I believe that the issue is no longer how to "fix" organizations that allow or enable oppression and injustice; rather, it is to grow new, and renew, organizations on the foundation of valuing diversity. If we want to *have* a future, we can do nothing less!

NOTE

1. This concept is the basis of the Appreciative Inquiry approach to organization change created and tested by Dr. David Cooperrider and his colleagues at the Mandrell School of Management, Case Western Reserve University, Cleveland, Ohio.

VI

VOICES OF ACTION

VOICES OF ACTION

To confront oppression successfully, we must transform our beliefs and behavior and act on our determination to value everyone's contribution. In our organizations and communities, we must reject old ways, embrace change, thrive on differences, and constantly adapt to new challenges. But how? What follows is a chorus of voices describing actions we can take.

Chapter Thirty-Nine

Bailey Jackson

Rita Hardiman

Multicultural Organizational Development

Bailey Jackson and Rita Hardiman

■

*Rita Hardiman, EdD, and Bailey Jackson, EdD, are part-
ners and cofounders of New Perspectives, Inc., a consulting
and training firm specializing in multicultural organization development.*

*Bailey Jackson is a professor of education and the dean of
the School of Education at the University of Massachusetts.*

*Rita Hardiman has also served on the faculty of Antioch
New England Graduate School and as a visiting faculty
member at the School of Education, University of Massachusetts, Amherst.*

M ulticultural organization development (MCOD) is a phrase
coined by Jackson and Holvino, based on the original work of
Jackson and Hardiman. This model and its related conceptual frames
and techniques are the result of more than 30 years of collective work
by Jackson and Hardiman as social-justice change agents and organization development specialists. The theory and practice of MCOD are
guided by these key assumptions.

1. Oppression, manifested by racism, ethnocentrism, sexism, classism,
   heterosexism, ageism, ableism, and religious oppression are
   thoroughly institutionalized in public- and private-sector
   organizations in the United States. Oppression is not an
   organizational aberration; it is systemic and entrenched.

2. Oppression in an organization cannot be addressed effectively by
   focusing only on changing the *individuals* in that organization.
   Individual development (i.e., consciousness raising, awareness, and skill
   development) *is necessary but not sufficient to create meaningful change
   in an organization.*

3. Striving to create multicultural organizations, by definition, requires
   that organizations work on both eliminating social injustice and

recognizing and valuing social diversity. Focusing exclusively on one or the other will be ineffective. Trying to create a multicultural organization by adopting a value-the-differences approach without confronting injustice in the organization is akin to trying to cure cancer solely by adopting sound nutritional practices.

4. MCOD asserts that optimal functioning of organizations cannot be achieved without addressing issues of oppression and maximizing the benefits of diversity. Organization development, which was initially intended to attend to various forms of inequity in organizational settings, appears to have moved away from this agenda.

STAGES IN THE DEVELOPMENT OF MULTICULTURAL ORGANIZATIONS

Work with organizations in the 1970s and 1980s led to the development of a model describing the six developmental stages that organizations move through in their transformation from being monocultural to being multicultural. This model was influenced by Robert Terry, Mark Chesler, Judith Katz, and numerous other social-justice change agents. After identifying the stages of development from monocultural to multicultural, we began to formulate a method of working with organizations to help them determine their stage, identify goals, and make interventions to move to the next stage of development. This approach, called *multicultural organization development*, involves the following four components as part of an organizationwide, long-term change strategy (see Figure 39–1):

1. The creation of a *multicultural internal change team.*

2. A *support building phase,* to establish a level of readiness to pursue both individual change and development and organizational development.

3. A *leadership-development phase,* to engage the senior management in leading the change effort.

4. A self-renewing *multicultural systems-change process.*

The following sections describe these components in the recommended sequence. Realistically, however, the MCOD effort may "start in the middle" or wherever the client is and proceed backward and forward as organizational realities dictate.

THE MULTICULTURAL INTERNAL CHANGE TEAM

The multicultural internal change team (MCIT) is the group within the organization that guides the multicultural organizational change

FIGURE 39-1
Multicultural Organization Development

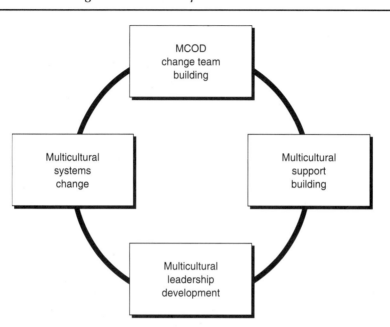

process. The team plays a vital role in the success or failure of an MCOD effort. This group truly "owns" responsibility for being a catalyst and leader of change. The change team becomes the change agent's internal contact with the organization. The change agents meld their experience and expertise with the team's to develop a plan for the organization. The MCIT is essential because its members have an understanding of the people, language, history, politics, and values of the organization and the ability to translate the consultant's concepts and approaches into terms that can be understood in their organization.

The MCIT should comprise people who meet as many of the following criteria as possible:

- Representation of diverse social groups (e.g., race, gender, age, disability, sexual orientation).
- Representation of different levels and roles in the organization.
- Willingness to participate and a personal commitment to principles of equity, fairness, and the value of diversity.
- Personal and professional competence in dealing with racism, sexism, and other forms of oppression in the organization.
- Respect from peers, subordinates, and superiors in the organization.

- Adequate time to participate in the team.
- Representation from both line and staff functions, with staff members in the minority. Ideally, people in the "lines of business" should outnumber those from the staff ranks.

Formation of the team takes time and is not always a straightforward process. Internal politics must be considered. It is not unusual for people to be on the team for political reasons, regardless of whether they meet the criteria.

Relationship of the Internal Team and External Consultants

Some organizations have an internal change team of some type in place—or at least the rudimentary beginnings of a group that could become a team. When this is not the case, building an MCIT is an early priority in the MCOD process. Once the team is formed, the MCOD models and process can be introduced.

Team development involves classic team-building techniques, as well as a focus on the diversity within the team and the team members' views about diversity, oppression, and creating organizational change. The goal is for the internal team and the external consultants to build a collaborative relationship. The first collaborative task is to assess the level of support for change that exists in the organization.

SUPPORT-BUILDING PHASE

The support-building phase of the MCOD process begins with an assessment of the level of awareness and concern for diversity that exists within the organization. This involves reviewing the history of the organization's efforts to respond to diversity issues: its history with EEO and affirmative action strategies, its history with training and awareness- or sensitivity-building activities, and its networks, support groups, or other groups organized by identity or class. At this point, the focus is on determining the level of support for and readiness to undertake interventions designed to move the organization along the path to being a truly multicultural organization. If the organization has had a history of efforts to comply with equal access statutes and increase awareness of diversity, it is clear that at some level there is attention being paid to diversity as an issue for this organization. Occasionally, organizations have little or no history of these types of support-building endeavors. Even more infrequently, an organization has not yet heard of the celebrated *Workforce 2000* report. Depending on the level of activity present at this point, it may be necessary to initiate activities at this phase to build awareness of diversity as an issue and build support for organizational change.

Many of the interventions are intended to raise the consciousness of individuals in the workplace about one or more social-justice and social-diversity agendas. Although these interventions do not affect the policies and practices of the organization, they are critical to the establishment of a climate and awareness level that will enable the organization to begin to change its systems, including its policies, norms, structures, personnel practices, and, perhaps, even its mission, values, products, or services.

We look for four indicators of organizational support in this phase (see Figure 39–2): (1) diversity in the personnel profile, (2) clear boundaries for determining appropriate behavior in the workplace and clear responses to inappropriate behavior, (3) sufficient educational opportunities for those interested in learning how to function well in a multicultural workplace, and (4) indications from the leadership that social justice and social diversity are a high priority and that the organization intends to "walk its talk."

LEADERSHIP-DEVELOPMENT PHASE

In the leadership development phase, it is important to help the senior management of the organization develop an understanding of

FIGURE 39–2
Support-Building Phase

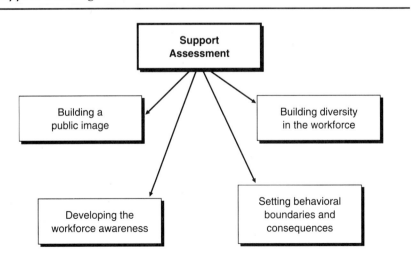

and commitment to MCOD necessary for success. The degree of impact of MCOD work correlates with the degree to which the leaders are involved and how knowledgeable and skilled they are in leading the organization through the multicultural change process.

The leadership development phase focuses on five objectives (see Figure 39–3):

1. *Developing a sense of team.* It is important that the leadership group, the top person and her or his direct reports, are in agreement on this agenda. It is inadequate if the top person champions the effort while others in the leadership group come along for the ride or drag their feet.

2. *Developing the leadership team's awareness.* Providing an opportunity for the leadership team to enhance its own awareness of and commitment to social justice and diversity issues will significantly enhance the overall effort.

3. *Developing a vision, mission, and/or values statement.* The leadership team must be intimately involved in developing a mission, vision, and values statement on diversity for its organization. Their creation of such a statement ensures top-level ownership.

4. *Developing a reward system that is congruent with the justice and diversity statement.* The leadership team rewards those who help the organization reach its goals and missions. If there is no reward system that serves the justice agenda, there will be no progress.

5. *Developing the leadership capacity to be role models.* In other words, help the leadership learn how to "walk its talk."

FIGURE 39–3
Leadership-Development Phase

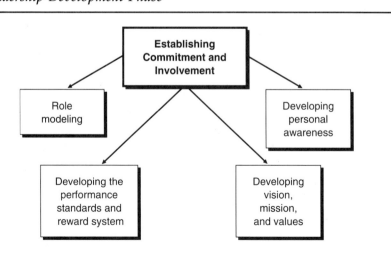

Having a leadership team that is even beginning to work toward these objectives sends a powerful message throughout the organization. As each of these objectives is accomplished and the support continues to strengthen through the ongoing activities of phase one, the climate is set for phase three, the MCOD systems change process.

MCOD SYSTEMS CHANGE PHASE

In the systems change phase of the MCOD process, individual units of the organization work on four steps to create changes that will bring that organization or subunit closer to its multicultural vision (see Figure 39–4). It is important to note that this phase is related to, and in some ways dependent upon, the first two phases. Without organizational readiness and support for interventions that will change the organization and without adequate leadership involvement and commitment, the systems change phase will have limited success—and may fail entirely.

As mentioned earlier, the multicultural internal change team has a particular role to play during this phase. Typically, the internal team has been shaped to guide all phases of the MCOD efforts and has oversight over all phases of the MCOD work. At this phase, however, depending on the size and complexity of the organization, several smaller change teams may be created within each organizational unit

FIGURE 39–4
Systems Change Phase

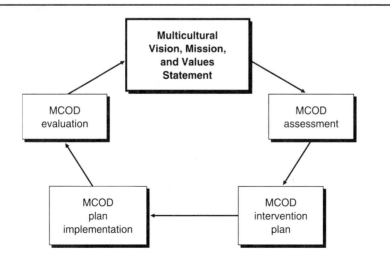

or division. These smaller teams usually report to the change team that has oversight for the whole organization. These smaller, or local, teams will have the responsibility for tackling the issues within their own units.

MCOD Assessment

The first of the four steps is the assessment of the unit. In concert with the team, the change agents devise a data-gathering strategy, using a variety of methods, including selected interviews, focus groups, paper-and-pencil instrumentation, and "incident audits." Together, they target the following five components of the system in the assessment:

1. *The mission, goals and values.* They examine the state of the unit's mission and values to ascertain commitment to diversity in the unit. They also determine the extent to which the stated and implied mission, goals, and values serve the system's diversity agenda.

2. *Personnel profile.* They examine the numbers regarding representation of staff according to race, gender, disability, age, etc. They also review turnover rates, intake and recruitment processes, and grade and salary level.

3. *Technology.* They examine the hardware, software, and human resources that are employed to produce and deliver the unit's product or service and look for bias and barriers in the processes used by the organization to do its work. The change agents and the team often pay close attention to the criteria used to select the technology used by the organization. Typically, they find implicit barriers to diversity built into the specifications or selection criteria used to identify the appropriate technology.

4. *Management practices.* The team works together with change agents to examine the management of human and financial resources—the decision-making processes, punishment and reward systems, career progression system—to determine the extent to which they inhibit or contribute to the organization's diversity agenda.

5. *Awareness and climate.* It is important to examine the support for diversity in the organizational climate. Attention is paid to the attitudes and behaviors of the work force. The focus is on the effects that these attitudes and behaviors have on the climate for each social identity group.

MCOD Intervention Plan

The second step involves analyzing the data gathered, setting priorities for necessary changes, and developing a plan that will effect change. It is critical that this plan be developed by the change team.

The plan should be a realistic road map for the organization. It should also be "owned" by the parties who live in the organization, not only by the consultant. The plan details goals, objectives, benchmarks, evaluation criteria, and accountability structures.

MCOD Plan Implementation

Implementation of the plan is usually not carried out solely by the change team members. Typically, the plans affect most subsystems of the organization and therefore are carried out by organizational members—managers, supervisors, teams, or individual contributors—not by a committee.

MCOD Plan Evaluation

Plan evaluation is part of the plan itself. Criteria for determining progress toward goals is built into the stated objectives. It is important that the change team devise a schedule of periodic monitoring of the system's progress. The evaluation step in this process is, in fact, almost indistinguishable from the first step, the assessment. After one plan has been implemented and evaluated, that evaluation provides a new assessment, which the change team can use to begin building the next plan.

This systems change phase is a never-ending, continuous-improvement process. Clients must understand that creating multicultural organizations is a long-range, far-reaching process, not a project. Changing the organizational mindset from short-term to long-term, from a problem to be solved to a process that is ongoing, is also important to ensuring the success of the effort.

CONCLUSION

The MCOD model described is but one model used by diversity consultants. While this model has unique characteristics embedded in its theoretical foundations and its practice, it shares one thing with several other diversity models—that is, the need to integrate issues of social justice and social diversity in both the individual and the organizational context.

There are many organizations that are ready to fully embrace the challenge and realize the benefits of becoming multicultural organizations. There are also organizations that are serious enough about the diversity agenda to want to invest the time, resources, and energy required to ensure a lasting and positive effect on the organization and its all-important "bottom line."

Chapter Forty

Mark A. Chesler

Organizational Development Is Not the Same as Multicultural Organizational Development

Mark A. Chesler

■

Mark A. Chesler, PhD, is a professor at the University of Michigan, Ann Arbor, in the Department of Sociology and the Center for Research on Social Organizations. He holds a PhD in social psychology from the University of Michigan. His interest in activist social science has led to research projects and change efforts focusing on racism, sexism, and other forms of oppression and discrimination in organizations and communities. He has consulted with organizations in the public and private sectors.

O rganizational development (OD) is a broad and diverse field, and because it has been rooted partly in the academy, many texts, anthologies, and review articles have been written that espouse its primary assumptions, principles, and tactics of change making.[1-5] Its principal goals generally have included the simultaneous increase of organizational profitability or efficiency and the full utilization of human resources, as well as the satisfaction of organizational members. In the pursuit of this agenda, it generally is assumed that individual goals, diverse individuals' goals, and organizational goals can be met with minimal conflict. Organizational conflict generally is not seen as inevitable or inherent but as the result of faulty communication, bureaucratic malfunctioning, and the distortions created by divisions of power and task or unit specialization.

The key principles of OD have been summarized as follows:[6,7,8]

- A long-range effort to introduce planned change.
- Based on a diagnosis that is shared by the members of an organization.
- Involves the entire organization or a coherent system or part thereof.
- Has the goal of increasing organizational effectiveness and enhancing organizational choice and self-renewal.
- Utilizes various strategies to intervene into ongoing activities of the organization in order to facilitate learning and to make choices about alternative ways to proceed.

The major tactics utilized by organizational development specialists and organizational managers to achieve these goals include:

- Training and coaching.
- Goal setting and planning.
- Process consultation.
- Survey (or other data) feedback.
- Intergroup problem solving.
- Technostructural intervention.
- Team building.
- Crisis intervention.
- Quality of work-life programs.
- Quality circles.
- Total quality management programs.

For the most part, these principles and tactics are consistent with a *consensus model* of organizations[9] and with what Bolman and Deal label the human relations or (techno)structural perspective.[10] They reflect the rational-empirical and especially the normative-reeducative models of change originally suggested by Chin and Benne,[11] the attitude-change strategy articulated by Walton,[12] and the professional-technical perspective suggested by Crowfoot and Chesler.[13]

To be sure, there are competing tendencies within this field, and some practitioners and theorists have advanced a view and practice of OD that is more tuned to a *conflict model* of organizations.[14–22] These authors have suggested a political approach to understanding and managing organizations,[23] one that emphasizes a political model of change,[24,25] or a "power strategy,"[26] and the relevance of power, conflict, and status hierarchies. Theorists and practitioners operating from this vantage point often see conflict as an inherent aspect of all organizations, starting with the difficulty of creating a harmonious fit between individuals' needs and organizational priorities. They are likely to focus on using or exposing structural conflict in the organization, to engender negotiations among units, among people of different social (or racial or gender) categories or statuses, and between workers or workers' labor unions and management cadres or owners. But this latter approach, and practical applications based upon it, is confined largely to union activists and academic rhetoric. It is a quite minor theme in orchestrated OD efforts at change making.

The distinctions between consensus-oriented and conflict-oriented models of OD occur on a continuum and not as a clear bifurcation; mixed models clearly are being utilized in practice.

WHAT IS MCOD?

Prior to the arrival of systematic works on MCOD,[27-29] and despite a few pioneering studies of race and gender relations in organizations,[30-34] reviewers pointed out that "many major works on OD do not emphasize issues related to race and minorities."[35] The field of organizational behavior also has been faulted for the "absence of research reports on the effects of race and ethnicity."[36] If issues of race and gender were rare in the OD literature, discussions of class issues were, if anything, even rarer.[37]

In practical work in the field, moreover, Jackson and Holvino argue, "Traditional organizational development (OD) efforts have not made the kind of impact on social oppression in the workplace that its founders had hoped."[38] In particular, individual consciousness raising about prejudice and discrimination was judged to have had limited success in creating lasting organizational change,[39] and training interventions in the 1970s generally were not seen as having led to comprehensive efforts to alter organizational power and culture.[40] Beyond training, relatively few research or practice efforts were undertaken that went beyond equal opportunity and affirmative action programs. Innovations occurred primarily around the recruitment and hiring of people of color and women. Indeed, Fine, et al., argue, "Early work on diversity in the workplace assumed that difference should be eliminated, that everyone, regardless of color or gender, should strive to be alike."[41] Those few efforts that did address organizational racism or sexism focused on policies aimed at controlling or reducing the most overt forms of prejudice and discrimination. These are important gains, to be sure, but they were quite limited. By and large, these change efforts were concentrated at the margins and at lower levels of organizations and avoided challenges to or changes in organizational (mono)cultures and race or gender power relations.

Authors concerned with MCOD begin with the problem of social diversity, variously stated. There are, to be sure, differences among the major writers and practitioners in this subfield: Some focus on diversity and the effort to understand and accommodate differences, while others focus on achieving equality and social justice. The difference is similar to the difference between consensus and conflict views of OD in general, of race and gender relations in our society and organizations, and between change that is driven by goodwill and enlightenment or by power. The distinction between the assumptions underlying consensus-oriented MCOD and conflict-oriented MCOD, like similar distinctions among OD variants, also occur as a continuum rather than a duality (see Table 40–1).

Among those MCODers who advocate a social justice agenda, there generally is agreement on several important propositions:

TABLE 40–1

Orientations and Assumptions of Different Approaches to Organizational Change

	Consensus	*Conflict*
Organizational Development	Common values	Disparate values
	Mutual organizational interests	Competing organizational interests
	Harmonious workplace	Contest and struggle in workplace
	Person-organizational fit	Authority is exploiter
	Authority is trustable	Coordinate via control
	Coordinate via collaboration	
Multicultural Organizational Development	Racial harmony near	Racial hostility here
	Gender bias treatable	Gender bias deep
	Prejudice is the problem	Organizational oppression is the problem
		Societal oppression supports the organization
	Diversity is the issue	Dominance/oppression is the issue

- Racial (and gender, class, etc.) differences have a powerful impact on people and organizations. This social diversity embodies differences in attitudes, behavioral styles, ways of thinking, culture, and the like.

- In a society that constantly translates differences into ranking systems, some of the characteristic styles of diverse groups are seen as better than others. Thus, when diverse styles encounter one another in an organization, white and male styles tend to dominate those of people of color and women. People of color and women (among others) have been systematically oppressed in the larger society, and thus in most organizations as well. In turn, white males are systematically privileged, empowered, and preferred.

- When the oppressed resist their oppression, overt interest group conflict (racial, gender, and class conflict) naturally ensues. This conflict is not primarily the result of poor communication, inadequate managerial structures, poor coordination of task roles, or poor fit between person and organization; it is primarily the result of systems of oppression and monopolies of racial and gender power in society and organizations.

Multicultural organizational development specialists generally articulate an approach to organizational change that is frankly antiracist and antisexist. The multiculturalism that is sought is not simply an acceptance of differences, nor a celebrative affirmation of the value of differences, but a reduction in the patterns of racial and gender oppression (racism and sexism) that predominate in most U.S. institutions and organizations. As one example, Cross makes it clear that her approach to "managing diversity" includes the amelioration of oppression and necessarily exposes intergroup conflict.[42]

A consensus-oriented approach to MCOD stresses the possibility of reform in organizational racism, sexism, etc. It is reflected in programs of understanding differences and valuing diversity. These programs may help organizations make important gains involving increased recruitment, support, and advancement for women and people of color and reeducation of white managers and elites. But they do not tackle issues of domination and oppression. Thus, in my view, OD—even OD that includes racism and sexism awareness programs—does not equal MCOD.

How is MCOD to be done? What are the tactics utilized by MCODers? The tactics are as varied as the tactics of OD specialists, but they generally include the necessity of challenging the culture and structure of white male oppression. Such challenge can be mounted via the following tactics:[43,44]

- Educational tactics to inform and enlighten white, male managerial cadres through awareness or bias-reduction training.
- Development and mobilization of leadership among employees/ managers of color and women and the formation of interest groups, cadres, and caucuses whereby members of oppressed groups can support one another in their efforts to change themselves and the organization of which they are a part.
- Change in human resource and personnel policies and programs in order to meet diverse populations' needs.
- Creation of new organizational mission statements, symbols and myths, and norms and alteration of reward systems so as to punish or reward managers for behavior on issues of racism and sexism.
- Creation of coalitions across race, gender, and status divisions.
- Negotiated decision-making and interest-based bargaining as ways of utilizing conflict productively.
- Generation of the power with which to influence, threaten, or coerce the change process and the use of pressure and threat, including whistle blowing, protests, and external agents.
- Multicultural forms of conflict resolution and dispute settlement.

Power, including racial and gender power, seldom is shared or given away, absent challenge and pressure. When power changes, it generally is "taken," and therefore the development of new sources of power among formerly oppressed and disempowered organizational members is vital to this approach.

Both OD and MCOD may use a variety of specific organizational change tactics, as suggested earlier. One of the key differences between the conflict and consensus models of change, whether practiced by ODers or MCODers, involves their relative emphasis on communication and trust, or on power and pressure, as tactics. Table 40–2 categorizes some common change tactics by their relative congruence with the consensus (olive branch or trust and communication) model or the conflict (two-by-four or power and pressure) model.

Careful choices must be made among the various tactics and tactical approaches. Consensus, or olive branch, tactics may work well in establishing a cooperative context for change, generating racial understanding, and creating change in a relatively equal power situation. But they may not work well in situations of great power difference. In fact, then they may easily lead to delay, co-option, tokenism, and agreements to make changes that are not implemented. Conflict, or power and pressure, tactics on the other hand, can bring long-repressed issues to the fore (especially when gulfs among groups are great or calcified), command attention, speed up action, and provide the framework for monitoring implementation efforts. They may not work well if backed by insufficient power; elites who experience threat may counterorganize and overwhelm a change effort.

Despite these contrasts, as with those in Table 40–1, this is a bifurcated and therefore simplified presentation. In the reality of organizational life and in organizational consultations for change, there is a much more complex continuum, with many mixed options. For instance, it may take pressure and threats of disruption by people of color and women (conflict strategy) to convince white male managers and executives to reeducate themselves (consensus strategy) regarding racism and sexism and to take action to counter institutional discrimination. By the same token, it may take sustained pressure to enable these white men to maintain the personal and organizational changes so generated. In my own work—as in the work of most MCOD theorists or practitioners, but to a lesser extent in the work of ODers—moving back and forth across these lines is common.

IS MCOD THE SAME AS OD?

The challenge of justice-oriented MCOD to OD occurs, thus, on several levels. First, there are assumptive and analytic differences.

TABLE 40-2

Ways of Thinking About Making Organizational Change

	The "Olive Branch" Approach:	The "Two-by-Four" Approach
	Trust and communication—consensus	Power and pressure—conflict
Assumptions	Everyone is in this together	Not everyone is in this in the same way or for the same things
	Decision-makers can and do want to improve the situation	Power brokers will not improve the situation on their own
	We do not have a lot to say or do about it	We can and do have a lot to say and do about it
	Not too much is wrong	A lot is wrong
	Conflict is unnecessary and can be overcome	Conflict is natural and can be a force for change
General Approach	Cooperative problem-solving	Constituency organizing and surfacing conflict
	Appeal to decision-makers:	Persuade and pressure power brokers:
	with information	with information
	with needs or concerns	with pressure
	with grievances/requests	with incentives
	with shared values	with demands
	Educate and persuade managers:	Threaten managers:
	with reason	with disclosure
	with information	with embarrassment
	with incentives	with disruption
	with support	with lack of support
	with new options	with a "way out"
Working "With"	Decision makers and staffs	Others of the constituency or interest group
	Internal informal influentials	Internal cadres External agents/agencies
	Consensus	Coalition

MCOD assumes that on issues of race and gender, power is so embedded in the white male hierarchy that white males have a strong self-interest in maintaining that power and privilege. It is hard to imagine serious change occuring around these issues without serious struggle and conflict. How much power sharing will be undertaken by those with most of the power and the privileges that come with power?

Typically, power sharing is rather quickly redefined by managers as democratic or participatory management and then further redefined in practice (and perhaps redefined right out of existence) as employee involvement. Second, in the face of these differences and conflicts of interest, it is difficult for anyone to ascertain and work on behalf of the interests of the entire organization. If the organization is conceived as a political system,[45] the good of the entire system is constantly in negotiation among competing interest groups. Thus, when consensus-oriented ODers or MCODers say they are working for the good of the entire system in a nonpartisan or neutral manner, they usually are working for, and for the good of, the managerial cadre—those who hire and fire consultants as well as underlings.[46] Inasmuch as managerial cadres are disproportionately white and male, this is a difficult stance from which to work for the interests of people of color and women in the organization.

Some of the major challenges that MCOD poses to traditional OD are summarized in Figure 40-1.

SO OD IS NOT THE SAME AS MCOD!

It is clear that MCOD utilizes some of the assumptions and many of the tactics of OD. But other traditional OD assumptions and many other OD tactics are not shared; they even contravene one another.

If MCOD is so different from OD in assumptions about the nature of society and organizations, in analyses of difference and oppression, and in tactics of change, what happens when OD assumptions, analyses, and tactics are employed in an MCOD effort? Can OD be effective in reducing institutional oppression? Not if it follows the basic principles of traditional OD outlined above and agreed to by many of the major writers and practitioners in the field. Can MCOD be done (and done well) without challenging the centers of monocultural power and norms? Not if it truly seeks socially just and antiracist/antisexist organizations. The degree of challenge, and its relative noise or threat level, may be highly variable, but some challenge—and therefore conflict—is crucial.

When OD, or a consensualist form of MCOD, is utilized in a true MCOD effort, change tactics are utilized that often prematurely seek consensus rather than reveal or explore conflict, that celebrate difference rather than challenge dominance or oppression, that help individuals adjust to monocultural norms and power systems rather than alter power structures and cultures themselves, that create individual changes while maintaining organizational structures and cultures of racial and gender power, that mask struggle with a patina

FIGURE 40-1
MCOD's Challenges to OD

- White males are unlikely to change without significant appeal (including threat) to their self-interest.
- Power must be taken to be shared.
- Race and gender oppression is the rule; it is a fundamental element in U.S. organizations.
- An organization is composed of units and people who differ from one another and are in (overt or covert) conflict with one another in important ways.
- Organizational norms (and thus reward systems) reflect the dominance of the white male culture and its power.
- People with power who are threatened by struggle will resist change and will counterattack (overtly or covertly).
- The core power for change will come from people of color, women, and other oppressed groups.
- On some occasions, some white males will vigorously support and join the MCOD effort.

---

of enlightened rhetoric and tokenism, and that maintain—if not solidify—organizational monoculturalism. Its current popularity, more-over, has led some observers to label Diversity and MCOD efforts as the new "race industry"[47]—an industry more interested in its own maintenance and profit than in combatting oppression and attaining social justice.

Realistically speaking, can managers and consultants survive economically and politically by using an MCOD approach that challenges white and male power structures and cultures, that reveals and utilizes race and gender conflict? The evidence is increasing that some leaders in major organizations in the United States are reading the danger of the current situation of race and gender oppression accurately. Whether prompted by notions of *Workforce 2000*, by economic market necessities, by increasing racial and gender conflict in workplaces and livingplaces, by notions of charity and goodwill to all, or by commitments to social justice and the "right thing to do," there are major players who understand the assumptions underlying the MCOD approach. Indeed, books on valuing or managing diversity and a diverse work force are selling apace,[48–51] and according to Cox's rather optimistic view, many corporate managers "are already convinced that the multicultural model is the way of the future."[52] Whether they can and will act on that conviction and how long they will invest in taking the risks and helping to make the changes that flow from this approach—and that one would hope flow from the work of MCOD specialists—remain to be seen.

On the other hand, there also is substantial evidence that major stakeholders in current U.S. organizations resist this approach and seek to defend their own and others' racial and gender privileges, especially when challenged. Then, MCODers have a hard time surviving—as academicians or managers or consultants. But oppressed groups in the United States are also having a hard time surviving right now, with or without MCOD. So the questions are: Whose survival? Survival at what level of economic and moral comfort or security? Eventually, none of us is very likely to survive in a society that is not able to respond proactively and progressively to continuing racial and gender privilege and oppression.

As long as we do not test these possibilities of justice-oriented MCOD work, or if we confuse traditional OD and MCOD, we fail in our vision and our struggle for a socially just and multicultural future.

NOTES

1. W. Burke and L. Goodstein, eds., *Trends and Issues in Organizational Development: Current Theory and Practice* (San Diego: University Associates, 1980).

2. Wendell L. French, Cecil H. Bell, and R. Zawicki, eds., *Organizational Development* (New York: Irwin, 1989).

3. F. Friedlander and D. Brown, "Organizational Development," *Annual Review of Psychology* 25 (1974), pp. 313–41.

4. M. Sashkin and W. Burke, "Organizational Development in the 1990s," *Journal of Management* 13 (Summer 1987), pp. 393–417.

5. Walter Sikes, A. Drexler, and J. Gant, eds., *The Emerging Practice of Organizational Development* (Alexandria, VA: NTL Institute/San Diego: University Associates, 1989).

6. L. Goodstein and P. Cooke, "An Organizational Development (OD) Primer," in *The 1984 Annual: Developing Human Resources,* eds. J. William Pfeiffer and John E. Jones (San Diego: University Associates, 1984).

7. J. William Pfeiffer and John E. Jones, "OD Readiness," in *The 1978 Annual Handbook for Group Facilitators,* eds. J. William Pfeiffer and John E. Jones (San Diego: University Associates, 1978).

8. J. Sherwood, "An Introduction to Organizational Development," in *The NTL Managers' Handbook,* eds. Roger A. Ritvo and Alice G. Sargent (Alexandria, VA: NTL Institute, 1983).

9. J. Crowfoot and Mark A. Chesler, "Conflict Control and Organizational Reform: Three Approaches," in *Conflict Management and Industrial Relations,* eds. Gerald B. Bomers and Richard B. Peterson (The Hague, Netherlands: Nijhoff, 1982).

10. Lee G. Bolman and Terrence E. Deal, *Modern Approaches to Understanding and Managing Organizations* (San Francisco, Jossey-Bass, 1984).

11. R. Chin and K. Benne, "General Strategies for Affecting Change in Human Systems," in *The Planning of Change,* eds. Warren G. Bennis, K. Benne, and R. Chin (New York: Holt, Rinehart and Winston, 1969).

12. R. Walton, "Two Strategies of Social Change and Their Dilemmas," *Journal of Applied Behavioral Science* 1, no. 2 (1965), pp. 167–79.

13. J. Crowfoot and Mark A. Chesler, "Contemporary Perspectives on Planned Social Change," *Journal of Applied Behavioral Science* 10 (1974), pp. 287–303.

14. D. Bowen, "Value Dilemmas in Organizational Development," *Journal of Applied Behavioral Science* 13 (1977), pp. 543–56.

15. W. Burke and H. Hornstein, *The Social Technology of Organizational Development* (La Jolla, CA: University Associates, 1972).

16. J. Crowfoot and Mark A. Chesler, *op. cit.*

17. J. Espinosa and A. Zimbalist, *Economic Democracy: Workers' Participation in Chilean Industry, 1970–1973* (New York: Academic Press, 1978).

18. F. Friedlander and D. Brown, *op. cit.*

19. Evangelina Holvino, "Organizational Development from the Margins: Reading Class, Race and Gender in OD Texts," PhD dissertation, University of Massachusetts—Amherst, 1993.

20. T. Patten, "The Behavioral Science Roots of OD," *The 1979 Annual Handbook for Group Facilitators,* eds. J. William Pfeiffer and John E. Jones (San Diego: University Associates, 1979).

21. R. Ross, "OD for Whom?" *Journal of Applied Behavioral Science* 7, no. 5 (1971), pp. 580–5.

22. K. Thomas, "Worker Interests and Managerial Interests: The Need for Pluralism in Organizational Development," Working Paper 76–120 (Los Angeles: UCLA Graduate School of Management, 1976).

23. L. Bolman and T. Deal, *op. cit.*

24. R. Chin and K. Benne, *op. cit.*

25. J. Crowfoot and Mark A. Chesler, *op. cit.*

26. R. Walton, "Two Strategies of Social Change and Their Dilemmas," *Journal of Applied Behavioral Science* 1, no. 2 (1965), pp. 167–79.

27. T. Cox, "The Multicultural Organization," *Academy of Management Executive* 5, no. 2 (1991), pp. 34–47.

28. B. W. Jackson and Evangelina Holvino, "Multicultural Organizational Development," Working Paper 11 (Ann Arbor: Program on Conflict Management Alternatives, 1988).

29. J. Katz, "Facing the Challenge of Diversity and Multiculturalism," Working Paper 13 (Ann Arbor: Program on Conflict Management Alternatives, 1988).

30. Clayton P. Alderfer, A. Alderfer, D. Tucker, and L. Tucker, "Diagnosing Race Relations in Management," *Journal of Applied Behavioral Science* 16, no. 2 (1980), pp. 135–66.

31. Rodolfo Alvarez and Kenneth G. Lutterman, eds., *Discrimination in Organizations* (San Francisco: Jossey-Bass, 1979).

32. John P. Fernandez, *Racism and Sexism in Corporate Life* (Lexington, MA: Lexington Books, 1981).

33. Rosabeth M. Kanter, *Men and Women of the Corporation* (New York: Basic Books, 1977).

34. Alice G. Sargent, ed., *Beyond Sex Roles* (New York: West Publishing, 1976).

35. C. Jennings and L. Wells, "The Wells-Jennings Analysis: A New Diagnostic Window on Race Relations in American Organizations," in *The Emerging Practice of Organizational Development*, eds. Walter Sikes, A. Drexler, and J. Gant (Alexandria, VA: NTL Institute/San Diego: University Associates, 1989).

36. T. Cox, "Problems with Research by Organizational Scholars on Issues of Race and Ethnicity," *Journal of Applied Behavioral Science* 26, no. 1 (1990), p. 6.

37. Evangelina Holvino, *op. cit.*

38. B. W. Jackson and Evangelina Holvino, *op. cit.*

39. *Ibid.*

40. J. Katz, *op. cit.*

41. M. Fine, F. Johnson, and M. Ryan, "Cultural Diversity in the Workplace," *Public Personnel Management* 19, no. 3 (1990), pp. 305–18.

42. Elsie Y. Cross, "Issues of Diversity," in *Sunrise Seminars*, rev. ed., eds. D. Vails-Weber and J. Potts (Washington, DC: National Training Laboratories, 1991).

43. B. W. Jackson and Evangelina Holvino, *op. cit.*

44. J. Katz, *op. cit.*

45. L. Bolman and T. Deal, *op. cit.*

46. D. Bowen, "Value Dilemmas in Organizational Development," *Journal of Applied Behavioral Science* 13 (1977), pp. 543–56; and R. Ross, "OD for Whom?" *Journal of Applied Behavioral Science* 7, no. 5 (1971), pp. 580–5.

47. C. Mohanty, "On Race and Voice: Challenges for Liberal Education in the 1990s," *Cultural Critique*, Winter 1989–90, pp. 199–208.

48. D. Jamieson and J. O'Mara, *Managing Workforce 2000: Gaining the Diversity Advantage* (San Francisco: Jossey-Bass, 1991).

49. W. Johnston and A. Packer, *Workforce 2000: Work and Workers for the 21st Century* (Indianapolis: Hudson Institute, 1987).

50. Marilyn Loden and Judy Rosener, *Workforce America!* (Homewood, IL: Business One Irwin, 1991).

51. R. Thomas, "From Affirmative Action to Affirming Diversity," *Harvard Business Review* 68, no. 2 (1990), pp. 107–17.

52. T. Cox, *op. cit.*

Chapter Forty-One

Judith Palmer

Diversity
Three Paradigms*

Judith Palmer

■

Judith Palmer, PhD, has been a pioneer in developing theory and practice to help people learn to value diversity through positive, adult learning methods. She is a member of NTL and the OD Network, with academic roots in the Case Organization Behavior Program. In 1978, she moved to a corporate position where she focuses on organization and management development and valuing diversity.

A few companies are working energetically to become truly multicultural organizations, leveraging diversity as a source of competitive advantage and employee satisfaction. These organizations are exploring fundamentally uncharted ground in undertaking such changes on this large a scale.

Change leaders in companies working toward this goal can usually all agree to a statement describing the ideal outcome, or vision, for their organizations. The generalizations and beautiful concepts expressed in such statements are usually created through a consensus process and thus are "close enough" that individual interpretations can fit into the general statement. But ironically, differences inevitably arise among the change leaders, sometimes leading to disagreements that can hamper their effort.

When change leaders disagree, in many cases the conflict arises from fundamental differences in their frames of reference, or *paradigms*.

There appear to be three different paradigms operating among today's organizational change leaders for diversity. They are: Paradigm I—the Golden Rule, Paradigm II—Right the Wrongs, and Paradigm III—Value All Differences. Each influences our interpretation of facts for action and generates a unique definition of diversity.

---

*The original version of this article appeared in OD Practitioner, March 1989. Used with permission.

PARADIGM I: THE GOLDEN RULE

The fundamental imagery of Paradigm I is that everyone is an individual and we are more similar than we are different. The dominant expression of this paradigm is the following notion: "I treat everyone the same. I believe any differences among people are due to individual characteristics, not to any 'group' a person is part of. I'm color-blind and gender-blind." A Paradigm I person typically is someone of good faith, whose self-image is one of a good and fair person. At the same time, a Paradigm I person does not usually explore his or her underlying unconscious prejudices or those of other people. In fact, Paradigm I would conceptualize prejudice as existing only among a few "bad" or "prejudiced" people in isolated incidents.

Paradigm I does not see diversity issues as systemic, nor does it perceive "typical" issues or behavior among various groups. For a Paradigm I person, diversity is a matter of individual responsibility and morality.

Vision and Preferred Approach to Change

Paradigm I change leaders want an organization where everyone can be an individual, where no prejudice or barriers exist to create disadvantages, and where all can contribute and be rewarded according to their abilities. The desired state is an effective organization and a pleasant work environment, where everyone can rise to her or his potential. Business results will improve through minimized interpersonal friction and better management. Each person will be empowered to contribute to his or her maximum.

Focusing on individuals getting along together, Paradigm I interprets any disharmony among people as being individually motivated. Paradigm I people do not perceive patterns among people or among "types" of people.

Paradigm I change leaders resist programs that separate out the issues faced by specific groups. They specifically resist awareness training, believing that this will provide negative imagery and put bad notions into people's heads. They are highly critical of special programs or numerical targets to increase the representation of selected groups, believing that these efforts are counterproductive, unfair to other organization members, and group people without regard to their individuality.

When morale is low or conflicts arise in the organization, Paradigm I change leaders recommend third-party consultations, team-building meetings, one-on-one counseling, and sometimes individual training in assertiveness, conflict management, or problem solving.

Meaning of Diversity

For Paradigm I, the word *diversity* means an atmosphere in which all the members of the organization are appreciated *regardless* of their differences. Paradigm I people are uncomfortable thinking about people based on what group they belong to and feel it is artificial to focus on the concerns of blacks, women, national groups, ethnic groups, etc. Diversity means everyone is an individual; each is special and different. For Paradigm I, diversity means the Golden Rule: "Do unto others as you would have them do unto you."

Organizational Impact

When the prevailing view of the change leaders is Paradigm I, the organization, over time, takes on some very predictable characteristics. Inside the organization, people perceive each other as being unique and different. They see themselves as sensitive to each other's character traits, personal quirks, individual backgrounds, family patterns, etc.

However, the organization's members usually have not stretched their experience by dealing with the deep issues of people who are significantly different from themselves. They apply the Golden Rule from their *own* frame of reference, usually with people rather like themselves. So in attempting to treat everyone the same, they don't usually know how to put themselves into the shoes of someone else who may be very different. An organizational culture of sameness is usually created by Paradigm I change leaders. This may not be an environment that different kinds of people consider welcoming or nurturing, even though the Paradigm I people mean well. Organization members do not see this, believing that "the door is open to all who are qualified."

PARADIGM II: RIGHT THE WRONGS

The fundamental imagery of Paradigm II is that there are specific groups in the organization, as in the larger society, that have been systematically disadvantaged. Paradigm II sets out to rectify these injustices.

The exact identification of the disadvantaged group (I will call it the *target group*) depends on the organization's environment. For instance, in Germany, the target group might be Turkish factory workers. In Japan, it could be ethnic Koreans. In San Francisco, it could be homosexuals; in Canada, Francophones. In U.S. organizations, two major target groups are African Americans and women of all races. Regionally, another target group in the United States could be Hispanics.

Vision and Preferred Approach to Change

Paradigm II change leaders want injustices corrected and want groups who were selectively and systematically disadvantaged in the past given respect and the opportunity to participate equitably in the rewards of the organization. They believe that business results and managerial and interpersonal effectiveness will be improved by the fresh perspectives of the target group.

Paradigm II focuses on removing the disadvantages and barriers of the target group. Success is measured when the target group's members are equitably deployed and rewarded throughout the organization, as shown by statistics on recruiting, salaries, rankings, job levels, turnover, etc., as well as by attitude surveys.

Training in Paradigm II centers on having the majority members learn how the target group feels, "walk a mile in someone else's shoes," and face up to their negative prejudices. Confrontation is seen as valuable in training to break down normal perceptual barriers so that real learning or change can take place. It is seen as crucial that the learning group contain enough target group members for dialogue to take place.

An important element of Paradigm II's preferred approach is that the effort should remain focused first on the target group. Later, the organization will apply the important skills and principles learned to respond to the concerns of the other groups. Paradigm II change leaders fear that the effort will be "watered down" if too many groups' needs are addressed at the same time.

Meaning of Diversity

For Paradigm II, *diversity* means the establishment of equality and justice for the specific target groups handicapped by systemic prejudice and differential treatment. In Paradigm II, diversity means "right the wrongs."

Organizational Impact

At times, when Paradigm II changes are being championed, tension and anxiety can develop to a significant degree because the change leaders are usually thrust into an adversarial role (or at least a teaching role) with peers in their own organization who do not share the Paradigm II perspective. Frustration and impatience can run high on the part of target group members, and people are prompted to take sides. At times, strong demands are made to management on behalf of the target group on the belief that "no one gives up power; you have to take it." Change leaders sometimes experience discouragement and burnout.

Paradigm II conveys a sense of a split world, a dichotomy, and a struggle to bridge the gap. The language that characterizes the Paradigm II outlook is reflected in "we/you" types of dialogue between target group members and those who appear to wield the power or to control access to what's desirable in the organization. Paradigm II language in the United States, for instance, characterizes "white males" versus "minorities and women." Separate formal or informal structures and programs to develop the target group are the appropriate way to foster the growth of the disadvantaged groups.

PARADIGM III: VALUE ALL DIFFERENCES

Paradigm III change leaders want people to be conscious of what makes each other different. Paradigm III expects everyone to appreciate the heritage and culture of many different groups and to respond to the self-image and uniqueness of each individual.

VISION AND PREFERRED APPROACH

Paradigm III change leaders envision an organization in which individuals reach beyond their own experience to understand and interact effectively with a wide range of others. Thus, all are able to contribute in their own unique ways. Creativity, the decision process, and organizational results improve exponentially. Outcomes and solutions are found that were not thinkable in a more homogeneous organization.

Paradigm III change leaders believe that to focus on only one or two target groups would mean having to do it all over again later with subsequent target groups. Meanwhile, the organization would not be striving to value all differences. Paradigm III encompasses a wide range of significant differences, including race, gender, and class, as well as nationality, native language, psychological makeup, organizational or functional home base, style, and more.

Systemic change in Paradigm III focuses on the inclusion and appreciation of many kinds of people leading to excellence in business results and organizational climate. This appreciation of differences is built into hiring, development, and reward systems.

Training in a Paradigm III framework emphasizes self-knowledge—learning the patterns of one's own prejudices—and interpersonal skills, as well as specific learning about the cultural history of many different groups. Confrontation and victim/oppressor dichotomies are downplayed. The lesson is that all must learn to appreciate each other's contributions to achieve better results.

Meaning of Diversity

In Paradigm III, *diversity* means consciously and sensitively deploying the talents of all the groups in the organization without emphasizing or putting priority on any specific difference or group. Paradigm III places importance on all kinds of differences: ethnic and racial heritage, gender, problem-solving and creative approaches, professional disciplines, native language, home organization, etc. For Paradigm III, diversity means "value all differences."

Organizational Impact

Paradigm III language patterns convey sensitivity and appreciation for difference and might not use "minorities and women" versus "white males," for example, as a dichotomy. People are interested and enthusiastic about learning about themselves and others, and all organizational systems are geared to maximizing diversity while honoring and pursuing the fundamental needs of the organization.

Whereas Paradigms I and II have been operating for some time and have established theory and methodology to move toward their vision, Paradigm III is relatively new. It does not yet have proven methods and a shared set of terminology to draw from. Even Paradigm III change leaders often do not know how to communicate with one another.

SOURCES OF DISAGREEMENT: PARADIGM CLASH

Clearly, all three paradigms have as their objective the creation of a high-performance, smoothly running organization in which members are neither penalized nor rewarded for the type of person they are perceived to be. Change leaders, operating from separate paradigms, can work collaboratively toward this end.

Too often, in a discussion of methods or goals, change leaders who think they're in alignment begin to feel a kind of craziness developing in their conversations; logic does not lead to the expected conclusion, and familiar terminology suddenly does not mean the same thing when used by different people. A predictable and very human outcome of "paradigm clash" is that individuals personalize these differences. When their paradigm is challenged, perceived (or real) irritations and oppositions begin to arise. People feel personally threatened and slip into blaming or disliking the other person ("shooting the messenger").

Paradigm I people value their "do as you would be done by" rule and believe they are already aware and sensitive; they are shocked and hurt when the "right the wrongs" Paradigm II people confront them on their lack of awareness. Paradigm II people are horrified with the "global" scope of Paradigm III, fearing that Paradigm III people will duck the tough issues facing the target groups. Paradigm III with its "value all differences" orientation believes Paradigm I is dangerously ethnocentric with its Golden Rule and that Paradigm II is serving the needs of a few at the expense of the many. Paradigm I people think they're the same as Paradigm III and can't understand why Paradigm III people appear impatient with them. These issues are rarely brought to light, but seethe beneath the surface.

COALITION BUILDING

A concept that can be useful in these situations comes from the field of community action, pioneered by Saul Alinsky and others. Groups with widely differing viewpoints and agendas can work together if they carefully define the areas where they are in alignment and where their agendas (paradigms) differ. It is not necessary to see the world in the same way or agree on everything. It is imperative, however, to define the common goals and clarify the "boundaries" between what people agree on and what they don't. Each can work independently on the separate part of their agendas, while cooperating on shared objectives.

Finally, change leaders should work to understand in some detail the approaches favored by the other paradigms, in order to develop new approaches that incorporate and go beyond everything that was known before.

Chapter Forty-Two

Catherine S. Buntaine

Developing Cross-Gender Partnership Competencies
Exploring the Seven C's

Catherine S. Buntaine

■

Catherine S. Buntaine, a vice president of The Kaleel Jamison Consulting Group, has worked as an organization development consultant since 1979. Her work focuses on assisting corporate, public, and not-for-profit clients in building the strategic foundations supporting high-performing and inclusive workplaces. She has extensive experience in cultural change, strategic planning, and executive team development and has developed technologies to improve synthesis following mergers and acquisitions.

W e live in an age of changing workplaces. Traditional ways of getting work done are disappearing as organizations flatten and transform in response to competitive demands and stakeholders' changing needs.

Increasingly, we are required to leave the security of our narrowly defined roles and comfortable cubicles, pack up our tools and skills, go where we are needed, and join others in a task. We may know what result is expected from our work, but in this world of teams, task forces, and committees, other questions are unanswered:

"Who is in charge?"

"How will decisions be made and conflicts resolved?"

"Will I get along with these new people?"

"How will I communicate and work with people so different from me?"

"What can I expect of these people, personally and professionally?"

"How much of myself will I be able to bring to the table?"

To work productively within dynamic and diverse organizations, a key competency we now require is the ability to *partner* quickly and effectively. But partnering is an unfamiliar skill for many people. Even the full bandwidth of meaning of the word *partner* is probably unfamiliar to most of us:

259

part•ner \pärt′ner\ *n* [Middle English *partener*] **1.** *archaic:* one that shares : PARTAKER **2. a.** ASSOCIATE, COLLEAGUE **b.** either of two persons who dance together **c.** one of two or more persons who play together in a game against an opposing side **3.** husband or wife : spouse **4.** one of the heavy timbers that strengthen a ship's deck to support a mast

Thinking of partners as people who share or partake suggests that *what* they share has value and is the focus of their coming together as associates or colleagues. But as women and men, we are much more familiar with other aspects of this definition, such as spouse or dance partner. Our focus shifts from *what* we share to *with whom* we share.

FAMILY PARADIGM

The tendency to shift from "what" to "who" in cross-gender work partnerships is rooted in our earliest training. From the moment of birth, our family systems define our relationships with members of the other sex. This socialization is reinforced in most of our intimate relationships and in many of our institutional experiences. We have far fewer lessons and few role models for the workplace.

Within the family framework, we learn our culture's accumulated wisdom, preferences, biases, and stereotypes about women and men. Family paradigms guide us as we struggle with intimacy and interdependency. They teach us the basic "rules of the game" in our personal relationships: how we communicate with each other, how we engage in conflict, how we come close, and who is responsible for which tasks. The rules define our "rank" in these relationships, letting us know who is to lead and who is to follow, who will initiate and who will shape the many aspects of our relationship.

The familial framework provides us with a deeply held set of norms and values about women and men, and also many of our sexist biases and prejudices. For thousands of years, interactions between women and men at work often reflected these models and their inherent ranking, as women became helpmates to men, or were put aside in the organization or community to do "women's work."

Family-based models of rank, interdependency, and intimacy function less well in today's workplace, where men and women come together as peers to accomplish organizational tasks. Our family-based skills, norms, and values actually prevent our work partnerships from functioning as effectively and productively as they could. We need to develop a new rulebook and a new set of skills that can enable us to move beyond a relational framework and work together as co-equals, co-contributors, co-creators (and even co-conspirators).

THE SEVEN C'S

The following competencies increase the potential for success of partnerships between women and men at work. Each reflects an important currency for cross-gender partnerships and a critical set of skills women and men must develop and practice.

Context: Creating a Strong Foundation for the Partnership

Successful women and men colleagues understand that "partnership" is different from "relationship." Partnership is about consciously choosing to *do* something together, not about the choice of *having* each other. It's a joining together to accomplish a task, not a task of joining together.

Figure 42–1 describes some of the basic differences between relationships and partnerships.

New partners too rarely invest the time and effort in laying a foundation for their work together: discussing and agreeing on the partnership's objectives, products, ground rules, and shared resources. Too often, in search of more personal points of connection, we overlook our shared objectives and fail to share our individual goals.

When faced with ambiguity and a lack of foundation, we may be tempted to return to the relationship mode. We can quickly diagnose this "relationship trap" by noting the focus of our attention. If we are focused on issues of comfort or discomfort, affection or dislike, we have probably lost sight of our common task.

Commitment: Committing to Reach Our Goals Together

Without commitment to a shared goal, there can be no commitment to partnership. But there must also be a commitment to hang in through the partnership's ups and downs, riding the initial learning curve required of any new venture.

We must recognize our tendency to personalize cross-gender partnerships. Few of us have been prepared to interact with people of the other gender outside social and familial roles, and we inappropriately fall back on these roles as a foundation for partnership. Behaving as peers is often a daunting task. Fear of being harassed or accused of harassment can have us walking on eggshells or trying to escape in any way we can—through avoidance, requests for transfers, quitting, or even precipitating conflict with our new colleague.

FIGURE 42-1
*How a Relationship Differs from a Partnership**

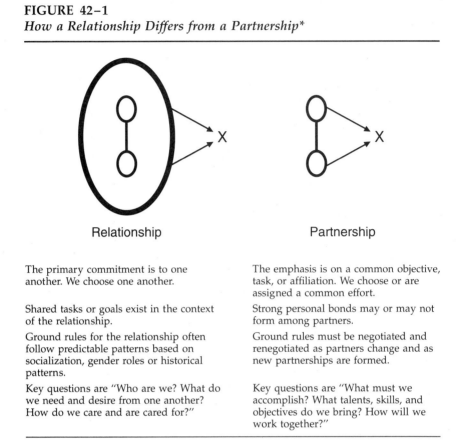

Relationship	Partnership
The primary commitment is to one another. We choose one another.	The emphasis is on a common objective, task, or affiliation. We choose or are assigned a common effort.
Shared tasks or goals exist in the context of the relationship.	Strong personal bonds may or may not form among partners.
Ground rules for the relationship often follow predictable patterns based on socialization, gender roles or historical patterns.	Ground rules must be negotiated and renegotiated as partners change and as new partnerships are formed.
Key questions are "Who are we? What do we need and desire from one another? How do we care and are cared for?"	Key questions are "What must we accomplish? What talents, skills, and objectives do we bring? How will we work together?"

*This diagram was developed with the help of my friend, colleague, coconsultant, and occasional coconspirator Kent Linder.

For many men, the struggle to establish protocols for interacting with women colleagues (e.g., about language, opening doors, carrying bags, picking up checks, etc.) remains a key task. The suppression of other behaviors, especially dominating or "sexualizing" their women partners, can be a struggle that makes these new partnerships seem exceedingly difficult.

For women, a lifetime of training to be "a good girl," not make waves, and protect the male ego can make honest participation difficult. "Hanging in there" may require dropping the search for the perfect nonsexist colleague. Overlooking awkward behaviors, such as a slip on the word *girl*, can sometimes reveal a potentially worthy colleague.

Women also must take some responsibility for their own inclusion in partnerships. While waiting to be invited "to the table," some may miss the open chair.

Communication: Learning Each Other's Language

As women and men partners, we have begun to talk about *how* we talk with one another. Women complain that men don't listen (i.e., they miss significant portions of women's communications by focusing on a single topic within the dialogue). Men complain that women don't get to the bottom line (i.e., they add information about process and context to a description of business results).

To communicate effectively, partners must accept that there is more than one way to talk. Cross-gender partners, indeed any partners of different backgrounds and cultures, must learn to value and interpret the emotional as well as the factual content of a communication, the contextual as well as the literal message.

This requires an aggressive acceptance of responsibility for *mutual* understanding: Have I understood and been understood? Am I able and willing to broaden my ways of sharing and my ways of listening?

Improving these skills can help us discover the various gifts of women's and men's communications and build a process of dialogue to support our partnerships.

Conflict: Managing Conflict Creatively

Partners joined in a common venture inevitably face differences in goals and approach. Negotiating and problem solving are key skills. Yet the rule book for effective conflict between women and men at work is short. It doesn't go far beyond:

"It's not safe/right/polite/appropriate to fight with a woman/man. Don't do it."

"If you have to fight, win—and take no prisoners."

Many of us have painful stories to tell about cross-gender workplace conflicts. The pain comes from our tendency to personalize these conflicts in a family/relationship mode. We are less likely to personalize conflicts with colleagues of our own gender.

Accepting conflict as a natural and productive consequence of working together becomes easier when we learn conflict skills:

• Remembering the goals of our partnership and using them as a reconciling force.

- Avoiding actions and words that create an unsafe climate, realizing that women and men both have safety issues about conflict.
- Recognizing that strong emotions may be present and signal the commitment we share.
- Understanding that our styles, processes, and needs for connecting and disengaging may differ, and letting that difference exist.
- Agreeing to "move on" with our partnership without grudges or recriminations when the conflict has passed.

Another challenge in cross-gender partnership is employing the counsel of others in situations of conflict. Those around us will often push us right into the relationship trap. Men in conflict are often told simply to get back to work. But for cross-gender pairs, the diagnosis is almost always personal, as are the solutions:

"Why don't you like her?"

"Can't you get along?"

"Do we need to separate you two?"

When in conflict, we must ground ourselves (and remind others to ground us) in the task we share and the hopes, skills, and value we seek to bring to the task. Learning to fight well signals to our colleagues that our partnership is invested with attention, energy, and care.

Competition: Dealing with Competition and Comparison

As with conflict, our unwritten rules urge us to avoid competing with the other gender. Because of this, cross-gender competition often takes surprising forms in the workplace. Men and women may compete by creating conflict, by feigning interest and collaboration, by avoiding one another, or by sexualizing the partnership.

Comparison can also be challenging because men and women often bring such different qualities to a particular role or task. Questions of relative competencies may shift from the traditional "Who is better?" to "With whose approach, style, personality, perspective, appearance, or attitude are we more comfortable?"

A strategy for addressing cross-gender competition is to view it as an opportunity for feedback and growth. A woman and man competing in the workplace may often discover different and complementary qualities in one another as they bring different skills to work. As in same-gender partnerships, competition can help us learn from each other's strengths and add to our own portfolio.

Competencies: Utilizing and Growing Each Other's Skills

Cross-gender partnerships have the opportunity to use gender-related differences as well as individual skills to broaden their success-producing resources. But to maximize potential, partnerships must also meet the needs of the individual members to grow and develop beyond narrow and "ranked" roles. Supporting one another includes helping each other acquire new competencies.

These supportive bonds among peers have been rare in the hierarchical workplace. A useful practice for cross-mentoring involves asking and answering the following questions:

"What do I/you feel competent to teach?"

"What do you/I want to learn?"

"How am I doing?/How do you think I'm doing?"

Closeness: Acknowledging and Managing Attraction and Sexuality

Collaboration often leads to affection and broadening of the personal bonds between partners, genders notwithstanding. But in cross-gender partnerships, closeness brings forth many family- and relationship-based behavior patterns.

If we find ourselves focusing on our partner's personality, style, or appearance more than our work together, how do we keep from confusing the personal and the professional? What is appropriate to do or say?

Feelings of affection and admiration may be accompanied by sexual interest. With no models for expressing these feelings, some partners may act upon them. Workplace romances occur, often with unwanted ramifications and consequences for the individuals, their families, their friends, and the organization. Others experiencing attraction avoid one another or even create conflicts to distance themselves.

People who are successful in forging effective cross-gender work partnerships often find affection becomes easier to manage when expressed in an open and collegial manner. Simple statements like, "I've enjoyed working on this project with you" or "I'm glad we had the chance to work together" can help us refocus on the task. Discussing feelings in the context of the task and the partnership can help us stop fantasizing and see our partners realistically again.

In other cases, it is necessary for the partners to acknowledge their sexual attraction and to make responsible decisions to address it. Partners may have to:

- Acknowledge the feelings out loud to each other.
- Decide whether to make the relationship or the partnership their primary commitment, considering career and organizational consequences.
- Engage in explicit problem solving, possibly with help from a third party.

WORTH THE EFFORT

There are no rule books for cross-gender partnerships. Each is unique, just as each individual is unique. Each partnership must continually invent itself as it goes along. Individually and collectively, we learn and grow through each interaction.

Much of the work of learning and practicing these new competencies involves simply checking out our partnering efforts on an ongoing basis and talking "out loud" with our partners.

Appreciating the currencies and acquiring the competencies for cross-gender partnering can add to our experiences as women and men. Freed from the demands of our interdependent, relational framework, we can explore our individual identities and contributions more fully and learn about ourselves through our interactions. Like the ship's "partners," which support its mast and sails, we can build partnerships that strengthen our individuality, enhance our joint efforts, and reinforce the rewards of our work.

Chapter Forty-Three

Lenneal J. Henderson

Managing Diversity in Organizations
Empirical, Normative, and Public Policy Issues

Lenneal J. Henderson

■

Lenneal J. Henderson, PhD, is currently Distinguished Professor of Government and Public Administration, Senior Fellow in the William Donald Schaefer Center for Public Policy, and a Henry C. Welcome Fellow at the University of Baltimore.

He has lectured or consulted in Europe, Canada, Somalia, Tanzania, Nigeria, South Africa, Swaziland, India, Japan, the People's Republic of China, the former Soviet Union, Brazil, Peru, Argentina, Egypt, Israel, and the Caribbean. He is also on the faculty of the Fielding Institute of California.

M uch of the empirical foundation for diversity studies is based on demographic projections of the American work force to the year 2000. Findings indicating that women, nonwhites, immigrants, the aging, and the disabled will constitute a larger and larger proportion of the work force are characterized as trends to which organizational management should be responsive. As Coates, Jarrett, and Mahaffie indicate, "the potential effects of a trend signal the needs for action and responses."[1]

However, if that action and response are to result in better-attuned and -performing organizations, the trend must be understood in more than merely demographic dimensions, which mask critical behavioral and institutional dynamics and nuances. Demographic analysis is an appropriate place to begin the assessment of diversity needs and strategies, but it is a dangerously inappropriate place to conclude such assessments.

Beyond the demographic paradigm are behavioral issues much more essential to management response. These issues include:

1. What are the socialization and actual cultural experiences of incoming women, racial, and ethnic groups as they either arrive at

the entry level of organizations or are promoted through the organizational ranks and hierarchies?

2. What structural and institutional dynamics in these socialization and cultural experiences reflect struggles with oppression, exclusion, or discrimination that may manifest themselves in the behavior of nontraditional groups *and* the behavior of traditional managers and employees of organizations?

3. Is there diversity within diversity? What are the variations in the socialization and cultural experiences among women, ethnic groups, the aging, and the disabled that dispel or refute tendencies to make groups culturally or behaviorally monolithic?

4. What are the experiences women, nonwhites, and other diverse groups have with task groups, organizational networks, professional organizations, and organizational leadership that do and can inform strategies of organizational response to diversity?[2]

ETHICAL/NORMATIVE AND STRUCTURAL/ INSTITUTIONAL ISSUES IN DIVERSITY

A second major challenge to the understanding of diversity in management is to clearly determine what the specific objectives of the management of diversity are in its various stages of development. Typically, at the initial stage of exhorting organizations to become aware of existing diversity in society and projective diversity in their own organizations, there is a strong ethical and normative undertone. "Organizations should ..." or "Management should ..." is the frequent refrain. The organizational response is often to capitulate to these ethical exhortations by referring to the organization's track record or current efforts to diversify or to comply with current public policy imperatives.

However, beyond the ethical/normative dimension are deeply entrenched and societal structural and institutional issues that the management and leadership of many organizations are often not equipped to perceive, characterize, or respond to.[3] These issues include:

1. Historical patterns of institutional treatment of women, people of color, and others grouped under diversity rubrics.

2. Maldistributions of financial, educational, technological, quality-of-life, and human resources based on these historical institutional and structural patterns.

3. Conscious and subconscious patterns of perceptions, attitudes, beliefs, and behaviors among both those in control of societal institutions and those subject to those controls, which too often

manifest themselves in the particular orientation and behavior of particular organizations and institutions.

4. Struggles played out within particular organizations over the distribution of economic, social, and political power in society.

These structural/institutional issues are indeed inextricably intertwined with the ethical/normative issues. But there is often such an emphasis on the moral imperatives of managing diversity that, paradoxically, deep, powerful, and visceral structural/institutional forces are seldom fully recognized. Strategic response to the challenge of diversity includes confrontation of structural/institutional dynamics.

THE MULTIDIMENSIONALITY OF MANAGING DIVERSITY

Another myopic approach to managing diversity is the exclusive or primary emphasis on work-force diversity. Although recognizing work-force diversity is fundamental, at least two other dimensions of managing diversity are essential:

1. Management of diverse clients, customers, constituencies, or organizations.

2. Management of diverse organizational network relationships, including vendors, organizational partners, conventurors, grantees, and consortia.

Organizations are diverse in terms of mission, mandate, scale, scope, size, and activities. Some organizations deliver goods and services to defined customers, clients, or constituents. A key issue is the extent to which the organization is culturally, behaviorally, and institutionally attuned to and responsive to diversity among its current and potential customers or clients. Do pizza delivery chains recognize that home delivery may be culturally offensive to ethnic groups for whom the sanctity of the home is paramount? Is the social services department aware of language differences and family attitudes among its Hispanic clients? These clients are technically part of the organization's field.

Similarly, do certain large manufacturers subcontract with and respect the diversity of women-owned or minority-owned computer or supply companies? Does the U.S. Department of Energy manage its relationship with a Hispanic American–owned chemical engineering firm with cultural, as well as financial, sensitivity and acumen? Or to what extent are state and local governments or local businesses inclined to enter into contractual relationships with nonprofit, community-based organizations operating in urban or rural areas that are predominantly African, Asian, Hispanic, or Native American? What are the mutual cultural presumptions that characterize those contractual relationships?

Clearly, effective management of diversity includes management of these external relationships beyond the immediate work force. Indeed, increasingly the management of internal and external relationships is correlated. Improved management of differences internal to the public, corporate, or nonprofit mainstream organization may facilitate improved management of external relationships with institutions representing diverse communities or constituents.

PUBLIC-POLICY DYNAMICS AND DIVERSITY

A fundamental element in the management of diversity for corporations, small businesses, and nonprofit, public, and international organizations is the extent to which they recognize, understand, and enforce current public-policy imperatives for affirmative action, prevention of sexual harassment, work with the differently abled, management of immigrant populations, and other mandates for managing differences. Although many diversity-oriented public policies are limited in scope or circumscribed by interpretation, they are often second only to public relations and marketing as compelling motives for establishing diversity programs in organizations. This public-policy dimension of diversity includes at least three interrelated challenges:

1. *Policy implementation:* Compliance with existing federal, state, and local policy mandates germane to issues of diversity.

2. *Policy interpretation:* The recurring need to reconcile many inconsistencies and conflicts in diversity-oriented public policies. For example, recent court decisions appear to shift the burden of proof in discrimination cases to the victim. The victim must establish discrimination in the *intent* of an individual or institution rather than rely on evidence that establishes the *effects* of past discrimination.

3. *Policy formulation:* The initiation of novel and creative approaches to both the interpretation of current diversity-policy mandates and the generation of new and more responsive public policies on diversity.

The significance of an effective response to these public-policy challenges lies both in their central role in behavior modification (including demographic changes) and in the fact that many oppressed populations are disproportionately dependent on govern ment for both protection from oppression and access to basic goods and services. For example, more than 90 percent of African American– and Hispanic-owned businesses and more than 60 percent of women-owned businesses depend on government contracts for at least 50 percent of their annual gross receipts. Consequently, public policy must be responsive to demographic, organizational, and policy dimensions of diversity.

THE HORIZONS OF ORGANIZATIONAL DIVERSITY

Current concerns with diversity must go beyond mere demographic analysis and projection. Individuals and institutions behave and decide in a variety of modes not necessarily consistent with the expectations of the demographic category to which they are assigned. These behavioral dynamics are the real essence and meaning of diversity in organizational environments.

Strategies for reducing oppression in organizations by pursuing diversity must therefore examine not only work force dynamics but also the current and future relationships organizations maintain with diverse institutions in their organizational environment. Coventures, joint ventures, subcontracting relationships, fair-share agreements, advisory networks, and clearinghouses are all institutional mechanisms for extending the range of an organization's awareness of diverse populations, for addressing structural inequities perpetuated by organizations, for relieving oppression in the institutional networks of organizations, and, indeed, for improving recruitment of diverse individuals to the work force of the organization. Consequently, existing and future public policy should emphasize not only recruitment of diverse individuals to the work force but also the development and management of relationships with networks representing diverse populations and constituents.

NOTES

1. Joseph F. Coates, Jennifer Jarrat, and John B. Mahaffe, *Future Work: Seven Critical Factors Reshaping Work and the Workforce in North America* (San Francisco: Jossey-Bass, 1990), p. 1.

2. Hermina Ibarra, "Personnel Networks of Women and Minorities in Management: A Conceptual Framework," *Academy of Management Review* 18, no. 1 (Jan. 1993), pp. 56–87.

3. Kenneth Prewitt, *Institutional Racism* (Chicago: University of Chicago Press, 1968).

Chapter Forty-Four

Donald C. Klein

Collective Dis-Identity

Donald C. Klein

■

Donald Klein, PhD, is currently on the faculty of Union Institute's Graduate School and has taught at Harvard, Johns Hopkins, and the University of Maryland. In his 40-year career, he has addressed such concerns as affirmative action, citizen participation, community change, employee empowerment, institutional racism, intergroup conflict, management development, power, preventative mental health, and social action.

*T*he author is white, male, Jewish, American, heterosexual, and middle class. Because there is no such thing as absolute objectivity—especially in matters of human diversity, conflict, and oppression—this chapter inevitably reflects perspectives and emphases that, although not intentionally incorporated into the text, reflect his own "collective identities" and "dis-identities."

Any identity, whether individual or collective, is a distinction created by one's mind. Distinctions draw lines between that which lies inside and that which lies outside a mental boundary. That is, for every "this" there is a "that." There cannot be heads without tails; they are two sides of the same coin.

The definitions of *me* that all of us carry around in our minds include both an inside and an outside. Inside is a set of words and phrases—both descriptive and evaluative—that have to do with who one is—the "me." Outside is a corresponding set of words and phrases that have to do with who one is not—the "not me." To think of oneself as smart, for example, means one must also think of oneself as not stupid, or whatever the opposite of smart happens to be in one's mind.

Erik Erikson speaks of the "not me" as negative identity. He says:

in any "normal" identity development . . . there is always a negative identity, which is composed of the images of that personal and collective past which is to be lived down and of that potential future which is to be forestalled.[1]

As Erikson points out, our definitions of *me* are both personal and collective. Personal identities are those ideas about ourselves that are based on perceptions of how significant others in our lives have responded to us as unique individuals.

COLLECTIVE IDENTITIES

Collective identities are those ideas about ourselves that are based on our perceptions of how we are viewed as members of significant groups with which we identify ourselves. They are, in other words, what we call *us* and are part and parcel of the *me* that each of us carries around in our minds.

IDENTIFYING CHARACTERISTICS

Certain collective identities are based on what some call *identifying characteristics*. They refer to ways in which people group themselves and others into categories that usually are obvious. Examples include skin color, age, and sex.

DEFINING ATTRIBUTES

Other collective identities are based on what have been called *defining attributes*. They refer to ways in which people group themselves and others according to characteristics that usually aren't apparent on sight.[2] Examples include attitudes on social, economic, and other issues; political affiliations and labels; religious beliefs; nationality; and sexual orientation.

ASCRIBED ATTRIBUTES

Collective identities do more than sort people by identifying or defining attributes. Each collective identity also includes what some call *ascribed attributes*. That is, one's identity involves an evaluative cognitive structure or mental picture of what one imagines people who share a particular collective identity to be like. In other words, in addition to being descriptive, a collective identity is also judgmental. It includes value or moral judgments, beliefs about how similar or dissimilar one is to other people, and how likable or unlikable other people are. It is these ascribed attributes that lead to put-downs and derogatory labels like *kike, nigger, faggot, welfare cheat, honky,* and *pushy bitch.*

Collective identities are stereotypes about ourselves and others that exist in our minds. At best, they help us to process information about the social world in which we live. At worst, they are prejudices we use to make us feel superior to members of another group and to justify racist, sexist, classist, and other discriminatory behavior.

IN-GROUPS

A collective identity is especially powerful when it involves a highly valued in-group. Powerful identities usually have well-defined boundaries between one's in-group and one or more distinctly recognizable out-groups made up of all those who differ from that in-group in certain important ways.

Most of us rely on in-groups with which to identify. Our self-definitions thrive based on groups with which we identify. In-group memberships help us feel that we have both personal significance and social meaning. Just to be a member of society-at-large is too anonymous for most of us.

GROUP NARCISSISM

Eric Fromm points out that group narcissism is more acceptable than individual narcissism. "Expressions of patriotism, faith in a cause, and loyalty to a group," he writes, "appear to be realistic and rational value judgments because they're shared by fellow countrymen, believers in the cause, or members of the group."[3]

Group narcissism also makes up for one's insignificance in the scheme of things.

> Even if one is the most miserable, the poorest, the least respected member of a group, there is compensation for one's miserable condition in feeling, "I am part of the most wonderful group in the world. I, who in reality am a worm, become a giant through belonging to the group."[4]

Collective identities, therefore, have a lot to do with how good we feel about ourselves. They also have a lot to do with how we feel about those whose collective identities are different from our own. If the latter make certain people part of distinct out-groups with reference to our own in-groups, we may well feel uncomfortable and even condemnatory about the differences that exist between "us" and "them."

COLLECTIVE DIS-IDENTITY

Just as for every "me" there is a "not me," so for every "us" there is a "not us"—that is, for every collective identity there is a psychological opposite, which I have labeled *collective dis-identity*. One cannot have a collective identity without, at the same time, having some picture in one's mind of what that identity is *not*. To the extent one takes pride in a certain collective identity—which is almost always the case for members of dominant groups—one is likely to hold the corresponding collective dis-identity in disdain. The tendency is to associate them with "minus" qualities, such as failure, abnormality, immorality, inferiority, social disapproval, and handicap.

Collective dis-identities can include both positive and negative attributes, and often do. This is especially true of members of oppressed groups, who are prone to identify with characteristics of those who dominate or oppress them. Minority racial and ethnic group members in the United States, for example, frequently hold certain characteristics of the dominant white majority as positive.

There is much evidence that before the 1960s and the "black is beautiful" movement, social status within the African American community was associated for many with light skin, straight hair, and "white facial features."

Growing up as a Jewish child in New England, I learned to model my behavior on Yankee restraint and modulation, at the same time rejecting and holding in contempt the unrestrained gestures and loud voices of New York "kikes."

The more one's view of how people ought to behave resembles the characteristics of those who share one's collective identity, the harder it is to understand those who are part of one's collective dis-identity. Sometimes it's possible even to look upon them as not fully human.

At the extreme is the attitude that William Graham Sumner called *ethnocentrism*. Sumner wrote:

> Ethnocentrism is the point of view in which one's group is the center of everything, and all others are scaled and rated with reference to it. Each group nourishes its own pride and vanity, boasts itself superior, exalts its own divinities, and looks with contempt on outsiders. The most important fact is that ethnocentrism leads a people to exaggerate and intensify everything in their own folkways which is peculiar and which differentiates them from others.[5]

MANAGING ONE'S COLLECTIVE DIS-IDENTITIES

To manage differences more effectively, it helps both to be aware of our collective dis-identities and to work on understanding how they color and limit our ability to empathize with people who are different from us.

The following self-study is offered as one way to begin to identify your collective identities and dis-identities. It would be especially helpful to do this exercise with three or four other people with whom you can compare viewpoints and discuss what you discover.

Part One

Step one. Down the left-hand side of a page list all the collective identities that help to describe who you are. Chances are, they'll include such things as gender, age, and nationality. How about race or national origin and religion? Don't forget social class, political orientation, groups that have to do with social issues of various kinds, fraternities, sororities, or other membership groups, the community and region in which you were born or are now living, groups with whom you share common interests or hobbies, and your sexual preference or orientation. Most of us have a great many groups with whom our identities are intertwined.

Step two. For each of the collective-identity items listed on the left-hand side of the page, think of at least one collective dis-identity that represents a "not us." List each collective dis-identity on the right-hand side of the page next to the identity with which it belongs. Some distinctions are easy and automatic; others require thought to determine what not-us group in *your* mind best fits a particular collective identity.

For example, for the collective identity *woman* on the left side, you probably would list the collective dis-identity *man* on the right. If you listed *conservative*, you would have more choices for the corresponding dis-identity, such as *liberal, radical, do-gooder, cosmopolitan,* or some other term that more exactly indicates what for you is the opposite of *conservative.*

Step three. Ask yourself how you feel about each dis-identity listed on the right side of the paper. Be especially alert to positively or negatively tinged reactions that support judgmental attitudes and emotional biases.

1. Consider whether any dis-identities are associated in your mind with "plus" qualities, such as *success, normality, superiority, morality, prestige,* or *special competence.* Put a plus sign (+) next to them.

2. Identify those that are associated in your mind with "minus" qualities, such as *abnormality, criminality, ugliness, immorality, inferiority, social disapproval, handicap, failure,* or *incompetence.* Put a minus sign (–) next to them.

You may notice an inclination to say that you don't have any particular negative feelings or biases toward any of them. That's a common reaction, especially on the part of those of us raised as members of dominant groups in which racist attitudes and practices were taken for granted who later in life learned to guard ourselves against prejudiced attitudes and discriminatory behaviors.

To move past such an initial disclaimer, think about each of the dis-identities in terms of the negative qualities that others in our society—especially friends and members of your immediate and extended family—ascribe to that group. What negative qualities have you heard them use to describe members of the group? What prejudices existed toward them in your family of origin? Among friends and acquaintances when you were growing up? Among colleagues and business associates today? Among individuals and groups of people with whose biases you're acquainted, if only from reading the daily newspaper?

Especially if you are male, heterosexual, middle class, and white, chances are that few, if any, of your dis-identities are totally free of negative associations. Even though you, yourself, may not consistently identify with such reactions, remember that you are the one who thought about them. Therefore, they are attitudes, beliefs, and biases that exist in your own mind, whether or not you consciously agree with them. Most anthropologists who study many different cultures agree with William Graham Sumner, who, as noted earlier, pointed out that few human beings are totally free of such negative associations to groups of people who are unlike themselves.

Part Two

The next phase of this self-audit has to do with the meaning collective dis-identities have for you. To begin with, pick two or three from the list that in your judgment are most important to think about further.

Step four. Consider each one in terms of the following sets of questions. (If you're working with a group, first think about your responses to each question individually. Then take time in the group to share, compare, and discuss every group member's responses.)

1. *Growing up:* What did it mean to me as a young person? What attitudes and beliefs did I pick up about it as a child or adolescent from family and friends?

2. *Today:* To what extent do I have trouble understanding or dealing with such people today? What confuses me about members of this group? If I have negative feelings about them, what am I reacting to in their attitudes or behavior? What positive qualities in me stand out in contrast to the negative qualities that I or others see in members of this group? If I have positive feelings about them, what negative qualities in me stand out in contrast?

Part Three

The next part of the self-audit has to do with exploring whether and how you might gain a more complete understanding of your collective dis-identities and thereby become more accepting of and enriched by the not-us parts of you.

Step five. Consider each of the two or three collective dis-identities in terms of the following sets of questions:

1. *Owning the collective dis-identity:* How do I imagine members of this group would describe themselves? How might they describe me as a member of this dis-identity group? How would I view myself and feel about life if I were a member of that group? Would I be or feel more or less limited in my attitudes and behavior?

2. *Gaining understanding of the collective dis-identity:* Given my upbringing, experiences, attitudes, and feelings about people like this, what more would I like to learn about them? How might I go about such learning?

Part Four

The final part of the self-audit is an opportunity for you to explore what life would be like if you claimed your collective dis-identities as part of who you are.

Step six. On separate sheets, write a letter to each of the collective dis-identities you've chosen. Explain why you've found it hard to accept each one as part of who you are. Tell what each dis-identity has to offer you emotionally and intellectually, in your personal relationships, at work, and in other aspects of your life. Describe at least one situation where this collective dis-identity may help you in the future. Describe the steps you plan to take to learn more about what each one has to offer you.

BECOMING MORE HUMAN THAN OTHERWISE

Judging by past participants' explorations of their collective dis-identities, the effects of owning the not-us aspects of one's collective self can be transforming. They include:

1. Discovery of potentially positive, useful qualities in one's self that previously had been denied, repudiated, and projected as negative characteristics of stigmatized groups.

2. A feeling of greater tranquility combined with a sense of heightened vitality due to liberation of energy that was required to maintain the separation and denial of the "not us."

3. Increased excitement about and interest in exploring the varieties of attitudes, perspectives, and behavior patterns reflected in the diverse groups in one's not-us consciousness.

4. Recognition that, as the famous American psychiatrist Harry Stack Sullivan put it, "We are all more human than otherwise."

NOTES

1. Erik Erikson, *A Way of Looking at Things: Selected Papers from 1930 to 1980*, ed. S. Schlein (New York: Norton, 1987).

2. E. Babad, M. Birnbaum, and K. Benne, *The Social Self: Group Influence on Personal Identity* (Beverly Hills: Sage Publications, 1983).

3. Erich Fromm, *The Anatomy of Human Destructiveness* (New York: Holt, Rinehart and Winston, 1973), p. 204.

4. *Ibid.*

5. William Graham Sumner, *Folkways* (Boston: Ginn, 1906), p. 13.

Chapter Forty-Five

Pat Callair

Peace Within, Peace Between, Peace Among
A Satir Model for Multicultural Change

Pat Callair and Jean McLendon

■

Jean McLendon

Pat Callair conducts interactive and long-term diversity training with groups and organizations. She is founder of the South Carolina Women's Consortium. Ms. Callair is director of community development and a faculty member of the Satir Institute of the Southeast in Chapel Hill, North Carolina.

Director of training for the Satir Institute of the Southeast in Chapel Hill, North Carolina, Jean McLendon travels extensively, applying the therapeutic system of Virginia Satir to organizational change. She is a member of the Resource Learning Council, part of the International Institute for the Study of Systems Renewal in Seattle, and is on the faculty of the Avanta Network.

T he late Virginia Satir, an internationally known pioneer in the field of family therapy, said, "We come together from our sameness and grow from our differences." But in the current culture of the United States, to be different is to be in jeopardy—to be wrong, outcast, perverted, unnatural. Differences are the building blocks of racism, genderism, prejudice, and bigotry. Not following the party line—or not following the party's attitude, look, dress, or culture—is often a recipe for personal and cultural disaster. In our great "melting pot," the stew is becoming more and more toxic. The incongruities that are continuously interwoven in our national fabric could ultimately destroy us.

One of these incongruities is that our basic human vulnerability, which has the potential for ensuring our compassion, can also trigger our weapons of prejudice, bigotry, violence, and greed. If we are to turn the tide of our times, we must resolve such incongruities. And to

FIGURE 45–1
The Satir System Model for Social Change

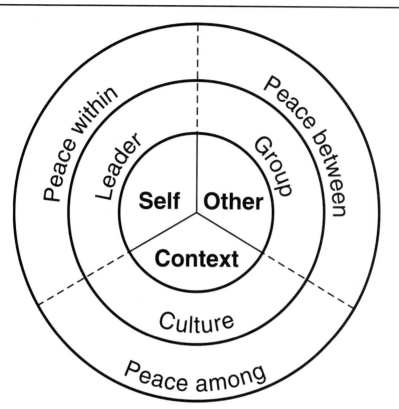

do this, we must find a way to discover and promote high self-esteem and high system-esteem.

Satir believed that we exist at three levels, the *self*, the *other*, and the *context*—or *within*, *between*, and *among*.[1] As she explained, we cannot truly value ourselves without valuing the other two aspects of our existence. All three are inextricably linked. Similarly, peace between and among must begin with peace within. Sustainable positive change must come from an internal awareness of the value of the whole system (see Figure 45–1).

PEACE WITHIN

Individuals with high self-esteem can find value in differences as well as in sameness. They can open their hearts, hands, and minds to the choices they have, and they can open and close doors as they need to, not as they feel they must because of arbitrary and shallow criteria fueled by fear.

Most of us live with internal and external oppression, afraid to trust our knowledge and experience and afraid to give voice to who we are. But if we can heal our wounds enough to attend to the issue of our esteem, we can do something about oppression, our own and our culture's.

To build esteem, we must learn how to accept our basic humanness and must be congruent, bringing our understanding, our beliefs, and our actions into agreement. Congruence is the ultimate Golden Rule that includes the whole system. It both requires and promotes self-esteem.

Conversely, expecting ourselves to accept on the outside more than we can accept on the inside would be shortsighted and unrealistic and would bankrupt us. We would be living beyond our spiritual means if we expected to honor in others what we could not honor in ourselves.

PEACE BETWEEN

Congruent living requires impressive intra-, inter-, and metapersonal skills. The prerequisite values can be stated simply but powerfully as follows: All human beings—no matter their culture, creed, color, or context—have the necessary resources to grow, learn, heal, and change. Being human means we are born with a spiritual, emotional, mental, and physical makeup and with basic needs that reflect our multiplicity of needs.

Being understood is a "megavitamin" for healthy human development. Being recognized for our differences as well as our sameness is empowering. We all have suffered loss; we all dream; we all have more capacity than we use; and we all do the best we can.

Even with the infinite number of ways that we are alike, our miraculous uniqueness suggests that there is always potential for our ideas and perspectives to be enlarged and enriched or modified by genuine contact with another human being or context.

The context is the container or structure that holds us to a place, time, and purpose. It is the foundation upon which we build our definition and understanding of who we are and why we exist at a particular moment. Acknowledging our thoughts, feelings, and sensations enhances the self and makes it possible for us to value the other or the context. We gain the freedom to see, hear, speak, feel, and connect without the influence of fear.

PEACE AMONG: DEVELOPING THE CONTEXT FOR MULTICULTURALISM WITHIN THE ORGANIZATION

Multicultural change is movement away from the traditional, homogeneous context, in which experience and reality are defined from one cultural point of view. Unfortunately, because of our history of racism and segregation, there have been few incentives for adding color or shape (diversity in race or gender) to the top levels of organizations. This situation has led to what we know as the glass ceiling, which keeps corporate leadership almost totally white and male. As a result, there is virtually no leadership at the top of our political, social, and educational institutions to help bring about multiculturalism.

Multiculturalism is also the acceptance, appreciation, and honoring of diverse cultural experiences. It means acknowledging that an organization is enhanced by the diversity of its members, and it involves creating an organizational atmosphere in which differences can thrive and grow. In a multicultural organization, diversity is valued in balance with sameness. Understanding and appreciating what is different allows space for a healthy celebration of what is the same.

This represents a major change in the way we as a society do business with one another because it redefines our relationships to one another. For those of us who have been major beneficiaries of the traditional system, such changes can be disturbing, to say the least.

Without bold and effective leadership, these changes are virtually impossible. Effective leadership is the conscious and strategic use of self to achieve desired and positive outcomes.[2] Therefore, a leader must change at the individual level before she or he can lead change at the organizational level. It is the new awareness and experience to which high self-esteem opens us that motivates a leader to facilitate organizational change.

In multiculturalism, the leader perceives differences as nonthreatening. Having accepted all parts of herself, the leader can be excited about the new possibilities that come with diversity. By becoming the author of her life and not being limited by rigid scripts that originate outside of herself, the leader experiences a peace within. That peace empowers her to take bold steps that will enhance the character of the organization.

The leader comes to understand the value of a multicultural context. She has made her first step away from the old status quo and is willing to introduce the foreign element, multiculturalism, the transforming idea.

She not only articulates this new awareness in verbal communications, but also becomes a visible model for the change she seeks within the organization. She "walks her talk"—she is congruent. She is able to apply her new awarenesses in her relationships with others and has the ability to expand her connections to include those from diverse cultural experiences, creating peace between.

According to the Satir model, introducing a foreign element into the old status quo inevitably creates chaos, placing every part of the organization in flux. Old structures no longer work for the new order, relationships change, and old rules and policies no longer apply.

During the chaos phase, effective leadership is essential. However, people inexperienced in planned intra- and interpersonal change cannot know about the human reactions they will face when they lead multicultural change.

Leading an organization through its chaos requires a steady hand at the helm. The captain of the ship must be confident, clear, consistent, and compassionate. She must offer a sturdy hand with a gentle touch and must hold a strong belief in the organization's efficacy and integrity.

From the chaos, the organization will move to integration and practice, the application of the transforming idea. As it does, the organization tries on its new character and makes adjustments in structure, atmosphere, and personnel to accommodate the new situation.

Because the leader has experienced change at a personal level, she understands that the process will involve chaos and is therefore able to coach the organization with wisdom and understanding. She is able to model congruence and support communication that honors the self, the other, and the context. She is able to maintain the vital balance between sameness and difference. She knows this is not change for the sake of change, but change that is intelligent, wholesome, and holistic, serving the overall mission of the organization (see Figure 45–2).

From integration and practice, a new status quo is created. The leader now presides over a new organizational culture, and the organization enjoys an atmosphere of acceptance, appreciation, and honoring of difference. Multiculturalism is the norm. The leader is the catalyst, the activist for maintaining the new context.

Within this multicultural context, the self-esteem of all members of the organization is enhanced. With this improvement comes high system-esteem, which is directly proportional to the number of individuals within the organization who experience high self-esteem.[3] High system-esteem is characterized by structures within the organization that are stable, safe, secure, and stimulating, and these qualities become more achievable as individuals within the organization feel better about themselves.

FIGURE 45–2
The Satir Multicultural Peace Process

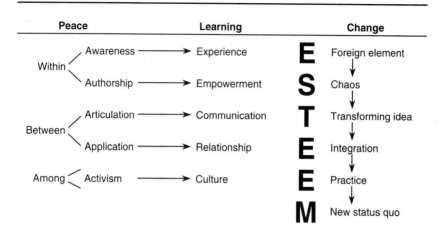

The leader who has high self-esteem will act to provide an organizational context that promotes stability, security, safety, and stimulation. These qualities enhance the peace among all members. The vital balance is maintained, and prejudice and racism cannot take hold. The system is flexible because all options are possible under the guidance of wise leadership that knows how to maintain the delicate interplay of self, other, and context.

NOTES

1. Virginia Satir, J. Banmen, J. Gerber, and M. Gomori, *The Satir Model* (Palo Alto, CA: Science and Behavior Books, 1991).

2. J. A. McLendon, "Changing Organizations in Change," presentation, Avanta Conference, Through the Family and Beyond: Full Esteem Ahead, Santa Clara, CA, 1991.

3. *Ibid.*

Chapter Forty-Six

A Model for Personal Change
Developing Intercultural Sensitivity*

Milton J. Bennett and Barbara R. Deane

Milton J. Bennett

Barbara R. Deane

Milton J. Bennett, PhD, is codirector of the Intercultural Communication Institute in Portland, Oregon, an educational foundation that sponsors programs in intercultural research, professional development, and graduate studies.

Barbara R. Deane is cofounder and editor of Cultural Diversity at Work *newsletter and* The Diversity Training Bulletin, *the first national periodicals to explore the opportunities and challenges of diverse people working together to achieve organizational goals.*

More and more organizations are recognizing that to remain productive they must adapt to the increasing diversity of the work force. This trend is reflected in the *Harvard Business Review* article "From Affirmative Action to Affirming Diversity," in which Roosevelt Thomas argues that recruitment of diverse personnel should be accompanied by efforts toward valuing diversity and managing diversity.[1] Successful recruitment strategies create the need for new management skills that more clearly treat difference as a valuable resource.

Intercultural communication has long considered the influence of difference on interpersonal, group, and organizational relations. The

*This article is a revised version of two previous articles, "Developing Intercultural Sensitivity" and "New Insights for Intercultural Sensitivity Model," both of which appeared in the May 1991 issue of *Training and Culture Newsletter,* now published as *Cultural Diversity at Work in Seattle.*

FIGURE 46–1
Development of Intercultural Sensitivity Model

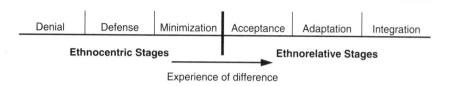

| Denial | Defense | Minimization | Acceptance | Adaptation | Integration |

Ethnocentric Stages   **Ethnorelative Stages**

Experience of difference

model of intercultural sensitivity presented in this article is based on several precepts from that field. For instance, *culture* is defined as the patterns of behaving, thinking, and valuing that are generated and maintained by groups of interacting people. Examples of groups that may be defined by this kind of subjective culture include nationality, ethnicity, regionality, gender, socioeconomic status, physical ability, sexual orientation, and vocation. According to the intercultural view, the foundation for valuing diversity is built on understanding and respect for one's own and others' cultures, on appreciating the strengths and limits of different cultures, and on developing special skills of intercultural communication.

This article is a short summary of a model developed by Milton Bennett to explain how people make sense of cultural differences.[2] It will give you some ideas on how to understand and develop intercultural sensitivity in both international and domestic contexts. Domestically, the ideas are particularly applicable among dominant groups. The model is valuable because it breaks the process down into a progression of stages people may go through, suggesting how they may resist development at various points and indicating strategies for helping them move from one stage to the next. Each stage has a range of behaviors associated with it, some far more subtle than we can describe in this short article. We recommend strongly that anyone who wants to use this model in training consult one of the original sources.

As you can see in Figure 46-1, the model is divided into ethnocentric stages and ethnorelative stages. *Ethnocentric* may be defined as using one's own set of standards and customs to judge all people, often unconsciously. *Ethnorelative* is a word coined to express the opposite of *ethnocentric*; it refers to being comfortable with many standards and customs and an ability to adapt behavior and judgments to a variety of interpersonal settings. The following are short descriptions of each of the stages.

DENIAL

"Tokyo is no different from New York: lots of cars and tall buildings."
"We have some women and people of color at the office. They fit right in."

People at the denial stage have few categories to distinguish differences. On the surface, they may seem accepting of different people, but basically they just don't want to think in complex ways about difference. People in denial probably live in relative isolation from cultural differences. When confronted, they may attribute sub-human qualities to those from different cultures and regard them with extreme prejudice.

Strategies

Use nonthreatening awareness activities, such as multicultural fairs, celebration of different holidays, entertainment by different ethnic groups, travelogues, talks on women's or African Americans' history, or exhibits. The purpose here is to help people begin to recognize cultural differences without provoking too much anxiety.

DEFENSE

"Women are so naturally passive; they'll never fit in at this level."
"We wouldn't have any problems at all if it weren't for underhanded Japanese trade practices."

People in the defense stage make statements that indicate they feel threatened. The most common reaction at this stage is to denigrate the differences or to create negative stereotypes. An alternative response may be to promote one's own cultural superiority. A few people may enter a "reversal" form of defense, wherein they vilify their own culture and become zealous proponents of an adopted culture. For example, some whites spurn their European roots while idealizing Native American cultures, and some Americans when traveling label many of their compatriots as "ugly Americans."

Strategies

Emphasize the things cultures and genders have in common and what is good in all cultures. Avoid the argument that cultures are not good or bad, just different; it tends to be ineffective at this stage. Because focus on commonalities is the goal, look for similar examples of ethnocentrism in other cultures. Be aware that some people may want to slip back to denial because change is uncomfortable and denial allows one to continue in familiar behaviors.

MINIMIZATION

"The best thing to do when being interviewed by a Japanese employer is just be yourself."

"I don't see race or gender, I just see employees."

People at the minimization stage believe that cultural differences are superficial because deep down, people are all just human beings. Certain cultural values are assumed to be universally desired. For instance, Americans may believe that people everywhere desire individual freedom, openness, and competition. Sometimes, people with overseas experience find a haven in this stage; it sounds culturally sensitive, and it allows them to avoid feelings of incompetence in the face of many cultural unknowns. Domestically, this view is expressed by a strong adherence to the melting-pot idea.

Strategies

Moving from minimization into the next stage represents a major conceptual shift from an ethnocentric position that avoids difference and relies on simple either/or principles to an ethnorelative stage where difference is sought out and answers are not so clear. For Westerners, handling this shift inductively seems best. Use simulation exercises, personal stories, and carefully chosen "representatives" from other cultures to show how behavior can be interpreted differently. Stress understanding one's own culture, including, when relevant, what it means to be European American.

ACCEPTANCE

"I know my boss, a black woman, and I, a white man, have had very different life experiences, but we're learning how to work together."

"Our new engineer is from Pakistan; where can I learn more about that culture?"

People at the acceptance stage enjoy recognizing and exploring differences. They are fairly tolerant of ambiguity and are comfortable knowing there's no one right answer (although there are better answers for particular contexts). *Acceptance* does not mean that a person has to agree with or take on a cultural perspective other than his or her own. Rather, people accept the viability of different cultural ways of thinking and behaving, even though they might not like them. This is the first stage in which people begin to think about the notion of cultural relativity, that their own behavior and values are not the only good way to be in the world.

Strategies

Stress recognizing and respecting behavioral differences; focus on verbal and nonverbal communication skills. Encourage the view that what is different is also appropriate. Learning to respect differences distinguishes this stage from the previous one; but moving too quickly to a discussion of cultural value differences may be threatening and result in a retreat to an earlier stage.

ADAPTATION

"To solve this dispute, I need to change my behavior to account for the differences in status between myself and my Arab colleague."

"I greet my male and female colleagues somewhat differently to account for cultural differences in the way respect is communicated."

People at the adaptation stage can intentionally shift their frame of reference (such as, in the example, considering the greater influence of status in some cultures). They can empathize, or take the other person's perspective. They can choose to act in various appropriate ways, based on their ability to use alternative cultural interpretations. Some of these people may be bicultural or multicultural. Most people at this stage are generally interculturally sensitive, but a few can still be ethnocentric toward cultures with which they are unfamiliar. For instance, some people who are otherwise interculturally skilled retain negative stereotypes of gay and lesbian cultures.

Strategies

Provide opportunities for people to practice their new ability in face-to-face interactions. Activities might include a task for partners from two different cultures or a problem-solving session for a multicultural group. Activities should be related to real-life communication situations.

INTEGRATION

"Sometimes, I don't feel like I fit in anywhere."
"I feel most comfortable when I am bridging differences between the cultures I identify with."

These two statements represent ways that people at the integration stage tend to handle multicultural identity issues. Some people become overwhelmed by the cultures they know and are disturbed that they no longer can identify with any one of them. Others at this stage achieve an identity that allows them to see themselves as interculturalists or multiculturalists in addition to their national and ethnic backgrounds. These people may seek out roles that allow them to be intercultural mediators and exhibit other qualities of "constructive marginality."[3]

Strategies

Establishing one's own "cultural core" or personal value system is a key step here. Developmental work should be focused on mastering the ethics of contextual relativism. As with all ethnorelative stages, integration requires conscious thought and effort.

APPLICABILITY OF THE MODEL

The stages summarized above do not completely describe the process of developing intercultural sensitivity for all people. For instance, there is some evidence that Japanese learners may reverse the order of the defense and minimization stages, proceeding in their development from assuming basic similarity to negatively evaluating differences. In the United States, people whose ethnicity has been oppressed by the dominant group may also deal with ethnocentrism differently.

To illustrate the domestic variation, Figure 46-2 shows the stages of ethnic and cultural development model by James Banks mapped onto the intercultural sensitivity model.[4] The comparison suggests that members of oppressed ethnic groups do not experience the denial or minimization stages of intercultural sensitivity. Indeed, denial is characterized by cultural isolation, a position more easily maintained by the dominant group through control of housing opportunities, media, etc. And minimization is likely to be offensive to people who have experienced "ethnic identity clarification" be-

FIGURE 46-2

Comparison of Dominant and Nondominant Experience of Difference

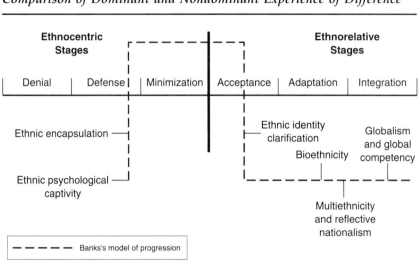

cause it trivializes the very cultural differences upon which a unique ethnic identity is built. Despite the divergence in their early stages, the latter stages of both models run parallel.

The implications of these cultural variations is that interpretations of behavior in terms of developmental stages should always be made in their cultural context. For instance, statements of cultural superiority from a European American male may indicate that he is threatened by a difference, and development would occur by minimizing the differences while maintaining or increasing the contact. Alternatively, the same statements of cultural superiority from an African American male might indicate "ethnic encapsulation." Development in this case might occur by temporarily maintaining separation and emphasizing issues of ethnic identity clarification.

ETHICAL ISSUES

Much of the controversy surrounding the development of intercultural sensitivity is about ethics. Some people seem to think that being interculturally sensitive means giving up any set of ethical principles or moral guidelines. They think cultural relativity is the same thing as moral relativism or situational ethics. To understand that criticism, we can turn to yet another developmental model, the Perry Scheme of Cognitive and Ethical Development.[5]

Perry outlines a process whereby people develop ethical thinking and behavior as they learn more about the world. The model describes movement from dualism (one simple either/or way of thinking) to multiplicity (many ambiguous and equally good ways of thinking) and then on to contextual relativism (different actions are judged according to appropriate context) and commitment in relativism (people choose the context in which they will act, even though other actions are viable in different contexts).

The people who are most critical of multiculturalism seem to be at Perry's stage of dualism. They think of ethics and morality as absolute, universal rules; you either abide by them or you don't. In this dualistic view, the acceptance of different cultures leads only to multiplicity, where all options are equal and ethical chaos reigns. As people develop more sophisticated ethical abilities, they become able to see how ethnorelativism and strong ethical principals can coexist.

The most difficult challenge for valuing and managing diversity in organizations may not be altering attitudes, skills, or institutional structure. Rather, it may be how constructively, respect for diversity can be integrated with respect for oneself.

NOTES

1. T. Roosevelt Thomas, "From Affirmative Action to Affirming Diversity," *Harvard Business Review,* March–April 1990, pp. 107–17.

2. Milton Bennett, "Towards Ethnorelativism: A Developmental Model of Intercultural Sensitivity," in *Cross-Cultural Orientation: New Conceptualizations and Applications,* ed. M. Paige (Lanham, MD: University Press of America, 1986); "Towards Ethnorelativism: A Development Model of Intercultural Sensitivity," rev., in *Education for the Intercultural Experience,* ed. M. Paige (Yarmouth, ME: Intercultural Press, 1993); and "A Developmental Approach to Training for Intercultural Sensitivity," *International Journal of Intercultural Relations* 10 (1986), pp. 179–96.

3. J. Bennett, "Cultural Marginality: Identity Issues in Intercultural Training," in *Education for the Intercultural Experience,* ed. M. Paige (Yarmouth, ME: Intercultural Press, 1993).

4. James Banks, "The Stages of Ethnic and Cultural Development," in *Multicultural Education: Theory and Practice,* 2nd ed., ed. James Banks (Boston: Allyn and Bacon, 1988).

5. W. Perry, *Forms of Cognitive and Ethical Development in the College Years* (New York: Holt, Rinehart and Winston, 1969).

Chapter Forty-Seven

Diversity Management
The Challenge of Change

Marilyn D. Loden

■

Marilyn D. Loden

Marilyn Loden is president of Loden Associates, Inc., a San Francisco–based management consulting firm. Her work in public and private institutions focuses on managing organizational change and valuing employee diversity. She is the author of Feminine Leadership, or How to Succeed in Business Without Being One of the Boys *(1985) and coauthor of* Workforce America! Managing Employee Diversity as a Vital Resource *(1991).*

Since the mid 1980s, when diversity began garnering attention in the American workplace, considerable time, money, and energy have been spent developing initiatives to raise organizational consciousness and pave the way for change. These initiatives have included audits to identify inherent institutional barriers that delimit human potential and educational efforts to help individuals deal more effectively with personal biases and destructive, institutional "isms." Underlying these efforts is the implicit recognition that *valuing diversity is a new paradigm for managing people,* one that requires awareness of the impact of core differences, management experimentation, and institutional reform.

Among the many changes required to support diversity, none is more fundamental than a change in assumptions about the importance of human differences. Historically, throughout the U.S. workplace, most managers minimized the importance that core differences such as age, ethnicity, gender, physical abilities, race, and sexual orientation played in shaping assumptions, expectations, and behavior. Instead of viewing cultural differences as the key to greater innovation, diversity was viewed as a liability, something to be suppressed. Today, U.S. institutions and their management teams are finally recognizing that *basic human differences make a powerful difference* in the ways people relate to each other and their environments. It is this acknowledgment of the importance of core differences in shaping assumptions, expectations, and behavior that is unfreezing the old diversity-as-liability mind-set and leading to a paradigm shift in the ways managers deal with people issues.

Effective management of differences—both visible and invisible—requires increased awareness and flexibility. Creating a climate that supports diversity is a complicated process. Once cultural diversity is acknowledged, managers can no longer assume that fair treatment always means the same treatment. They can no longer "manage for fit" by encouraging assimilation and discouraging behavioral styles and methods regarded as counter to the culture. Now they must demonstrate a willingness to consider the new and unfamiliar. Managers must create a safe environment for experimentation. In short, they must balance the organization's ongoing need for common goals, quality performance, and employee commitment with newly recognized realities created by diversity in experience, desires, styles, and methods.

Thus, when the cultural audits and awareness workshops are concluded, questions about how to manage diversity for greater innovation and productivity still loom large. When to focus on sameness and when to celebrate differences become fundamental management challenges. Providing appropriate coaching and support for people of diverse cultural backgrounds is recognized as a more complex undertaking than simply applying the one-size-fits-all approach of the past.

CHOOSING CHANGE OVER COMFORT

As people who have mastered the unwritten rules and prospered in the organizational system, most managers exhibit some resistance to letting go of old assumptions, traditions, and practices, even as they recognize the need to value diversity in the present. Despite the desire to change the culture, managers are often reluctant to give up the "knowns" and embrace the new and untested. Unless they recognize this dilemma and work against the human tendency to choose comfort over change, their own socialization will restrict their ability to innovate and manage diversity as an asset.

Moving beyond the boundaries of one's own socialized experience, then, is an ongoing challenge for managers committed to valuing diversity. Regardless of one's particular age, educational background, ethnic heritage, gender, organizational role, physical abilities, race, sexual orientation, etc., every manager faces some internal tension between the natural desire to maintain comfort and the status quo *versus* the need to embrace change. As they develop long-term goals and devise strategies to leverage diversity, managers must remain cognizant of their own desires for both comfort and change. More important, they must recognize that these underlying needs will have a direct bearing on the ways they position and manage diversity in the future.

NEW DIVERSITY MANAGEMENT CHALLENGES

Today as never before, these conflicting desires are creating new management challenges. These critical challenges require that managers choose between:

* Assimilation versus integration.
* Tolerating versus valuing diversity.
* Maintaining innocence versus becoming accountable.
* One-dimensional diversity focus versus multidimensional focus.
* Rugged individualism versus systems perspective.
* Diversity for increased productivity versus diversity as the right thing to do.

Assimilation Versus Integration

Among the early challenges that managers face in dealing with diversity, none is more fundamental than choosing between two distinct, managerial mind-sets: assimilation and integration. Proponents of assimilation deal with diversity as an issue of *fit*. Emphasis is on helping those outside the cultural mainstream learn the existing insider rules in order to achieve full membership.

Because assimilationists view acculturation as the critical factor in determining failure and success, their primary focus is on changing people to fit the culture. Although many assimilationists are also committed to increasing visible diversity (e.g., in age, ethnicity, gender, physical ability, and race) within their organizations, they are reluctant to give up the old assumptions that define *appropriate behavior* and support greater behavioral diversity. Thus, they often do not recognize or encourage more subtle, stylistic differences that are an inevitable by-product of increased diversity.

This desire for visible diversity, then, becomes more symbolic than real. Instead of adding new zest to organizational life, the perspectives of those outside the mainstream *remain* outside, even as more people from diverse cultural backgrounds move in. Despite the demographic changes that occur, no new models of leadership, followership, teamwork, or process innovation emerge as a result of this change. Instead, people of diverse cultural backgrounds participate and prosper by adopting the styles, values, and standards previously established by those in the mainstream.

Integrationists employ a different diversity management mind-set. Because they see the institutional culture as a construct that supports and validates its mainstream creators, their primary focus is on modifying the culture to support greater human diversity. This emphasis on culture change leads to different conclusions about how to develop, evaluate, reward, and manage people. Instead of emphasizing fit, flexibility becomes the critical element.

Like assimilationists, integrationists recognize the fundamental need for creating common goals and commitment. However, they believe that common ground can be established only with widespread acknowledgment of and respect for core differences. Thus, their approach to leading and managing diversity is grounded in multicultural education and awareness building.

Integrationists focus on developing a multicultural perspective. They use this perspective to examine the impact of formal organizational systems (policies, practices, rules, standards) and informal systems (norms, traditions, networks, etc.) on employees, clients, customers, publics, and other stakeholders. Although eliminating cultural bias is a major goal in integrative change, the primary objective is the creation of a new, more inclusive culture, grounded in the experiences of all, where diversity in its many varieties is recognized, sought, and supported. Is there still a need for performance standards, rules, and conformity in a diverse, integrated culture? Certainly. However, here the common goals and common expectations are linked to the basic mission of the organization rather than to the styles and perspectives of select people.

Tolerating Versus Valuing Diversity

As they search for a balance between assimilation and integration, managers must also grapple with the question: Is increased diversity merely unavoidable or actually an asset? If cultural diversity is regarded as merely unavoidable, it is more likely to be dealt with as an externally imposed change requiring greater tolerance. As such, managers and their organizations will devise ways to cope with this new reality (while maintaining their comfort), rather than welcome it as an opportunity for new learning and growth. Conversely, if managers believe that *increased diversity is intrinsically valuable* as a source of innovation and renewal, then they are more likely to actively pursue it and encourage it to flourish.

As with the glass that is either half-empty or half-full, the value that diversity can offer is truly in the eye of the beholder. If managers choose to merely tolerate this change, then the long-term benefits of increased diversity will be severely limited. However, if they choose to actively support diversity and seek ways to maximize its positive impact, then the benefits that it can offer—in increased cooperation, respect, commitment, and quality performance—will continue to grow. Deciding how to position this change is a critical management responsibility that requires both an understanding of the subtle benefits that diversity offers and a recognition of the ways in which its potential can be *restricted* through tolerance and *enhanced* through active support.

Maintaining Innocence Versus Becoming Accountable

In creating cultures that value diversity, managers must also decide where they stand and *when they will take a stand* on issues of workplace bias and discrimination. Are they willing to examine and acknowledge the pain that prejudice and discrimination cause, or do they tend to minimize these problems? Do they take ownership for their *own* biases and stereotypical assumptions? Do they work to increase their own multicultural awareness and encourage candid feedback about their behavior, or do they proclaim themselves prejudice-free?

Although historical patterns of discrimination can be found in virtually every organization in the U.S. workplace, most institutions and many individuals remain locked in denial. Because there is widespread reluctance to acknowledge prejudice and discrimination in many organizations, it is not surprising that little energy is used to address the real and persistent issues of ageism, heterosexism, racism, sexism, etc. Instead, many managers and employees spend their time and energy proclaiming their support for diversity *and* attesting to their own innocence. Yet, if individuals and organizations were as innocent as some claim, discrimination would cease to exist and diversity would already be valued throughout the American workplace.

To break the cycle of denial and inertia that exists today, managers who value diversity must be among the first to acknowledge the problems of bias and destructive institutional isms. At the personal level, they must allow themselves to be vulnerable to feedback and work to change their own behavior. To grow, they must be willing to venture into new and unfamiliar relationships with *others* (people of different core identities)—to risk, discover, and learn from their own missteps. In short, they must be models for other employees in their organizations and lead the way to enlightenment and justice by demonstrating that they, too, are unfinished, open to new learning, *willing and able* to change.

One-Dimensional Diversity Focus Versus Multidimensional Focus

Once the real problems of discrimination are acknowledged, managers must then determine how best to address them. If managers decide to focus on a single "ism" rather than look for patterns in assumptions and behavior across the spectrum of diversity, they run the risk of becoming single-issue agents of change. Similarly, if their energy and interest in fighting injustice is limited to "isms" that affect their own core identities, they are likely to be perceived by *others* as insensitive, lacking commitment, and even self-serving.

To be models of multiculturalism, managers must advocate as strongly for fairness for *others* as they do for fairness for themselves and their own core identity groups. By being we-centered as opposed to me-centered, they can build coalitions among people of diverse cultural backgrounds and raise the collective consciousness regarding similarities in the patterns of treatment and assumptions that run through *all* forms of social discrimination. Rather than dealing with the problem one "ism" at a time, managers can simultaneously address the need for inclusion, respect, and cooperation across many dimensions of difference and build multicultural partnerships in support of institutional change.

Rugged Individualism Versus Systems Perspective

Dealing effectively with issues of discrimination also demands that managers challenge the myth of "the level playing field" and help their organizations recognize the ways in which some groups continue to be systematically disadvantaged because of differences in age, disability, educational background, gender, race, sexual orientation, etc. For those in the mainstream who believe in their own ability to transcend all external obstacles on the path to success, the concept of powerful systematic barriers that derail and delimit *others* is often difficult to comprehend, let alone accept. Nonetheless, if one considers the demographic profile of middle and senior management in most U.S. organizations in the 1990s, evidence of exclusion (based on differences such as race, physical abilities, and gender) is still apparent.

As long as mainstream managers use their own experience as the yardstick for measuring the experiences of others, they will fail to recognize the powerful ways in which organizational systems work to give them advantage and force disadvantage upon those outside the mainstream. Managers will also contribute to *others'* frustration with every new assertion that their organizations are meritocracies, in which the playing field is truly level.

To create a culture of respect and fairness, mainstream managers must give up the myth of rugged individualism and, with the help of a systems perspective, recognize the privileges they receive because of their dominant position. Once this is done, they must then decide if, for the sake of fairness, they are willing to give up these privileges and create a truly level field on which to compete. Unless the invisible advantages of dominance cease to exist, the concept of a real meritocracy will continue to be just that: a concept, not a reality.

Diversity for Increased Productivity Versus the Right Thing to Do

Finally, after resolving these challenges, managers must reassess the very arguments that they themselves use in making the case for increased cultural diversity within their organizations. Do they argue the value of diversity as a tool for greater innovation? If they work in institutions that are driven primarily by short-term, economic considerations, do they avoid discussions of valuing diversity as the right thing to do?

Within the many organizations where moral and ethical arguments in favor of valuing diversity are dismissed or viewed with cynicism, managers use productivity improvement as the sole rationale for supporting this change. Indeed, one can make a strong case for diversity purely on the basis of the potential it offers for increased innovation, teamwork, and quality performance. Nonetheless, viewing the value of diversity as a short-term, opportunistic strategy for productivity improvement diminishes its importance as a powerful, sustaining change. Because valuing diversity is good for organizations and good for people, it is a change that can and should be positioned in both pragmatic, productivity-related terms and in enduring, moral/ethical terms. To view it only as a productivity tool is to miss the important role that diversity can play in making the workplace more spirited, more humane, and more vital.

Chapter Forty-Eight

Edith Whitfield Seashore

Feedback
*Making a Difference in a World of Differences**

Edith Whitfield Seashore

■

Edith Whitfield Seashore has consulted to industrial, military, educational, and voluntary organizations for 25 years. She is a social psychologist concerned with organizational change, team building, strategic planning, and multicultural organizations. In addition to her consulting practice, from 1974 to 1979 she was president of the NTL Institute for Applied Behavioral Sciences. In 1979, with Morley Segal, she founded the American University/NTL Master's Program in Human Resource Development. She is a coeditor of this book.

The concept of feedback comes from cybernetics, the theory of control. However, as influential as feedback may be, it doesn't necessarily control anything. How often have we received or given the same feedback repeatedly without anything significantly changing? Feedback may not be a very good tool for change, but without it, we might never understand or influence human interactions.

Why is feedback important? If we want to build, maintain, or test our relationships, feedback is our only source of information. Without feedback, we would not be able to test the reality of our perceptions, reactions, observations, or intentions!

The psychologist Carl Rogers observed that one of our most powerful needs is to be heard and to be understood. Without feedback, we would have difficulty distinguishing between what's going on internally and what's going on externally.

Feedback is fundamental to helping people improve their performance, reach an objective, or avoid unpleasant reactions. Feedback enables people to work together and achieve more through cooperation.

---

*With permission of the authors, portions of this article have been extracted from the recently published book *What Did You Say? The Art of Giving and Receiving Feedback,* by Charles N. Seashore, Edith Whitfield Seashore, and Gerald M. Weinberg (Douglas Charles Press, 1992).

Feedback distinguishes the important from the irrelevant and reality from distortions. It helps us see patterns in a series of specific instances. Feedback creates new information and maximizes the opportunities to share thoughts and feelings.

Some very important personality theories help us to understand the concept of feedback. Sigmund Freud's concept of defense mechanisms talks about the way we defend ourselves against messages as if survival were at stake.[1] The Freudian term *projection* refers to the way we place an image of what's inside of us onto others. Projection leads us to send messages that reveal more about ourselves than others.

Virginia Satir's Interaction Model[2] is another insightful way of looking at feedback. The feedback model is (1) a message is sent, which (2) you perceive and interpret in any way you choose; you then (3) have your own feeling about your interpretation, and immediately thereafter (4) have a feeling about that feeling. You may share none, any, or all of these reactions. Depending on what is shared or not shared, it will not be clear what happened to the original message sent until there is some behavior, which is then perceived and interpreted. Then the cycle continues: a message sent, perception and interpretation made, a feeling produced, and, immediately after, a feeling about that feeling.

Many interactions start as simply as, "What time is it?" And the time is told. We don't need Freud's defenses or Satir's interaction model to decipher this kind of interaction, yet this kind accounts for about 99 percent of all our interactions during a typical working day. However, simple, straight interactions do not account for 99 percent of our time during the working day because they happen in a few seconds and then are forgotten. The most complex interactions account for probably less than 1 percent of our interactions during a typical working day. However, complex interactions and misunderstandings take a great deal of time to resolve—50 percent or more of our time.

Many of these complex interactions occur when we interact with people we perceive as very different from us. Why are we so reluctant to give them feedback? Often it is because we fear getting involved.

Telling them—giving feedback, can be a way to play "If one of us is going to change, why don't you go first?" Telling them can be a way of testing their willingness to change. But not everybody is willing to play that game. If we play the game, we may wind up only learning something about ourselves—and that could be the most significant learning of all.

Sometimes we avoid giving direct feedback because we fear learning the truth about ourselves. We avoid telling them out of fear of being known. Telling them exposes us to the possibility of surprise and therefore to the possibility of change. By definition, discovery is not predictable. Although we may have set out to change the other person, we might wind up changing ourselves.

The less we invest in changing the other person, the more likely it becomes that each of us will grow. This paradoxical fact is one good reason for letting go of the fantasy that we can change another person. Being realistic, we might admit our inherent selfishness and substitute the goal of exploring and discovering something new about ourselves. Being even more realistic, it takes a mighty effort to admit we're doing something for ourselves. It's so tempting to revert to the pretence that we're giving them feedback for their own good.

In a world where most of our interactions have been with people whose upbringing and ways of living have been somewhat similar to ours, we could project a lot of ourselves onto others and find a somewhat predictable response. However, in today's world, where we are interacting more and more with others who were brought up in less familiar cultures, we have ever more opportunities to be misinterpreted and perhaps to be less and less influential. Our socialization and theirs lead to unfamiliar responses. Our biases and theirs lead to more and more resistance and confusion. Feedback necessitates our understanding about what we have heard. We must find creative ways to understand our socialization and biases in order to help each other grow, to build and maintain more meaningful relationships, and to test the reality of our perceptions, reactions, observations, intentions, and behaviors.

The following are three examples of the difficulties of giving and getting feedback with others who are very different from ourselves.

1. I was present when a white male, sixtyish senior executive gave feedback to a much younger African American employee. It was intended as a compliment of the highest order. "You work so much the way I did at your age. You remind me so much of me that I never notice your color."

   To the shock and amazement of the white male, his employee responded after a few moments of silence. "You couldn't insult me more. I can't believe that you don't notice my color, of which I am very proud." Between the two of them, it took many hours of discussion with a third person's assistance to make sense of this totally misunderstood piece of feedback, in this case coming from both directions.

2. Another curious relic of my past was feedback I received when I was completing a year at college as president of the student body. The dean of students told me how wonderful it was working with me closely all year. His comments were, "It was wonderful working with you this year; you think just like a man." I was incredibly flattered.

It was only upon reflection that I realized how utterly ridiculous this compliment was. Many years later, in a conversation with the then-retired dean, I recalled this compliment with greater awareness. He protested his statement, but I assured him it had a very positive effect at the time it was given to me and only seemed ridiculous in retrospect. He was fortunate that I, too, was unaware back then.

3. The next incident was related by a Hispanic student of mine, who is an executive in a corporation. He said that he and some of his Hispanic colleagues at work were having a discussion in Spanish when another employee, who didn't speak or understand Spanish, told them it wasn't appropriate to speak in Spanish in front of him and their other colleagues. He said he didn't understand why that was and that he had received that feedback before. The person replied, "We assume you are talking about us." My Hispanic friend said he was astonished and replied, "We are never talking about you; why would we want to talk about you? It is just a more familiar, intimate way for us to communicate." This was enlightening to the colleagues who had always felt suspicious before.

Our concerns about using feedback in a world of differences make it impossible for many to continue to receive valuable information that will help them lead the kinds of lives and make the kinds of choices that are essential for their development. In a world of differences, devoid of feedback, we face the grave danger of living in a world lacking information and therefore living in a world of unreality. Because of these possible pitfalls, we avoid giving important feedback information to those whose reactions and responses are less familiar.

One of our major concerns in giving feedback to those whom we perceive as different from us in race, gender, etc., is that we could reveal our own racist or sexist biases, so that the feedback would tell more about the giver than about the receiver. In most instances, the receiver is much more aware of the impact of the feedback and its relevancy. Therefore, it is increasingly more important to understand the receiver's reactions and to be able to look more closely at ourselves regarding our preconceptions.

The giver's fantasy: If feedback is clear, specific, timed right, nonjudgmental, and speaks only to behavior, it will be accepted as given.

The giver's fact: No matter what it appears to be, feedback information is almost totally about the giver, not the receiver.

The receiver's fantasy: The receiver is controlled by the giver's feedback. Whatever receivers do with the feedback is totally within their control. They can reject it, swallow it whole, distort it, adore it, hate it, forget it, or remember it forever.

The receiver's fact: The receiver is totally in control of feedback, but the control is not necessarily conscious. It's the "not necessarily conscious" that makes it hard for us to believe that we are totally in control, for we are often not conscious that we are in control. And until there is a conscious exchange between the receiver and the giver, what happened to the feedback will remain a mystery.

Among the many factors contributing to possible misunderstandings are different perceptions. We may be similar, but in the end we are different people, so our perceptions differ. We extract different information from the situation, so what you send is not what I receive. Different time: We can get confused when part of the feedback doesn't refer to the present, but to the past or future. Different place: We may be mystified because part of the feedback refers to some other context. Someone else: We'll also be thrown off center when part of the feedback refers to some other person. Inner feelings about myself: My feelings about myself have a powerful influence on how I respond. If I feel bad about myself, I may be more critical of things. If I feel good, I may be more inclined to see things in a favorable light.

All of these confusing factors—different perceptions, different time, different place, different people, as well as my inner feelings about myself—tend to combine to produce the most confusing feedback situations.

Giving feedback is often a way of exercising influence via the Trojan horse. Feedback may look as though it is for the benefit of the receiver, but it disguises the payoff to the sender. Regardless of its usefulness to the receiver, such feedback serves as a convenient vehicle for avoiding, displacing, attacking, gaining status, and justifying the status quo for the sender.

There are four factors that can take priority over the substance of a feedback message. In hierarchical order, they are:

1. The perceived *power* of the sender.
2. The *"intention"* or influence attempt.
3. The strength of the *emotion* from the giver.
4. The substance of the *message.*

No wonder it is so difficult to give and receive feedback that can be useful.

Although some of us may grow up to be big and powerful, we were all children at one time, little and weak, surrounded by powerful giants. When the giants spoke, we listened. The principal problem about giving feedback derives from these childhood experiences. When feedback was given to us by those more powerful, we were supposed to take it, believe it, and change our behavior accordingly.

The use of formal power—that is, the power inherent in a position—is key to the way feedback will be received. People in powerful positions can make demands, be heard, exercise control, be coercive, or intimidate us. In a world of differences, power is a powerful ingredient.

Intention/influence refers to how the sender wants the message to be heard and what particular response the sender expects. Receivers will resist change and misinterpret the intent if the giver gets disturbed or upset. The more we try to control, the less influence we are likely to have. Giving feedback starts with your intention, though good intentions may not be enough. You may want to persecute me, exploit me, hinder me, confuse me, victimize me, diminish me, disarm me, immobilize me, or demolish me. On the other hand, you may want to help me, inform me, encourage me, enlighten me, or improve me.

Delivery is like an outer wrapping. Once we've successfully stripped it away, there may still be a hidden emotional layer of anger, warmth, sadness, or whatever. If the message is wrapped in anger, we might alert our system to be ready for an attack. A wrapping of warmth may open our hearts or set off alarms depending on our past experience. Often we filter the content of a feedback message according to the emotional state we perceive in the sender. Our preferences for different emotions may differ drastically, and this may influence unique interpretations.

As for style, each of us is unique. Although we may think our style is clear and straightforward, to others it is frequently full of distractions, confusions, or new strategies that may draw our attention to the style and not the substance of our message.

At long last, we have come to the content, the substance of what a person has wanted to communicate—an idea, an opinion, a fact, or an observation—which, depending on all the other factors, can be received with curiosity and seen as an opportunity to grow or can be seen as criticism, threatening one's relationship or very survival.

Whether giving or receiving feedback, the most important thing is acknowledging, understanding, and accepting what's going on inside the giver—then checking out what the receiver did with the feedback.

Feedback is a challenging tool for helping us to continue to learn, grow, improve our relationships, and really understand each other. In a world of differences, whether they be in gender, skin color, religion, or sexual preference, successful feedback can make a difference.

NOTES

1. Sigmund Freud, *A General Introduction to Psychoanalysis* (New York: Pocket Books, 1975).

2. Virginia Satir, *Meditations and Inspirations* (Millbrae, CA: Celestial Arts, 1985).

Chapter Forty-Nine

Michael F. Broom

Diversity, Synergy, and Transformative Social Change

Michael F. Broom

■

Michael F. Broom, PhD, is an organizational psychologist with 15 years of experience consulting with organizations toward productivity improvement. He is a senior faculty member of Johns Hopkins University's Fellows in the Management of Change. He teaches in Georgetown and American universities' programs in human and organizational development. A member of NTL's board of directors, Broom chairs that organization's Transformative Social Change Committee.

S ocial change is simple. Watch!

Adversity as a function of social diversity = Social dysfunction

Synergy as a function of social diversity = Social well-being

Therefore, positive social change requires the transformation of adversity into synergy.

See? That's all there is to it—transformative social change.

OK, let's break this verbal calculus down to something understandable and doable. Imagine that our goal is to convert our world—our local, national, and global communities—into systems that fully support the interdependent physical and emotional well-being of all individuals and peoples. That would be a world without wars, poverty, hunger, homelessness, crime, drug abuse, or oppression.

Most efforts to date to produce such a world have been attempted by creating, in one way or another, a single, right mold into which you fit or didn't fit. If you fit by virtue of birthright (e.g., apartheid and other ethnic-based efforts) or assimilation (e.g., how women and people of color can succeed in modern corporate America), you were allowed the benefits of well-being. If you didn't fit—by birthright or assimilation—you were impoverished, jailed, enslaved, exterminated, or otherwise denied the benefits of social well-being. Current examples of the latter include the ethnic conflicts in Eastern Europe, women in many societies, and the poor, hungry, and homeless (most of whom are also ethnically different) of most societies.

It is no news that such fit-or-die efforts at social change either have failed (the former USSR), are failing (Bosnia-Herzegovina), or are struggling to survive (the United States). The sources of their struggles have been their own ineptitude and/or the concentrated challenges and social cost of those who "don't fit." More important, whatever successes fit-or-die efforts have achieved have only been on behalf of those who fit—at best, an exclusionary definition of social well-being. Our world is diverse and has proved intractable. Our differences of ethnicity, color, religion, gender, age, sexual orientation, nationality, occupation, and class—to name just a few—are not going to melt away into any singular pot.

To convert our world—our local, national, and global communities—into systems that fully support the interdependent physical and emotional well-being of all individuals and peoples, how we deal with the intractability of diversity requires change of a particular nature. The particular form required is transformation.

We know how to change mud into bricks, we know how to change our clothes, and we know how to change a gathering of people into a cohesive group. Transformation is needed when you "change water into wine," "get blood out of a turnip," or get synergy rather than adversity out of diversity. In these latter examples, ordinary change is insufficient.

Something is needed beyond the normal formulations and structures of change as defined by our belief systems. That something is transformation, which occurs beyond (*trans*) the structures (*form*) of our normal belief systems. To create effective, pervasive, and permanent social change, we must go beyond the forms and structures of our beliefs about diversity. Those forms and structures about diversity, however, are held in our beliefs about power.

Any change requires power, the use of energy; and diversity is a key coin in the realm of power. Therefore, to transform our beliefs and behavior regarding diversity, we must transform our beliefs and behavior regarding power. Table 49–1, adapted from Broom and Klein's *Power, the Infinite Game*,[1] contrasts our current, finite, and problematic view of power with an alternative, infinite view that would be more supportive of the social change we are after.

The belief that power is abundant is a transformation from the belief that power is scarce. Each supposition supports a complete, logically consistent, and very different system of corollary beliefs and behaviors. Highlighted in italics are three beliefs about differences and diversity that are subsequent to the two fundamental

TABLE 49-1
Contrasting Paradigms of Power

The Finite (Current) Paradigm	An Infinite (Alternative) Paradigm
Fundamental supposition: Power is scarce.	Fundamental supposition: Power is plentiful.
Power is a zero-sum game. No one can win in the long-run.	Power is a positive-sum game. Everyone wins.
The purpose is to establish who is winner and who is loser.	The purpose is to maintain the game and the players.
Differences are used to determine who wins and who loses.	*Differences are cause for curiosity and learning.*
Diversity is threatening and dangerous; conformity is safe.	*Diversity is valued and safe; conformity is a matter of personal choice.*
Diversity leads to adversity.	*Diversity leads to synergy.*
Destroys partnerships through distrust and hostility.	Supports partnerships through curiosity and learning from differences.
Ignorance condemned as different from knowledge.	Ignorance valued as necessary precursor to curiosity, learning, and knowledge.
A game played very seriously when individual or group identity is perceived as at stake.	A game to be played well and joyfully as no one's survival is at stake.
A self-fulfilling prophecy because potential partnerships are temporary and limited.	A self-fulfilling prophecy because potential partnerships are secure and unlimited.
The paradigm of choice when survival is a moment-to-moment issue.	The paradigm of choice when growth and learning are primary goals.

suppositions. When diversity is valued and safe, differences can be used as a source of curiosity, learning, and the synergy needed for social change. When differences determine who wins and who loses, diversity is threatening, unsafe, and cause for adversity; and we can never gather the systemwide synergy needed for social change.

Synergy is in evidence when the results of the components of a system working together are greater than the sum results of those components working separately. Synergy can occur when the components working together are different. The amount of synergic energy possible within a social system is directly proportional to the amount of diversity within that system. If I were to be in a room of clones of me, I would be very comfortable and at ease.

However, genius that I am, no learning or synergy could occur because each of us only knows what each of the others knows. Hence, the amount of synergy possible is directly proportional to the amount of difference available. So if we have a system full of differences—ethnic differences, gender differences, religious differences, age dif-

ferences, class differences, etc.—there is a great deal of synergy possible. However, to change the possibility into reality, another change
is necessary. In the late 1960s and early 1970s, many cities sponsored
charrettes, in which many components of those communities' systems came together to figure out what to do about the disenfranchisement and poverty of the inner-city African Americans. Not a whole
lot came from these charrettes, where much synergy was possible,
but little was actually created. This failing occurred because they
used their differences as a cause to fight over what should be done
and who was going to be in charge of what. The amount of synergic
energy created for change within a social system is directly proportional to the degree to which the system implicitly and explicitly
values and learns from its diversity.

The creation of synergy must be preceded by a transformative shift
from the finite paradigm in which "differences are threatening and
dangerous" to the infinite paradigm in which "differences can be
used as a source of curiosity and learning." Likewise, "ignorance
condemned as different from knowledge" must transform to "ignorance valued as a necessary precursor to curiosity, learning, and
knowledge." Only when we perceive power as abundant rather than
scarce will we learn to create synergy rather than adversity from our
diversity.

There are five principles of synergy in social systems that include
the key points made above:

1. Sufficient resources and energy for substantive change exist within
   any properly defined system.

2. Such resources and energy will only be sufficient for substantive
   change when used synergically.

3. The amount of synergic energy possible within a social system is
   directly proportional to the amount of diversity within that system.

4. The amount of synergic energy created for change within a social
   system is directly proportional to the degree to which a system
   implicitly and explicitly values and learns from its diversity.

5. All general components of social systems will willingly contribute to
   the synergy if they perceive a process sufficient to lead to a
   practicable possibility of maintaining or enhancing the well-being of
   that system.

Transforming the use of diversity for synergy rather than adversity is one of several still-developing ideas this writer has regarding
the processes of transformative social change. The issues of synergy
and diversity are included in Number 2 and are considered the most
important. The others are as follows:

1. *Create a sense of possibility* regarding the desired change. Some thinking requires a leap of faith from one fact-of-reality to another fact-of-reality for transformation to occur. However, such a requirement is daunting, at best. An intermediate step requiring a sense of possibility regarding the transformation rather than a fact-of-reality is offered. For example, many of the social dysfunctions that we desired to change are seen by many to be part of human nature and thus immutable. Because the Bible says that the poor will always be with us (Matthew 26:11a), some may think that work to eradicate poverty, hunger, and homelessness is fruitless. War is often described as sad, but unavoidable. For transformation to occur, the belief that any particular social change is impossible must first shift to a sense that the desired state is possible, though not a fact-of-reality. Once people believe that change is possible, they may become involved in bringing about a transformation that would have otherwise been impossible.

2. Transform the idea that differences are an occasion for overt or covert conflict to the idea that the valuing of differences is required to develop the synergy necessary to create the desired change. This transformation must occur within the change-initiating system before it can occur within the larger system.

   To create effective social change, we must emphasize learning, as we have little pertinent experience with it. Peter Senge's *The Fifth Discipline* urges companies to become organizations committed to learning if they wish to continue to thrive.[2] Likewise, if we are to create thriving communities, the same commitment to learning must prevail. Ironically, we can only learn from our differences, and our prevailing paradigm—the finite—has us afraid of differences.

3. Engage all the major components of the social system (e.g., corporations, media, government agencies, related nonprofit organizations, people with low income, etc.) as partners in the desired change and related transformations.

   This relates to the issue of synergy. Items 1 and 5 of the principles of synergy are relevant here. Item 1 says, "Sufficient resources and energy for substantive change exist within any properly defined system." These are the resources (brainpower, personpower, money, skills, etc.) that must come together synergically if we are to create the solutions to our social ills.

   Item 5 says, "All general components of social systems will willingly contribute to the synergy if they perceive a process sufficient to lead to a practicable possibility of maintaining or enhancing the well-being of that system." Many corporations of our social systems perceive getting involved with social change issues as fruitless and a waste of time and money. Accordingly, they stay away or at best provide financial donations to maintain their identity as good citizens. Such mediocre involvement is insufficient to the goals of synergy creation. However, corporations will involve themselves to sufficient depth if they are presented with some process that they believe could be successful.

4. Identify the *covert and exclusionary processes* that maintain the status quo and turn them into *overt, inclusionary, and modifiable processes.*

Decision making is a good example here. In many communities, decisions regarding social issues are often made behind the scenes or openly by a very small but influential group of public and corporate officials. Where a housing project is going to be built or how much funding a homeless project will receive might be cases in point. Decisions made in this manner not only contravene the democratic process but also are made with motivations different from those of social well-being. To move such decision making into an open, inclusive forum provides the opportunity for broader diversity and more effective synergy.

5. Support awareness and management of any shadow issues regarding the change goal. This is a difficult and undocumented issue concerning social change. In essence, this idea proposes that we—the *haves* of our communities—will not effectively manage the social issues of hunger, homelessness, drug abuse, and criminal violence until we decide to become aware of and manage the hungry, homeless, self-esteem-seeking, and outraged parts of ourselves. In one testing of this idea with a group of middle-class antihunger leaders, most acknowledged the existence of these issues within their everyday lives. They mentioned their hunger for fuller love lives, their loss of a sense of neighborhood or extended family, their sense of powerlessness in the face of our bureaucracies, and their rage at the society that has "forced" all these difficulties upon them.

These issues within middle America have become shadow issues because we have obeyed the social contract that says we must pretend we are happy because we have so much. As we deny our own happinesses, we must as a group blind ourselves to the despondency and needs of the *have-nots* in our communities. To do otherwise would be to open ourselves, not just to their unhappiness, but also to our own. In truth, we do not know how to deal with either. And we cannot learn as long as we keep ourselves blind and in the thrall of the finite perspective of power that says that we dare not speak our anguish for fear of being seen as different and, all too possibly, losers.

6. Identify and transform any other beliefs and assumptions that are in the way of the desired change from hindering beliefs to supporting beliefs. There are many of these. The antihunger leaders, while doing an exercise on the assumptions they have that hinder them from inventing the end of hunger, listed: "Corporate America is the enemy," "Poor people are too difficult to work with," and "No one's interested in hunger but us." These highlight just a few of several dozen beliefs of which they became conscious and cited—much to their consternation and excitement for the opportunity for change that

such awareness provided them. Clearly, these beliefs had kept them
isolated from the larger community, including the community they
themselves created to serve. They are now actively working at building partnerships with the corporate world, the poor, and the bureau-
crats on behalf of creating a systemwide synergy to invent the end of
hunger.

The work of transformative social change—transforming how we
deal with diversity, delving into our murky shadows, and building
systemwide synergies—is daunting, not to mention complex, mysti-
fying, and sometimes terrifying. At the same time, it is energizing
and enlivening as we give our lives a surpassing meaning. And as
we tackle these tasks with passion, patience, and persistence, we will
find ourselves with an enormous sense of humble personal power,
and we will build a world that supports the well-being of all individuals and peoples.

NOTES

1. Michael F. Broom and Donald C. Klein, *Power, the Infinite Game* (Washington,
   DC: HRD Press, *in press, 1994*).
2. Peter M. Senge, *The Fifth Discipline* (New York: Doubleday/Currency, 1990).

Chapter Fifty

Jeanne Cherbeneau

Diversity in the Workplace

Optimizing the Value of Individual Differences Through an Organizational Systems Approach

Jeanne Cherbeneau

■

Jeanne Cherbeneau, PhD, is president of Cherbeneau and Associates, a management and organization development consulting firm located in Berkeley, California. Cherbeneau specializes in organizational change management and designing successful efforts to enhance the valuing, productivity, and satisfaction of diverse work forces. Organizations served vary in size, stage of development, and industry—from 800,000 employees to small business start-ups, and in the public and private sectors.

A mind is a terrible thing to waste.

T hat well-known slogan packs a powerful emotional punch, and its applications are many.

Daily, organizations waste not just the minds of their people but the intrinsic human desire and the capability of people to achieve and perform at their highest possible level. With that loss goes physical and emotional energy, drive, stamina, and creativity, the very human resources organizations need most to survive and thrive in today's complex, ever-changing world.

THE WORK FORCE OF THE 1990s

The changing work force is reshaping organizations. Increased numbers of women, people of color, people of various ethnic and national groups, the disabled, singles, single parents, and dual-career couples have brought different values, skills, and motivations to traditional organizations dominated by white, married males. A major stumbling block to organizational and individual high performance has been the inability to: (1) recognize, (2) value, (3) manage well, and (4) fully develop, utilize, and benefit from the individual differences people bring to the workplace.

The challenge for organizations in the 1990s is to both advance equal employment opportunities and move beyond the previous color/gender/ethnic/age/religion–blind phase that had been advocated in the 1970s. The assumption underlying the color-blind concept was that biases existed *against* nonwhites, women, and individuals in various ethnic, religious, or age groups. Therefore, to achieve equity or neutrality, one should be blind—that is, not take into account those factors—in any evaluation of or decision making regarding a person's qualifications for employment or advancement, housing, loans, and so on. At the same time, paradoxically, organizations subject to federal regulations were required to adjust the mix of their employee population to reflect, in particular, the percentage mix of gender and race of their local community. This requirement meant, of course, that gender and race *had* to be taken into account in hiring decisions in order to correct inconsistencies. Within communities, similar requirements were reflected in school busing and housing issues. Needless to say, the issue of affirmative action "goals" rages on today within organizations and communities alike.

Dr. Price Cobbs, coauthor of *Black Rage* and one of the nation's leading organization consultants and educators in improving race relations and managing and valuing cultural diversity in the workplace, has described this next phase of organization development as moving from a deficit to an asset model. In this phase, the individual and organization must move beyond viewing the gender, race, ethnicity, and age differences as deficits (i.e., regarding a given individual as lacking something important that the majority has) and view the differences as assets (i.e., the individual brings something valuable that the existing majority does not have).

Some of the more obvious benefits of differences that the changing work force brings to the workplace are the addition of multiple perspectives, as well as experiences and skills that can enhance innovative and creative ways of solving problems, achieving goals, and motivating/energizing people to commit themselves fully to individual and organizational success and excellence.

These changes make it possible to optimize the value and benefits of a diverse work force, as well as ameliorate human oppression and *repression* of potential.

SUCCESSION PLANNING: A KEY TO ORGANIZATIONAL VIABILITY AND HUMAN VITALITY

Succession planning is the conscious, systematic, long-range planning for and development of successors for functional and general/

executive management positions, as well as professional and technical specialty positions, throughout an organization. Succession planning is both lateral and vertical.

An effective succession-planning and career-development system can play a key role in creating and maintaining organizational effectiveness, viability, and success; increasing human effectiveness, satisfaction, and vitality; reducing the waste of human possibilities; and ameliorating human oppression in organizations.

Continuity and integration are two key concepts related to succession planning. *Continuity* is defined as an "unbroken course; without interruption; change without disruption; uninterrupted succession" or "following in order of sequence."

Integration is defined as "making into a whole by bringing all parts together; unifying; uniting; joining with something else." Succession-planning and career-development systems are designed to meet the organization's ongoing human-resource needs and to manage organizational change with minimal disruption. Succession-planning systems and functions are integrated and aligned with the organization's vision, mission, strategy, goals, values, cultures, and priorities.

WHY SUCCESSION PLANNING?

Effective succession planning must take into account the impact of the organization's diverse work force and the members' differing values, needs, and lifestyles.

Many organizations have discovered that most managers and professionals who are in the early and middle stages of their careers, particularly those who might be considered "diverse," believe that developmental opportunities and career advancement are more important than an unusually attractive paycheck in cases when the immediate given job has no implied advancement prospects. Future opportunities may well be the determining factor in accepting a position offer, as these people are not just taking a job, they are joining an organization and looking toward a career in which they believe who they are and what they have to offer will be recognized, valued, supported, developed, and rewarded.

Although a primary organizational purpose of succession planning and career development is to assure that a sufficient source of well-prepared candidates can be identified and that those candidates are readily available for all management, professional, and technical positions, several other important purposes are served as well: (1) an increased ability to compete and to develop and retain capable and diverse people for all targeted positions; (2) an increased preparedness for major organizational changes, such as growth, new ownership or alliances, downsizing, or restructuring; and (3) an increased ability to respond to changes in the external environment (government regulations, the economy, international relationships, etc.).

Growth or Contraction

The growth of many organizations, particularly many start-up companies, has propelled them into organizational sizes that can no longer function effectively with their original leadership, management styles and practices, communication systems, and structures. These organizations risk collapse if they are not able to anticipate, recognize, and respond quickly to changes resulting from the organization's movement from one stage of development to another and to the specific needs for change in management, personnel, structure, systems, and practices.

Such organizations hear and feel the effects of demands for planning and change from many sources: the workplace, regulatory and legal agencies, stakeholders, and their own employees, who want to know if and where their own futures lie in the organization. Organizations frequently lose high-performing or high-potential people when there is minimal observable or stated commitment to the development and promotion of people from within. A well-developed and managed succession-planning and career-development system that is *known* to current employees as well as communicated to potential employees can be a powerful deciding factor in both attracting and retaining capable and diverse people.

For organizations in a contraction, downsizing, or retrenchment mode, there is an increased need for exceptionally capable managers. Given that downsizing tends to reach down into the ranks of middle managers (in addition to staff), the decrease in middle managers usually means larger and/or broader spans of control and more-complex management demands for those who assume these responsibilities. Managers must effectively manage more people and often more functions. In addition, with reduced resources, they must be able to find ways to increase productivity, increase cost-effectiveness, and respond quickly and effectively to change and competition. These increased demands mean competition with other organizations for exceptionally competent and creative managers.

The Marketplace

Changes in the economy, deregulation, global politics, and international competition are additional factors influencing organizations today. These factors have led to both the growth of some organizations and the spawning of multiple new alliances: expansions, start-ups, acquisitions, mergers, joint ventures, and so on. These changes frequently have necessitated: (1) careful selection and deselection among current managers and/or staff when two or more organizations join; (2) more managers, executives, and professional and technical specialists due to growth or new ventures; (3) whole new executive teams for starting up new regional offices or organizations; and (4) reconfigurations of executive and management teams and departments, especially when organizational mergers or international or multicultural alliances require a representative mix of both organizations and cultures.

KEY COMPONENTS AND ROLES

There are seven key components of a successful succession-planning and career-development system, which will advance the valuing and optimization of a diverse work force: (1) strategic human-resource planning; (2) organization design and needs assessment; (3) career-development systems; (4) recruitment and orientation; (5) performance management and appraisal systems; (6) assessing potential; and (7) training and development.

A few points should be highlighted about these components as they relate to work-force diversity. For example, it is essential that human-resources planning occur at every stage of the organization's strategic and business planning in order to achieve the organization's desired mix of diverse employees.

Second, education and training, conferences, and team building may focus on attitudinal change and/or skills development, particularly related to areas of valuing and managing diversity. It is essential that human relations, communication, conflict management, and motivational skills be applied to diversity-related issues. Additional developmental efforts include orientation, acculturation, mentoring, and sponsorship programs.

The complexity and political dynamics of mentoring or sponsorship programs targeted for women, people of color, or immigrants should not be underestimated. Because of the origin and nature of the concept of mentoring—that is, that it has been a "natural," self-selected, informal process that implicitly occurs between two people—it often is assumed that a structured program should be relatively easy to implement. In fact, there can be a great deal of confusion, resentment, resistance, and awkwardness if the intentions, objectives, expectations, etc., of such programs are not carefully and effectively thought through, communicated, structured, and followed through.

Finally, assessing potential is by far the most difficult of all the components. It is an attempt to predict an individual's capabilities for growth, development, achievement and ability to "fit" in specific positions. This component is a particularly sensitive area, as it can be highly vulnerable to the influence of personal biases, stereotypes, and limited views of the best ways to do things. The "assessors" must truly value differences in styles and approaches of those being assessed.

KEY PROCESSES AND SYSTEMS

There are two critical ongoing processes and systems to maintain the overall succession-planning and career-development system. They are: (1) the development and continual review of succession plans; and (2) the ongoing assessment of the compatibility of the succession-planning and career-development system with the organization's vision, mission, strategy, goals, values, structure, policies, practices, systems, and culture.

The ongoing review of the effectiveness of the system needs to address the question "Do our policies, practices, structures, systems, culture, etc., support the effective recruitment, identification, development, and placement of the right people in the right jobs at the right time, and is the valuing and inclusion of diversity clearly reflected in the results?"

Frequent issues are rigidity, inconsistency, inequity, inadequacy, and/or conflicts in systems and among people. These issues are related to such areas as the availability of relevant, accurate, and comprehensive information; short-term and long-term organizational needs and goals; AA/EEO goals; compensation structures; benefits and employee support services such as day-care and employee-assistance programs; recruitment- and relocation-cost reimbursement; policies related to work schedules (e.g., flextime, job sharing, part-time status) power, control, and decision-making processes; values and biases; culture and norms; and personal relationships.

The resolution of these issues and responsibility for these processes involve the CEO, all levels of management, human-resource specialists (particularly in areas of compensation and benefits, training and development, career development, employee assistance, AA/EEO, labor relations, personnel policy), organization-development specialists, strategic planners, and financial and legal advisers.

CAVEATS AND CONCLUSIONS

The success of any succession-planning and career-development effort depends on the attitude, understanding, leadership, behavior modeling, personal involvement, and support of top management.

Succession-planning and career-development systems are not just formal technical systems but very personal and political "informal systems." Their success is dependent on how the following issues are resolved and how things really work in an organization:

- How truly open and participative the system is; who and what levels are involved in the design of the system, decision making, and the extent of information shared.

- How roles, status, and reporting relationships affect the responses to the above questions.

- How flexible the organization and its structure, policies, practices, and systems are; critical areas include compensation and benefits, position-grading structures, policies on reimbursement of relocation and recruitment costs, timeliness in decision making, support for creativity, experimentation, risk taking and innovation, and the use of positions for developmental purposes.

- Which values take priority. Particular areas of values differences include cultural, ethnic, religious, racial, gender, and sexual orientation differences; AA/EEO goals; competence; immediate and long-term needs; personal loyalties and friendships; and what behavior is rewarded—for example, individual/departmental success and competition versus teamwork and collaboration for the good of the whole.

Clearly, a succession-planning and career-development system involves many functions, departments, and individuals. The success of the system depends to a large degree on the level of true integration (unity) of the human-resource and organization-development functions. Not only does integration advance the purposes of succession planning and career development, it advances the integration of human-resource and organization-development functions with other key functions in the organization and with the mission of the organization itself.

Concurrently, top management must be the steward, the guiding and monitoring force, in order to create a smoothly functioning and well-integrated system that is understood and supported by all. Every manager must ensure the availability of capable successors to her or his position. Human resources, organization development, strategic planners, and financial and legal advisers play critical and unique roles, but management at all levels is the implementor and driving force.

Integrated succession-planning and career-development systems align staff functions with all levels of management in common purposes: to value and realize the full range of human possibilities, to create and maintain long-term organizational viability and human vitality, and to ameliorate needless and destructive oppression within the organization.

SOURCES

AMACOM (division of American Management Association), "Conversation with Reginald M. Jones and Frank Doyle," *Organizational Dynamics,* Winter 1982.

Jeanne Cherbeneau, "Self-Esteem and Diversity in the Workplace: An Interview with Price Cobbs, M.D.," *Vision Action* (Journal of the Bay Area OD Network), Vol. 9, No. 3 (Sept. 1990), pp. 22–24.

Chapter Fifty-One

Flex Management
A New Mind-Set for Today's Work Force

David Jamieson and Julie O'Mara

■

David Jamieson

David Jamieson, PhD, is president of the Jamieson Consulting Group and an adjunct professor of management in the Master of Science program in organizational development at Pepperdine University. He is a past president of the American Society for Training and Development and coauthor of Managing Workforce 2000: Gaining the Diversity Advantage.

Julie O'Mara

Julie O'Mara is president of O'Mara and Associates, a full-service development consulting firm formed in 1972. Julie and her associates work with clients primarily on leadership and managing diversity processes. A former national president of the American Society for Training and Development, she also teaches at the University of California Extension at Berkeley and John F. Kennedy University.

D aily, managers are confronted with new, complex challenges as they try to balance the wants and needs of a highly diverse work force. Laws and organizational policies constrain managers' options, dictate ineffective action, or simply make it too difficult to try new approaches. The times create so much frustration, stress, and defensiveness that many managers would like to return to the stability and sameness of the past.

Employees grow increasingly alienated from organizations that don't value them, understand their needs, or care about their quality of life. Employees who are not part of the majority work force have struggled for years with subtle demands to adapt and fit in and sometimes not-so-subtle biases and discrimination. Still others have grown frustrated by the apparent inability of organizations to respond to their changing lifestyles.

Situations such as these create an adversarial climate between management and employees. Perhaps even more critical, managers and employees alike are experiencing an escalation of frustration, often over the same issues.

It is important to understand work-force differences, their impact on the workplace, and what is needed to move beyond the "one-size-fits-all" model of management. A fundamental shift in attitude is needed. This shift must recognize the interdependencies among an organization's policies, systems, and practices. It must acknowledge the need for both individual and organizational change. And it must understand that individualizing means paying attention to differences and providing options and choices.

UNDERSTANDING THE MANAGEMENT MIND-SET

It is not difficult to understand how the mind-set of the past may have developed. Consider the following scenarios:

- With a growing labor force adding new bodies to the pool of workers and a capital-intensive emphasis on plant and equipment, people could be seen as expendable or replaceable, as an expense needed for production. Consequently, labor costs, wages, benefits, and investments in people were minimized.

- Because information, knowledge, experience, and age resided in the management hierarchy and not in the employees, the separation of "thinking" from "working" became strongly ingrained, and the concept of "managing" and controlling work and employees could flourish. Scientific management, widely practiced at one time, broke all work into its smallest, most routine components. Employees were placed in a more passive role and were forced to follow the rules inherent in a high-control orientation.

- The vast majority of the work force was homogeneous, and those who were different were forced to adapt and assimilate; therefore, an understandable one-size-fits-all mentality developed.

- With little influence from women or employees with diverse cultural backgrounds, only the white, male mentality of the time was available to create the values and behavior of the work culture. As a result, importance was placed on being tough, macho, competitive, militaristic, and paternal.

The mind-set of the past has increasingly become out-of-sync with today's work force and organizational demands. Needs aren't being met, frustrations are growing, and performance often suffers. Ultimately, productivity, job satisfaction, and hiring and retaining competent employees are at stake. As employees acquire a greater voice, they will choose to work in organizations that at least attempt to meet their needs and preferences. Organizations that offer greater flexibility will have a competitive advantage when it comes to recruiting and retaining the highest quality employees.

A MODEL FOR CHANGE

Flex management is a new mind-set—a different philosophy of management.

At the heart is a deep appreciation of individual differences and the understanding that equality does not mean sameness. Although diverse needs and wants are equally respected, they are not met by treating everyone the same. Instead, more-individualized policies, systems, and management practices meet diverse needs. The mind-set of flexibility is the antithesis of a one-size-fits-all viewpoint. This concept is not a replacement of one paternalistic system with another; instead, it recognizes that one system cannot work across today's diverse workplace.

It requires management to tune in to people and their needs, create options that give people choices, and balance diverse individual needs with the needs of the organization.

Figure 51–1 graphically relates the dynamics of three components of management—policies, systems, and practices—to four strategies for individualizing—matching people and jobs, managing and rewarding performance, informing and involving people, and supporting lifestyle and life needs.

The goal is to use policies, systems, and practices to create options and flexibility within the four strategies so that the strategies can be individualized within the work force.

MANAGEMENT COMPONENTS

Policies

All too often, policies become shackles. They force sameness when customizing is needed. With a long history of developing policies from the top, managing with a control orientation, and investing little authority and trust with middle- and lower-level managers, upper management used policies as a central tool. What is needed are fewer, broader policies that aid in individualizing, provide wider latitude and choice, and support desired organizational and employee values.

FIGURE 51–1
The Flex Management Model

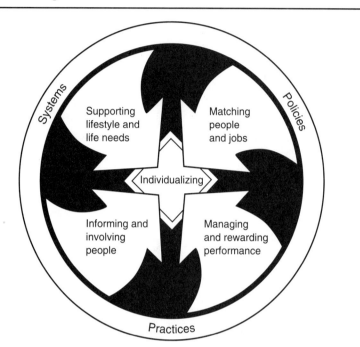

Systems

Human-resource systems and programs—the organized, "formal" tools, processes, and procedures provided by the organization for use in managing people—have long followed the sameness, or one-size-fits-all, notion. They need to be redesigned to have a less prescriptive focus and to allow more options, adaptations, and avenues of implementation. Variation is needed in how goals are set, the number of goals implemented, and the time frames used. Management must be free to customize rewards and to create special opportunities to "try out" jobs. Systems are often tied to policies, so change in one of these areas usually goes hand-in-hand with change in the other.

Practices

The day-to-day practices of managers working with both individuals and groups require much flexibility. The face-to-face work of managing diversity will involve negotiating, facilitating, and balancing production with compassion.

Some employees may require more direction, whereas others may perform better with greater autonomy. Even with greater participation, managers still need to control some aspects of work. Questioning and listening to employees will be important in trying to understand differences, as will versatility in coaching, training, and development.

STRATEGIES

Matching People and Jobs

This strategy focuses on ways to match a variety of different individuals, their skills, and their work preferences with real job characteristics. Matching involves paying attention to both the objective and subjective sides of work and people in order to individualize job profiles, assessment methods, orientation, and careers.

To do this, policies and systems related to transfers, promotions, rotation, job posting, job designs, and descriptions may have to be changed. Career-development systems may need review, management practices of interviewing, recruiting, development planning, and career coaching may demand new emphasis.

Managing and Rewarding Performance

This strategy recognizes that people don't work in the same ways and are not motivated by the same methods or incentives. It is used to consider different approaches to planning work goals, managing the process of work, and rewarding people in meaningful ways. Variables that can be individualized include choosing the work to be done, the people who participate, the amount of time they spend on a project, and the steps or approach they use to perform the work tasks.

Policies related to performance appraisal, disciplinary processes, and rewards are candidates for greater flexibility. In order to be effective, practices such as regular coaching, written evaluations, informal feedback sessions, and structured development meetings will vary greatly as they are applied to different people.

Informing and Involving People

This strategy recognizes the significant desire among people to be more informed about and involved in their workplace. It also appreciates that some employees may not wish to be highly involved and that some persons who come from different cultures may find it difficult to participate when their bosses are present or to assert their views in a group setting. Therefore, this strategy creates opportunities for people to choose to participate, develops vehicles for the flow of information, and keeps people informed.

Policies may deal with the use of work time or the establishment of participation groups. Suggestion systems, surveys, or focus groups can be used to offer flexibility in input. And everyday practices—such as delegating, asking for ideas, or running staff meetings—can be varied.

Supporting Lifestyle and Life Needs

Life needs and lifestyle preferences vary greatly. Issues include ways of getting to work, productivity at work, work-time flexibility, and satisfying life and family needs. This strategy identifies people's needs and interests and, where possible, creates supportive options—ways to obtain needed assistance, such as child care or substance-abuse counseling, or to meet lifestyle preferences related to such issues as work hours, fitness facilities, or leave options.

An Integrated Approach

Flex management integrates much of what we have known, but have rarely used, in a systematic way. Its essence is in rethinking what can be controlled—policies, systems, and practices—as they relate to the four strategies to be used in the management of people.

The three components and the four strategies are not mutually exclusive; in fact, they have many interconnections and can reinforce each other. One of the most common mistakes is to attempt to solve complex problems with simple solutions that ignore these interdependent connections.

It's not enough to train only those who manage employees from different cultural groups to improve cross-cultural understanding and opportunities for advancement. Outdated career-progression systems or co-worker prejudice could still hinder the outcome. It's not enough to promote women into management positions and ignore their support and development or to hire a worker with a disability without helping to build his or her relationships with co-workers.

A NEW ORGANIZATIONAL PARADIGM

If organizations can meet the challenge and capitalize on the opportunity, what might the new organization look like and do differently?

In the "new" organization, function, department, or role structures vary in type, levels, spans of control, and permanence, depending upon the specific work to be done and the workers who are used. Policies are minimal and are focused on intent or outcomes, not on constraints. Systems that involve working with people have basic and alternative ways of operating. They focus on outcomes and provide a variety of tools to aid managers. Management practices are based on accepting individual differences, valuing people, and providing choices.

People throughout the organization have great multicultural awareness and understand how to use the strengths of diversity. They feel appreciated and have a strong commitment to the organization's mission. They influence the type of support they receive, the way they are rewarded, and the way their jobs are designed and carried out.

People at all levels have the opportunity to participate in planning and problem solving. They understand the larger goals of their organization and can move among jobs as their skills, preferences, and life situations require.

In the new organization, people have worked out a balance between work and home and have support for handling issues that might keep them from being at work and being productive. If they need assistance, training, or special help, they can find it easily.

Transforming the way an organization operates requires a systematic, planned approach to change. Action must be taken to analyze the profile and characteristics of the work force, investigate implications, and identify individual and organizational modifications that are affordable and desirable. The Flex management approach is comprehensive. The interrelated strategies may be ineffective as isolated solutions or as ways to implement only a few or partial changes. Mandates, fragmented activities, and piecemeal programs rarely generate desired outcomes.

As a mind-set for the new organization, Flex management enables managers to develop inspiring organizations in which people are valued, supported, and satisfied as individuals, where high performance is a way of life and employees are committed to their work and their workplace.

NTL'S HISTORY REGARDING INCLUSION

Chapter Fifty-Two

Edith Whitfield Seashore

Judith H. Katz

NTL's Road to Multiculturalism

A Diverse History

Edith Whitfield Seashore and Judith H. Katz

■

Edith Whitfield Seashore has consulted to industrial, military, educational, and voluntary organizations for 25 years. She is a social psychologist concerned with organizational change, team building, strategic planning, and multicultural organizations. In addition to her consulting practice, from 1974 to 1979 she was president of the NTL Institute for Applied Behavioral Sciences. In 1979, with Morley Segal, she founded the American University/NTL Master's Program in Human Resource Development. She is a coeditor of this book.

Judith H. Katz, EdD, has focused her 20-year career in organizational development on linking strategic initiatives with diversity efforts. Her book, White Awareness: Handbook for Anti-Racism Training *(1978) was one of the first works to address racism from a white perspective. A respected educator, consultant and writer, she is also the author of* No Fairy Godmothers, No Magic Wands: The Healing Process After Rape *(1984) and numerous articles on diversity, oppression, and empowerment. She is a vice president of The Kaleel Jamison Consulting Group, Inc. and a coeditor of this book.*

I n the 1930s, several social psychologists joined together to help bring noted social researcher Kurt Lewin to the United States to escape Germany and Nazism. After witnessing the devastating impact of Nazism and Fascism, these social scientists, Ron Lippett, Lee Bradford, and Ken Benne, along with Lewin, began to use applied research to foster democracy through principles of participative leadership, group dynamics, and experiential learning. NTL and its mission were born.

333

NTL's core technology, the training group (T-group) emerged in 1946 as a by-product of the NTL founders' involvement with a State Workshop in Intergroup Relations held at the Connecticut State Teachers College in New Britain, Connecticut. The workshop's purpose was to address issues of anti-Semitism and intergroup relations in Connecticut schools. Each evening, the staff and researchers would meet to discuss the day's activities. Participants were invited to attend. As the staff and researchers shared their observations, participants would often offer quite different perceptions. In the course of the evening meetings, a rich dialogue evolved, focused primarily on the process of group development. This experience led directly to the birth of the Training Group, a learning laboratory in which group members can explore and learn leadership and group membership skills by participating freely, sharing different perceptions and feedback.

To the researchers, this method of stimulating and supporting learning seemed more effective than any tried before. Based on their experience with it, Benne, Bradford, and Lippett organized the National Training Laboratory in Group Development and held their first residential laboratory in the summer of 1947 at Gould Academy in Bethel, Maine. (Kurt Lewin had died earlier that year.)

Lee Bradford became NTL's first CEO. Under Bradford, the organization's membership comprised mainly academicians from the behavioral sciences. On Bradford's retirement in 1972, Vladimir Dupre became NTL's new director and CEO. Within two years, Dupre shifted NTL from a 500-member organization to a consulting firm with a central office and a core group of training and organization development (OD) consultants. NTL's uniqueness had been its network of professionals, its membership. With the network disbanded and its lifeline severed, NTL began to wither and die.

By 1975, NTL had no financial credit, could no longer get loans, and was close to bankruptcy. NTL's board of directors, made up of white businessmen, could no longer sustain the organization and began looking for ways to dissolve it. At this point, Vladimir Dupre asked four longtime NTL members to volunteer their time and expertise to develop some solutions to save the organization. The four were Barbara Ben Bunker, Hal Kellner, Edith Whitfield Seashore, and Peter Vaill, all of whom were trainers and OD consultants.

The Four Horsemen, or Horsepeople, as they were nicknamed, decided to reinvent NTL as a multicultural organization. They planned to bring back many of the outstanding former members along with a group of newer entries into the field of OD, especially white women and women and men of color. This cadre faced the task of helping to rebuild NTL by volunteering their time to develop and staff programs, work on organizational committees, and contribute to the direction and leadership of the organization.

Committed to diverse membership, the Four Horsemen asked 75 old and new professionals in the field to come together for a three-day meeting to develop the structure for a multicultural organization, with the caveat of retaining NTL's original philosophy and values. Sixty-five members actually took part, with proxies from the other ten. In three days, they reframed the organization, selecting a multicultural structure for its 12-person board of directors (half the members men, half women; half white, half people of color), and developing multicultural staffing policies, membership requirements, and training capabilities.

Prior to the gathering, the NTL board had asked for a reorganization or a plan for dissolution. They were presented with the plan for reorganization, and they chose it. But their choice mattered little. The Four Horsemen had acquired NTL, and whether it was to live on or dissolve, the first step was for the current CEO and board of directors to resign.

They did, leaving only two members of the old board as holdovers as required by the NTL bylaws. NTL had taken a revolutionary step in reframing itself as a multicultural organization. At the helm were Edith Whitfield Seashore, as the new president, and Elsie Y. Cross, as chair of the board. The organization had shifted from an all-white, all-male institution to one whose future was in the hands of a white woman and a black woman.

As a result of their leadership, with contributions from members and renewed investment from other organizations valuing the rebirth, NTL was out of bankruptcy within 18 months. All this at a time when organizations were seriously questioning if a pluralistic organization were possible to achieve and, if achieved, could be productive.

In many ways, NTL could provide a case study for other organizations struggling with oppression, affirmative action, and social justice. The leadership and membership of NTL have always thought of themselves as committed to principles of democracy and humanness. However, like many organizations, the leadership and most of the program staff were white and male.

NTL has always mirrored the issues of the society at large. In the beginning years, the staff and participants attending NTL programs were largely white men. As social-justice and civil-rights issues received greater attention throughout the 1960s, NTL also found itself needing to address these issues in its methodology, public programs, and organizational leadership. The shift was not easily accomplished.

In 1967, a laboratory was held for leaders from major U.S. cities. During the workshop, participants aggressively confronted the staff, demanding changes in NTL's programs and policies. As a result, the Black Affairs Center was founded, under the direction of Leon West. The purpose of the center was to increase the number of black participants in NTL programs, to provide adequate scholarships and funding to enable blacks to attend, and to work toward increasing the diversity and availability of black professionals to staff NTL programs and labs.

NTL also struggled to address women's issues and concerns. By 1973, efforts were under way by Jane Moosbrucker and others to form a women's caucus and begin to look at the issues of women in NTL and in the field. This group presented a list of demands to the board of directors, and the board agreed to the list. In 1974, Elaine Kepner's efforts to create a more formalized women's support network led to a second women's caucus. But it was not until 1975, after years of pressure and struggle, that NTL reemerged with a concern and commitment to respond aggressively to issues of civil rights and social justice. This major shift led to the reshaping of programs, policies, and organizational structure to ensure the organization's ability to incorporate more white women and women and men of color.

NTL continues to address issues of oppression as it evolves technologies to assist organizations and individuals in many areas. In addition to knowledge and experience in the behavioral sciences and competencies to facilitate T-groups, members also must demonstrate their knowledge and skills in addressing racism, sexism, and other issues of oppression.

The editors of this book wish to thank the NTL board of directors for supporting this effort. In addition, the editors wish to express their appreciation to the NTL founding fathers—Benne, Bradford, Lippett, and Lewin—and to acknowledge the 75 NTL members who in 1975 made the difficult transition of changing NTL Institute from a monolithic organization to one of diversity. The struggle continues . . .

LITERATURE REVIEW OF THE EVOLUTION OF OUR THINKING

Chapter Fifty-Three

Nancie Charme Zane

Theoretical Considerations in Organizational Diversity

Nancie Charme Zane

■

Nancie Charme Zane is a visiting lecturer at the University of Haifa, Israel, while finishing her doctoral degree in applied social psychology from the University of Pennsylvania. Her research includes the organizational politics of race and gender, educational change, and building democratic work structures. Zane has worked as an organizational consultant in the philanthropic and public sectors in such organizations as the Philadelphia Foundation, the Philadelphia Schools Collaborative, and the National Institute of Corrections.

Although the area of organizational diversity is a dynamic one, whose meaning is constantly expanding,[1] most of the existing research has focused on issues related to race, gender, and, to a lesser extent, ethnicity. This article provides a brief historical analysis of a number of the major studies conducted on race and gender within organizational contexts and identifies some of the theoretical concerns across the organizational behavior, sociological/feminist, and organizational development (OD) practitioner literatures.

From a historical perspective, the various organizational literatures paint a painful picture, filled with the shadowy clouds of racism and sexism. Whether one reads the findings of the first organizational study on race—Stouffer's 1949 documentary on race in the military—or more current corporate survey data,[2] the racial intergroup dynamics read similarly: Whites view race relations more favorably than people of color do and have little insight into the kind of interactions that are oppressive to people of color. In most studies, white employees have difficulty relating to "group-level phenomena" and are less able to see the systemic barriers that disadvantage people of color and privilege whites. Similarly, the gender literature highlights the double-binds with which women are constantly confronted—for example, the lose-lose situation in which neither acting the "same as" nor "different from" white men ultimately changes access to the important positions in organizations. Only recently—with the documentation of longer-term, more systemic interventions—have both the practitioner and academic literatures offered some brighter perspectives on these persistent organizational problems.

ORGANIZATIONAL BEHAVIOR LITERATURE

Research in organizational behavior has only recently focused on the importance of race and/or ethnicity as issues worthy of study. Early industrial studies, particularly those conducted between the 1930s and 1960s, tended to avoid overtly examining the impact of race and ethnicity within an organization.[3] Exceptions were studies focused on public sector organizations, particularly the military and public schools.[4]

The civil rights movement of the 1960s was a pivotal time in American society, and it subsequently had a significant impact on race relations within organizations. The Civil Rights Act (1964) and the development of the concept of equal opportunity provided a legal and moral mandate to end discriminatory practices against societal "out groups," particularly blacks and women. Gradually, over the next 25 years, researchers became more attentive to group-based differences and began to explore in more depth their impact on organizational dynamics.[5]

During the 1980s, there was a proliferation of studies that focused on the experience of blacks—particularly black male managers[6]—in primarily white organizations.[7] While not agreeing on appropriate strategic interventions, most studies observed the overwhelming barriers that blacks face in corporate life (e.g., impenetrable "glass ceilings" and "glass walls" and exclusion from informal social and political organizational networks), as well as the internal stress that blacks experience as a result of these obstacles.[8]

Some recent studies go beyond merely analyzing the experience of blacks within organizations by developing an analytic framework for diagnosing race relations and creating change strategies in predominantly white organizations. Alderfer, building on existing theories of social identity and intergroup relations, introduced intergroup theory, which attends to the importance of organizational context in the intergroup interaction.[9] The theory says that individuals have memberships in both organizational (role and status) and identity (biologically and historically rooted groups such as race, gender, etc.) groups and bring all their various memberships into any encounter. The key, however, is that certain group memberships become salient depending on the particular context in which she or he is found.

Consequently, individuals may find themselves representing different parts of their "selves" as their situations vary. Out of this theory developed a diagnostic methodology that utilized two strategies as a way to get a handle on the nature of the intergroup dynamics operating within the entire organization and to devise systemic interventions: outside race- and gender-balanced consulting teams and microcosm groups (organizational members chosen to replicate the variety of groups and identities in the organization).[10]

Embedded intergroup theory offered a further theoretical development by describing how a group's experience is affected by the dynamics within both the larger organizational system and the external environment in which the group is located.[11] To understand race relations within an organization, one must also develop a theory about racism and its impact on organizational life. A researcher must be clear about his or her values "and avoid the illusion that one can study race relations in this society from a neutral or value free position."[12]

By the end of the 1980s, there were a number of studies reflecting on the progress of affirmative action policies instituted during the 1970s and '80s.[13] The three most important messages emerging from these are:

1. Although affirmative action policies have played an important role in raising African Americans' and women's occupational status, they have not eradicated the injustices that they were intended to correct ("discrimination still reigns"). In fact, in many male-dominated organizations, the attention to numbers has masked the multiple levels at which racism (and sexism) infects the lives of white and black workers.

2. African Americans experience a kind of "triple jeopardy," which negatively impacts them at the recruitment, entry, and evaluation stages of organizational life.

3. There continues to be a strong need for outcome-based affirmative action policies (i.e., policies focused on demographic alignment) that seek to remedy both historical and modern structural barriers to equal employment opportunities.

These studies document the lack of good faith that undercuts many affirmative action initiatives, white resentment at such policies, and the problems confronted by the designated beneficiaries of such actions. They note the importance of government support for affirmative action to continue fighting overt—as well as the more subtle forms of—racism and sexism, and they emphasize the need for gaining a "critical mass" of people from individual minority groups so that the problems of tokenism would be alleviated. Not only do they suggest a number of "microremedies" to provide incentives for recruiting, hiring, and promoting minorities, they also insist on "macro" solutions intended to realign structural relations within the organization.

In reviewing the research to date, the overall focus has been on black–white organizational relations, particularly at the managerial level. Further research on nonmanagerial levels—as well as the experiences of other racial, ethnic, and cultural groups—remains to be done.[14]

SOCIOLOGICAL AND FEMINIST LITERATURE

Kanter's ground-breaking work on women's and men's experiences in the corporation in the 1970s[15] identifies the ways in which existing organizational structures reproduce gender inequities within society. The segregation of men and women in particular roles with their own norms and responsibilities (women in clerical roles, and white men in managerial roles) produces behaviors that are then used to justify the ghettoization of women and men in the corporation. In response, Kanter recommends the long-term goal of dismantling large, impersonal bureaucratic structures in favor of more flat, democratic organizations. In identifying structural barriers as the explanation for behavioral differences between women and men to the exclusion of possible psychological or social psychological differences, Kanter seeks to minimize differences between the sexes, thus eradicating the justification for discrimination.

Other feminist analyses of organizations, however, borrow from Chodorow and Gilligan's work[16] to validate psychological differences between women and men and demonstrate the impact of socialization on male–female management styles.[17] This approach treats "female" leadership qualities (being team-oriented, concerned about people and quality, intuitive in their problem-solving approach, etc.) as a valuable asset that should be affirmed as complementary with male management strategies. Sargent lobbies for a more androgynous model in which men and women combine the best of their characteristics to become more whole and ultimately more effective in their managerial roles. Several works link the possibility of transforming alienating and oppressive organizational structures with a shift from a competitive, aggressive male organizational culture to a less hierarchical, feminist model that values public and private connections.[18]

Some feminists have injected concern with issues of race and class into their analysis of the workplace. Bell Hooks criticizes the feminist discussion of women and work for reflecting the concerns of privileged white women who are beginning to compete for the managerial jobs previously dominated by white men, but being oblivious to the issues and problems of poor women of color. In this way, traditional feminism has sometimes replicated the oppressive dynamics it intended to change. The further critique by post-modern, white feminists and African American women that the middle-class white feminist movement's presumption of a universal "women's experience" based on themselves has made the unique experience of women of color invisible.[19] For the organizational researcher, it is critical to differentiate the experience of white women from women of color so as to capture the multiple realities that women confront inside and outside the organizational context. To avoid collapsing the experiences of a less powerful group into the experiences of a more dominant group, Phelan and Mouffe remind us of the multiple components and group memberships that constitute everyone's identity as well as the social and political context in which each particular aspect is located. Phelan also suggests that the element of "difference" within one's identity be understood not only in contrast to the norm of white, male culture but also in positive ways that capture the uniqueness of the various components of one's self.[20]

ORGANIZATIONAL DEVELOPMENT PRACTITIONER LITERATURE

Since the advent of the report *Workforce 2000* and its demographic projections of an increasingly diverse work force, corporations have been alerted to the potential economic consequences for failing to (1) hire, professionally develop, and promote white women and people of color,[21] and (2) train managers and employees to work effectively with and across diverse work teams. As the publicity about the impact on the bottom line and participation in the global economy has increased, discussions about the significance of diversity within the workplace have become more common. A recent book on organizational diversity described a study of 645 firms in which "74% of the respondents felt that diversity affected their corporate strategy."[22]

Although acknowledgment of the issue has not necessarily translated into corporate action[23] many OD practitioners have attempted to introduce various technologies into organizations that would help them shift from being monocultural to multicultural.[24] Not surprisingly, however, both the vision and strategies that consultants engage vary widely. These efforts may include educating organizations to understand the importance of diversity and cultural differences within employee populations on the interpersonal and group levels.

For some practitioners, education and change within organizations require a more systemic analysis, one that exposes the oppressive nature of racism and sexism within an organization's policies, procedures, practices, etc. Cross identifies the sociopolitical phenomenon (i.e., the intersection of individuals' multiple group memberships with societal power relations) that results in most individuals' occupying both victim and oppressor roles simultaneously. She also points out the insidiousness of "internalized oppression" and the ways in which people unconsciously collude with their subordination. Katz—who has researched the tendency of whites to negate their white identities and disown their participation in perpetuating racism—stresses the need for developing new paradigms—that speak to the deep-seated tensions in the society between opportunity and discrimination and that highlight the contradictory impulses of celebrating diversity while simultaneously trying to quash it.[25] For Cross, Katz, and others, combatting race and gender discrimination must be coupled with the creation of new organizational cultures that value a range of differences and that practice more inclusive ways of operating.

Some models for supporting multicultural organizational transformation are developmental,[26] providing both a long-term vision toward which organizations can strive as well as a diagnostic tool for identifying an organization's present status. A critical element in the transformation of organizations is to link the commitment to diversity to an organization's overall mission, daily operations, and quality of services produced.[27] Morrison's research in 16 organizations leads her to underscore the role of top management in increasing leadership diversity—that is, the participation of white women and people of color at key levels of the organization and the incorporation of a balanced "education, enforcement, and exposure" strategy throughout the organization.[28]

Thomas highlights the importance of developing an "empowered work force" that has the managerial capability for creating a work environment that "works naturally for everyone."[29] He, like others, cautions against the notion of organizations expecting a quick fix, and he foresees the stabilization of a truly diverse work culture as a 10- to 15-year change process. Jackson, Holvino, and others' visions of a diverse or multicultural organization acknowledge the larger social context that produces oppressive practices and is committed to combatting oppression in both the organization and the larger community.

Historically, the practitioner literature has said far too little, beyond the anecdotal, about the methods and outcomes of implementing these conceptual ideas or about the relationship between diversity and organizational structure. More-recent publications have attempted to document and analyze various organizations' experiences with diversity, providing practitioners and consumers with at least initial data about the multiple issues to be considered in regard to diversity initiatives.[30]

IMPLICATIONS

Much of the foundational research summarized here reflects the specific concerns, interests, and methodologies of various disciplinary and professional communities. As new work in the area of organizational diversity struggles to integrate the various approaches that have developed to date and a truly multidisciplinary approach to this issue begins to emerge, the conflicting theoretical assumptions in the field also need to be reexamined and clarified. These include:

1. *Degree and location of change.* Researchers do not agree on whether partial reformation of an organization is sufficient to reach the goals regarding diversity or whether total transformation is necessary. Authors focus their change efforts at different levels within the organization: the individual, group, and intergroup relations within the organization, organizational structures, and/or external environment. Many recognize the need to be working systemically and at multiple levels simultaneously. Researchers also differ on the primary location of change efforts. Most assume the change needs to be from the top down in order for managers and staff to be held accountable.

2. *Measure of change.* Although there is relative agreement about the fact that white women and people of color have been excluded from entering and/or fully participating in the corporate world, there is little discussion about how inclusion is measured. For example, in some instances, monitoring *employment processes* that build equal employment opportunity and/or equal access is seen as sufficient, while in other situations *employment outcomes* that recast the organizational demography to equal that of the local labor market are the measures of change.

3. *Duration of change.* There is disagreement on whether change is a limited or ongoing process. Some assume that once the "right" policies and procedures are put in place or the "right" feminist structure is created, the organization will be free from oppressive dynamics and individuals will be able to bring their "full selves" to the organization. Others have a more process-focused orientation, which suggests that managing diversity needs to be viewed as a long-term, ongoing process.

4. *Justification for change.* There is no underlying conflict in the literature about the meaning of diversity, multiculturalism, pluralism, and

integration and the most appropriate terms and models to use when discussing the future of diverse organizations. Much of this literature uses the terms *diversity, multiculturalism,* and *cultural pluralism* interchangeably. In both the academic and practitioner literature, multiculturalism and cultural pluralism sit in opposition to the concept of assimilation. In fact, there is little ambiguity that assimilation—the melting away of ethnic and cultural differences in order to blend with the dominant culture—is a deeply problematic paradigm of the past.[31] Although assumptions about white male hegemony have not disappeared, concerns about the best ways to employ all the human resources available to the work force have surfaced as well.

NOTES

1. Although issues of race and gender are the most commonly referred to in regard to diversity, there is little consensus about the meaning of *diversity*. It is discussed in a variety of ways: as narrowly as the coexistence of individual style differences (e.g., being an extrovert, conflict avoider, or autocratic decision maker) or as broadly as managing differences that reflect both the intersection of demographic (e.g., age, race, gender, ethnicity, sexual orientation) and experiential (e.g., educational background, parental status, occupational experience) variables. A number of organizational consultants discuss diversity in the context of individual differences, while others posit a more systemic analysis embedded in the historical sociopolitical power relations in the United States. Diversity has also been written about in the context of organizational mergers and the problems that arise from bringing two or more disparate cultures together.

2. Samuel A. Stouffer, Suchman, Devinney, Star, and Williams (1950) in Clayton P. Alderfer and David Thomas, "The Significance of Race and Ethnicity for Understanding Organizational Behavior," in *International Review of Industrial and Organizational Psychology,* eds. Cary L. Cooper and I. Robertson (New York: Wiley, 1988), pp. 1–35.

3. Clayton P. Alderfer and David Thomas, *op cit.*; B. Ferdman, "The Dynamics of Ethnic Diversity in Organizations: Toward Integrative Models," *Issues, Theory and Research in Industrial/Organizational Psychology* (Amsterdam, Netherlands: North Holland, 1991). Kurt Lewin and others founded NTL in the late 1940s in an effort to study and improve intergroup relations, with subjects such as race and ethnicity in the foreground. However, their initial technology removed people from their work settings and focused on helping individuals and groups learn about race and ethnicity in a "laboratory" context. It was only in the mid-1960s that experiential education moved into the organizational environment to help work groups and organizations to explore these issues contextually.

4. Clayton P. Alderfer and David Thomas, *op. cit.* In the chapter "Negro Soldier" in their 1949 study *American Soldier,* Samuel A. Stouffer, Suchman,

DeVinney, Star, and Williams document the racist attitudes, behaviors, and practices of the military. The effects of racism on black children's self-concept were documented by Clark and Clark in 1958 and may have influenced the *Brown* vs. *The Board of Education* decision to desegregate public schools—a critical policy as well as organizational intervention.

5. For example, Clayton P. Alderfer and David Thomas note that during the late 1960s and the 1970s there were several studies conducted that explored blacks' opportunities within organizations and their relationships to unions. The research indicated that while unions were not forceful in their advocacy for their membership around issues relating to racism and other forms of discrimination, nonmembership in a union guaranteed lower salaries. Purcell and Cavanaugh, 1972; Small, 1976; Almquist (1979), in Clayton P. Alderfer and David Thomas, *op. cit.*

6. Ella Bell, *The Bicultural Life Experience of Career Oriented Black Women* (New Haven: Yale School of Organization and Management, 1988). Bell's work is a notable exception in her description of the multiple stresses on black women in white organizations.

7. Clayton P. Alderfer, A. Alderfer, D. Tucker, and L. Tucker, "Diagnosing Race Relations in Management," *Journal of Applied Behavioral Science* 16, no. 2 (1980), pp. 135–66; John P. Fernandez, *Racism and Sexism in Corporate Life* (Lexington, MA: Lexington Books, 1981); John P. Fernandez, *Managing a Diverse Work Force* (Lexington, MA: Lexington Books, 1991); George Davis and Glegg Watson, *Black Life in Corporate America: Swimming in the Mainstream* (New York: Anchor Press, 1982); Alderfer and Smith, "Studying Intergroup Relations Embedded in Organizations," *Administrative Science Quarterly* 27 (1982), pp. 35–3. Clayton P. Alderfer and David Thomas, *op. cit.*; David Thomas and Clayton P. Alderfer, "The Influence of Race on Career Dynamics, Theory and Research on Minority Career Experiences," in *Handbook of Career Theory*, eds. Michael B. Arthur, D. Hall, and B. Lawrence (London: Cambridge University Press, 1988); Clayton P. Alderfer, D. Tucker, A. Alderfer, and L. Tucker, "The Race Relations Advisory Group: An Intergroup Intervention," in *Research in Organizational Change and Development*, vol. 2, eds. Richard W. Woodman and William A. Pasmore (Greenwich, CT: Jai Press, 1988), pp. 269–32.

8. David Thomas, "Racial Dynamics in Cross-Race Developmental Relationships," *Administrative Science Quarterly.* David Thomas's work on cross-race developmental (i.e., sponsor-protege and mentor-protege) relationships provides some insight into the conditions that support positive cross-race experiences. Whether such incidences can be translated into positive systemic change has yet to be determined.

9. For work on social identity theory, see Henri Tajfel, *Human Groups and Social Categories: Studies in Social Psychology* (London: Cambridge University Press, 1981); Henri Tajfel and J. Turner, "The Social Identity Theory of Intergroup Relations," in *Psychology of Intergroup Relations*, eds. S. Worschel and Austin (Chicago: Nelson-Hall, 1986). For work on intergroup relations, see Muzafer Sherif, *Intergroup Conflict and Cooperation: The Robbers and Cave Experiment* (Norman, OK: University Book Exchange, 1961); Lewis A. Coser, *The Func-*

tions of Social Conflict (New York: Free Press, 1956). Intergroup theory work was discussed in Clayton P. Alderfer, A. Alderfer, D. Tucker, and L. Tucker, *op. cit.* See also Alderfer, Tucker, Alderfer, and Tucker, *op. cit.*

10. Alderfer, Tucker, Alderfer, and Tucker, *op.cit.*

11. Alderfer and Smith, *op. cit.*

12. Alderfer, Tucker, Alderfer, and Tucker, *op. cit.*

13. Pettigrew and Martin, "Shaping the Organizational Context for Black American Inclusion," *Journal of Social Issues: Black Employment Opportunities: Macro and Micro Perspective,* (1987); Braddock and McPartland, "How Minorities Continue to Be Excluded in Equal Employment Opportunities," *ibid.*

14. The inclusion of Native Americans, Asians, and Hispanics in the study of corporate race relations and the consideration of women's experiences in corporations appeared in John P. Fernandez's *Racism and Sexism in Corporate Life* (Lexington, MA: Lexington Books, 1981). Fernandez documents the discriminatory treatment of people of color and women within corporations. Although he presents useful advice for increasing employee satisfaction by addressing questions of participation and sensitivity within an organization, his suggestions do little to help redistribute organizational power. In Fernandez's latest book, *Managing Diversity* (1992), he offers a more structural analysis of race and gender problems rampant in the competitive atmosphere of hierarchical organizations and bureaucracies. For additional work focusing on Hispanics, review Ferdman (1992) and A. Reyes, PhD dissertation, University of Maryland, 1992.

15. Rosabeth Moss Kanter, *Men and Women of the Corporation* (New York: Basic Books, 1977).

16. Nancy Chodorow, *The Reproduction of Mothering: Psychoanalysis and the Sociology of Gender* (Berkeley: University of California Press, 1978); Carol Gilligan, *In a Different Voice: Psychological Theory and Women's Development* (Cambridge: Harvard University Press, 1982).

17. Alice G. Sargent, *The Androgynous Manager* (1987); Marilyn Loden, *Feminine Leadership, or How to Succeed in Business Without Being One of the Boys* (New York: Times Books, 1985); S. Tucker, "Women in Organizations," in *Making Organizations Humane and Productive,* eds. H. Meltzer and Walter R. Nord (New York: Wiley, 1981).

18. Kathy E. Ferguson, *The Feminist Case Against Bureaucracy* (Philadelphia: Temple University Press, 1984); Suzanne Gordon, *Prisoners of Men's Dreams: Striking Out for a New Feminine Future* (Boston: Little, Brown, 1991).

19. Katherine Jones, "The Trouble with Authority," *Differences: A Journal of Feminist Cultural Studies* 3 (1991); Phelan and Shane, "Specificity: Beyond Equality and Difference," *ibid.*

20. Phelan and Shane, *ibid.,* pp. ; C. Mouffe, "Feminism, Citizenship, and Radical Democratic Politics," *Cultural Studies* (1990).

21. Greenhaus, Parasuaman, and Wormely, "Effects of Race on Organizational Experiences, Job Performance Evaluations, and Career Outcomes," *Academy of Management Journal* 33, no. 1 (1990), pp. 64–86. The lack of job and career

development is stultifying for the individual and has been correlated with lowered motivation and productivity. Equally problematic is the relative reduction in the pool of those prepared to step into senior and executive management positions.

22. S. Jackson, ed. *Diversity in the Workplace: Human Resources Initiatives* (New York: Guilford Press, 1992).

23. Marilyn Loden and Judy Rosener, *Workforce America! Managing Employee Diversity as a Vital Resource* (Homewood, IL: Business One Irwin, 1991); A. Morrison, *The New Leaders: Guidelines on Leadership Diversity in America* (San Francisco: Jossey-Bass, 1992); Elsie Cross, "Making the Invisible Visible," *Healthcare Forum Journal* 10 (1992).

24. The OD practitioner literature yields little consensus concerning the meaning of diversity and multiculturalism. Although the focus is usually about the inclusion of those who are not part of the majority culture by race and gender, the literature also mentions people who are "different" along other demographic, lifestyle, or physical dimensions. For example, see the following: (*a*) B. W. Jackson and R. Hardiman, "Racial Identity Development: Implications for Managing the Multiracial Work Force," in *The NTL Manager's Handbook,* eds. Roger A. Ritvo and Alice G. Sargent (Arlington, VA: NTL Institute, 1983), pp. 107–19. (*b*) J. Howard, "Pluralism and Professional Development: Minorities, Women and the Psychology of Performance," in *Managing Development and Diversity* (J. Howard and Associates, 1987). (*c*) B. W. Jackson and Evangelina Holvino, "Working with Multicultural Organizations: Matching Theory with Practice," *OD Practitioner* 20, no. 3 (1988). (*d*) J. Katz and F. Miller, "Between Monoculturalism and Multiculturalism: Traps Awaiting the Organization," *ibid.* (*e*) C. Halvorson, "Managing Intercultural Differences in Work Groups," *ibid.,* pp. (*f*) J. Katz, "Valuing Diversity on Campus: A Multicultural Approach," in *College Unions at Work* (Bloomington, IN: Association of College Unions International, 1989). (*g*) Marilyn Loden and Judy Rosener, *Workforce America! Managing Employee Diversity as a Vital Resource* (Homewood, IL: Business One Irwin, 1991). (*h*) Elsie Cross, "Making the Invisible Visible," *Healthcare Forum Journal* 10 (1992). (*i*) S. Shea and R. Okada, "Benefitting from Workforce Diversity," *ibid.,* pp. 23–6. (*j*) A. Morrison, *The New Leaders: Guidelines on Leadership Diversity in America* (San Francisco: Jossey-Bass, 1992). (*k*) S. Jackson, ed. *Diversity in the Workplace: Human Resources Initiatives* (New York: Guilford Press, 1992).

25. J. Katz, *White Awareness: Handbook of Anti-Racism Training* (Norman: University of Oklahoma Press, 1978); J. Katz, "Valuing Diversity on Campus: A Multicultural Approach," in *College Unions at Work* (Bloomington, IN: Association of College Unions International, 1989).

26. B. W. Jackson and R. Hardiman, "Racial Identity Development: Implications for Managing the Multiracial Work Force," in *The NTL Manager's Handbook,* eds. Roger A. Ritvo and Alice G. Sargent (Arlington, VA: NTL Institute, 1983), pp. 107–19; J. Katz and F. Miller, "Between Monoculturalism and Multiculturalism: Traps Awaiting the Organization," *OD Practitioner* 20, no. 3 (1988).

27. B. W. Jackson and Evangelina Holvino, "Working with Multicultural Organizations: Matching Theory with Practice," *ibid.*; J. Katz, "Valuing Diversity on Campus: A Multicultural Approach," in *College Unions at Work* (Bloomington, IN: Association of College Unions International, 1989); Marilyn Loden and Judy Rosener, *Workforce America! Managing Employee Diversity as a Vital Resource* (Homewood, IL: Business One Irwin, 1991); Elsie Cross, "Making the Invisible Visible," *Healthcare Forum Journal* 10 (1992); S. Shea and R. Okada, *op.cit.*

28. A. Morrison, *op.cit.*

29. R. Thomas, "Managing Diversity: A Conceptual Framework," in *Diversity in the Workplace: Human Resources Initiatives,* ed. S. Jackson (New York: Guilford Press, 1992).

30. A. Morrison, *op.cit.*; S. Jackson, ed. *op.cit.*; Marilyn Loden and Judy Rosener, *op.cit.*

31. References concerning the displacement of assimilation as the major cultural paradigm include the following: (*a*) D. Taylor, "Should We Integrate Organizations," in *Integrating the Organization: A Social Psychological Analysis*, eds. Howard L. Fromkin and John J. Sherwood (New York: Free Press, 1974). (*b*) Gajendra K. Verma and C. Bagley, "Multicultural Education: Problems and Issues," *Race Relations and Cultural Differences*, ed. Gajendra K. Verma (New York: St. Martin's, 1984). (*c*) Elsie Cross, *op.cit.* (*d*) J. Katz, "Valuing Diversity on Campus: A Multicultural Approach," in *College Unions at Work* (Bloomington, IN: Association of College Unions International, 1989). (*e*) David Thomas, "Mentoring and Irrationality: The Role of Racial Taboos," *Human Resource Management* 28 (Summer 1989). (*f*) John P. Fernandez, *Managing a Diverse Work Force* (Lexington, MA: Lexington Books, 1991). (*g*) Marilyn Loden and Judy Rosener, *op.cit.* (*h*) B. Ferdman, *op.cit.* (*i*) R. Thomas, *op.cit.* (*j*) A. Morrison, *op.cit.*

FURTHER READING

Argentine Saunders Craig

Recommended Reading

Argentine Saunders Craig

■

Argentine Saunders Craig, PhD, is a professor, consultant, facilitator, and mentor with over 20 years' experience in teaching human-resource development. Craig has consulted extensively in the United States, Bermuda, Trinidad, Kuwait, Kenya, and South Africa. She specializes in diverse work teams in organizational settings through International Management Development Associates, where she serves as president. Her PhD is in higher education, and she serves on the board of directors of NTL.

BOOKS

Allport, G. W., *The Nature of Prejudice* (Cambridge, MA: Addison-Wesley, 1954).

Amott, Teresa, and Julie Matthaei, *Race, Gender and Work: A Multicultural Economic History of Women in the United States* (Boston: South End Press, 1991).

Anderson, A., and P. H. Collins, eds., *Gender, Race and Class* (New York: Wadsworth Press, 1991).

Anderson, Margaret, and Patricia Hill Collins, *Race, Class and Gender: An Anthology* (Belmont, CA: Wadsworth Publishing, 1992).

Bowser, Benjamin P., and Raymond G. Hunt, *Impacts of Racism on White Americans* (Newbury Park, CA: Sage Publications, 1981).

Brittan, Arthur, and Mary Maynard, *Sexism, Racism and Oppression.* Oxford, England: Basil Blackwell, 1984).

Davis, George, and Gregg Watson, *Black Life in Corporate America* (Garden City, NY: Anchor Press, 1982).

Dickens, Floyd, and Jacqueline B. Dickens, *The Black Manager: Making It in the Corporate World* (New York: AMACOM, 1982).

Essed, Philomena, *Understanding Everyday Racism: An Interdisciplinary Theory* (Newbury Park, CA: Sage Publications, 1991).

Ferdman, Bernardo M., "The Dynamics of Ethnic Diversity in Organizations: Toward Integrative Models," In *Issues, Theory, and Research in Industrial Organizational Psychology,* ed. K. Kelley (Amsterdam: North Holland, 1992).

Gerber, D. A., *Anti-Semitism in American History* (Urbana: University of Illinois Press, 1990).

Goldberg, David T., eds., *Anatomy of Racism* (Minneapolis: University of Minnesota Press, 1990).

Gutek, Barbara A., *Sex and the Work Place* (San Francisco, CA: Jossey-Bass, 1985).

Hacker, Andrew, *Two Nations: Black and White, Separate, Hostile, Unequal* (New York: Scribner, 1992).

Hall, Edward T., and Mildred R. Hall, *Understanding Cultural Differences* (Yarmouth, ME: Intercultural Press, 1990).

Herdt, Gilbert, ed., *Gay Culture in America: Essays from the Field* (Boston: Beacon Press, 1991).

Hodge, John L., Donald K. Struckmann, and Lynn Dorland Trost, *Cultural Bases of Racism and Group Oppression* (Berkeley, CA: Two Riders Press, 1975).

Hofstede, Geert, *Culture's Consequences: International Differences in Work-Related Values* (Newbury Park, CA: Sage Publications, 1984).

Katz, P. A., and D. Taylor, eds., *Towards the Elimination of Racism: Profiles in Controversy* (New York: Plenum, 1988).

Kitano, H., and R. Daniels, *Asian Americans.* (Englewood Cliffs, NJ: Prentice Hall, 1988).

Knouse, Stephen B., Paul Rosenfeld, and Amy Culbertson, eds., *Hispanics in the Workplace* (Newbury Park, CA: Sage Publications, 1992).

Lewin Kurt, *Resolving Social Conflicts: Selected Papers on Group Dynamics* (New York: Harper Brothers, 1948).

Lucash, F., ed., *Justice and Equality Here and Now* (New York: Cornell University Press, 1986).

Marinelli, R. P., and A. D. Orto, *The Psychological and Social Impact of Disability* (New York: Springer Publishing, 1991).

Morrison, Ann M., *The New Leaders: Guidelines on Leadership Diversity in America* (San Francisco: Jossey-Bass, 1992).

Morrison, Ann M., Randall P. White, and Ellen van Velson, *Breaking the Glass Ceiling* (Reading, MA: Addison-Wesley, 1987).

National Council on Disability, *Americans with Disabilities Act* (Washington, DC: The Department of Justice, Civil Rights Division, Coordination and Review Section, 1991).

Palmore, E., *Ageism: Negative and Positive* (New York: Springer Publishing, 1990).

Pinderhughes, Elaine, *Understanding Race, Ethnicity, and Power* (New York: Free Press, 1989).

Rhode, D. L., ed., *Theoretical Perspectives on Sexual Difference* (New Haven: Yale University Press, 1990).

Rose, P. I., *They and We: Racial and Ethnic Relations in the United States,* 4th ed., (New York: McGraw-Hill, 1990).

Rose, Stephen, *Social Stratification in the United States* (New York: New Press, 1992).

Rothenberg, P. S., *Racism and Sexism: An Integrated Study* (New York: St. Martin's, 1988).

Thiederman, Sondra, *Bridging Cultural Barriers for Corporate Success* (Lexington, MA: Lexington Books, 1990).

Vanneman, R., and L. W. Cannon, *The American Perception of Class* (Philadelphia: Temple University Press, 1987).

Weinberg, Meyer, *World Racism and Related Inhumanities: A Country by Country Bibliography* (New York: Greenwood, 1992).

Welsing, Frances Cress, *The Isis Papers: The Key to Colors* (Chicago: Third World, 1991).

Zenner, Walter, ed., *Persistence and Flexibility: Anthropological Perspectives on the American Jewish Experience* (Albany: State University of New York Press, 1988).

JOURNAL ARTICLES

Aramburo, D., "Celebrating Diversity," *Senga* 1, no. 3 (1991).

Cross, Elsie Y., "Managing Diversity—A Continuous Process of Change," *The Diversity Factor* 1, no. 1 (1992).

Gorden, Jack, "Rethinking Diversity," *Training,* Jan. 1992.

Pheterson, G., "Alliances Between Women: Overcoming Internalized Oppression and Internalized Domination," *Signs* 12 (1986), pp. 146–60.

Thomas, R. Roosevelt, "From Affirmative Action to Affirming Diversity," *Harvard Business Review,* March/April 1990.

Woodson, William B., "A Vision of Excellence Through Diversity: The Competitive Opportunity for the 1990's," (1991, unpublished); available from Brooks Woodson, 444 Central Park West, New York, NY, 1991.

Index

A

Acceptance in developing intercultural sensitivity, 289–90

Accountability
in achieving diversity, 29
in maintaining innocence, 298–99

Action, 229
challenge of change in, 294–300
collective dis-identity in, 272–79
developing cross-gender partnership competencies in, 259–66
diversity, synergy, and transformative social change in, 308–14
feedback in, 301–7
flex management in, 323–29
managing diversity in, 267–71
model for personal change in, 286–93
multicultural organizational development in, 231–39, 240–49
optimizing value of individual differences through an organizational systems approach in, 315–22
Satir model for multicultural change, 280–85

Acton, Lord, 26

Adaptation
in developing intercultural sensitivity, 290
in silencing feminine leadership, 192

Adversity as function of social diversity, 308

Affirmative action, 10, 70
in creating equity, 184

African Americans, 18, 89, 92, 128, 179, 182, 217, 270. *See also* Black cultural style; Black identity development
and business ownership, 271
and civil rights movement, 4, 6–9, 340
and labor unions, 5
and sense of entitlement, 134
stereotypical treatment of, 131

Aggressive communication in inclusive organization, 41

Agitated organizations, 215–16

Agriculture, U.S. Department of, 16

Alban, Billie, 11

Albee, Edward, 94

Allen, Dwight, 13

Americans with Disabilities Act (1990), 19

Androgyny, 189

Anger as stage in black identity development, 153

Apartheid, 11

Apple Computer Co., 19

Appreciative Inquiry approach to organization change, 227

Argyris, Chris, 9, 93

Arizmedndi, Padre José Maria, 224

Art metaphor for racism, 72

Asch, Solomon, 211

Ascribed attributes of collective identities, 273–74

Asian Americans, 4, 6, 18, 32, 47, 128, 270
and coming to terms with racism, 133
discrimination against as students, 166
and sense of entitlement, 134
stereotypical treatment of, 131, 132–33
values of, 42

Assimilation
versus integration, 296–97
as stage in black identity development, 153

Assumptions versus focus groups, 42

Atlantic Bridge, 89–90

AT&T, 13–14
sexual orientation policies at, 144, 147, 148

Attribute, ascribed, of collective identities, 273–74

Authenticity, 73, 113–14

Authoritarianism and preference for male applicants, 182

Ayman, R., 188